Cutting Edge
WEB AUDIO

ISBN 0-13-080753-2

9 780130 807533

90000

Cutting Edge

WEB AUDIO

Ron Simpson

To join a Prentice Hall PTR Internet mailing list, point to
http://www.prenhall.com/mail_lists/

 Prentice Hall PTR, Upper Saddle River, NJ 07458
http://www.prenhall.com/mail_list/

Editorial/Production Supervision: Mary Sudul
Acquisitions Editor: John Anderson
Editorial Assistant: Kristy Schaack
Marketing Manager: Miles Williams
Buyer: Alan Fischer
Cover Design: Scott Weiss
Cover Design Direction: Jerry Votta
Interior Design: Gail Cocker-Bogusz
Composition: FASTpages

© 1998 Prentice Hall PTR
Prentice-Hall, Inc.
A Simon & Schuster Company
Upper Saddle River, NJ 07458

The publisher offers discounts on this book when ordered in bulk quantities.
For more information, contact
Corporate Sales Department,
Prentice Hall PTR
One Lake Street
Upper Saddle River, NJ 07458
Phone: 800-382-3419; FAX: 201-236-714
E-mail (Internet): corpsales@prenhall.com

Printed in the United States of America

10 9 8 7 6 5 4 3 2 1

ISBN 0-13-080753-2

Prentice-Hall International (UK) Limited, London
Prentice-Hall of Australia Pty. Limited, Sydney
Prentice-Hall Canada Inc., Toronto
Prentice-Hall Hispanoamericana, S.A., Mexico
Prentice-Hall of India Private Limited, New Delhi
Prentice-Hall of Japan, Inc., Tokyo
Simon & Schuster Asia Pte. Ltd., Singapore
Editora Prentice-Hall do Brasil, Ltda., Rio de Janeiro

I would like to dedicate this book to my wife Kerrie Anne.
I'm the lucky one!

Contents

Contents

Contents

Contents

Contents

Contents

Contents

Contents

Foreword

Internet Audio production may at first glance appear a radical departure from audio production practices of the past. Yet, in fact, the process and approach for success remains the same.

The 'Net is a new audio distribution medium, similar in respects to other media including 78 RPM, 8-track tape, audio cassette, LP, CD, and the Digital Video Disk (DVD). Yet, unlike it's predecessors, the Internet doesn't provide a static audio format sanctioned by committee and adopted universally. Technically, any digital audio format can be transferred over the 'Net.

In practice however, the best Internet audio formats address the bandwidth limitations of the typical user's network hookup. Currently, bandwidth reduction methods employ 1) event-driven performance data, 2) audio compression proper, and 3) CD-ROM/Internet hybrid schemes. Any combination of these techniques can also be merged. In the coming years, newer technologies will continue to appear that further optimize audio fidelity while simultaneously requiring less data to be transferred over the network.

Also, due to bandwidth limitations, a complete paradigm shift is occurring in how and where audio is processed and delivered. As an example, software-based synthesizers now run on a user's machine, reconstructing the artist's MIDI performance data on site, where previously an artist recorded the synthesizer in the studio.

Similarly, certain browser plug-ins enable a real-time mix of audio data at the client end of a network. The line between the home and studio is becoming less defined, and with that a corresponding power shift and struggle as the Internet now allows anyone to be a record company in the traditional sense.

This book provides the tools and information to make intelligent choices to author audio for the Internet today. It provides an extensive background on audio basics with a complete survey of the currently available authoring tools. Given the number of variables involved (highest quality, lowest bitrate, audio delivery, streamed media, budget, and so on), there is no right way to author audio for the Internet. Though, as a producer—large or small—the rules of audio production for this complex new medium remain the same: Have a thorough knowledge of the technical issues of the process and work within your personal limits to achieve the desired end-user experience.

Brian Balthazor
Director of Audio Technology
Waking Dreams
brian@wakingdreams.com
http://www.wakingdreams.com

Acknowledgments

This is a tough one as there are so many people that helped me in one way another on this book. The biggest thanks goes to Ralph Moore, who besides being a great Editor is responsible for this book being where it is today (on the shelf). I'd also like to thank Prentice Hall for having the vision to publish this book.

There are so many companies and individuals that were of great help both supplying information and the software tools I needed to make this book happen. I really need and want to thank all of you so I'll just start at the top of the list.

- Arboretum Systems: Richard Lee
- BIAS: Andrew Calvo
- Digidesign: Jennifer Barrier and Mary Stevens
- Headspace: Mary Coller
- Liquid Audio: Tom Murphy
- Macromedia: Leona Lapez, Suzanne Mattis, Suzanne Porta, Buzz Kettles and Brett Stewart.
- Opcode: Paul DeBenedictus and Lori Carsillo
- QSound: Scott Willing
- Sonic Desktop: Kevin Klinger

- Sonic Foundry: Stacey Moran
- Syntrillium Software: Bob Ellison
- Waking Dreams: Brian Balthazor and Kelli Richards
- Waves: Marsha Vdovin at Marsha Vdovin Public Relations for getting the Waves NPP to me for use in the book.
- Mike Overlin and Mike D'Amore at Yamaha.

Also I'm not going to forget Nancy Dunn, Pat O'Brian, Andy Cummings, Juliana Aldous, and the rest of you who hung in there with me during the early development of this book. I'd also like to thank my entire family, especially my Mom and Stepdad (Jack and Judy Vorfeld) for all your support.

At Prentice Hall: Thanks to John Anderson, Christy Schaack, and Jeffrey Pepper for all your help. Also, there's a lot of you that I won't see or hear, but I thank you all the same for your contribution.

Last but far from least I've got to thank "Boz" and "Micus"(my fearless Golden Retrievers) for guarding the fort and alerting me to the impending arrival of UPS and FedEx deliveries.

Introduction

Welcome to *Cutting Edge Web Audio*! At last, a chance to not only separate fact from fiction, but to also get a hands-on guide to the tools you need to cut to the front of the line. My own curiosity and the lack of any one detailed resource about creating sound for the Web is what started this journey for me. Every 40 or 50 years, a new medium for the information delivery comes along. The radio and television are a couple of good examples that come to mind. Imagine what it must have been like being one of the first to own and operate a radio station. There were no rules, you just made them up as you went along! Guess what—We're there again.

For the first time in the history of the world, almost anyone with a computer has the opportunity to reach millions of people all over the planet through the World Wide Web. Sound and music are two of the most powerful tools available to help get your message across and the Web is the new delivery system. In the last year or so, it has finally become possible to deliver high-quality streaming audio through the Internet in a number of different ways. *Cutting Edge Web Audio* is your guide to the when, where, and how of integrating sound and music into this exciting new form of interactive multimedia.

What's This Book About?

The title says it all. Regardless of your level of expertise, I will walk you through the many levels of creating and assembling the components needed for adding sound to your Web site. Along the way, if I'm able to pass along a little conceptual wisdom as well, so much the better. For all practical purposes, this form of content delivery is relatively new and there are many limitations (especially our old nemesis, bandwidth). This is not a problem. Through the creative genius of many forward-thinking developers, the rules as they once existed are being broken almost on a daily basis.

 ## How This Book Is Organized

This book is broken down into three main sections.

Part 1, "Getting Started," covers all of the basics, including browser and audio plug-in capabilities, file formats, copyrights, licensing, clip music, and contracting talent for your project.

Part 2, "The Tools," is where we really dig in and you get a chance to gets your hands dirty. We'll look at many of the development tools available and through a series of in-depth tutorials take an idea and turn it into sonic reality for your Web page. In this part of the book, you will be able to find out which streaming (or downloadable) technology best fits your needs and budget. Whenever possible, save-disabled versions of the recording and editing software used in the tutorials will be available on the CD-ROM.

Part 3, "Back To the Future," is a look at the future of sound on the Web. I'll talk about how advances in bandwidth are changing the way we educate, entertain, communicate, and sell our products and services to the rest of the world. For those of you who are content developers, this book should be able to help you identify emerging markets and give you the jump on the rest of the competition.

What This Book Isn't About

This book will not teach you about designing a Web page or go into much depth about HTML. It will, however, give you the basic information needed to embed sound and the necessary controls to your Web page. As much as I'd like to, in *Cutting Edge Web Audio*, I won't cover recording a MIDI sequence or dealing with music theory or performance. Instead, I will concentrate on basic editing and set-up principles using the MIDI and audio clips provided on the CD-ROM. Because the main thrust of this book is about creating Cutting Edge Web Audio, I will stay away from the development tools geared toward Internet telephony.

The Mac/Windows debate will not be fought here. Everyone has their favorite development platform and tools, and I'll do my best to cover both sides of the coin.

 ## Who Should Read This Book?

If you work (or want to) in the field of Interactive Multimedia and Web Design, this book has your name written all over it. All of the principals and tools involved apply to almost every area of development in Interactive Multimedia, including intranet applications. If you're a Musician, Composer, or Recording Engineer who would like to figure out where he or she might fit into this rapidly expanding marketplace, you can use this book as a reference guide.

I haven't forgotten the little guy either. You have no budget or you're just curious about how it's done. On the CD-ROM, I have included original music and sound effects in a variety of formats that are completely royalty-free for performance on the Web or for multimedia presentation (see Chapter 4, "The Music License," for specifics). When I'm able to find the appropriate freeware, shareware, or demo software, it will be either included (on the CD-ROM) or I'll let you know where you can download it. So, in theory, for the cost of this book you could have your Web site sonically enhanced with quality audio, making *Cutting Edge Web Audio* a bargain at any price!

Conventions Used in This Book

There is some information presented in this book that deserves special attention. For this reason, I've employed textual conventions to help this type of information stand out. This section overviews the types of conventions that I've employed in this book and tells you what you can expect from them.

Icons

I use five icons in this book:

Tip

Tip icons point out expert advice on tricks and techniques.

Warning

Warning icons will help you avoid trouble.

Note

Note icons point out specific details that require special attention.

CD-ROM

The CD-ROM icon points you to demo software, tutorial sound files, and examples that reside on the CD-ROM.

Web

The Web icon points you to specific examples, plug-ins, freeware, shareware, and demo software available on the Web.

Sidebars

Every once and a while, I'll need to take you to a Sidebar to clarify a concept or process. The sidebars can be extremely helpful to those of you who are new to some of the audio basics needed to successfully complete the tutorials.

Tutorials

The tutorial files are the heart of this book. Even if you don't have the software (or the correct platform) to complete a tutorial, by simply following the steps and clicking on the corresponding tutorial files, you can hear the results of each step of the process. Each tutorial and tutorial step is numbered.

Here's an example of how it works. During a tutorial step, you've been instructed to add some sort of effect (say, Reverb); you are then asked to save it as CH?EX?.WAV. By going to the tutorial file folder for that particular chapter on the CD-ROM and clicking on the file with that name, you can hear the results of that step. So in theory, you can start with the first tutorial file in a series and by clicking each file and listening, you can hear the results of the different steps. With the exception of some really long files (10 MB), there are duplicate Mac and Windows files for each tutorial step regardless of the platform and software that was used to perform the tutorial. That way, even if you have none of the software, you could follow most of the tutorials and hear the results.

The Glossary

On occasion, you will probably run into terms that are unfamiliar to you. These are covered in the glossary and should make it easier for you to navigate through areas that are a little new to you. Some of the terms are pretty standard, but just in case I'll make sure they're covered.

System Requirements

Many of the newer software applications require the use of a Pentium (for Windows) or PowerMac (for the Mac OS) to accomplish their magic. However, some of the development tools were designed to run on a 486 or 680X0 Mac and that will be noted whenever it applies. To successfully playback audio from the Web, it is necessary to use Netscape Navigator (3.0 or better) or Microsoft Internet Explorer (3.0 or better). In most cases, for tutorials I used Navigator because of the similarity and compatibility between the Windows and Mac versions of this browser.

Disk space

Disk space can also be an issue when dealing with digital audio. If you are recording or editing CD-quality audio files (16-bit, 44.1 kHz, stereo) you will be using up 10 MB of disk space per minute. In the world of pro audio and multimedia, it is quite common to use a separate AV drive (audio visual). These drives are generally hold between 1 and 9 gigabytes of data and are lightning quick in retrieving audio files. However, the need for an AV drive will be determined by the audio recording/editing application you are using and its specific requirements. In many situations, I simply use the main drive on my computer and archive the files to an Iomega Zip drive. The application you choose for your work and it's specific system requirments will be the determining factor in this situation.

◼ Speakers and Soundcards

Because we are dealing with sound in this book, you're going to need a pair of computer speakers. While I could recommend one of my favorites (Bose), all I can really say is get a pair that sounds good to you. A decent pair of computer speakers will probably cost more than $10. You might want to remember that. Windows users also need a sound card to playback both MIDI and WAVE files. The lowest common denominator would probably be a Creative Labs SoundBlaster 16 or its generic equivalent. Most, if not all, Windows machines now come with a sound card pre-installed, but all the same don't take anything for granted. With the exception of the really old Macs (pre 68030), all Macs and PowerMacs come with built-in audio capabilities. MIDI, however, is a different situation altogether. Fortunately, after installing Quicktime 2.1 (or better), you will be able to playback MIDI files with no external synthesizer via QuickTime Musical Instruments. See Chapter 15, "QuickTime," for more on that.

The CD-ROM

The CD-ROM included with this book is a Windows/Mac hybrid. I've split the CD-ROM into three main sections, as follows.

> **Note**
>
> While I initially thought it was important to put as many audio-based browser plug-ins on the CD-ROM, I've since changed my mind. Most of them have a time-out and wouldn't be usable by the time you got your hands on the book so instead you'll need to take a trip to the Web and download the latest version of each plug-in. The relevant URLs can be found at the end of each corresponding chapter.

Demo software

Much of the demo software I was able to get for this CD-ROM is full-featured with one exception—It's save-disabled. However, you'll still be able to do many of the steps in the tutorials while using it (the demo software).

Miscellaneous software

This includes all the usual suspects as well as a number of original music files from my own collection. Probably the highlight in the shareware department is Cool Edit 96 (for Windows) from Syntrillium Software.

Tutorial files

With the exception of a few large files, I've duplicated the tutorial files so you can listen back to them on either a Mac or Windows machine regardless of which platform or application was used for each specific tutorial. The files have been saved as either WAVE (Windows) files or System 7 Sound files. All you need to do to initiate playback is to double click the file to hear what's going on.

For a more in-depth look at what's on the CD-ROM and a description of it's contents, go to the CD-ROM appendix.

 ## And Last but Certainly Not Least ...

It is my sincere hope that the tutorials, software tools, and information featured in this book give you everything you need to go out there and create Cutting Edge Web Audio.

Ron Simpson
January 6, 1998

The home page for this book is at: `http://www.prenhall.com`
To contact the author, send e-mail to: `ronsimpson@uswest.net`

About The Author

You're probably wondering exactly who I am, where I came from, and how I got around to writing this book. Me too. After growing up in the rain-soaked forests of the Pacific Northwest (the first 30 years), I migrated to a warm and sunnier climate in Phoenix, Arizona where I now reside. In the world of life, I've majored as a professional musician/composer for the last 21 years with a minor in computers. After being bitten by the computer music bug back in 1985 and turning it into a profession, the migration to music and sound in multimedia and the Web was a natural step in my evolution. In 1996, I co-authored and published my first book on sound on the Web for another publisher (who shall remain nameless). By then, I was hooked and felt this book, *Cutting Edge Web Audio,* was going to be the book I would have written the first time around had the technology existed at the time. Instead of going for a general-purpose overview of the state of Web audio, I felt it was time to get down to the nuts and bolts of content creation using the best of the most current and coolest applications available. Timing is everything, and this book couldn't be more well-timed because of the audio explosion on the Web.

Anyway, as I've worked in the world of audio content creation for multimedia and Web developers, I've used the questions and inquires that my colleagues and clients are always dumping in my lap as the basis for the tutorials in this book. The upside is that you will get a lot of useful information. The downside is that anyone buying this book won't need me to do the audio for most of their projects anymore. Such is progress. So I guess I'll need to sell a lot of books to make up the slack. As I stand here with both feet planted equally in both camps, it's my hope that this book will help to bridge the communication gap between the world of the musician/composer and that of the multimedia Web designer and developer. Good luck, and do send me e-mail (ronsimpson@uswest.net), I really will answer it!

Part 1

Getting Started

To start this book out, we'll take a look at a little bit of everything. The game of sound on the Web is easy to follow if you know who the major players are and you'll get a look at who's doing what and why in this part of the book. You'll also take a run through the gauntlet where I'll cover the basics on file formats, licensing, clip music and sound as well as going through the process and pitfalls of hiring and recording talent for a voice over session. This section will be helpful as it does address issues such as copyright law that are often ignored and can end up costing you the big bucks.

The Basics

In This Chapter

- Technology overview
- Web resources to bring you into the future

Imagine this. You're excited! You've just purchased *Bob's Mondo Music and Sound Effects Library*! Over 6,000 audio files! Not only will you elevate your site to the exalted status of *sound-enabled*, but you are going to embed more sound files in your site than anyone in the history of Web design—possibly putting yourself in the running for the *Guinness Book of World Records* and the cover of *Wired* all at the same time!

At the very same moment ... your six-year-old nephew has just noticed there is a gallon of his favorite ice cream in the freezer and while you're not looking, he's going grab it and eat until he explodes! There is a parallel here. Just because you can, doesn't necessarily mean you should. Too much of anything (even something good) can cause at the very least a stomach ache!

There's a lot out there in terms of Web audio technology. For most of you reading this book, even the concept of Web audio is a new one.

In this chapter, I'll take you through a brief overview of what's going on out there in the world of Web audio as well as who is making the most noise.

Fearing the Unknown

For the most part, the combined musical experience of most Web developers and designers falls somewhere between a stint in junior high school band and being able to operate a car radio. (Okay, so a few of you took piano lessons and played drums in a garage band during high school.) This is okay. Using this book as a guide, you can avoid the musical pitfalls that can so often cause elements of tension in one's day.

Here's a hypothetical situation. You are a busy and talented Web designer and you're getting ready to meet with one of your most valued (AKA revenue-generating) clients. So far, there has been an incredible working relationship. Fred, the owner and president of a very successful auto dealership, is known for his hands-on approach in dealing with all aspects of his business and likes to think of himself as very progressive. After the preliminaries, Fred announces, "I've been thinking. I'd really like to have the main theme music from our television and radio spots play right from our home page."

At this point your mouth gets dry, there's a knot in your stomach, and you get the urge to run screaming from the building. When it comes to designing Web pages, you are it, but your knowledge of Web audio is zip. So what are your options? You could be honest and tell Fred that what you know about Web audio could be written on a postage stamp; or you could stretch the truth a little and scare him away with an astronomical cost estimate. There is, however, a third option and you're looking at it now.

Using *Cutting Edge Web Audio* as your guide, you'll be able to give Fred (or anyone else) the complete lowdown on how you're going to turn a great-looking Web site into a great-sounding interactive experience.

Technology Is Your Friend (or Is It?)

You hear everyone saying that it's an exciting time to be in the business of creating products and services for the Web, and it is! It's also confusing and frustrating. There's so much new technology being jammed down our throats, it's sort of difficult to know the difference between the real deal and yesterday's old news in a new package. Using this book as a starting point, you'll be able to assemble the right combination of technology and audio content to make sure your site is out there on the cutting edge.

It's been a long time coming, and creating audio content for the Web is going to be a major growth industry in the next few years. You're going to need sound and music if you want to compete. There are a lot of unscrupulous individuals who would love to take advantage of your lack of experience in this department. Fortunately for you, using this book (and a little common sense) as your guide, these Internet hucksters will be out of luck!

The pipeline

The bottom line is bandwidth. Even the most innovative compression technology is only going to be so good. The reality of our current situation is that the majority of Web users both now and in the near future are going to be dealing with connecting to the Web with a 28.8 modem. Even with 33.6 and the fabled 56K modem, you're still not going to be guaranteed a fast connection. There will be a small minority connecting at high-speed with the mini satellite dish and cable modems, but for now we're still in the 28.8 mode and we're going to have to live with it. Just remember we're pioneers and we can handle the hardships of being the first ones there!

Streaming audio

The most significant event in my life on the Web was the advent of streaming audio. Initially the sound quality was really bad and there were skips and hiccups in the stream that created a listening experience not unlike fingernails dragging across the blackboard. Still, the experience was probably similar to that of our forefathers as they listened to their first radio broadcasts. It was way too cool.

Streaming audio is just what the name implies—a stream of audio. Here's a layman's explanation of how it all works. You arrive at a sound-enabled Web site and, being worldly wise, you have already downloaded and installed on your system a number of plug-ins and players that will enable you to request, receive, and playback streaming audio from a remote location on the Web. Right before your eyes is a link that says "Click here for music". Being the adventurous soul you are, you do just that. In this case, it's a RealAudio-enabled site and your request is sent to a RealAudio server. Then the compressed data is sent in a stream through your modem where it is decoded by the RealAudio Player and converted into music, instantly. So, rather than waiting for an entire file to download before you can listen to it, streaming audio enables you to hear the file *as it is being dowloaded!* It's really simple: All you've got to do is ask and it's there for you to hear.

Downloadable audio

With the different streaming audio technologies popping up, you would think that downloadable music and sound files would be a thing of the past; but in fact they're not. MIDI (Musical Instrument Digital Interface)-based music is very popular and because of the small file size, provides a very quick download time. While it's also possible to download a standard audio file (AIFF, AU, or WAVE for instance) for playback, unless the user has an extremely fast connection (T1 or cable modem), it just takes too long. Beatnik (from Headspace) may be an exception to the rule of streaming versus downloadable audio. Read on to find out more!

 Formats

There are a number of different file types and formats that are specifically designed to make sound on the Web a reality. Chapter 3, "File Formats," delves a little deeper into the specifics of many of the different formats available. To give you a taste of what's out there, I've broken it down into two categories: streaming and downloadable (not-so-streaming) audio.

Streaming at you!

Streaming audio is changing the way we entertain, educate, and do business over the Web. Here's a quick overview of what's out there and why you need it!

RealAudio

When it comes to being first out of the starting gate, RealNetworks (formerly Progressive Networks) is second to no one. Cutting to the front of the line with RealAudio and again with RealVideo is no small feat. RealAudio 2.0 was in fact my first experience in listening to streaming audio over the Web. It didn't sound all that great, but it sure was cool. I was able to listen to a radio broadcast from my home town, and an archived performance of NPR's "All Things Considered." If that wasn't enough, I was able to preview the latest releases of a number of bands via an on-line music store.

Fortunately, the sound quality has improved considerably and there is more content available every day. The recently released RealPlayer 5.0 and RealPlayer Plus 5.0 make it possible to playback RealAudio 3.0 and RealVideo 1.0. In Chapter 11, "RealAudio," you'll have an opportunity in a series of tutorials to use the RealAudio Encoder (it's included on the CD-ROM that comes with this book) and convert your audio files into RealAudio! If that's not enough, in Chapter 17, "Embed Audio," I'll show you how to embed a RealAudio file in a Web page and play it back! All for the mere price of this book.

Shockwave Audio

Shockwave audio (SWA) was released at the end of July 1996 and has made some pretty large waves in the world of Web audio. There were a number of advantages right out of the starting gate and good sound quality was only one of them. SWA was and is a bargain, as you don't need to purchase or use a dedicated SWA server, but can stream audio directly from your Web page. For those of you that are Macromedia Director users, it's possible to create your own custom SWA player although we've got one or two (players) available for your use and abuse included on the CD-ROM that comes with this book. In Chapter 12, "Shockwave Audio," I'll take you on a step-by-step tour of the conversion process from sound file to Shockwave Audio with a series of fairly comprehensive tutorials.

Liquid Audio

With the entry of Liquid Audio into the mix, the record industry may never be the same. Not only is the sound quality excellent (thanks to Dolby Digital sound), but it just might be the complete solution for music distribution on the Web. Not only is Liquid Audio a great way to preview new music, but with the click of your mouse you can purchase the music you've been listening to. The Liquid Music Player is free and gives the listener quite a few very cool options.

While you're listening to a piece of music using the Liquid Music Player, it's possible to check out the album cover art, read the lyrics to the songs, and take a look at what used to be referred to as the *album liner notes*. There's also a volume control slider and with the click of your mouse, you can purchase the music on-line, have it downloaded to your computer via the Web, and record it directly to an audio CD. With the price of CD recorders coming down, this option is a reality and makes it very easy to create your own custom audio CDs.

In Chapter 13, "Liquid Audio," I'll give you an in-depth look at the components that make Liquid Audio one of the most exciting options for music sales and distribution on the Web. If you're an independent musician looking for an alternative way to sell your music, Chapter 13 will be a valuable how-to in preparing and converting your music files using the Liquifier Pro. While I doubt the big record companies are quaking in their boots just yet (don't worry, they will be), Liquid Audio is the first step in a completely new direction for the recording industry. If you want to be part of the revolution, I'll see you in Chapter 13.

■ MPEG

The mystery of MPEG (Motion Pictures Experts Group) audio has been plaguing me ever since I started researching this book. The mystery to me is why this superior-sounding audio format has not caught on in a bigger way as a form of delivering streaming audio over the Web. It could be the cost of setting up a server or it could simply be the name/product recognition factor. While quite a few people have downloaded the AudioActive streaming MPEG player and the Xing Streamworks player, there is just not an abundance of MPEG-enhanced sites out there. While MPEG very well may be the future of streaming audio over the Web, it is currently being overshadowed by RealAudio and several others. For a more in-depth look at streaming MPEG and where it's going on the Web, check out Chapter 18, "The Future."

Downloadable audio (not so streaming!)

The other side of the mountain is of course the formats that involve downloading a file before initiating playback. There are the old standbys (if there is such a thing) and there's always the new kid on the block. I'll give you a quick look at what they each have to offer and then send you to their respective chapters for the in-depth information and tutorials.

■ QuickTime

Apple's QuickTime technology is what many consider the cross-platform solution for developing sound on the Web and multimedia. The release of QuickTime 3.0 is just around the corner as we're about to go to press, and there will be complete equity between the Mac and Windows in features. One of the really cool features in QuickTime (2.1 and later) comes in the form of QuickTime Musical Instruments. This software-based General MIDI (GM) synthesizer enables playback of MIDI files without a MIDI sound card. It's also possible to combine a MIDI and an audio file for simultaneous playback. If that's not enough, there is now an MPEG extension available as well. In Chapter 15, "QuickTime," you can explore a few of the developments possibilities with QuickTime.

■ Beatnik

One of the up-and-coming new development tools for cool Web sound is Beatnik from Headspace Inc. The Beatnik browser plug-in is a really good example of how downloadable sound technology can really work for playback of music on the Web. Because the actual sound source resides in the Beatnik browser plug-in, the file size isn't all that much larger than a MIDI file, giving the listener almost instant gratification. There are also a number of very cool possibilities with Beatnik, including the ability to load and edit custom sound samples into the Beatnik Editor. In Chapter 14, "Beatnik," you'll get a chance to see just how the Beatnik editor works with a series of tutorials and a short tour.

■ MIDI

MIDI is still one of the most economical ways (both in file size and overall expense) to get music on your Web page. Small files equal a fast download and almost instantaneous playback for the listener. Now, with the emergence of a few decent-sounding software-based General MIDI (GM) synthesizers, there is a little more uniformity as to what the end user will actually hear. Granted, if you have a 200 mHz MMX Pentium, that extra processing power will give you an edge over that old 486/66, but what do you expect?

The Yamaha MIDPLUG is an excellent example of soft synth (software synthesizer) technology. Based on Yamaha's XG format (Yamaha's extended version of the GM spec), the MIDPLUG is a Netscape-compatible browser plug-in that provides high-quality playback of General MIDI files.

The Internet Music Kit (Wildcat Canyon Software) and Crescendo from Live Update are yet two more ways for you to get MIDI files to playback from your site. I'll cover all this and more in Chapter 16, "MIDI on the Web."

Resources

Let's face it – the Web is an ever-changing entity, and in some cases plug-ins go through new versions so fast it makes you want to slap your granny. Instead of including *today's* latest and greatest version of each of these Web audio plug-ins on the CD-ROM accompanying this book, I encourage you to take a little side trip to each of the Web sites listed in Table 1-1; you never know what you might find.

Table 1-1   Audio plug-ins on the Web

Product	Web location
Beatnik by Headspace Inc.	`http://www.headspace.com`
Crescendo by Live Update	`http://www.liveupdate.com`
Internet Music Kit by Wildcat Canyon Software	`http://www.wildcat.com`
Liquid Audio by Liquid Audio	`http://www.liquidaudio.com`
MIDPLUG by Yamaha	`http://www.ysba.com`
QuickTime by Apple	`http://www.quicktime.apple.com`
RealAudio by Progressive Networks	`http://www.real.com`
Shockwave Audio by Macromedia	`http://www.macromedia.com/shockwave`
Streamworks by Xing	`http://www.streamworks.com`

Looking Back to the Future

Remember, there's a lot more to this book than meets the eye. I'll take you on a guided tour through a number of CD-ROM collections featuring Music and Sound Effects designed specifically for Interactive Multimedia. I'll also unravel the mysteries of licensing music for the

Web. You will experience first-hand how 3D sound and other similar technologies can enhance your Web site. With in-depth tutorials on Pro Tools 4.0 and Sound Forge 4.0 (to name a few), learn the power of the many sound effect and enhancing plug-ins and listen to aural examples of the before and after on the CD-ROM. History will always repeat itself and those of you who've jumped on the bandwagon are part of a late 20th Century gold rush. Sound and music will increasingly become a larger part of the equation (remember, silent films are ancient history!) and if you're not part of the revolution, you'll be left in the dust. *Cutting Edge Web Audio* gives you the ammunition you need to cut to the front of the line!

Chapter 2

The Browser Battle

In This Chapter

- Microsoft and Netscape: The Final Conflict
- Native sound features
- Plug-ins may be the way to go

When it comes to the Web, there are two main contenders in the world of browsers: Netscape and Microsoft. The big question is—in the world of Web audio, do they both deliver and if so, what? When I go online, whether it's with my Mac or Windows machine, I expect the same sound quality and features regardless of the machine or the browser I'm using. There are, however, differences—some small and others maybe a little larger—that we'll be looking for (and at) in this chapter. The release of both Netscape Communicator and Internet Explorer 4.0 have added more fuel to the fire of the controversy.

This chapter is going to be short and sweet as far as length, as many of the development and playback technologies are covered with their own chapters. Whether anyone likes it or not, the *plug-in* is still the heart of what you can or can't do with sound in the browser. Eventually, ActiveX and Java controls will change that, but for now the plug-in is the gateway to hearing and being heard on a global basis. While UNIX and even OS/2 (what about my Amiga!) are important to some, in this chapter we're going to concentrate on working within the mainstream of the Windows and Mac operating systems.

I've spent enough time using both browsers on both platforms to say there is as of now no big winner in the sound department. To make things even worse, I go back and forth between browsers and platforms all the time because there isn't one that I've come to accept as *the* one. There are some cross-platform and plug-in compatibility issues that still need to be addressed before equality will be achieved, but as long as Microsoft and Netscape continue to nip at each other's heals, the real winner is going to be the end user—and that's you!

 ## The Playing Field

Microsoft (like the rest of us) doesn't like playing on a level playing field—and why should they? In terms of operating systems, it only makes sense that, using Windows 95 and Internet Explorer (3.0 or better), you're going to have a leg up when it comes to extending the native sound capabilities of your browser. The Mac version of IE 3.0 (and 4.0) is great, but it's pretty feature-disabled in comparison to its big brother. Navigator, on the other hand, can match itself feature for feature regardless of OS and hardware. Granted, users of Windows 3.1 or the 68K Macs are slowly being left out in the cold, but that's progress.

What it comes down to is that using a PowerMac and Internet Explorer is not going to be as rewarding of an experience as using a Windows 95 machine with Internet Explorer will be. For most of you, this should be no big surprise. If you're running Navigator, you really won't notice much of a difference regardless of which OS and hardware you're running. Still, I've always thought that one of the cool aspects of the Web was equality among platforms (and operating systems). So what does a Mac or PowerMac user do when arriving at a site where there are Windows-only ActiveX controls? The same could also be said for a Windows user showing up at a site where the ActiveX controls are Mac-only. For the time being, the only thing any of us can do is to sit back and see what falls out of the trees.

ActiveX controls

Unless you've been living on a desert island, you've heard of ActiveX and are probably curious about the overall impact it's having in the battle of the browser. For those of you who don't know what ActiveX is, let me give you a brief and simplified explanation. ActiveX controls are little self-contained software applets that are automatically loaded into your system when viewing a Web site that utilizes them, providing you're using IE 3.0 (or better). This beats taking a side trip to download a plug-in and going through the install/restart process. ActiveX controls also take up less operating memory than a plug-in, which means more RAM left over for important stuff.

So where do we stand amongst the browser population and ActiveX? Obviously, IE (3.0 or better) for Windows is the shining example of what ActiveX plug and play controls can do; but what about the rest? The Mac version of Internet Explorer does support ActiveX but, for it to work, separate ActiveX controls have to be written for the Mac. So, in other words, at the early stages of the game, ActiveX is mostly there in name only for the Mac OS. Because most of the cool ActiveX controls are written by third-party developers, there's a better than even chance that you'll never see much developed for the Mac in the way of ActiveX controls.

Netscape Navigator plug-ins are compatible with Internet Explorer, so how about the other way around? Although as I write this it's a resounding no, with the release of Netscape Communicator (and Navigator 4.0) there should eventually be complete compatibility with ActiveX controls. Again, I'm wondering—Where does this leave users of the Mac? I guess we'll just have to wait and see.

Native sound

So, who wins the battle of best overall native sound capabilities? As you might imagine, in the 3.0 (and later) releases of the usual suspects, it's *almost* a toss up. I would have to say that the ActiveX plug-and-play controls do let IE 3.0 cut to the front of the line. Both browsers support playback of AIFF, AU, MIDI, and WAVE audio out of the box.

15

Internet Explorer, however, needs no plug-in to playback RealAudio, QuickTime movies, or MPEG audio (or video). I guess this is an advantage, but by simply loading QuickTime 2.5 (with the MPEG extension) with Navigator, you've solved that one. Also, with the release of the RealPlayer 5.0 from RealNetworks, you now have audio, video and RealFlash animations on the same player, which also sort of negates the IE advantage. You could go back and forth between the two and even the score almost every time with the addition of a plug-in.

Native MIDI and the Soft Synth

Here's an area where Netscape is gonna get whumped upon heavily: the Microsoft Synthesizer. As part of the IE. 4.0 package, the Microsoft Synthesizer offers an option for those listeners of MIDI who are not going to go out and purchase a decent-sounding full-featured MIDI sound card. The Microsoft Synthesizer is a Soft Synth (software-based synthesizer) with a sound set licensed from the Roland Corporation. It is GM GS compatible, and when it comes down to it, it sounds pretty good. It is available in 8 and 16 bit versions. Of course, there are a few plug-ins that can easily counter the Microsoft Synthesizer, such as the MIDPLUG from Yamaha, which is essentially a GM XG software synthesizer. And the soft synth that is QuickTime Musical Instruments (QuickTime 2.1 or better) offers yet another alternative to the Microsoft Synthesizer. Not to mention with the release of QuickTime 3.0, Apple has also licensed the Roland Sound Canvas for their software synthesizer. Currently of the three mentioned in this paragraph, the MIDPLUG is my hands-down favorite for sound quality and again it works equally well with a Windows 95 machine or a PowerMac.

While there is a certain convenience to having a soft synth, it does rob processing power and slow your system down. The MMX technology counters some of this problem, but for better overall performance, a separate soundcard is going to make the serious gamer or multimedia enthusiast happier in the long run. But again, when it comes down to Native MIDI capabilities, until we see the Netscape Synthesizer, Microsoft definitely has a big check in the plus box with this one.

> **Note**
>
> GM is the abbreviation for General MIDI. GS (Roland) and XG (Yamaha) are extensions of the General MIDI format and, while remaining completely compatible with the GM standard, offer some enhanced sound features that really do sound good. Interestingly enough, XG synthesizers respond to GS commands, though you're out of luck the other way around.

Streaming at you

Well, I got sort of adventurous in the streaming audio category and decided I'd check out the Netscape Media Player (1.1). I was hoping to find a player (with controls) that would playback both streaming audio and work as a stand-alone player for playback of local files as well. Unfortunately, while the plug-in was properly installed, not a single one of the sites suggested by Netscape was able to actually play any streaming audio via the Netscape Media Player. This included the Netscape Site as well. Apparently while the Media Player is functional, the Netscape Media Server is still in beta (12/97).

Using Internet Explorer for Windows was also an interesting experience when it came to streaming audio. RealAudio would sometimes playback using the RealPlayer and at other times (even though the Real-Player was present) would playback directly through the browser. Playback through the RealPlayer was considerably smoother and it was nice to be able to control the start and stop of a file. Using the IE default playback, I never really knew when streaming audio playback would start or stop, much less for how long the file would actually play.

My suggestion (for the near future anyway) is to use the third-party plug-ins, discussed next, for streaming audio playback. It's my opinion that you'll be way more pleased with what you hear as well as the consistency of the performance. I was.

Third-Party Plug-ins

Table 2-1 is an overview of just a few of the available audio plug-ins for these browsers. Some you will have heard of, and are cool enough to even rate their own chapter; others are a bit more obscure. Use Table 2-1 as your guide to the audio-enhancing third-party plug-ins. There are more plug-ins out there than could be possibly featured in this chapter. With very few exceptions taken, if it doesn't run on both browsers and the Mac and Windows operating systems, you probably won't see it here.

Table 2-1 Audio Browser Plug-ins

Product	Description	IE or Navigator (3.0 or better)	Windows	Mac
Audioactive by Telos	Stream MPEG Layer III files from the Internet	both	3.1, 95, NT	68k, Power Mac
Crescendo by Live Update	MIDI plug-in	both	3.1, 95, NT	68k, Power Mac
Liquid Audio Player by Liquid Audio	Streaming audio player	both	95, NT	Power Mac only
MIDPLUG by Yamaha	Soft synth MIDI plug-in	both	3.1, 95, NT	68k, Power Mac
Netscape Media Player 1.0 by Netscape	Synchronized audio and multimedia	Navigator only	3.1, 95, NT	Power Mac only
QuickTime by Apple	Audio, MIDI and animation	both	3.1, 95, NT	68k, Power Mac
RealAudio Player 3.0 by Real Networks	Streaming Audio Player	both	95, NT	Power Mac only
RealPlayer 5.0 by RealNetworks	Streaming Audio/ Video Player	both	95, NT	Power Mac only

Table 2-1   Audio Browser Plug-ins *(continued)*

Product	Description	IE or Navigator (3.0 or better)	Windows	Mac
Shockwave by Macromedia	Streaming audio with the Shockwave audio plug-in	both	3.1, 95, NT	68k, Power Mac
Tool Vox by Voxware	Audio plug-in	both	3.1, 95, NT	Power Mac only
WebTracks by Wildcat Canyon	MIDI plug-in	both	3.1, 95, NT	68k, Power Mac
Xing by Xing Technologies	Streaming MPEG player	both	3.1	68k, 68k emulation

 Go Find It!

It's time to load your browser up with every available audio plug-in known to man. Use Table 2-2 as your guide to finding and downloading what you need! Many of the companies offer free plug-ins with an upgraded version available for sale. The choice as always is yours.

Table 2-2   Audio Plug-ins

Plug-in	Description	URL
Crescendo by Live Update	MIDI plug-in	`http://www.liveupdate.com/crescendo.html`
Crescendo Plus by Live Update	Streaming MIDI plug-in	`http://www.liveupdate.com/crescendo.html`
MIDPlug by Yamaha	MIDI browser plug-in	`http://www.ysba.com`
Netscape Media Player 1.0 by Netscape	Synchronized audio and multimedia	`http://www.netscape.com`

Table 2-2   Audio Plug-ins *(continued)*

Plug-in	Description	URL
QuickTime by Apple	Audio, MIDI and animation	`www.quicktime.apple.com`
RealAudio Player 3.0 by Rea Networks	Streaming Audio Player	`http://www.real.com/ products/player/`
RealPlayer 5.0 by RealNetworks	Streaming Audio/Video Player	`http://www.real.com/ products/player/`
Shockwave by Macromedia	Streaming audio with the Shockwave audio plug-in	`http://www.macromedia.com/ shockwave`
Tool Vox by Voxware	Audio plug-in	`http://www.voxware.com/ download.htm`

Developmental tools

This is where Microsoft is the hands-down winner. The Microsoft Interactive Music control is an ActiveX control that makes it possible to create an interactive music environment (via MIDI) on a Web page. You can use either the sound card installed in your PC for playback or download an 8 or 16 bit version of the Microsoft Synthesizer. To use the Microsoft Interactive Music control, there's no need for musical ability. It works in a similar fashion to the old Wurlitzer organ my Aunt used to have (remember the Teen Tango Waltz button?). For the developer, there are a number of options (or presets) including 27 different styles and 110 personalities to choose from. You can also choose the length and activity level of the music. In essence, you choose from a wide palette of presets and the computer creates a MIDI file that plays back and can be programmed to change at random. Just press a button (so to speak) and go. For the non-musical, this tool is pretty cool as you can create a unique MIDI file on-the-fly that conforms to your taste. However, most musicians and those who appreciate listening to music will find the results annoying at best. Still, it's an interesting option to say the least and definitely worth checking out.

So, who's the winner?

Taking a realistic look at where the cutting edge is and where it will be, I'm going to say that Microsoft is putting a lot more effort into developing native sound capabilities than Netscape is. Microsoft isn't just developing and selling the technology; they're creating some interesting tools that give content developers on all levels something to work with. Still, it seems as though the bottom line is going to be the universal plug-ins and controls created by third-party developers. While you can hardly fault a company for making it easier to develop products for their proprietary system, I'm still bothered by the no/low Mac approach to advanced controls.

I, like probably everyone else out there, have a love-hate relationship with Microsoft. They definitely have a certain edge; I'm just not sure who other than Microsoft will benefit from this advantage.

When the dust is settled and the final versions of Communicator and IE 4.0 are out, how will everything sound? My guess? About the same. With Netscape scrambling for complete compatibility with ActiveX controls and Microsoft already having achieved compatibility with the Netscape-compatible plug-ins, who got there first? It looks like Microsoft. Well, sort of. There's so many angles and opinions here, all of which are valid at some point. If you're a Windows 95/NT user, then the advantages to using Internet Explorer are obvious—It fits your OS like a custom-made glove. As the two integrate and become one, if you're not part of the Windows/IE experience, it could be like hearing about a really cool party but not getting invited.

Then there's Communicator. I like the multi OS/hardware compatibility thing that is going on here. I know when developing sound and music content for my (Web) clients that the audio files are going to sound and work pretty much the same (Windows or Mac) when using Navigator as the browser. With Internet Explorer, unless your target audience is strictly limited to Windows 95/NT users, there's no real advantage (at least for the time being) using Internet Explorer for playback of Web audio. While I do tend to use Navigator a little more often (than IE) for streaming audio development (testing and playback), that could change.

I've spent more hours than I care to confess to using both browsers (IE and Navigator) on the PowerMac and Windows machines. Though the clock speed in my Pentium is considerably faster than that of my Power-

Mac, in most situations I got a much smoother performance in regards to streaming audio from the Apple machine using Communicator. RealAudio is the exception and pretty much sounds and performs the same in both browsers and both platforms.

On paper, both Netscape and Microsoft have very convincing arguments why each of their respective products are better. Strictly in the terms of using audio plug-ins, Netscape seemed to crash less and run smoother. I have a lot of friends and acquaintances who would argue that point and some of you probably will too. As far as native sound capabilities are concerned, for both development and playback IE 4.0 is the winner. However, when running third-party plug-ins, I could go either way. I tend to use Communicator on both my Windows 95 and PowerMac more than I use Internet Explorer, but that could change as more stable versions of IE 4 are released. If I were adding up points for sound and interactivity (regardless of platform), I'd have to begrudgingly say Internet Explorer wins.

Table 2-3   The Browsers

The Browser	URL
Internet Explorer by Microsoft	`http://www.microsoft.com`
Navigator by Netscape	`http://www.netscape.com`

Chapter 3

File Formats and Conversions

In This Chapter

- Learning about sound file formats
- Converting sound files
- WaveConvert
- SoundEdit 16

File formats and conversions. That's easy, right? If you're familiar with the process, it's a walk through the park. If you're not, it can be as confusing as calculus is to most first graders. In this chapter, you get the practical information you need to prepare your sound files for multimedia and Web playback. I'd like to tell you there's one sure way to convert and sample files down to different formats and resolutions, but there's not. Just when I think I've got it down, new information drops into my lap and once again, somebody's telling me they have a better way to do it. Don't get me wrong: All the old techniques work just fine, but there's always a few new tricks that can sometimes help to retain a higher sound quality when converting or sampling down a file. Like real life, everyone has an opinion as to what works best.

 File Formats

Listed in Table 3-1 are many of the file formats commonly used in sound recording and playback for computers in regards to multimedia and the Web.

Table 3-1 Sound file types and descriptions.

File Type	Description	Extension
AIFF	The Audio Interchange File Format is a standard audio file supported by most Macintosh sound applications.	AIF
Amiga SVX File	This file format was created for use on the Commodore Amiga.	SVX
Liquid Audio	The Liquid Audio file format is a high-quality compressed audio format enhanced by Dolby Digital sound.	LA1
MIDI	Musical Instrument Digital Interface has been a standard of the music industry since 1982.	MID
MOD files	With MOD files, digitized sound samples are an actual part of the file. This format started life with the Amiga and has migrated to the PC, as well.	MOD
QuickTime	The QuickTime Movie format from Apple playback standard audio (such as AIFF) or MIDI files as a QuickTime movie compatible with both the Mac and PC.	N/A
Raw Files	A Raw sound file can be composed of any sound data.	*
RealAudio	The progressive Networks RealAudio format is a compressed format designed for real-time streaming over the Internet.	RA
RMF	The Rich Music Format comes to you from Headspace. This hybrid file format allows the user to import and process sound from a variety of different sources including WAVE, AIFF, and MOD files. Web TV uses the RMF format.	RMF

Table 3-1 Sound file types and descriptions. *(continued)*

File Type	Description	Extension
Shockwave Audio	SWA is compressed streaming audio format from Macromedia.	SWA
Sound Designer II	The file format used by Sound Designer II (SDII) from Digidesign.	SD
System 7 Sound	This format is used on Macintosh for the alert sounds in System 7 and above.	SND
Sun .au	The .AU file format is native to Sun/Unix systems and is also used for playback over the Web.	AU
Video for Windows	This digital video for Windows format supports multiple audio channels.	AVI
VOC File	The Creative Labs VOC file format is commonly used for playback on both 8- and 16-bit Soundblaster audio cards.	VOC
VOX File	The Dialogic VOX file format.	VOX
WAVE	This format from Microsoft is used for playing back sampled sounds through Windows. It has become one of the most used sound formats.	WAV

> **Note**
>
> Okay, so you may notice there's a few of the old standards (and I do mean *old*) missing. I'm hoping the days of 8-bit 11kHz mono files are behind us and with any luck, you do too.

There are so many file formats bouncing around in the world of computers and sound that it's hard to know where to begin (or end). For the most part, we will stay away from the obscure proprietary sound formats unless they are actually in wide use today. The most commonly used file formats used for recording and editing sound are AIFF, WAVE, and MIDI. For ease of playback, all tutorial files in this book are in two formats, System 7 Sound for the Mac and WAVE files for the PC. The exception would be when the application being used for the tutorial requires a different format.

> **Tip**
>
> To playback System 7 Sound files on the Macintosh, simply double-click the file you wish to hear. No additional player is needed.

Preparing a File for Conversion

To save disk space and prepare for playback through a streaming audio format, sound files are sometimes sampled down to a lower bit resolution. Unfortunately, there's always a significant (and noticeable) loss of audio quality on the way down. Using a few simple tricks (and the right tools), you can minimize and, on occasion, partially restore this sonic degradation. Depending on which platform I'm working with, I quite frequently use SoundEdit 16 version 2 from Macromedia (Mac) or Sound Forge 4.0 from Sonic Foundry (Windows) to convert or sample a sound file downward. They are both reasonably priced and work well—not only for the file conversion process but for editing and recording as well. You will see a lot of both of these applications and the audio plug-ins that make them break the sound barrier in this book.

For the first tutorial, I'm going introduce you to WaveConvert (from Waves), a really cool multi-platform conversion utility.

WaveConvert for Windows and Mac OS

WaveConvert is more than a standard audio utility and contains many audio processing features designed to compensate for the loss of sound quality during the conversion process. With Tutorial 3-1, I walk you through the process and give you some before-and-after examples that you can compare for both sound quality and file size.

In Tutorial 3-1, we'll be using the Mac OS version of WaveConvert. It is somewhat different in both appearance and features from the Windows version, but the results are the same.

Note

The current Windows version of WaveConvert only supports AIFF and WAVE file formats.

■ Tutorial 3-1: Down conversion

In this tutorial, we are going to lower the bit depth and sample rate of a WAVE file. See Table 3-3 for tutorial sound file (before-and-after) information.

What you need

To do this tutorial, there are several components needed, as follows:

- WaveConvert Mac OS version
- Tutorial file CH3EX1.WAV
- Macintosh (68040 or better) Computer

CD-ROM

The tutorial file CH3EX1.WAV resides in the Chapter 3 tutorial folder on the CD-ROM accompanying this book.

File format conversion

1. Open the application WaveConvert for the Mac. Figure 3-1 shows the main screen. To load the tutorial file, click the *Add Input File* button at the top left of the main screen.

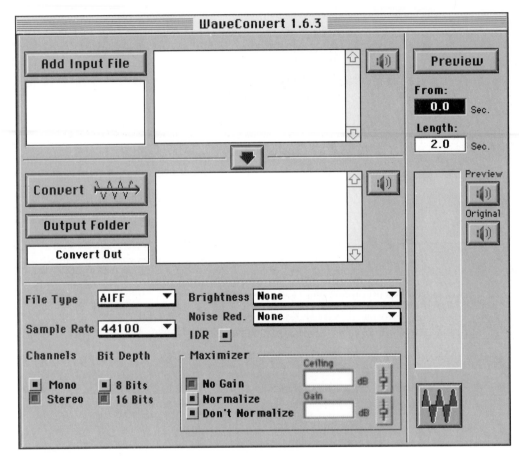

Figure 3-1
Click the Add Input File button to load tutorial file.

2. Select the file or files you wish to add to the input list and click Open. As shown in Figure 3-2, WaveConvert (Mac) can save, load, and convert between six different file formats. As the tutorial file is a WAVE file, be sure to check the .WAV box or the tutorial WAVE file will remain invisible. For this tutorial select the file CH3EX1.WAV (found in the Chapter 3 tutorial folder on the CD-ROM) and click Open.

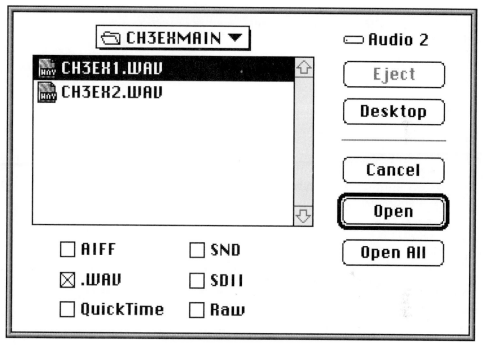

Figure 3-2
WaveConvert saves, loads, and converts six different file formats.

3. With tutorial sound file CH3EX1.WAV loaded into the Input File, you can now begin the conversion process. You will note that in Figure 3-3, the attributes of the highlighted file are displayed in the window at the top left of the screen.

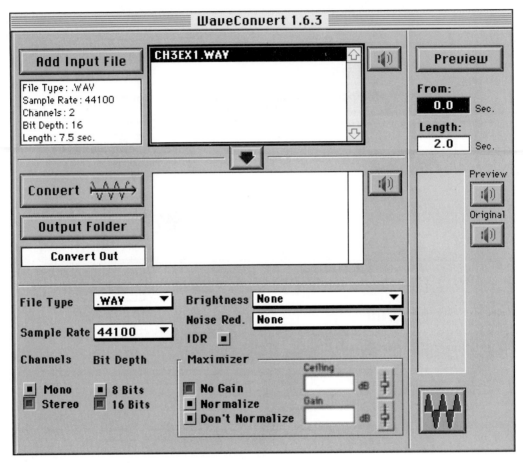

Figure 3-3
The pre-conversion attributes of your loaded sound file are displayed in the top left-hand corner of the screen.

4. The purpose of this step is to convert the sample rate and bit depth of the file CH3EX1.WAV, as well as change the file from stereo to mono. This will considerably reduce the overall file size. With WaveConvert, there are a number of control options available. In Figure 3-4, note that the conversion attributes I chose for this tutorial are pretty straight ahead. Go to Table 3-2 for the pre- and post-conversion settings. Using this table (3-2) as your reference, make the appropriate changes and click the Preview button in the top right corner of the main screen of WaveConvert. This will create a preview file (1) you can use to reference and recall the settings before you convert the file.

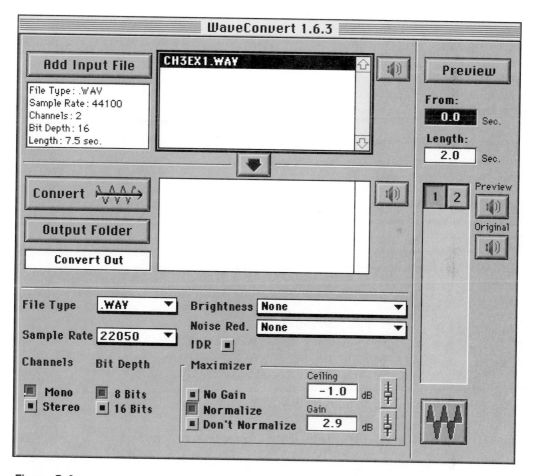

Figure 3-4
The Preview function can be used to preset and recall the post conversion control functions.

Table 3-2 Tutorial 3-1 pre- and post-conversion settings

	Pre-conversion	Post-conversion Preview 1	Post-conversion Preview 2
File Type	WAV	WAV	WAV
Sample Rate	44.1 kHz	22.050 kHz	22.050 kHz
Channels	Stereo	Mono	Mono
Bit Depth	16 bit	8 bit	8 bit
Maximizer	n/a	Normalize	Normalize
Ceiling	n/a	–1.0 dB	–1.0 dB
Gain	n/a	2.9 dB	2.1 dB
Brightness	n/a	n/a	Brightness – Soft
Noise Reduction	n/a	n/a	Quant. Gate Hard
IDR	n/a	n/a	Yes

Note

IDR is an acronym for Increased Digital Resolution.

Tip

Use the Preview feature to build a series of preset options for comparison.

5. Do an A/B comparison between Figure 3-4 and Figure 3-5 and note the difference in the control settings. Toggling between Preview 1 and 2, you are able to compare the subtle differences between the two files and decide which is best suited for final conversion. In this case, the preset conversion information in Preview 2 is the choice for best overall sound quality.

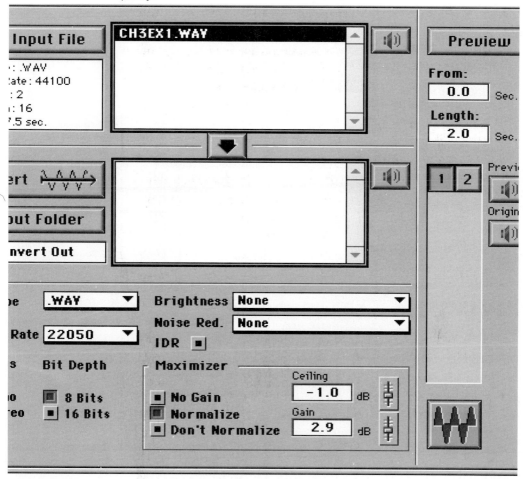

Figure 3-5
Notice the subtle differences in the control settings from those in Figure 3.4.

6. Select file CH3EX1.WAV and click the down-pointing Add Arrow (shown in Figure 3-6) to move the selected file to the output list. Select the Output Folder by clicking the Output Folder button. If you don't select or create an output folder, WaveConvert will do it for you automatically. Click Convert (take a short break while it's converting—it takes a moment).

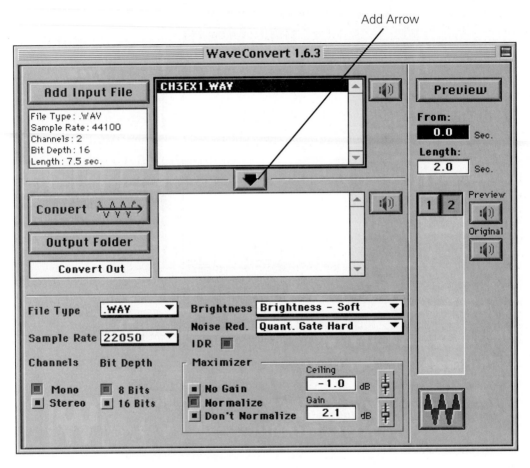

Figure 3-6
Click the Add Arrow to move file CH3EX1.WAV to the output folder.

7. The converted file now resides in the destination folder. Repeating Step 1, load the converted file CH3EX1A.WAV to the Input List (shown in Figure 3-7) for a complete A/B comparison to the original sound file.

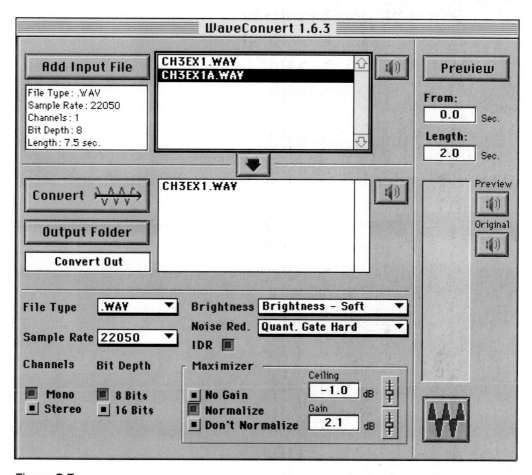

Figure 3-7
The pre- and post-conversion example sound file now resides in the Input Folder.

To Convert or Not to Convert; That Is the Question!

For the near future, down sampling and converting audio files to a lower bit depth is going to be a way of life if you want to put streaming audio on the Web. Taking a 16-bit 44.1kHz stereo file and converting it to a 16-bit 22.050 mono file reduces the file size by 75 percent, but sometimes even that is only a start. Using WaveConvert, you can minimize the loss of audio quality on the way down to manageable file size for playback on the Web. The WaveConvert process does take a little getting used to, but all in all it is a very useful application specifically designed just for handling the pitfalls of file conversion. If you're dealing with converting a large number of files, Wave Convert can be a real time saver.

Which Is the Best?

What I'd like to do here is address a question that has been asked of me quite a bit: "Which application is the best for converting a file down to a lower sample rate and bit resolution?" Tough question—and an even tougher answer. In addition to using WaveConvert, I've also used Sound Edit 16 (Version 2) for the Mac and Sound Forge 4.0 for Windows for quite a lot of file conversions. The process and audio tools involved are different with each application. If you tried to mimic the process and steps used with Sound Forge 4.0 in Sound Edit 16, it just wouldn't work. The same goes with WaveConvert. The problem is that each application takes the audio file through the conversion process in a slightly different way. Once you know each application and how they work, you can get pretty much equal results. So I guess the answer is: Use what is most comfortable for you. (I should be a politician). In all honesty, I usually use the application I happen to be working in at the time the work needs to be done. The exception is if I'm processing a large number of files at the same time; then I go with WaveConvert.

Note

File CH3EX2.WAV is a voice-over clip processed in much the same way as the preceding example. Do an A/B comparison between the high- and low-resolution sound files and listen to the difference. See the chart in Table 3-3 to compare file size and attributes.

Table 3-3 Tutorial Sound File Information

File Name/Type	File Size	Sample Rate and Bit Depth	Notes
CH3EX1.WAV	1.3 MB	16 bit 44 kHz stereo	Music file, 7.5 seconds in length, CD quality preconversion.
CH3EX1A.WAV	224 K	8 bit 22 kHz mono	Music file, 7.5 seconds in length, low quality sound resolution.
CH3EX2.WAV	256 K	16 bit 44 kHz mono	Voice file, 2.4 seconds in length, CD quality preconversion.
CH3EX2A.WAV	96 K	8 bit 22 kHz mono	Voice file, 2.4 seconds in length, low quality.
CH3EX3.WAV	704 K	16 Bit 22 kHz stereo	SFX high quality, converted from audio CD.

Note

The examples in this chapter are available for playback on the Mac as System 7 Sounds. The .SND extension is tagged to the end of each of these files.

WaveConvert Pro

Just as I was about to turn this chapter into production, the FedEx guy brought me a little surprise: WaveConvert Pro (for the Mac). One of the new features that I really like is plug-in support. Those of you with the Waves Native Power Pack can now use this arsenal of plug-ins directly with WaveConvert Pro. This can be especially handy for those of you who don't have a stand-alone recording/editing application such as Sound Edit 16 or Pro Tools. Another feature exclusive to WaveConvert Pro is preprocessing filters designed for RealAudio and Shockwave Audio encoders. Just another step in the right direction for this already powerful sound conversion tool.

Tutorial 3-2: Converting CD audio

On more than one occasion, I've needed to move a few sound effects into my computer from a standard audio CD. I prefer to keep all my audio in the digital domain whenever possible to eliminate the unsightly noise that can sometimes get picked up during the digital to analog and analog to digital conversion process. So, using the *Convert CD Audio* Function in SoundEdit 16 (Mac), I'm ready to rock and roll. This is an easy and painless process that enables you to convert an entire (or partial) track from an audio CD into an AIFF file. Don't worry; the conversion process from AIFF to WAVE is quick and easy. If you use a non-Apple CD player (with SoundEdit 16), you may not be able to successfully complete this procedure.

> **Note**
>
> Sonic Foundry has just released CD Architect as a plug-in for Sound Forge 4.0 and Sound Forge XP, or as a stand-alone application for Windows 95/NT. While the main application of CD Architect is burning Red Book CDs, one of the many cool features is Extract Audio From CDs.

■ What you need

Due to the nature of this tutorial, the demo version of SoundEdit 16 will not work because it is save-disabled. While I have used a specific audio CD for the tutorial, any standard audio CD can be used to get similar results. The following components are needed to complete this tutorial:

- SoundEdit 16 Version 2
- Macintosh (68040) Computer With CD-ROM
- Audio CD

Web

The Hollywood Edge offers a demo Sound Effects CD for free. For more information, visit: www.hollywoodedge.com.

■ CD audio conversion

Let's get started. For this tutorial, I'm extracting around six seconds of a jet flyby from the Super Single Volume 2 (Hollywood Edge) SFX CD. After loading the audio CD into the machine in question (in this case, PowerMac 8500/120), I'm ready to begin.

1. Start the application Sound Edit 16 Version 2 and select Xtras@(Convert CD Audio from the menu bar, or click the CD icon in the tool bar, as shown in Figure 3-8. This opens the Track directory box for the contents of the audio CD.

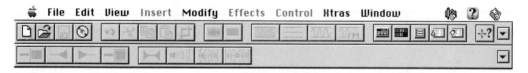

Figure 3-8
Convert CD Audio can be accessed by clicking on the CD icon in the tool bar of SoundEdit 16.

2. Select the audio CD track you wish to convert (as shown in Figure 3-9) and click Open.

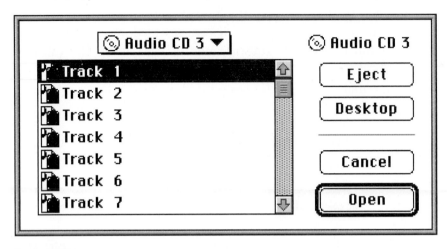

Figure 3-9
Select the track to be converted and click Open

3. Rename the audio track, choose the destination folder, and click Options, as shown in Figure 3-10.

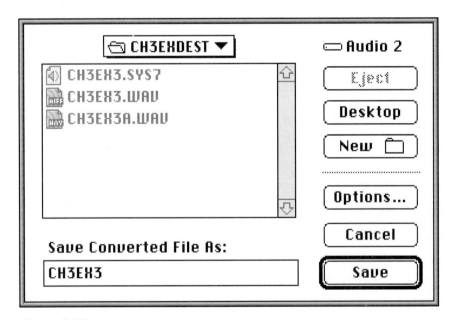

Figure 3-10
Remember to rename the audio file and set the destination folder.

4. In Settings (shown in Figure 3-11), choose the proper sample rate and bit
    depth, as well as between Mono and Stereo. Under Audio Selection, you
    can preview the entire track and choose which section to Import. Once your
    selection has been made, click OK.

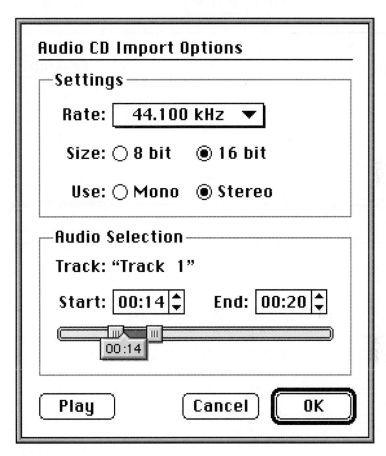

Figure 3-11
Choose the proper settings for conversion in the Audio CD Import Options
window.

5. Click Save to convert the file CH3EX3, as shown in Figure 3-12. Figure 3-13 shows the converted file in SoundEdit 16.

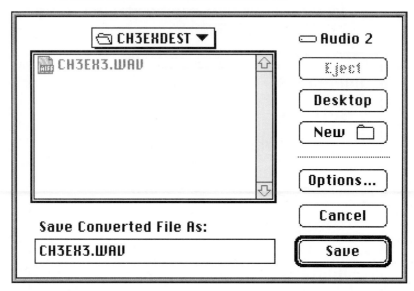

Figure 3-12
Click Save to convert the tutorial sound file.

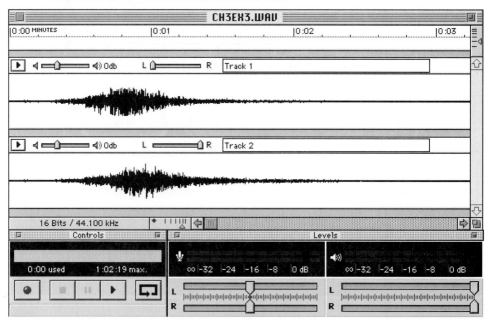

Figure 3-13
The file CH3EX3 in SoundEdit 16.

6. In Figure 3-14, you can see that SoundEdit 16 automatically saves the converted file to AIFF.

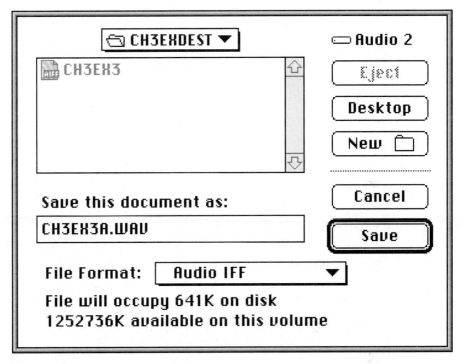

Figure 3-14
The file CH3EX3 is automatically saved as a AIFF file.

7. With WAVE being one of the 10 different file format options available with SoundEdit 16, converting the file CH3EX3 into a WAVE file is a simple process. Simply add the .WAV extension and resave the file under the WAVE file format, as shown in Figure 3-15.

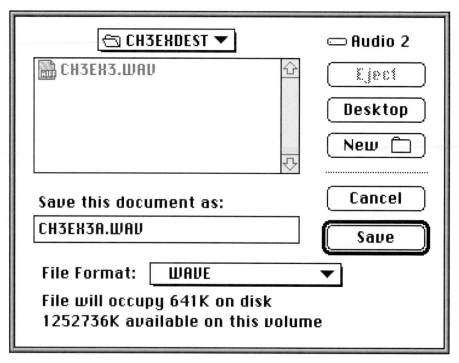

Figure 3-15
Changing an AIFF to WAVE file is as easy as resaving the file.

CD-ROM

The final results of Tutorial 3-2, CH3EX3.WAV resides in the Chapter 3 tutorial folder on the accompanying CD-ROM.

SoundEdit 16 is a very useful and user-friendly sound editing and recording tool. In Chapter 12, "Shockwave Audio," I'll show you some of the more powerful native features in this program. As a bonus, we'll dive head first into using some really cool third-party plug-ins, including my personal favorite, the *Native Power Pack* from Waves.

A Few Final Words

Regardless of which platform you use for development, the conversion process is basically the same: Crunch large great-sounding files into small (hopefully) decent-sounding ones. In Chapters 11, "Real Audio," and 12, "Shockwave Audio," as well as a few others, I'll use some of the favorite software development tools the developers of these products use and abuse on a daily basis.

One of the main points of the Web is that many platforms are able to look at and listen to the same content without prejudice. The new streaming audio file formats that are popping up are turning the dream into reality. While WAVE and AIFF will more than likely remain the standard for creation and development of audio files, it's the cross-platform streaming audio file formats that will change the face of what we listen to on the Web. The developers of new file formats geared toward the Web who don't address the playback and development needs of both Mac and Windows users will end up going the way of the dinosaurs—ancient history.

Table 3-4   File conversion and editing programs mentioned in this chapter.

Product	Platform	CD Audio Conversions	Cross Platform Conversions	3rd Party Plugins	URL
Sound Forge 4.0 by Sonic Foundry	Windows	yes	yes	yes	http://www.sfoundry.com
SoundEdit 16 (Version 2) by Macromedia	Mac	yes	yes	yes	http://www.macromedia.com
WaveConvert by Waves	Mac/Windows	no	yes	no	http://www.waves.com

Chapter 4

The Music License

In This Chapter

- Learning About the Music License
- Deciding Which Type of License You Need
- Understanding Basic Copyright Law
- Finding License-Free Music

For all practical purposes, a music license is a very simple document. It's basically an agreement between the owners of a musical work and the end user (for our purposes, you). Of course, quite often the wording of such a license can be more than a little confusing. Together in this chapter we'll stumble through the complicated maze of legal mumbo jumbo and make an attempt to decipher the sometimes confusing Music License.

About the last thing anyone needs is a lawsuit. The rules and regulations in regards to copyrights, music licensing, and performing rights organizations are confusing to those who deal with it on a daily basis. As millions of people flock to the Web for commerce, entertainment, and education, a unique set of problems have arisen and no one is exactly sure what to do about it. Is the music on a MIDI file considered a performance in the same way as a phonograph record? If so, by whom? There certainly are very few if any laws on the books nor are there many court rulings dealing with the varied types of sound delivery over the Web. What I'm hoping to do in this chapter is raise your awareness level and recommend using common sense when using intellectual property of any type. Let's start with the copyright.

The Copyright

United States Copyright Law is the saving grace for those of us who develop content considered to be intellectual property. Material developed by Authors, Composers, and even Sound Designers fall under the protective wing of copyright law. If you plan to use music and sound for playback on the Web (or anywhere else), you must make sure you don't violate these laws. You screw up with copyright law and it gets expensive. For the most comprehensive and up-to-date information on copyright law, go to the Library of Congress Web site at: `http://www.loc.gov/copyright/`.

An example: It could happen to you!

Here's a situation that actually happened to me: A multimedia content developer contacted me and needed some original music for a project. There was not enough of a budget for me to compose and record something from scratch, so I licensed several music cues from my personal library for a set price. The license I wrote clearly stated that the music was to be used for this project and this project only. These requirements were made perfectly clear both in conversation and in writing. Any other use (or reuse) would require another license and additional payment. There was no mystery here; it was all laid out in black and white.

Unfortunately for me, this multimedia developer decided to use some of the same music for a different project without my permission, perhaps without realizing he was doing anything wrong. Quite often, the attitude is "I've paid for it once, why should I pay for it again?" It could even be a situation where the project had no music or sound budget and they just inserted a few seconds on the front and back of a multimedia presentation to fill things out a little bit. Which leads to another prevailing attitude—my old favorite—"Who's gonna know?" It's not very wise to assume that nobody's going to find out.

In my situation, I was alerted to the potential violation by a friend working at the same company that was producing the project. After a quick phone call to the project manager, we easily resolved the situation and everyone ended up happy (even me!). It's always better to assume that it was an honest mistake and give the potential violator an easy way out.

> **Note**
>
> So, you're probably wondering if it's illegal to use or even give music away if you're not making any money. Without the permission of the copyright owner, use of the music and the musical performance is in violation of United States Copyright Law.

So what if . . .

Time for a hypothetical situation: I hear a piece of my music somewhere and I know for a fact that the individual or company using it was not given permission to use it. I call, I write, and I even knock on their door, and I'm completely ignored. Now what? Under current U.S. Copyright Law, the courts allow a minimum fine of $500 per violation! While the maximum allowed is $20,000 per infraction, it can go higher if the offender was found to act willfully in the theft of the intellectual property in question. While I've never run into this situation personally, I know that it does happen.

Warning

Here's another potential violation of which you need to be aware. What if a piece of music is sold to you by a less-than-scrupulous individual and it just so happens that this person doesn't even own the copyright or the performance? Let's say you convert it to a RealAudio file and it's the first thing that anyone and everyone going to your Web site hears. Not your problem, right? Wrong! You're still in violation of US Copyright law and are liable.

Where Do You Fit?

There are a number of classifications for music and sound on the Web. There are also performance rights organizations with the sole function of collecting royalties for music played from their repertories. Three such organizations—ASCAP, BMI, and SESAC—are the predominant players in the game (see Table 4-1).The traditional sources of revenue for these organizations have been concert halls, restaurants and bars, radio, TV stations—and even Girl Scout camps! I believe it was the summer of '96 that singing around the camp fire was banned at a Girl Scout camp in California until the annual fee that covered performance of the copyrighted material was paid. This is a pretty good indication that they will be interested in your sound-enabled Web site, as well. As you can imagine, the Web is seen as a great potential source of new revenue.

Note

The easy way to avoid this whole licensing thing altogether is to purchase music that is royalty-free for playback on the Web. See Chapter 5, "Clip Music and Sound Effects," for more on royalty-free music.

If you play it, you might have to pay for it

Time to get hypothetical again. You're a small business owner with two employees. You have a combination CD player/radio at your business location and you and your employees listen to music every day while working. No big deal. One day, you get a bill in the mail for $300 from ASCAP or BMI (you fill in the blank). Because you own a place of business and people are listening to music (even the radio or on-hold music on your phone system count here), you've got to pay—it's the law.

I know this sounds pretty crazy, but in most cases when you buy a tape or CD, you have merely paid for the permission to use the music for private performance (your home and your car, for instance). You don't own the contents of that CD of your favorite recording artist, only the right to listen to (but not broadcast) it. It sounds pretty ridiculous, but it does happen all the time. While it's even more confusing that you should have to pay for listening to a radio broadcast in a place of business, it's still the law.

The Web is the real world, too

You might be wondering what this has to do with sound and music on the Web. Well, the copyright laws and the rules and regulations that apply to those of us in the real world are also valid on the Web. Whenever possible, use music that is royalty-free for playback over the Web and save yourself the headache.

There are many descriptive categories for Web sound and music. Knowing where you fit in the big picture will help to determine whether your site will be subject to performance royalty payments.

▧ Music on demand

Imagine an online jukebox where the listener can choose from a selection of thousands of tunes. How about an online Karaoke Machine where the user chooses, pays for, and then downloads a music file from a server. These are two very good examples of what is referred to as *music on demand*. If a user can go to your Web site and choose a specific musical performance, then you fall into this classification. This an area that will be a strong future source of revenue for the performance rights organizations.

▉ Promotional music

While promotional music is legally considered to be another example of music on demand, it is still a very gray area. Should the owner of an online music store have to pay a performance royalty because a visitor to his (or her) site can listen to sample music clips of the products for sale? You would think the answer would be no, but it isn't. The prevailing opinion (with the exception of the performance rights organizations, of course) is that, in this case, the fee should be waived. Granted, money is possibly changing hands here, but they're also trying to sell a product, which makes a profit for the artist. Hopefully, the lawmakers in this country will use a little common sense and enter the twentieth century before it's over. (Better hurry up, guys!)

Now, here's an interesting little twist: The owner of a copyrighted song or performance can choose to waive the collection of fees by the performance rights organization in any specific instance. This will not do any good for the Web site owner who pays a blanket fee to each performance rights organization, but it could save a few bucks for owners of sites that are set up to promote a specific artist (or artists).

Webcasting

Don't you just love these new buzz words that keep popping up? With the advent of streaming audio, many radio stations are now rebroadcasting over the Web. This is the classic example of *Webcasting*—broadcasting on the Web. However, as time goes on, there will be content exclusively developed for broadcast over the Web. So, if you're involved in a Web-based venture that will be delivering content with music by either rebroadcast or push technology, then you're more than likely a candidate for paying a fee to performance rights organizations.

Downloadable audio files

When you offer downloadable audio in any form from your Web site— unless you have the permission of the copyright owner of the song and the performance—you are breaking the law. While it's great to be a rebel, at $500 per violation (the minimum amount allowed by law) you might want to reconsider. If it's your original music and you are the owner of the performance and you really want to give it away, knock yourself out! Otherwise, be careful.

In my research, I spoke to a few individuals who've been making audio files available for free download off their personal Web sites. Each and every one of them were shut down by the record labels that owned the music they were giving away. None of them could understand what the problem was, because it wasn't as though they were charging money for the music. When you sell or give away someone else's property, it's not only illegal—it's in really bad taste as well. They were lucky that the record labels and artists involved chose not to take them to court. Remember, you might not be that lucky.

Royalty-free considerations

So how can you play sound and music on the Web and avoid having to pay a performance royalty? Use royalty-free music! Here's an example: When I compose and record music for my Interactive Multimedia clients, I factor the performance royalty into the overall cost. In most cases, I write the license to be completely royalty-free for playback on the Web or for a multimedia presentation. Even though I am a member of ASCAP, I have the option of waiving the collection of the performance royalty. If you plan on having custom music composed for your Web site, negotiate royalty-free playback.

Some clip music libraries are royalty-free, letting you tell ASCAP and the others to go take a hike. Quite often, you will see *Royalty-Free* on the cover or in the advertising. That can be (and usually is) a misleading statement, as they are only royalty-free in select situations. The owner of a musical selection can decide when and where it is or isn't royalty-free. While there are certain laws that do apply, it is the right of the copyright owner to pretty much regulate how the music can be used. The fine print in the license could read "Music performance is royalty free-on the second Wednesday of every month (national holidays excluded)." This would be stupid, but legal.

Performance Rights Organizations

I have a mixed opinion on these organizations. The idea and intent are good, but in the case of ASCAP and BMI, we may have a classic example of the tail wagging the dog. Will the fees collected from sound on the Web actually make it to owners of the music being performed? If your name is Paul McCartney, maybe; but in most cases probably not. The little guy just isn't getting decent representation by these organizations. Many of the content providers and developers of music libraries have expressed an opinion that performance rights organizations need to go the way of the dinosaur (and some, in fact, already have). For non-broadcast applications (pretty much anything other than radio and television), users of these libraries are exempt from paying a performance royalty to these organizations (except where noted on the individual licenses).

If you have unanswerable questions in this arena, contact either the owner of the music collection you plan on using or one of the performance rights organizations listed in Table 4-1.

Table 4-1   Performance rights organizations

Organization	Description	URL	Phone
ASCAP	The Society of Authors Composers and Publishers	`http://www.ascap.com/`	212-621-6000
BMI	Broadcast Music Inc.	`http://www.bmi.com`	212-586-2000
SESAC	N/A	`http://www.sesac.com`	800-826-9996
Register of Copyrights	US Copyright Office	`http://www.loc.gov/copyright/`	202-707-3000

The Clip Music and SFX License

In Chapter 5, "Clip Music and Sound Effects," we'll take a look at a few of the Music and SFX libraries that are commercially available. What we're going to do right now is look at some of the licensing rules and regulations that you're going to come up against when using these collections.

Common ground: Restrictions!

So what do all these music and sound effects libraries have in common? Restrictions. When purchasing a sound and music library, remember this: You don't own the content; you're leasing it. Let's take a look at some of the more common restrictions that you'll find in each of these libraries.

▪ The multiuser license (yeah, right!)

Unlike many office applications, it is rare if nonexistent altogether to be granted a multiuser license for a music library. One user on one computer at a time—end of story. This is one of the reasons a multimedia music library can be purchased for between $50 and $200. Put any of these libraries on an in-house server, and you are in violation of the license. It's okay for millions of people to listen to it (over the Web, for instance), but not for multiple users to have access to it (while developing content) at the same time.

▪ Reproduction of content

Making copies of any music and sound content (from any library), for resale or distribution in another package or library, can get you into legal trouble up to your ears. This (especially) includes making files available for download off of your Web site.

Here's an example: You need music and sound for a computer game you are developing. To save time and money, you purchase a multimedia music library for $100. The big question: Can you use the music and sound effects from this library for the game? In most cases, yes; but buyer beware. What you can and can't do will vary between each individual library, depending on the license. In Table 4–2, take a look at some of the licensing restrictions and quirks from six different libraries reviewed in Chapter 5.

Table 4-2   Common licensing restrictions

Product	Royalty Free Reproduction*	Royalty Free Multimedia Playback	Royalty Free Web Playback	Royalty Free Broadcast (Radio and TV) Playback	Royalty Free ASCAP, BMI and SESAC
CyberTunz	500 copies	Yes	Yes	*No*	Yes
Digital Jukebox	Unlimited	Yes	Yes	*No*	Yes
Janus Professional Sound Library	Unlimited	Yes	Yes	*No*	N/A
Java Beat	Unlimited	Yes	Yes	*No for Radio†*	No
Music Bytes	Unlimited	Yes	Yes	*No*	Yes
Presentation Audio	100 copies	Yes	Yes‡	*No*	Yes

*   This does not include repackaging music or sound effects for another collection nor does it include making any of these files available for download from the Web. It is, however, royalty free as part of a multimedia presentation or game on CD-ROM.

†   When the music or sound is synchronized (integrated) with a movie or multimedia presentation. The sound file (by itself) must not be available for download from the Web.

‡   The copyright owners OK this collection for use with television and video, but not for radio.

■ Enforcement of the Law

You would think that the Federal Copyright Police would be standing by ready to arrest, prosecute, and convict any person or organization with the gall to violate U.S. Copyright Law. Well, they're not. It's entirely a civil matter. If you find someone in violation, you (or your attorney) will have to handle it. If you're proven to be in the right, you can win big (and maybe even collect, too); though in most situations it can prove difficult and more expensive than it's worth.

So who's gonna know? How are they going to find out? Now that's a really good point, too. What if some 12-year-old kid embeds Yoko Ono's latest release on his or her home page for all to hear? Will Yoko go after him or her? That's one only Yoko can answer.

The bottom line is . . .

When you use someone else's copyrighted intellectual material (music, print, graphics, photos, or even video) without the proper permission, you can be sued for a lot of money. If you're going to use music or sound on your Web site, be sure to get written permission (from the rightful owner) in the form of a license. Remember, a minimum of $500 per violation is allowed by U.S. Copyright Law. I don't know about you, but for me that would hurt!

 One Last Thought

The Web is changing the way we do everything in our lives, and music and sound is becoming an increasingly larger part of the big picture. Using common sense and asking questions when in doubt will keep you out of legal trouble 99 percent of the time, as far as sound on the Web is concerned. Music libraries can be an inexpensive and simple way for Webmasters to keep it simple and inexpensive.

In the next chapter, I'll show you some of what's out there and let you be the judge. At this time, it does make sense to keep it simple and inexpensive. The most cost-effective way to way to get musical content for your Web site is lurking just around the corner in Chapter 5. See you there!

Clip Music and Sound Effects

In This Chapter

- Prerecorded audio resources
- Comparing music libraries
- Choosing sound effect resources

Production Music Libraries have been around for a long time and for good reason—the law of economics. The cost of hiring a composer, musicians, a recording studio, and the various support personnel needed as well as paying royalties to everyone involved is rarely in the budget. Since their inception, music and sound libraries have always been a reasonable alternative. It only makes sense that a concept that has been so successful in radio and television would move on up the evolutionary ladder to take its place in the world of Interactive Multimedia, which includes the Web.

Because of the broadcast connection, there are more music and sound effects libraries than you can shake a stick at. In this chapter, I'll take you through a fairly in-depth look at five specific music libraries available on CD-ROM. For the purposes of this book, I'll concentrate on CD-ROM collections versus those in the form of (Red Book) audio compact disks. The one exception will be in the area of sound effects. Because I was only able to find one complete collection of sound effects in CD-ROM form, I'll give you a quick look at some of the more traditional options as well.

> **Note**
>
> While as a general rule I try to avoid coming off like a reviewer, in the case of the music and sound effects libraries there's really no way to get around it. My goal (in this case) is to give you enough good basic information so you don't end up spending money on a collection of music or sound effects on the sole merit of the packaging or advertising.

 The Music

What we now call *clip music libraries* fall into two basic categories. Category one was developed for radio and television, while the second is more modern in both content and concept. Understanding the strengths and weaknesses of both schools of thought is important in helping to decide what works for you.

Production Music has, for the most part, always been predictable and safe, designed not to offend or even be all that noticeable. There were more often than not 30- to 60-second radio and TV spots that needed to be filled and the music would usually convey positive happiness in a generic sort of way. The longer thematic pieces had an upbeat, winning feeling inspiring the listener to sell Amway or join the army and storm the beaches of Normandy with John Wayne. The music was boring and has been slowly driving the general public nuts in a quiet, Lawrence Welk sort of way for years. The old guard had a formula that worked and there was no reason for them to push the edge of the sonic envelope by creating innovative musical content.

Then came the Web.

The vast reaches of Cyberspace have a completely different set of needs and rules as far as music and sound is concerned. Just like the software industry, small companies (sometimes one-person companies) are starting up and offering really great-sounding affordable libraries of clip music. Most are even royalty-free for Web and multimedia playback and unlike their overpriced ancestors, some have a street price in the neighborhood of $50. You've got to love the concept of free enterprise.

Unlike their conservative broadcast-oriented counterparts, this new breed of music developers are taking chances and doing it their own way. The result is, at the very least, interesting and will undoubtedly inspire the creation of even cooler Web content. So how does a Web developer find out about these products? The cost of advertising these libraries in the trade magazines is too prohibitive for most of these small companies and thanks to the lack of shelf space, you won't find any of these products in the traditional retail outlets. Currently, catalogs, direct mail, and the Web are about the only places you could find these products—until now, that is! I looked, I listened, and here's what I found.

 ## The Players

There were two main prerequisites that the following products needed to get into this book. The first was that I had to be aware of their existence and the second was that the developer needed to send me a review copy. Each of these five products have their individual strengths and weaknesses, and I'll be sure to let you know what they are. A slick interface is all well and good and certainly looks pretty cool, but the bottom line is the music must sound good and be usable. Whenever a demo is available via the Web or any other source, I will point you in the right direction so you can make the final decision yourself.

Here's where we take a look and a listen. Just to set the mood, I'll be listening to the product I'm reviewing as I write. What could be more fair than that? Because Java Beat has been around the longest, that's where I'll start.

Java Beat

Java Beat from Jawai Interactive was the first music library on CD-ROM to make it to my desktop way back in March of 1996. This is a mixed-platform CD-ROM with the music available in four file formats (AIFF, WAVE, MIDI, and QuickTime). You can also purchase Java Beat in the form of a standard (Red Book) audio compact disk.

While the two have nothing to do with each other, this product was released at about the same time the Java programming language was becoming the buzzword of the computer industry. If that isn't marketing genius, I don't know what is. Figure 5-1 shows the main screen of Java Beat.

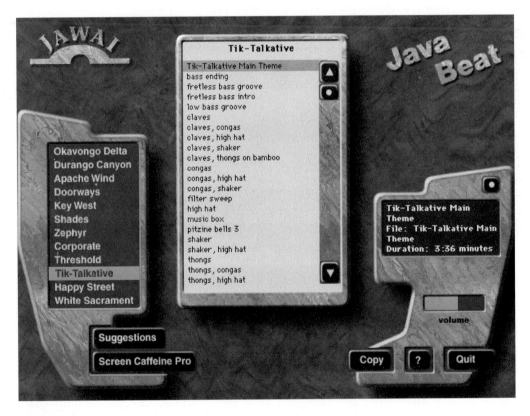

Figure 5-1
Each musical theme and its modular components are accessed through the main screen in Java Beat.

Java Beat's interface is about as straight forward as you can get. On the left side of the screen, you have the option of 12 musical selections. Just highlight the tune of your choice and the center screen fills with a large number of options. From there, pick one (the main theme is usually a pretty good place to start), click on it, and you're off to the races. At this point, you may wonder what exactly is in all those files in the center window; I sure did. In a nutshell, they are the components of each particular song. Most of those files are a short solo recording (between 1 and 15 seconds) of each individual instrument. While there are a few usable files in each song, for the most part they just seem to be taking up space. I really like the idea of assembling the song in individual components, but it would have made more sense to me for this to be different sections of the song itself (Intro, A, B, and so forth). With a little thought, I think the modular concept could be a very useful and flexible tool for the end user. Creating your own custom music files by assembling the components in the order and length that fit your personal taste and needs would be a wonderful option.

Moving back to the interface, we get to the box in the lower right-hand side of the screen. I found the window in this box very useful as it shows the name and the length of the file that's playing. The button at the top of this box is used to stop playback of the current sound file and of course there's the slick little volume slider. This may sound dumb, but I really liked the volume control in this window; it actually worked. I found that to be sort of a problem with other products in this chapter.

Now it's time to get down to the file types and bit resolution. The music in Java Beat comes in four different flavors: AIFF, WAVE, MIDI, and QuickTime. The AIFF and WAVE files are all 8-bit 22 kHz stereo files. The good news is smaller file size. The bad news is the overall sound quality is very poor. It's very rare when you can get a music or sound file with this low a resolution to sound very good and the selections in Java Beat are just too grainy and flat-sounding for my taste.

Okay, just when I'm beginning to fear for my life here, I'm going to come to their defense for a second. When Java Beat was released, the 8-bit 22 kHz stereo thing was not all that uncommon in the world of Multimedia. Music and sound in general was sort of secondary to the graphics in a multimedia presentation and always more of an afterthought. Times have changed, and high-quality sound is now the norm. Even as I write this, I'm listening to the Java Beat audio CD so I know the original recordings are good. Oh well, you've got to call them as you hear them.

Both the MIDI and the QuickTime files come up a little short quality-wise as well. There is a warning in each of the read-me files stating neither (the MIDI or the QuickTime files) accurately recreate the Java Beat music. I'm sort of wondering if that was the case, why bother? It would have been helpful to the end user if the MIDI files would have been converted and optimized to fit the General MIDI format. That would have made it possible for the rest of the world to play the files back with a minimum amount of hassle. The QuickTime movie files are really just MIDI files using QuickTime Musical Instruments for playback.

Jawai was one of the first to come out with music geared strictly for the multimedia developer. Great idea, a well-designed interface, and well intentioned. The best thing they could do at this point is to re-release Java Beat with the files at a higher sampling rate (at least 16-bit 22 kHz stereo). Today's end user likes to hear high-quality music and with Shockwave audio and all the other options available in both streaming and downloadable audio, there really isn't a place for grungy low-resolution music files. If the reason for MIDI and QuickTime files was just to fluff the file count, I say lose them or improve them. All in all, I really like the music; I just can't live with the poor sound quality and I don't think you could either.

Presentation Audio from Network Music

I first heard about the "Presentation Audio" series from Network Music by way of a review in Macworld. That in itself is sort of strange since the series is currently a Windows-only product. Not a problem, however, as most Macs read a WAVE file without so much as a second thought. Network Music is currently working on porting Trakfinder (see Figure 5-2) over to the Mac (more about Trakfinder later). There are five different volumes available separately or as a collection. The content of this series is more from the old school of broadcast music and sound. However, in this case, it works quite well and in fact it's sort of retro. The market targeted by Network for this series is more of the corporate user (PowerPoint, for instance) with little or no sound editing experience. As an added bonus, Trakfinder (utility) is included and makes it possible to change sample rates, set loop points, and set a fade in and out point. It's a great search tool as well.

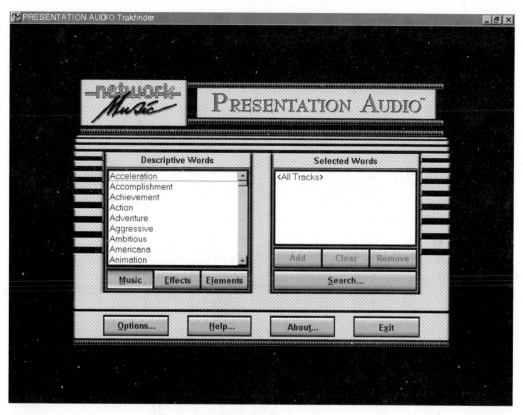

Figure 5-2
Trakfinder narrows the search with many search options.

Nothing in this collection is new and in fact is taken straight from Network Music's extensive broadcast library. However, this is not a bad thing and both the recording quality and the music are pretty good. If you're looking for something that covers a lot of ground and would qualify as a best buy, I would have to say this is it. You also must take into consideration that as reasonably priced as this series is, the license does limit use to multimedia presentations only. If you're worried (and you should be), take another look at Chapter 4, "The Music License," to make sure you don't break US copyright law and totally lose your assets (so to speak).

One of the major differences between this series and all the others we're looking at is the instrumentation on the recordings. For the most part, the music in this series was recorded using live musicians. All of the others were done completely in a computer-based environment. This is neither good nor bad, just different. When you hear a guitar or a harmonica on a Presentation Audio file, without a doubt you are listening to the real thing.

As I mentioned, these are Windows-only CD-ROMs, but the files can be imported into a Mac without any problems. I did, however, find that the files played back a little smoother on a Mac when I converted the files from WAVE to AIFF.

Each CD-ROM consists of three different components. The first one is 30 different music beds pre-edited to 60- and 30-second lengths with a looped and short tag version as well. The second is Effects, and has 100 different sound effects in two separate file resolutions (16-bit 22 kHz stereo and 16-bit 11 kHz stereo). The third area is Elements (as in production elements) with 100 files also in two different resolutions. These can be drones, stingers, or just about anything and run from between 2 to 20 seconds in length. To say the least, there's a lot of usable music and sound for one CD-ROM.

Trakfinder is an easy-to-use utility included on each Presentation Audio CD-ROM. Choosing the category in the Descriptive Words window, you can make your search as broad or as narrow as the situation calls for; Figure 5-3 illustrates the options in the Music Search Window.

By clicking the search button in the Trakfinder Music Search Window, you can view each relevant title and get a realistic description of what the file actually is. In the music search, you can easily audition each file and choose the length and resolution as well. Click on the Export button and you're in the Export window (Figure 5-4). If you have no sound editing software, the Export window can save your butt. You can export audio files as stereo or mono 22 kHz or 11 kHz ,16-bit or 8-bit WAVE files. It is also possible to set loops and fade in and out times. There is much more powerful sound editing software available, but the fact that Trakfinder comes as part of a very usable reasonably priced music library is icing on an already delectable cake.

OK, its time to take a close look at the music.

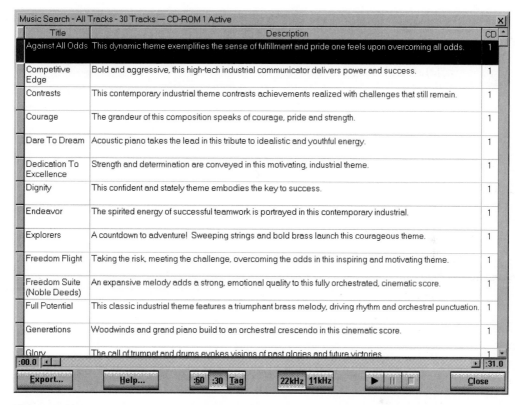

Figure 5-3
The Music Search Window lets you search for and audition files easily.

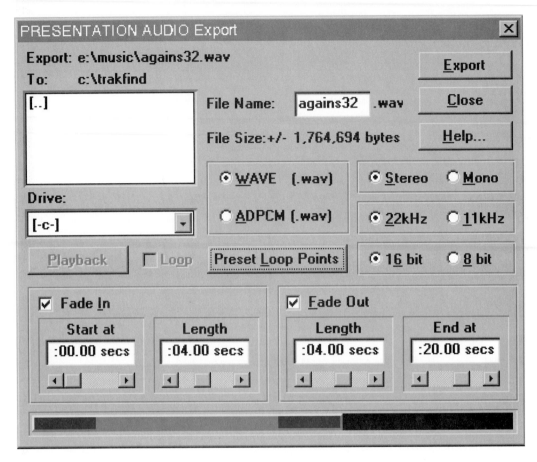

Figure 5-4
The Export Window includes basic sound editing features.

▧ Business and Office (Volume 1)

If I were looking for a way to describe the music in this volume, it would be: Majestic and maybe a little cheesy. I can visualize Dudley Do Right riding to rescue Nell from the evil Snidely Whiplash, an injured Olympic hopeful going for (and winning) the gold, or Lassie rescuing Timmy from some unknown peril (a rabid badger, perhaps). The music here is orchestral with a really big sound and is almost a little too positive and uplifting. However, the music in Volume 1 is a great example of what corporate production music should be. The sound effects and elements in this volume are good (though not great) and really do add an overall value to the package.

Pop Culture (Volume 2)

The music in Volume 2 is a lot more contemporary in an analog sort of way. The guitar stuff on this volume rocks pretty hard and I really like it. I'm sort of amazed at the actual amount of content that's available at this price. This one runs the gamut from Rock to Reggae to Grunge. If there is one thing I don't like about Volume 2, it's that some of the cuts are a little too corporate-sounding for my tastes. Now back to what I do like—the bluesy sounding Ray Charles piano piece and all the steel guitar tracks are really cool and not like anything you're going to find in multimedia-style music collections. The SFX in Volume 2 are good and there is a wide variety that I find very usable. The Elements are great in this one and are easily worth the cost of the volume by themselves. In short, they rock.

High Tech Electronics (Volume 3)

Five or six years ago, the music in Volume 3 was state of the art. Don't get me wrong—I like it, but there's quite an underlying sense of safety and conformity that almost puts me to sleep. Listening to similar music from other collections, the musicians and composers are stretching out more and breathing some life into the tracks. I'm sure I've heard excerpts from Volume 3 late at night on the Discovery Channel. The bottom line, however, is that I would have a lot of use for the music in this volume for my corporate multimedia clients and chances are you will too. The SFX in this volume are really mid-1970s-sounding stuff. The same goes for the Elements. With the re-release of Star Wars, maybe the retro Sci-Fi thing is a good thing.

Environments and Atmospheres (Volume 4)

This one's kind of different. It's open and airy sounding with a sort of pastoral new age feeling about it. The music in Volume 4 is very intro-spective and moving, but there's no fire in the performance. I do the like the SFX in this volume, although the Elements sound very dated and there's not much sparkle in the recording (of the Elements).

Comedy and Animation (Volume 5)

This one is definitely from another era. I'm not sure where I could use most of the material in this volume, but I love it. It's totally whacked-out cartoon stuff that reminds me of a simpler time in my life. I'm sure it has the same effect on everyone who hears it. The SFX in this volume really appeal to my juvenile side and will crack you up. Lots of animal sounds and a few offensive body noises as well, so my only warning is that Mom probably won't like it—She's always discouraged this kind of juvenile behavior (especially from adults). The Elements in this one are sort of unremarkable. The bottom line: I like it.

And finally. . .

The entire collection is a smoking deal and if you develop content for corporate multimedia, buy it. There were some small things I didn't care for in a few of the volumes, but there's so much material here you can't go wrong. For overall usability, Volume 2 is my hands-down favorite. If you develop for an unhip corporate environment, Volume 1 has your name written all over it. Three and Four don't knock me out, but are very usable all the same. Five is my favorite, though I don't know exactly where I'd use it. Now for the good stuff. If you're curious (and I know you are), every single sound file in this entire collection is available for playback (via the Web) using RealAudio.

Web

To preview each and every sound file available in the Presentation Audio collection, take a little detour to www.presentationaudio.com.

Music Bytes

My first taste of Music Bytes (Volume 1 from IQ Media Productions) was via a demo played off the IQ Media Web site. I liked what I heard and thought the entire library might be worth checking out. I'm pleased to say that it was. This is a mixed-platform CD-ROM with the contents available as WAVE and System 7 Sound Files. To audition the different sound files on the Mac, it's as easy as double clicking your mouse on the file of your choice. For the PC, there's an easy-to-use interface that offers features such as HELP, COPY, and Technical Information. For you Mac users, there's an ultra cool multimedia presentation showing off Music Bytes. It's my understanding that a second volume is on the way and will be available by the time you read this. Music Bytes is definitely a good combination of the old school production music concept with a mix of new music and sound. Accessing and auditioning the music files was definitely easier on the PC than with the Mac with this mixed-platform CD-ROM. The reason being there was no interface or description available for the Mac. With the PC, you're given a very simple interface where the music is looking at you in alphabetical order with a one-sentence description for each tune (see Figure 5-5), making it easy to find and select the right music clip. To audition the music files on the Mac, you simply choose a style folder, double click on the file you wish to hear and . . . music (see Figure 5-6). You can also print out the table of contents if you don't mind more paper laying around. The Music Bytes demo (Mac only) is an impressive presentation and would be a great advertising tool if it was located somewhere the general buying public could get a look and a listen.

Okay, so what does it sound like? Well, both the music and the recording quality are really good. One of the advantages with recording in a completely digital environment (as was the case with Music Bytes) is no tape hiss or other ambient garbage will show up on your sound files. Quite often when sampling a file down to a lower resolution (and it's done all the time to save disk space), background garbage that was not previously noticeable shows up and gets in your face. Just to see if the claims of sonic cleanliness in the recording process made a difference, I converted a few of the files down to 8-bit 22 mono. I was surprised, as they sounded pretty good. Now for the bad news. If you want stereo, forget it. All of the Music Bytes sound files are monaural. Granted they're 16-bit 44 kHz, but mono all the same. I'll make an educated guess the

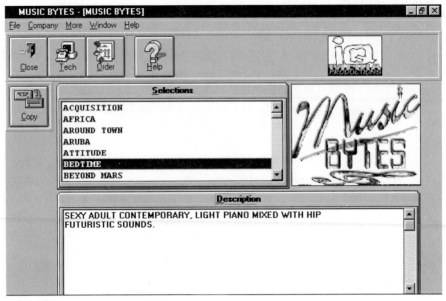

Figure 5-5
The Music Bytes main screen in Windows provides a description of each
sound file for a more intuitive selection.

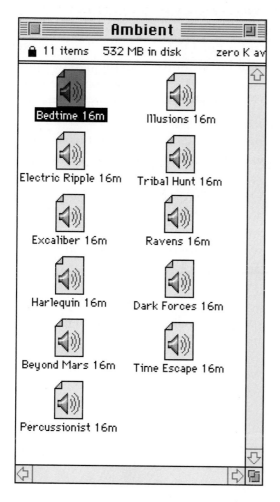

Figure 5-6
Auditioning a sound file on the Mac is a double click away.

reason was to open up more disk space. Still, it's way easier to convert a stereo file to mono than the other way around and I like having options.

As far as content, there are over 80 music beds that each run in the area of 30 seconds in length. I did, however, find an occasional exception to the rule. The music is divided into 12 different categories and for the most part is high-quality in all respects. There are a couple of real minor exceptions that can probably be chalked up to my personal taste more than anything else. I not so silently wish that some of the files in Music Bytes were a minute or more in length. Many of them would make great background spots for radio and TV commercials. Unfortunately, this collection is not licensed for broadcast through the traditional venues. Does this apply to Webcasting as well? Should you purchase Music Bytes, be sure to read the license carefully and make sure your use is in compliance.

There are two more areas of interest in Music Bytes that are a small sound effects collection and some short musical stingers known as workparts. Both are a nice addition and are very usable, but don't really add much to the overall value.

So now we get to the bottom line: I really do like Music Bytes and don't have any reservations recommending it at all. The musicianship, the quality of the recording, and the engineering are excellent, although I'm not real thrilled with the monoaural-only sound files; but again, for the price it's a good deal. This is the only professional clip music library I've seen that uses System 7 Sound instead of AIFF, but there's probably a good reason for it. Because it doesn't affect sound quality, I'm really just thinking out loud anyway. When it comes down to it, Music Bytes offers a lot of bang for the buck and I'd buy it.

Digital Jukebox

Digital Jukebox from Select Media is just that—a Digital Juke Box (see Figure 5-7). It is available for both the Mac and PC, although I only have the Mac version for review. The interface is put together like a Jukebox and offers a variety of musical styles as well as a few effects. In addition to the main themes, each song is broken down into components of the individual instruments. Saving a file is simple and Digital Jukebox even asks you if you'd like to save it as a 8- or 16-bit file.

I've gotta admit, I really like the concept of Digital Jukebox. The interface looks great and the different selections are easy to choose from. I was able to save the file of my choice to the hard drive right from the Digital Jukebox. To my relief, it was 16-bit 44 kHz stereo (Did I mention I like stereo?). I did find something a little confusing. When choosing a song (in this case, it was "Summer On Sunset"), the bottom center window gave me a duration time of 4 minutes and 21 seconds. When I saved it off, the piece ran more like 1:30. I also noticed on my review copy (Mac) that the volume control was not functional.

Figure 5-7
The interface on Digital Jukebox works just like a real jukebox. Scroll
through the menu, click the song you want to hear, and you've got music!

Let's get to the music. There are 12 main selections (one of them being effects). In each selection, you have the option of playing the Main Theme or one of 15 different files that are basically chunks of the song. Some of the alternate sound files are set to loop seamlessly in playback and run in length anywhere from one second to the length of the song. Like in Java Beat, the purpose of many of these files seems to be just to fill space. Unlike Java Beat, enough of these small chunks of the main theme were actually edited in a way to make them useful. So I'd have to say I'm in favor of this feature in the case of Digital Jukebox.

So let's get down to the actual musical content for a minute. There are 11 different main themes in several distinct styles including Latin, Reggae, and Contemporary Jazz. As a composer/ musician myself, I tend to be critical of what I listen to and I like almost everything I hear in Digital Jukebox. Jose Alves (the musician/composer in this case) sounds pretty good and in all honesty I like both his playing and musical ideas. The overall recording quality is pretty good, but maybe lacks the clarity and presence found in Music Bytes. There are a couple of the main themes that I wasn't wild about, but you can more than likely pass that one off to my personal taste (or lack thereof, depending on who you talk to).

There's nothing that really stands out and grabs me in the Effects section. Each one of the 16 choices are ambient synthesizer sounds and could be useful in a variety of situations.

Overall, I like Digital Jukebox and think it's a solid product. There are a few minor bugs in the program, such as the volume control and the sound file Roll 'n Disco wouldn't allow me save it to disk from the main screen, but I've been assured they will be corrected before you read this. To me, Digital Jukebox does seem a bit pricey in comparison to the competition, but again that's only one man's opinion. By the time you read this, there should be a Web demo of Digital Jukebox. To go take a listen, go to: www.directortools.com/mmwshop/jukebox.htm. There's no opinion like your own and the bottom line is always what you hear and not what I or someone else writes.

CyberTunz

Last but certainly not least is CyberTunz (see Figure 5-8). This is where someone a little more ethical than myself could run into a conflict of interest. Confession time: In the case of CyberTunz, I am the content developer (I composed, performed, and engineered the music). In the interest of fair play, I'll make it real easy for you the reader. The CD-ROM (with this book) includes a light version of CyberTunz at no additional cost to you. You may use any of the musical components in CyberTunz demo folder (on the CD-ROM) royalty-free for all Web (and most multimedia) playback. In the interest of journalistic integrity (if there really is such a thing), when it comes to CyberTunz, I'll report the facts and let the demo speak for itself.

I'll do my best to take the Joe Friday approach (at least in this instance)—just the facts. CyberTunz is a mixed-platform CD-ROM con-

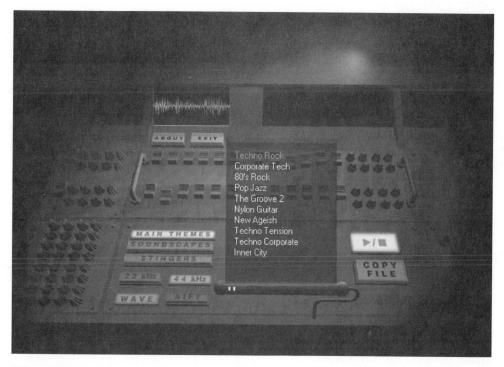

Figure 5-8
The CyberTunz main screen gives you access to three main musical styles:
Main Themes, Soundscapes, and Stingers.

sisting of three main musical components: Main Themes, Soundscapes, and Stingers. The interface is straight forward with each function labeled for the user's convenience. The music is available as AIFF or WAVE files in 16-bit 44 kHz stereo or 16-bit 22 mono (1/4 the file size). To audition the music, choose one of the three main musical components and pick a file from the description that shows up in the center of the screen. All that's left to do at this point is click on the play button and you're in business. To transfer a file to your hard drive, just press the copy button, save, and you're there.

There are 10 Main Themes that each run an average of one minute in length. The 12 Soundscape files are a bit more relaxed in nature and are between 15 and 30 seconds long. There are 32 Stingers that stylistically run the gamut from timpani rolls to a string quartet. As far as recording quality and content, you get to be the judge. Go to the CyberTunz demo folder on the CD-ROM and take a listen.

Last Dance

The first part of this chapter was a tough one for me to write. It's easy to come off like a bitter know-it-all wanna-be musician trying to impress readers with my vast knowledge of music by taking a negative approach. At least in my case, nothing could be further from the truth and I truly hope I don't come off that way. I like at least something about each of these libraries and, with the exception of Java Beat, I have no problem recommending any one of them without hesitation. If the music files on Java Beat were 16-bit (instead of 8), I would probably withdraw my protest as I do happen to like the music—just not the sound quality of the files. Again, I truly hope you carefully read Chapter 4, as it's important to get a good handle on the music/software license and how it can affect you. Make sure the music you purchase is available for the use you intend. I've used the licenses from each of the mentioned clip music products from this chapter as examples in a hope to enlighten, entertain, and inform. (Was that cheesy or what?)

 ## Sound Effects

Sound effects can be as important as music in trying to convey a message or set a certain mood. We'll take a look at few of the options available in the search to create cool Web sound. Several of the clip music libraries reviewed in this chapter had sound effects in addition to music. The Presentation Audio series had 100 sound effects files on each volume and was probably the only one mentioned that really had enough files and variety to merit a mention (at least in the world of SFX). At the time of writing this chapter, I was only able to find one complete sound effects collection on CD-ROM that was designed specifically for the multimedia market, so here it is. . . .

Janus Professional Sound Library

So what is the JPSL (you should have figured out this abbreviation by now)? It's a collection of 5,000 digitally recorded and mastered sounds. This mixed-platform CD-ROM is an obvious choice for the user who has no desire to deal with converting sound effects over from a Red Book audio compact disk into an AIFF or WAVE file.

This sound library is comprised of six separate CD-ROMs and the effects are listed alphabetically and by category. The main screen (which happens to be the only screen—see Figure 5-9), is also a very easy-to-use search tool. Everything is labeled so well even I could understand it. There are three windows from which to choose in the main screen: Categories, Sound List, and Playlist. Here's an example: If you were to highlight, say, Animals in the Categories window (as shown in Figure 5-9), all of the choices available in that category would appear in the Sound List window. At this point, playback is possible by two methods—highlighting the description of your choice, or dragging each sound you wish to hear into the Play List window. You can then trigger playback in sequential order from the VCR type (start/stop) controls at the bottom of the list window.

Tip

There is a Find feature and Volume Control directly beneath the Categories window. I thought I'd give them both a try. Using Find, I typed in *Cats* and even though there were a number of cat noises in Volume 1, no cats were to be found. Changing the search to *Cat* in the singular, 11 cat sounds showed up in the playlist. Now I'm pretty sure a Kitten is also a Cat (or at least distantly related), but alas none of the Kitten sounds showed up in the **Cat**egory. The moral of this little tail is to be very specific when searching for sounds.

Saving a single sound (or group of sounds) is as simple as moving the files from the Sound List to the Play List and using the Save PlayList function. I tried it and it worked flawlessly whether with single or multiple files. You are also given the option of saving the file at 16-bit 44 kHz stereo or 8-bit 22 kHz mono.

Moving right along to the actual sounds themselves . . . . The files are all 16-bit 44 kHz stereo and the original source recordings are generally

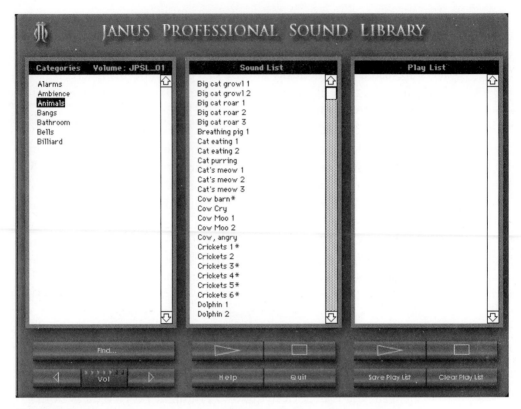

Figure 5-9
In the JPSL main screen, drag files from the Sound List to the Play List to
hear the music.

good. There is a lot of variety here and I find more than enough useful
material to make it worth the new lower cost of this collection. I won't
bother to get into the individual sounds (I mean, there are 5,000 of
them), but as I really get to learn my way around the content of this collection, I'm finding I like it more and more. Granted, there are a lot of
sounds I will never use – though you never know. The interface and
controls are really useful and are about as bug-free as any sound-based
program I've seen. The exception would be the volume control (in my
copy, at least), which didn't always work. Again, this feature, while con-
venient, is one most of us can live without.

If you were to compare the JPSL with the high-end professional sound
libraries designed for broadcast, it might come up a little short. When you
consider the cost versus performance, it's another story altogether. The
convenience of the search program coupled with the easy access of hav-

ing it all on CD-ROM makes the JPSL a real time-saver. If your needs are multimedia and you want an easy-to-use reasonably priced sound effects library, I would recommend the JPSL.

Other SFX Options

If your sound effects needs are a little more specific and high-end, then there are some other options for you. Two of the most predominant players in the world of commercially available sound effects would have to be The Hollywood Edge and Sound Ideas. For years, I have owned and been using SFX libraries from both of these companies. They have paid for themselves many times over.

Buying any one of these libraries can set you back a few bucks ($500, $1,000, or more), but I've found they offer such a wide variety of options that they are well worth the cost. For myself, I will normally purchase a SFX library only when a specific need comes up. As an example, one of my clients needed bird sounds for a project. Not your run-of-the-mill generic birds chirping in the background sort of ambiance thing, but a whole bunch of real specific birds. Animal Trax from Hollywood Edge was the solution to my problem (and the only one I could afford), with two of the CDs in the collection being nothing but birds. While it's doubtful I'll ever have that deep of a need for bird sounds again, I've added it to my collection and if the need should ever arise, I'm there. Instead of me going into depth on all the available libraries from these two companies, I'll just send you to their respective Web sites (see the end of this chapter). The Hollywood Edge site is sound-enabled with RealAudio 2.0. If you're really curious, both of these companies will send you a demo CD. More free stuff is a good thing!

 # The MIDI Connection

Believe it or not, for as little as 10 bucks, you can purchase a collection of MIDI files for playback on your Web site. In Chapter 16, "MIDI on the Web," I will not only show you the many different MIDI options for playback on the Web, but also where to buy them and how much you'll expect to pay. Another example of one-stop shopping and why this book is such a great deal!

Now That You Know

Table 5-1 presents the products featured in this chapter and their Web locations.

Table 5-1 Music and SFX Library URL

Product	Description	Web Location
CyberTunz	Music	http://www.monsoon.org/sound_advice
Digital Jukebox	Music	http://www.directortools.com/mmwshop/ jukebox.htm
Hollywood Edge	Sound Effects	http://www.hollywoodedge.com
JPSL	Sound Effects	http://www.janusinteractive.com
Java Beat	Music	http://www.jawai.com
Music Bytes	Music	http://www.iqm.com/music.html
Presentation Audio	Music and SFX	http://www.presentationaudio.com
Sound Ideas	Sound Effects	http://www.sound-ideas.com

The market for clip music and sound is going to explode over the next couple of years with every style and quality known to man showing up for all to hear. It is my sincere hope that now that you've become aware of a few of the current options, you'll be armed with enough knowledge to make the right purchase for your needs. I purposely omitted the retail and or street prices of these products because, like everything else in life, they're subject to change. However, I have it on good authority that you can expect to pay a minimum of $25 for the least-expensive single CD-ROM library.

Chapter 6

Voice Talent

 In This Chapter

- Desktop Recording Tips
- Hiring Voice Talent
- Recording Tutorials
- Voiceover Examples

Because this book is about working with sound content for the Web, you knew that sooner or later we'd have to deal with the hiring, recording, and editing of the human voice. The once silent regions of Cyberspace are now alive with all types of sound and music, and now more then ever the spoken word is part of the mix. This chapter contains much of what you will need to know when working with voice talent, including how to handle script management, contract voice talent, produce and direct a voiceover session, as well as how to edit and prepare the sound file for its final destination. For those of you who can't get the *do-it-yourself* recording thing out of your system, there are some aural comparisons between low-, medium-, and high-end recording solutions in this chapter.

Recording Quality

For the life of me, I'll never figure out why a company will spend as much as $100,000 on a project and record the voiceover on a $20 microphone using one of the guys from the sales department who seems to have a really good voice. State-of-the-art graphics, animation, and music—topped off with the crackle and hiss of a really bad voiceover recording. What's that all about? Even if the final destination of the audio is as a low-resolution RealAudio file, the quality of the original source material will dictate whether the overall sound quality ends up being good or really ugly. If the audio file sounds bad to begin with, do you think it will get better when you down sample and convert it? While life, multimedia, and the Web are a series of compromises, my mission is to make sure the audio you create and then playback from your Web site sounds as good as possible. So let's go listen to an example.

An example of the Good, the not so Bad, and the Downright Ugly

Sound quality is the name of the game, and if you're even half as stubborn as I am, the only way to get the message across is with an example that's too obvious to ignore. So, here's what I've done. I've recorded a sample voiceover using a combination of three different sound systems, and through the miracles of modern technology, I've pasted them all together to give you a chance to listen and compare. The entire example has been recorded in three parts and will be played back as a 16-bit 44 kHz mono file. Even though the sound file is of CD quality, as you will soon find out the components used in the recording process will definitely have an impact on what you'll end up hearing.

▪ The three systems

1. The first system consists of the free microphone that came with my Power Mac 8500 going direct to the audio input of the computer without any preamp or EQ to boost or alter the sound. This microphone probably has a street value of about 50 cents and other than the fact that it does work, it serves no practical purpose. Still, it was free!

84

2. The second system would be considered more of a low-budget semi-pro home recording set up. I used an Audio Technica ATM63HE microphone ($200) running into a Mackie 1202 VLZ 12 Channel Microphone Mixer ($469)with the sound finally making its way to the computer through the analog inputs of an AudioMedia III (PCI) card ($995) from Digidesign.

3. Overkill is what I'm going for in this last system, but with any luck you'll get the point I'm trying to make. Going to my favorite professional recording studio, we start with a standard of the industry—a Neumann U87 Microphone ($3,000) running into a Peavey VMP2 tube Stereo Microphone preamp, and EQ ($1,000) running into a TLA C1 Tube Compressor ($1,375.00), going straight to DAT (Digital Audio Tape). Tube gear has become very retro in the recording industry as of late because of the warmth and depth that can be achieved with its use.

As you can see and are about to hear, the price between these three systems is probably about as great as the sound quality will be. Does more expensive really sound better? Load tutorial file CH6EX1.WAV or CH6EX1.SND and find out.

CD-ROM

In the Chapter 6 tutorial folder on the CD-ROM accompanying this book, you will find (and hopefully listen to) the file CH6EX1.WAV (PC) or CH6EX1.SND (Mac).

Okay, you've listened. What do you think? System 1 was an obvious ploy on my part to teach you a lesson. You get what you pay for, or there's a reason why that microphone was free. System 2 on the other hand, while certainly not state-of-the-art, is more than adequate for many a situation, especially a low- or no-budget scenario. If you know what you're doing and pay attention, it's amazing what you can get away with and still come up with really good sound. System 3, however, is it! You just can't go wrong with the best. While I wouldn't recommend you go out and purchase the most expensive recording gear you can find, booking time in the right recording studio is always a good solution. Not only will you be able to use expensive state-of-the-art equipment, but you'll also have a trained audio professional assuring you'll get the most bang for your buck and superior quality as well.

■ The tradeoff

After listening to this first oral example, by now (I hope) you probably have enough sense not to go with a cheap microphone. This is good. At the same time, you're probably not going to go out and drop $25 grand on recording equipment either, and this is all right too. For most of you, the middle ground is going to do just fine, and a setup along the lines of System 2 will get the job done. Sure it's a tradeoff, but when you think about it, it's a good one.

Desktop recording

Many of you work on your own cars and repair your own homes, so no matter how much I try to persuade you, you're going to record the voiceover yourself. In fact, you might even use yourself or an unsuspecting friend or family member as the voice talent. For those of you new to all of this, you may need to be patient and have an adventurous spirit to achieve optimum results. Using myself as the guinea pig, I'll walk you through the pitfalls and triumphs of recording it yourself.

■ Mr. Microphone

Remember, we're keeping it low-cost and simple here. In the music biz, a favorite mic of the famous and not-so famous alike is the Shure SM58. Not only is it virtually indestructible, but if you look around, you can often find a used "58" for around $50. The street price of a new "58" will run in the ballpark of $120. Audio Technica is another company that makes good-quality reasonably priced microphones that fit into the $100 to $200 price range. I have half a dozen different microphones that fall into this category and while I mainly use them for live vocals in a band situation, they are more than adequate for the low-budget voiceover job as well.

> **Warning**
>
> Without a mixing board or microphone preamp, even a great microphone will end up giving you less than acceptable results.

Mixers

Depending on your overall needs, there are a bunch of desktop mixing boards (or micro mixers) that have a list price of under $500. My longtime favorite in this category has been (and still is) the Mackie 1202 VLZ. This handy little mixer has many features that are standard on much more expensive professional mixers including 4 pretty decent mic preamps built into 4 of the 12 channels. While getting into all of the features of this mixer is beyond the scope of this book, the 1202 VLZ is one unit that I highly recommend. For those of you looking for a smoking deal, there are also quite a few of the original Mackie 1202 Micro Series mixers out there in the used market. The street price seems to run in the area of $200. While the original doesn't have all the bells and whistles of later VLZ versions, it still sounds and works great.

Other options in the micro mixer category include products from Peavey Electronics and Yamaha. For more info about all three of these companies and their products, go to Table 6-1.

Table 6-1 Micro Mixers on the Web

Company	Description	URL
Mackie	Compact Mixers	`http://www.mackie.com`
Peavey Electronics	Compact Mixers	`http://www.peavey.com`
Yamaha Pro Audio	Compact Mixers	`http://www.yamaha.co.jp/` `product/proaudio/homeenglish/`

Recording/editing software

In the interest of affordability and simplicity, we're going to do all the slicing and dicing of audio in the virtual realm. Most software-based sound recording and editing applications have all the basic DSP tools needed to successfully record and edit a simple voiceover session. In Tutorial 6-1, the DSP tools we'll be using are compression and a noise gate.

Tutorial 6-1: Recording and Editing a Voice File

Simple and uncomplicated is the name of the game. Using a basic microphone, mixer, and computer, we're going to record and edit a small voiceover file. To make it easy, I'm going to assume that you have absolutely no experience whatsoever in recording. The application we will use in this tutorial is Sound Forge 4.0 from Sonic Foundry.

Time for me to confess: I was raised in a non-Windows environment and my home is littered with various vintages of Macs and Power Macs. Fortunately, in the past I had put in many long hours with Sound Forge 3.0 and I'll admit it, I really like 4.0 and my new Win 95 machine. There, I said it; I don't mind Windows 95 (when it works). Sound Forge is reasonably priced and so loaded down with both basic and advanced features, I hardly know where to start. So let's get on with it.

■ What you need

The items that you need to perform this tutorial are:

- ■ Sound Forge 4.0
- ■ A Windows 95 compatible PC (486/66) with 16 MB of RAM
- ■ A professional Microphone, Stand, and Cable
- ■ A small desktop mixing board
- ■ Audio cable to connect the mixer to the soundcard.
- ■ Headphones

■ But first...

There could be quite a few of you who have little to no experience with microphones, mixers, and recording in general. If you fit into this category, this next little section is for you. Because every mixer and microphone is a little different, there's no easy way to give exact setup instructions. What I'll do instead is give you a simple explanation of how to set up a basic chain of audio events. What I have listed here is merely some common-sense basic rules. Strap yourself in and good luck!

1. The microphone must be in the mic stand and connected to the mic cable. Also, be sure the microphone is not facing the speakers or you'll find out what a feedback loop is (and why it's a bad thing).

2. Connect the mic cable to an input channel of your mixer (channel one should do fine). You now have two volume controls to worry about: the master (or main) volume and the channel volume. The master volume should always be set higher than the channel volume. If the opposite were to occur, you would get distortion. This can be wonderful for guitar but not so good for your voice. On some mixers, the individual channels may also have a trim pot that will need to be adjusted as well. Start with the trim pot at a low setting and while speaking into the microphone, slowly raise the level until you achieve a full clean sound. Again, if it's distorting, you went too far.

3. Connect the main output to the input of the computer's sound card. At this point, if your mixer is actually plugged in and turned on, it is possible you might be able to make some sort of sound.

Those of you who actually didn't listen to the first tutorial file in this chapter are probably asking "Why can't I just hook up the microphone directly to the soundcard?" Well, you can but it will probably sound pretty bad. The mixer will boost the signal (via the microphone preamp) and give you more control over the sound quality. Go direct and you have no real control over the signal that leaves the microphone and enters the soundcard. If the signal is weak with no presence, the end result will be audio garbage.

For those of you who absolutely don't get it, I'm going philosophical on you for a moment. (For those of you who do, don't laugh too loudly). Here's another way to look at it: Think of your mouth as a giant reservoir of sound. When you talk into a microphone, you're sending a stream of sound down a series of audio canals to the ocean known as your hard drive. Your job is to make sure the pathway is clean and clear all the way to your computer and software. Stop, take a deep breath, and contemplate life for three or four seconds. You are now ready to proceed.

CD-ROM

In the Demo Folder (PC) is a save-disabled copy of Sound Forge 4.0. It can be used to perform most of Tutorial 6-1.

Recording and editing

1. Start the (Demo or) Application Sound Forge 4.0. The main screen is shown in Figure 6-1.

The Record
Button

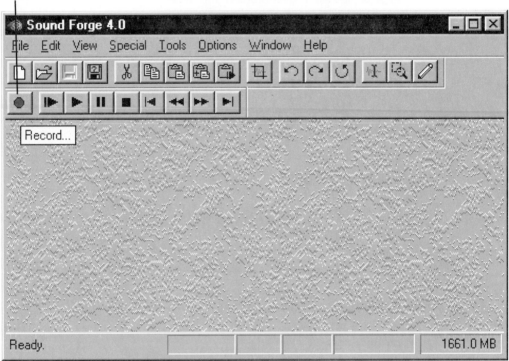

Figure 6-1
Open Sound Forge 4.0 to see the main screen.

2. On the Transport, click the red Record button. This action opens the Record dialog window.

3. The Record dialog window shown in Figure 6-2 is where you choose the
    what, when, where, and how (so to speak). First, you need to set the
    Recording attributes. For the purpose of this tutorial, record at a sample
    rate of 44 kHz, sample size of 16 bit, and in Mono. Click on the New button
    to access the Recording attributes in the New Window dialog box shown in
    Figure 6-3. Change your settings (if necessary) and click OK to continue.

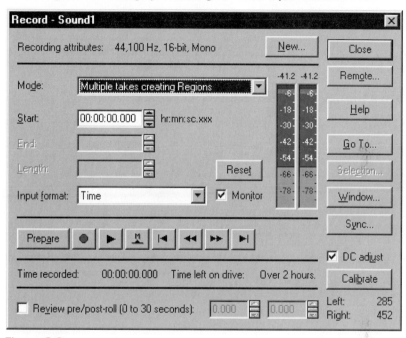

Figure 6-2
The Record dialog window in Sound Forge 4.0

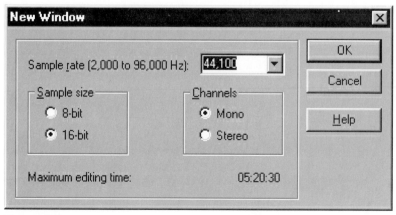

Figure 6-3
You can change the Recording attributes in the new Window Dialog box.

4. The next step is to select which Mode you choose to record in. There are five you can choose from as shown in Figure 6-4. Select "Multiple takes creating Regions" for this tutorial.

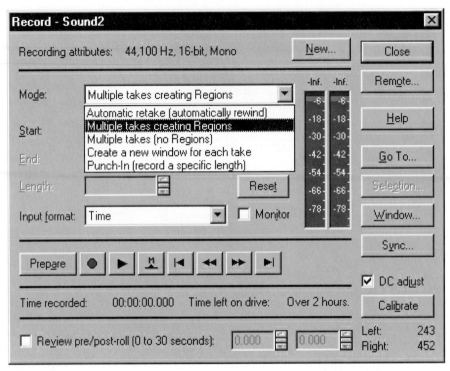

Figure 6-4
Choose "Multiple takes creating Regions" as the Mode for the tutorial.

5. Now let's get ready to record a take. The Record Meters are very important to this process. Notice in Figure 6-5 that I have checked the Monitor function box. This enables you to monitor the audio input levels while recording. Your peak levels should not go into the red (-6 dB) or you will get distortion, which is not good. If you are red lining the input levels, then lower the input level on the mixer channel to which the microphone is connected until the situation is corrected. If you can, keep the levels in the green occasionally jumping into the yellow.

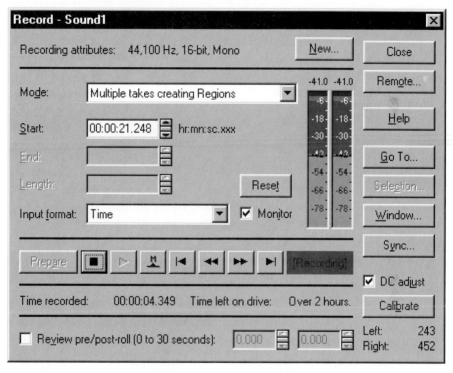

Figure 6-5
To enable the Record Meters, check the monitor box.

While we're here, I'll explain the meaning and use of the Prepare function (accessed through the Prepare button located at the far left of the Transport shown in Figure 6-6). When you enable the Record function, there is a slight delay before you can actually start recording. Click on Prepare first, and then when you hit Record, there's no delay; recording is instantaneous. So, click Prepare and you're ready to record a take.

Figure 6-6
To start recording, click the red Record button (directly to the left of the Prepare button).

> **Note**
>
> If you're going to record a voice file, it sort of helps to have a script. While I will grant you the artistic license to record what you want, here's what I used: "Cutting Edge Web Audio from Prentice Hall Professional Technical Reference, the only comprehensive up-to-date guide to sound on the Web. Anything else is just a book". There you go.

6. Using the short script that I prepared (or one of your own design), place yourself in front of the microphone. Options are important, so read the script three times in a row while you record so you have a slight variation on your performance. Okay, click the Record button (located directly to the right of the Prepare button shown in Figure 6-6) and start talking. When you've finished, press the space bar to terminate the record process. Click the Close button in the top right-hand corner of the Record window to get yourself back the WAVE edit window in Sound Forge.

CD-ROM

For those of you who don't have a microphone or mixer but still want to continue with this tutorial, you're in luck. In the Chapter 6 tutorial folder (on the CD-ROM accompanying this book) are my results from Step 6. Load the tutorial file CH6EX2.WAV to continue with Step 7.

7. You now have some sort of recording. If this is your first time, you'll probably need to experiment a little before you achieve optimum results. Be patient and give it a few passes.

I guess it's time for you to take a listen to your work. Press the space bar to initiate playback of the file. If you're curious to hear what I came up with, load the tutorial file CH6EX2.WAV (you can find it on the CD-ROM). Figure 6-7 shows my results of our exercise, which is three different takes of the voiceover script.

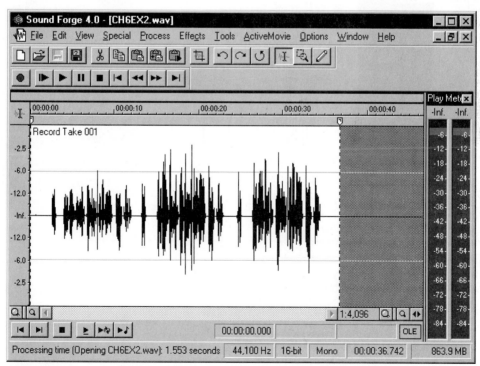

Figure 6-7
Press the space bar to initiate playback of the voiceover script. There are three separate takes residing in the tutorial file CH6EX2.WAV.

8. We now need to choose the best performance of the three and send the others into the twilight zone. Using the file CH6EX2 as my work file, I'm going to go with the first take because it seems a little less perky and more natural sounding than the other two. Place your cursor at the beginning portion of the audio you wish to select and, holding down the left mouse button, drag over the entire area as shown in Figure 6-8. Under the Edit menu, select Trim/Crop (Ctrl + T). This will delete the sections of file CH6EX2.WAV that were not selected. Save this new file (shown in Figure 6-9) as CH6EX3.WAV.

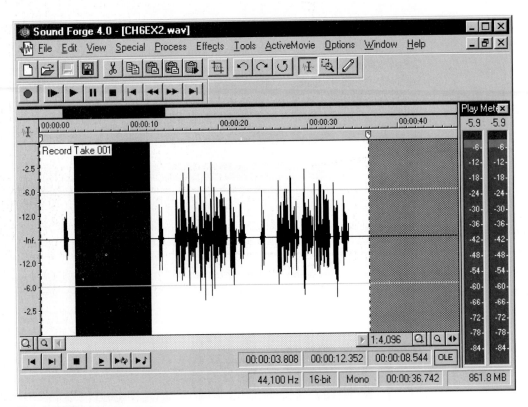

Figure 6-8
Select the portion of the file you wish to keep by dragging the cursor over it while holding down the left mouse button.

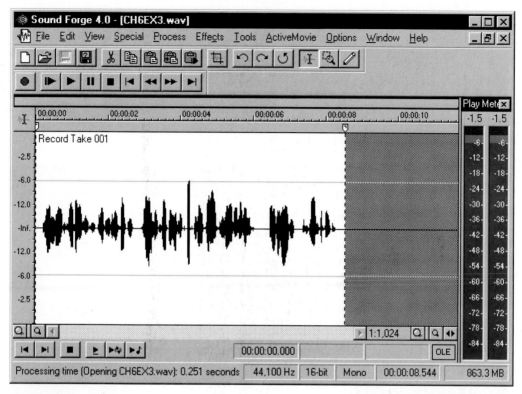

Figure 6-9
After editing the file with the Trim/Crop function, save it as CH6EX3.WAV.

9. It's time to add a little compression! Not to be confused with compressing the size of a file when saving it, the Compressor in Sound Forge is found under the Effects menu under Dynamics (Graphic). What Dynamic Compression does is it lowers the peaks and raises the valleys on an audio file, sort of a smoothing-out process. Depending on the settings you use, you will notice an overall jump in volume and presence. There are a number of compressor presets available in the Graphic Dynamics window. For this step, we'll use the preset 2:1 compression starting at -18 dB as shown in Figure 6-10.

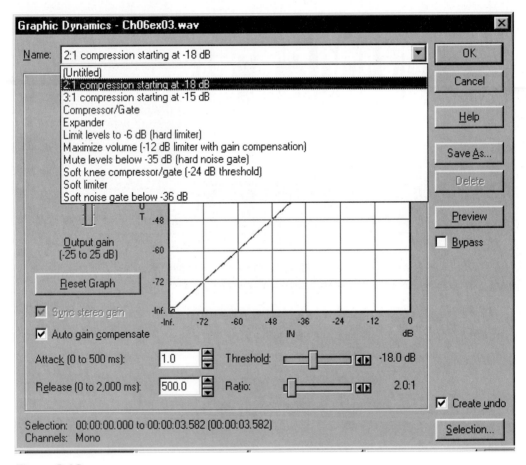

Figure 6-10
The many options found under Graphic Dynamics include basic compressor functions.

As in previous steps, you can audition the changes in the sound file by clicking on the Preview button. Fortunately, the preset compressor we're using was tailor-made for this particular voiceover file so all you need to do is click OK to proceed. When you've completed this process, save the file as CH6EX4.WAV. As you can see in Figure 6-11, the tutorial file has changed as a result of using the compressor.

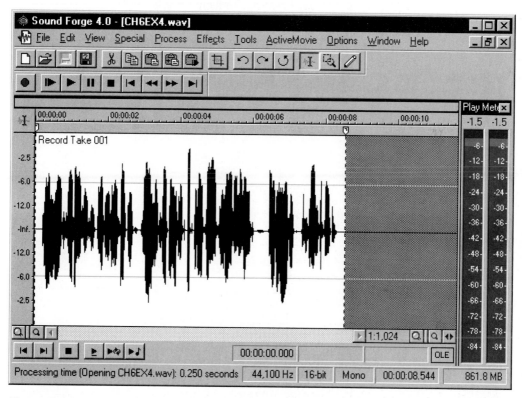

Figure 6-11
Notice the visual changes in the sound file after adding Dynamic Compression.

10. Well there's one more stop we need to make to get this WAVE file ready for playback on the Web. We need to shrink this file down just a bit more in overall size to get it ready for conversion to one of the many Web audio formats featured in this book.

Select Process@(Resample. What we're going to do is resample this file from 16-bit 44 kHz mono to 16-bit 22 kHz mono, cutting the file size in half. In the Resample window, select 22,050 Hz with anti-alias filter as shown in Figure 6-12. Click OK to initiate the process. Press the space bar to listen to the new version of the file. You will probably notice little to no difference in the overall sound quality, but you have just reduced the file size by half. When you're done, save the file as CH6EX5.WAV.

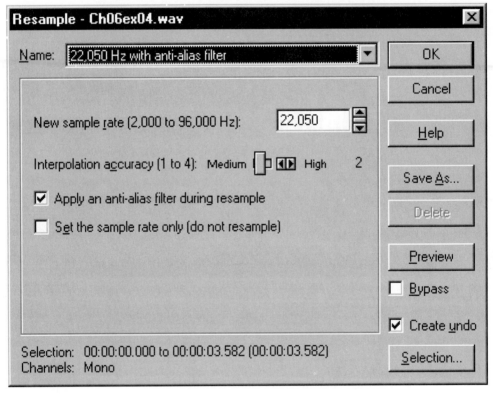

Figure 6-12
In the Resample window, select 22,050 Hz with anti-alias filter then click OK.

Note

The anti-alias filter will help to filter out unwanted sonic garbage that shows up during the down sample process.

◾ In retrospect

There are many editing options available when using Sound Forge 4.0 and I only touched on a few in Tutorial 6-1. Even if you don't choose to install and use the demo software (Sound Forge 4.0), you can still follow the process and listen to the four different tutorial sound files (CH6EX2 through CH6EX5) to hear the results of the different steps for yourself. Many of you will find some of the software-based DSP tools a little unfamiliar. A great way to help understand how the different processes work is to go back and experiment with the presets. A good example would be in using the Dynamic Compression in Step 9. There are a number of different presets that will bring varied results when used. Check some of them out and at the very least you'll probably be amused and you'll probably understand the inner workings of Dynamic Compression a whole lot better.

Sound Forge is one of the more popular sound design tools for the PC and while there are limitations (only two tracks at a time, for instance), it's easy to record high-quality audio files using it. You'll be seeing a lot more of Sound Forge throughout this book.

 # Gathering Your Resources

One of the problems often associated with strolling into uncharted territory is not knowing the rules of the game. Knowing the who, where, and how much do I pay for it can make all the difference in the world. In the real world, every project and situation will be different in so many ways it's almost hard to imagine. Even though this section deals with finding, recording, and editing the human voice, many of the principles can be applied to hiring musicians as well. (They usually work cheaper, too!) No one has all the answers, but this section can be a good starting point.

Finding a studio

Doing the wise and prudent thing, you have chosen to use a professional recording studio to record your voice talent. So now you ask yourself (and me) where, how, when, and who? That I can answer.

There are recording studios that specialize in handling voiceover sessions usually for broadcast. It has been my experience that they are usually very expensive and more often than not, the quality of their equipment is no better than what I have in my home studio. "How can that be?" you ask. Location, location, location! A studio that is affiliated with a broadcast facility (in the same building, for instance) is able to charge exorbitant rates. I've heard the old "They must be good, look where their studio is" line more than once. So essentially, if you want to pay twice as much for less, go for it.

Your best bet, however, is a recording studio that specializes in music. You will find a better variety of microphones and outboard gear as well as an hourly rate that is more than likely half that of the studios that specialize in doing voiceover for broadcast. As an example, a small- to medium-sized studio that specializes in music production in Phoenix, AZ can run $30 to $50 an hour depending on the facility, time of day, and engineer. This is a great deal. On the other hand, the going rate seems to be around $100 an hour (or more) to use a relatively lame and under-equipped studio that caters to the pre- and post-production broadcast crowd.

Another definite reason to use the music facility is more toys (tools). Most decently equipped music studios can burn audio and (or) data CDs on the spot, giving you a permanent and quick storage solution for the raw data from your session. It's also become standard to have Mac or PC hard disk editing systems on site and many facilities are able to edit your raw voiceover tape into a finished product on the spot. Quite often, I'll record my voiceover sessions straight to the hard disk and save the data on a CD-ROM.

Enough about the why; let's move to the where. I've used two resources over the years that have yet to fail me—the Yellow Pages and the Classifieds in the local Music and Entertainment Newspapers. Also, word of mouth is a good way to go as well. If you hear something you like, find out who did it.

Note

Recording studios want Web pages, and Web designers doing sound-enabled Web sites need audio. There's a good chance that, as a Web designer, you can work a trade out with a studio (or studios) looking for exposure on the Web. For those of you who've got a little hustle, you might even be able to get a few recording studios as permanent accounts. Think about it!

Hiring talent

How do you find a voiceover artist? It's not like you can look in the Yellow Pages—or is it? There are a number of tried and true methods that have worked for me.

1. **The Agencies**: Normally listed in the Yellow Pages under "Talent Agencies," this is probably your best resource for finding seasoned professionals. Hiring through an Agency is more expensive, but you have access to a wider variety of talent.

2. **Recording Studios**: Even a studio whose main client base is music will handle the occasional voiceover session. This is a good place to look as you will find quite a few Recording Studios that are listed in the Yellow Pages. Most studios have a working relationship with at least several voiceover artists and can give you recommendations and an idea of what the entire hourly rate will be.

3. **Radio Stations**: To me, this is the logical place to look for voice talent. On-the-air talent often supplement their meager wages with freelance work. Radio personalities are probably going to be out of the range of most budgets, but the not-so-famous (those working the midnight to 4 AM shift) can probably do the job just fine. One of my favorite voiceover artists works for the local NPR station in Phoenix.

4. **Trade Publications**: There are a number regional media resource publications springing up. These books usually contain listings of voiceover artists, composers, studios, and just about anyone else you could ever think of using on a project. Many of these publications are now setting up Web sites that contain much of the same info as their books or magazines.

5. **Word of Mouth**: This has been my most reliable source of voice talent. Often, when I need someone, I ask friends in the business who they would recommend for my particular project.

6. **The Web**: As time goes on, more and more companies will be building sites that cater to production for Interactive Multimedia. You may even be able to audition a number of voiceover artists (and musicians) right from a sound-enhanced Web site. That opens up some interesting possibilities.

■ The cost

So, what should you expect to pay? That's a tough one. In my local market (Phoenix, AZ), the standard agency fee for voice talent seems to run around $350 for the first hour and $150 for each additional half hour. This does not include the additional 20–percent agency fee that is tacked on to the total. The costs are going to vary regionally and, as you well know, nothing is ever set in stone. Another option is to bypass the agencies altogether and go straight to the source. I've gotten hourly rates from professional talent that have varied from $200 to $400 an hour. Remember that every situation is different and some will be more flexible on additional hours than others.

One tactic that I take on a regular basis is the concept of *piece work*. I'll have a client come to me with a script and a budget and I'll go to the voice talent with a proposal of "Can you do this project for $X amount?" When the amount is reasonable, I seldom get turned down.

Another factor to remember: A great voice doesn't necessarily mean a great reader. Make sure the talent you use fits the project. Someone used to doing 30- to 60-second commercial TV and Radio spots might not do so well reading documentary-type material. If you're running on an hourly basis and the amount and depth of the material is causing a major vapor lock on the voice talent's brain, it can get expensive in both studio time and the talent's hourly rate. It's important to foresee potential problems before they ever get a chance to happen.

Performance rights organizations and royalties

This is going to be an interesting situation as it develops. SAG (the Screen Actors Guild) and AFTRA (the American Federation of Television and Radio Artists) are probably going to figure into this equation at some point. There is a policy in regards to royalty payments for performance over the Internet. What that policy is, no one would really tell me. While researching this book, everyone sort of passed the buck to someone else and I was never able to get a straight answer. Sort of like politics. One of the current problems concerning performances, copyrights, and intellectual property in regards to the Web is that many of the laws are so vague and outdated it's next to impossible to for anyone to come up with a set policy. For the most part, SAG and AFTRA agreements only cover rebroadcast of film, radio, and television over the Web, although the rules and regulations vary from state to state.

■ The signoff sheet

Just to be safe, I always get a written release from any voice talent that I hire stating that with the agreed-upon payment (fill in the amount), said talent has been compensated in full. The *signoff sheet* is a protective device used so there is no later misunderstanding about such issues as royalty payments for performance. Both parties sign a simple and easy-to-understand agreement explaining the terms. While it might not be legally binding in a court of law, it certainly can show the intent of both parties if a future dispute were to end up in court.

Unions and their rules for performance (not to mention laws) can vary from state to state and city to city. It is always good to do a little research and see how they will effect you and your specific project. If using Union talent, you may not even be allowed to use a signoff sheet.

Preproduction

The key word here is *preparation*. Never go into the recording studio until you know exactly what you and your client want. If you're the client, so much the better. There are times that even when you show up prepared, you're still stuck with a bunch of changes. Make sure before you get to the studio that the script is finalized and you know how any of those really strange words are properly pronounced.

Recording and Editing in a Virtual Environment

Because we are dealing with Cyberspace in a disconnected sort of way, I usually record and edit in a virtual environment. What that means is many of the traditional recording tasks done in the analog domain of a recording studio have been bypassed in favor of software-based DSP and editing. In the case of working on a voiceover project, it's possible to take a sound file and clean up background noise, replace individual words or phrases, and generally turn a lump of coal into a diamond. This section presents a few software tools I've been using as of late to accomplish this task.

The Native Power Pack from Waves has a number of effects plug-ins for both the Mac and the PC. Using Sound Forge 4.0, I'll run you through some of the basics. You can also do these tutorials using SoundEdit 16 (Version 2) and the Mac version of the Waves Native Power Pack. While the screens and a few of the basic functions are slightly different, if you're of slightly above average intelligence and aren't afraid to get your feet wet, it shouldn't be a problem. So, even if haven't run out and purchased the Waves Native Power Pack just to do this tutorial, follow along anyway and you'll get an idea of what to expect.

Tutorial 6-2: Virtual editing tools

Using the right tools for the right job is very important. In Tutorial 6-2, we'll use a few of the components of the Waves Native Power Pack to clean up an audio file.

The compressor that comes as part of Sound Forge 4.0 is pretty cool. However, the compressor in the Native Power Pack (Waves) is just a little bit better.

▥ What you need

The items that you need to perform this tutorial are:

- Sound Forge 4.0
- A Windows 95 compatible PC (486/66) with 16 MB of RAM
- Tutorial sound file CH6EX3.WAV
- The Native Power Pack from Waves

◼ Breaking the waves

1. Start the application Sound Forge 4.0 and open the tutorial file CH6EX3.WAV (let's beat this file up one more time), shown in Figure 6-13.

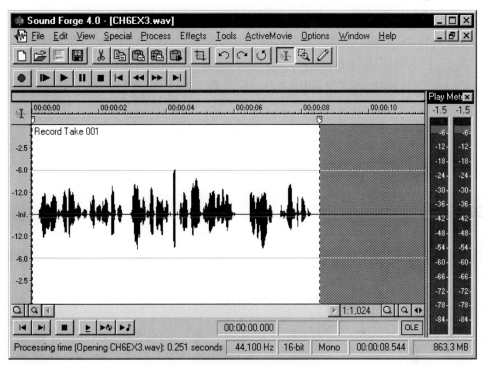

Figure 6-13
This tutorial starts with CH6EX3.WAV, from Tutorial 6-1.

> **Note**
>
> In step two of this tutorial (as well as throughout the book), notice the reference to ActiveMovie. This is a plug-in environment that has been accepted as a standard for cross application audio plug-ins in Windows. Microsoft has recently reclassified the meaning of ActiveMovie. So what once was an ActiveMovie plug-in is now a DirectX plug-in. Many software companies are still calling the DirectX plug-in environment ActiveMovie in regards to their audio software and it could be some time before the industry totally makes the change. In any case any reference in this book to either an ActiveMovie or DirectX plug-in is referring to the same thing.

2. Select ActiveMovie@(Waves C-1 Compressor, which puts you in the main window of the Wave C1-Compressor. What you need to do next is to choose [preset C] Speech Compressor, as shown in Figure 6-14. Quite often, I use the presets as a basic template. In this case, Preset C is in fact not only a good place to start, but without any adjustments will complete the task we need to accomplish, which is to add subtle compression to a speech file. Click the Preview button to hear what the file will sound like after it has been processed. By checking and unchecking the bypass box (directly under the preview button), you can do a before and after comparison. The Waves C1-Compressor alters the character of the entire file by increasing the volume in the quiet sections as well as smoothing out and limiting the peaks. Unfortunately, any previously unnoticed background noise may become more noticeable as well. However, that's what a Noise Gate is for, as you'll find out in the next step. When you're ready to proceed, click OK and save the file as CH6EX6.WAV.

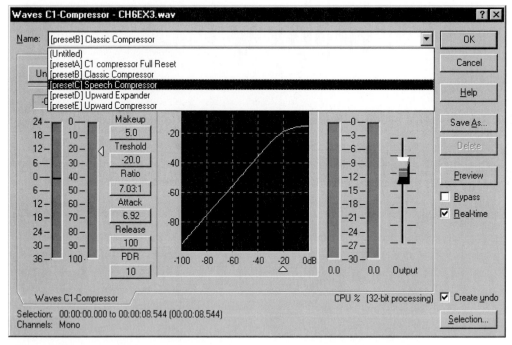

Figure 6-14
Choose [preset C] Speech Compressor and click the Preview button to hear what the file will sound like after conversion.

3. After compressing a file, you may notice previously unheard background noise in the silent spots between the dialog. This is where the noise gate comes in. For this next step, choose Waves C1-Gate from the ActiveMovie menu. To start the process, you'll need to load [preset B] Classic Gate, as shown in Figure 6-15. Using the Preview feature, you can hear that the gate is opening and closing fast enough to cut off any unwanted background noise that may reside between the dialog, while still leaving the speech unaltered. Click OK to gate the file and press the space bar to playback and listen to the results. When finished, save the results as CH6EX7.WAV.

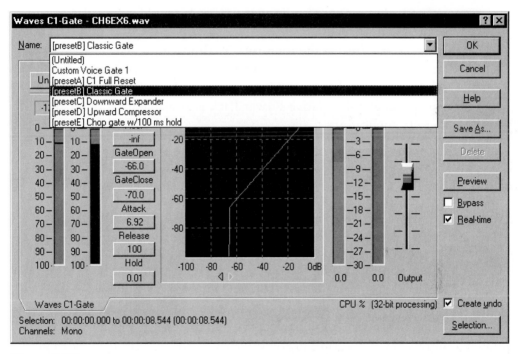

Figure 6-15
Load [preset B] Classic Gate as the Noise Gate solution for file CH6EX6.WAV.

Note

I'm going to really encourage you to check out the different presets in the Waves C1-Gate. This will give those of you who are inexperienced with the use and overall concept of a Noise Gate a little bit better idea of the how and why of gating a file.

Do the wave

I truly am in love with the Waves Native Power Pack. It features a complete arsenal of very good sounding, very usable DSP tools that give the user an affordable alternative to the really expensive DSP plug-ins. While the $500 price tag is a little steep for those who just play around with sound for fun, in the semi-pro and pro audio arena this is a smoking deal! The many presets that come standard with each of the separate plug-ins are also great templates for building your own custom settings and the ability to save these custom settings can save the power user a lot of time in the long run. With the great overall sound quality and ease of use, I would recommend the Native Power Pack for anyone who is serious about working with sound in the Mac or Windows environment. The Native Power Pack is available for a number of Mac and PC applications.

The voice heard 'round the world

It wasn't that long ago that even suggesting you wanted to put voice files up on your Web site would have gotten you burned at the stake. No one was going to wait around for 20 minutes or so to hear what you had to say. Now, we're streaming (pun intended) right along and this whole voiceover thing becomes one more component in a tangled web (I did it again) that the well-rounded Webmaster will have to deal with. The idea of this chapter was to give you some of the basics to help you understand what you'll be up against so it won't all be an overwhelming surprise. The human voice is a very effective tool in helping to get the point across on your Web site, or anywhere else for that matter. Now, not only can millions of people see what you have to say, they can hear it as well.

Part 2

The Tools

This section is full of tutorials using many of the latest audio development tools for both the Mac and Windows. Not only will you learn how to take an audio file and bend it to your will, but you'll learn some of the tricks needed to optimize your sound and music for playback on the Web. This section of the book has something for everyone from the home hobbyist all the way up to the seasoned audio professional. If you want to know how to encode and playback a RealAudio or Shockwave Audio file, then Part 2 is your ticket to success. In other words, everything you wanted to know and even a few things you didn't want to know about creating, converting, and generally squeezing some extra mileage out of a sound file is found here, in Part 2.

Chapter 7

Recording Editing Software and Hardware

In This Chapter

- An Overview of Software Products
- An Overview of Hardware Products
- Adding Power to Your Studio
- Putting It All Together with Tutorials

The kid in the candy store is a visual that comes to mind when thinking about currently available software and hardware for sound folks (at least for me).

In the beginning, computer-based audio was pretty much a novelty. It didn't sound very good, but at least it worked. Lately, however, there seems to be a surge of hardware and software resources available for turning some pretty cool tricks with Web-based audio.

In this chapter, you get some basic info on what to look for in hardware and software for creating and editing Web-based audio. Chapters 8 and 9 take this discussion even further with big-time tutorial action for working with the software on both the PC and the Mac, respectively.

This chapter begins with general coverage of what's currently available—from the lowest common denominator (that is, shareware, when applicable) all the way up to the best of the best. (To keep it simple, however, we will stay away from $100,000 work stations and stuff none of us will ever realistically be able to afford.) In addition, there exist a few cool applications with which you can do some pretty cool things with your audio files. This chapter ends with a look at two of them, complete with tutorials, so you can get an idea of some of the exciting extras that are out there.

So, let's take a run past the basics.

Introducing . . . The Software

Two tracks? Eight tracks? Digital audio with MIDI? What exactly do I need to record and edit sound for my project? Everyone's needs (and budgets) are different, so I've split this section into three different parts. For simple recording and editing of a file, two tracks are quite often just what the doctor ordered. There are occasions when eight or more tracks are needed to do it right. Then of course it's always possible that combining MIDI and digital audio at the same time (especially if you're a musician) is what you need. Read on and take a look at a few of the tools that are available to cover these three categories.

Two-track tools

When is two tracks not enough? Almost all the time anymore, but yet some of the most popular and successful recording and editing programs are only capable of using two tracks at a time (see Table 7-1). This is still okay for our needs because, in most cases, you can mix (or combine, if you like) two or more stereo files into a single (stereo or mono) file.

So what is it you (we, us) exactly need to create cutting edge Web sound? For starters, being able to tweak a sound file in a variety of ways is a big help. Your basic program should have native plug-ins such as Reverb, Noise Gate, and a Compressor, not to mention a graphic EQ (Equalization) of some sort. Because we are developing for the Web, it wouldn't hurt to be able to import and export a minimum of 10 different file formats (both Mac and PC).

Table 7-1 Two Track Editing/Recording Software

Product Name	Suggested Retail	DSP Effects	Mac/ Windows	Number of File Formats Supported	CD Audio Capture (digital)	Additional Information
BIAS Peak by Berkley Integrated Audio Software	$499	Premiere	Mac	n/a	Yes	
CoolEdit 96 by Syntrillium Software	$50	Native	Windows	25	no	Shareware
SoundEdit 16 Version 2.4 by Macromedia	$399 (with Deck 2.5)	Native and Third Party	Mac	10	Yes	Comes bundled with Director Multimedia Studio (Mac)
Sound Designer II by Digidesign	$495	SD II and Third Party	Mac	6	no	
Sound Forge 4.0 by Sonic Foundry	$499	Native and DirectX	Windows	19	Yes (with CD Architecture plug-in)	
Sound Forge XP by Sonic Foundry	$149	Native	Windows	16	no	Also bundled with Director Multimedia Studio (PC)
WaveLab by Steinberg	$495	Native DirectX	Win95/NT	2	Yes	16 to 24 bit audio

Note

To contact any of the companies listed in Table 7-1, or any company mentioned throughout this chapter, refer to Table 7-9, "Contact Info," at the end of this chapter.

▓ BIAS Peak

Running down the list from Table 7-1, we start at BIAS Peak from Berkley Integrated Audio Software. Peak is a very new entry to the game; so new, in fact, that it's still a little rough around the edges. However, after putting Peak through its paces, I'm impressed enough to add it to my collection of sound design tools. For those of you wanting to give it a try, I've included a demo version of Peak 1.5 in the demo software folder of the CD-ROM that accompanies this book. In Chapter 10, you can get your feet wet with a tutorial featuring Peak.

▓ CoolEdit 96

Without a doubt, CoolEdit 96 is the most useful, inexpensive sound program on the market today. To be honest, I'm surprised that something in the $50 range could have so many functions and be so usable. While the Reverb and some of the other DSP effects are average sounding, no other product in the price range comes even close. In Chapter 8, "Recording and Editing Tutorials for the PC," we'll dig deeply into CoolEdit 96 and the soon-to-be-released CoolEdit Pro (64 tracks instead of 2) with an overview and tutorials.

▓ SoundEdit 16

SoundEdit 16 has saved me on more than one occasion, and I've gotten to know it pretty well. While I would never consider doing multi-track recording with SoundEdit, you can stack tracks up and playback more than two tracks at a time. However, you need to mix the files down to stereo or mono before saving them (except in SoundEdit 16's own file format). In preparing Shockwave Audio files for conversion (and actually doing the conversion process itself), my copy of SoundEdit 16 has been getting worked overtime.

▓ Sound Designer II

Sound Designer II has been one of the standards for the music and sound design industry since before there was sound on the Web. Sadly, it may be on its last legs as Digidesign has integrated many of the plug-in features into AudioSuite for Pro Tools 4.0. For those of us with PCI Power Macs, none of the DSP plug-ins such as DINR currently work (unless you're using Pro Tools III hardware with TDM). According to Digidesign, there are no plans to upgrade SD II at this time. You never know, though—if enough people scream and yell, it may make a comeback with plug-in support for PCI.

Sound Forge

Speaking of standards of the industry, in the wonderful world of Windows, Sound Forge 4.0 is it. This program is loaded with really cool editing features and has more third-party plug-ins than I could ever afford. I've been using Sound Forge in its various incarnations for over two years and am really pleased with the progression of features in each new release as well as the good support. If you're looking for a powerful editing tool for your Windows 95/ NT machine, Sound Forge 4.0 is a good choice. If you're not in need of quite as many features (or you don't want to spend the bucks), Sound Forge XP is a good way to go. You can also upgrade at a later date.

WaveLab

WaveLab is a very powerful two-track editing/mastering tool. While currently only capable of dealing with AIFF and WAVE files, there are a lot of native features that make this application one of the most powerful I've ever seen for preparing music and sound for its final destination. You can actually burn a red book audio CD without any additional software. There is also a wide variety of DSP plug-ins available both native and DirectX.

In Table 7-2, you can see who supports what in terms of Web sound file format conversions. In the real world of Web sound, AIFF and WAVE files are most frequently used during the creation process.

Table 7-2 File Format Support

Software	Liquid Audio	Quick Time	Real Audio	Shockwave Audio	Sun.au
CoolEdit 96	No	No	Yes	No	Yes
Peak	No	Yes	Yes	No	Yes
Sound Designer II NUBUS	No	Yes	No	No	No
Sound Designer II PCI	No	Yes	No	No	No
SoundEdit 16 Version 2	No	Yes	Yes	Yes	Yes
Sound Forge 4.0	No	No	Yes	No	Yes
Sound Forge XP	No	No	Yes	No	Yes
WaveLab	No	No	No	No	No

Multi-track audio recording software

If you imagine yourself a power user (and don't we all), then this is where you need to be. In the beginning, the Mac ruled the arena of music and sound while the PC was used by office workers and geeks with thick glasses. This is changing, and while it's true that Pro Tools is probably the standard of the industry (especially with the release of 4.0), it's a brave new world out there and it's up for grabs. Windows machines are providing some low-cost and surprisingly high-end options for what was once a Mac-dominated world. Use Table 7-3 as a jumping-off point. Don't worry, I'll dig a bit deeper with the tutorials in Chapters 8 and 9.

Table 7-3 Multi-Track Editing/Recording Software

Product Name	Suggested Retail	DSP	Mac/ Windows	Tracks	System Requirements	Recommended Hardware
CoolEdit Pro by Syntrillium Software	$399	Yes	Win95	64	486/66	Layla from Event Electronics
Deck 2.5 by Macromedia	$399 (with SoundEdit 16)	Adobe Premiere	Mac	8	System 7 16MB RAM	AudioMedia (NUBUS) Korg Sound Link DRS 1212 I/O (PCI)
Digital Wings for Audio by Metalithic	$799	Native	Win95	128	Pentium P90 24MB RAM	Hardware included
Pro Tools 4.0 Software by Digidesign	$795	Audio-suite	Mac	8	System 7.5 32 MB RAM	Audiomedia II or III
Pro Tools 4.0 PCI Audiomedia III/Pro Tools Project by Digidesign	$795/$2,495	Audio-suite	Mac	8	System 7.5 32 MB RAM	Audiomedia II or III 882 or 888 I/O Audio Interface
Pro Tools 4.0 w/ TDM Core System NUBUS Core System PCI by Digidesign	$4,995	Audio-suite TDM	Mac	up to 64	System 7.5 32 MB RAM	882 or 888 I/O Audio Interface
Pro Tools 24 (4.1) 24 bit Workstation Digidesign	$7,995	Audio-suite TDM	Mac	up to 64	System 7.5 32 MB RAM	888/24
SAW Plus 32 Innovative Quality Software	$700	Native	Windows	24	90mHz Pentium 16 MB RAM Win 3.1 or 95 EIDE HD	Windows compatible Soundcard
TripleDAT by Creamware	$1,798 to $1,998	Native	Windows	between 8 & 20	Pentium, 16 MB RAM, Win 3.1 or 95, EIDE or SCSI HD	Part of the package

CoolEdit Pro

CoolEdit Pro was released in August of 1997. Plug-in DSP effects using DirectX and up to 64 tracks of digital audio are just a few of the features offered. I've actually had a chance to put Cool Edit Pro through its paces and was impressed (see Chapter 8, "Recording and Editing Tutorials for the PC") with all the native features and the low learning curve. Cool Edit Pro is without yet another winner for Syntrillium Software.

Deck 2.5

Deck 2.5 (from Macromedia) has come a long way and is now being bundled with the new SoundLink DRS 1212 I/O digital sound card from Korg. This application is geared toward the musician/recording enthusiast and uses Premiere plug-ins for DSP. Deck 2.5 is also bundled with SoundEdit 16 and is available as a component of Director Multimedia Studio (also from Macromedia).

Pro Tools

Without a doubt, Digidesign has been the major player that has been around the longest with the largest variety of software and hardware. Being a Pro Tools editor is now considered a job description. No one has yet to seriously challenge Digidesign's lead (as far as installed base, anyway) but it's coming. In Q4 of 97 Digidesign released Pro Tools 24, which in essence is a hot-rodded 24-bit version of Pro Tools TDM.

More Stuff

Every time I turn around lately I hear someone mentioning SAW 32 Plus. Radio stations and recording studios seem to be the most likely locations that you'll find SAW. TripleDAT from Creamware seems to be another strong contender in the Windows multi-track digital audio circus. Unlike some manufacturers who lower their prices, Creamware has kept theirs about the same. They just keep adding more features and not raising the price.

Another relatively new entry is Digital Wings for Audio (from Met-althic Software). This is a Windows-based product that is an all-in-one hardware/software combination with 128 track capability. In the crowd-ed field of digital audio multitrack software and hardware, it's hard to say what will happen; but the unique look and feel of the interface in Digital Wings for Audio will certainly make it stand out from the rest of the crowd.

MIDI

"MIDI," you're asking yourself, "What does MIDI have to do with recording digital audio?" Well, as of late, many of the MIDI-only sequencers of the not-too-distant past have added digital audio to their arsenal as well. Some support many of the same plug-ins and hardware as their big brothers in the audio recording/editing world. While the world of creating MIDI files is generally (although not always) the world of musicians, it's good for everyone to know the options. There's no way to list them all, but Table 7-4 shows a few from both the Mac and Windows world.

Table 7-4 MIDI Options

Product	Suggested Retail	Mac	Windows	Audio Tracks	MIDI Tracks	DSP Plug-in Support
Cakewalk Pro Audio 6.0 by Cakewalk Music Software	$399	no	3.1 and Win95	*	256	Yes
Cubase XT Steinberg	$399	no	3.1 and Win95	32	unlimited	Yes
Cubase XT VST Steinberg	$399	Power Mac	no	32	unlimited	Yes
Digital Performer 2.0 by Mark of the Unicorn	$895	Mac 68k and Power Mac	no	Up to 64	*	Yes
Logic Audio by Emagic	$399	Mac 68k and Power Mac	Win95	32	unlimited	Yes
Studio Vision 3.5 by Opcode	$995	Mac 68k and Power Mac	no	Up to 64	unlimited	Premiere TDM

* The number of tracks available are only limited by the hardware configuration.

Hardware: An Overview

While many computers are capable of playing back and recording sound, the overall sound quality just isn't going to be very good if you don't add professional hardware. If you're going to record from scratch, it's a good idea to match your system with the hardware that lets you take full advantage of the software you're using. While the Mac and PC have different needs, there are now audio interfaces available (PCI) that work on both types of machines. Using Table 7-5 as a reference, you can get an idea of what will work with your favorite software and how much it will set you back.

Table 7-5 Audio Interfaces

Product	MSRP	Mac/Win	Type of Slot	Inputs/ Outputs (Analog)	Optical I/O Balanced I/O	AES/EBU	S/PDIF
AudioMedia II by Digidesign	$1,295	Mac	NUBUS	Inputs: 2 Outputs: 2	Balanced	no	Yes
AudioMedia III by Digidesign	$795	Mac Win95/NT	PCI	Inputs: 2 Outputs: 2	Balanced	No	Yes
Audiowerk 8 by Emagic	$799	Mac Win95/NT	PCI	Inputs: 2 Outputs: 8	Balanced	No	Yes
CardD Plus by Digital Audio Labs	$795	Win95/NT	ISP	Inputs: 2 Outputs: 2	No	No	Optional
Darla by echo	$349	Windows*	PCI	Inputs: 2 Outputs: 8	No	No	No
Fiji by Turtle Beach	$299	Win95/NT	ISP	Inputs: 2 Outputs: 2	Optical	No	Optional
Gina by echo	$499	Windows*	PCI	Inputs: 2 Outputs: 8	No	No	Yes
Layla by echo	$999	Windows*	PCI	Inputs: 8 Outputs: 10	Balanced	No	Yes
Multi!Wav Pro24 by AdB International	$499	Windows	ISA	Inputs: 4 Outputs: 4	Balanced	Yes	Yes

Table 7-5 Audio Interfaces *(continued)*

Product	MSRP	Mac/Win	Type of Slot	Inputs/ Outputs (Analog)	Optical I/O Balanced I/O	AES/EBU	S/PDIF
SoundLink DRS 1212 IO by Korg	$1,295	Mac	PCI	Inputs: 2	Optical 8 ch ADAT Balanced		
StudioCard by Antex	$1,595	Win95/NT	PCI	Inputs: 4 Outputs: 4	Balanced	Yes	Yes
882 I/O Interface by Digidesign	$995	Mac	NUBUS PCI	Inputs: 8 Outputs: 8	Balanced	No	Yes
888 I/O Interface by Digidesign	$2,995	Mac	NUBUS PCI	Inputs: 8 Outputs: 8	Balanced	Yes 8 channels	Yes

★ Future Macintosh compatibility

Because of deadlines, it wasn't possible for me to obtain and review all the hardware featured in Table 7-5. Do note that the Audiomedia III (from Digidesign) and the Audiowerk8 from Emagic both work on either Mac or Windows machines. This is for sure a step in the right direction.

 Finishing Touches

The icing on the cake has got to be the DSP plug-ins. While some plug-ins come standard with many of these programs, it's quite often the third-party stuff that will put a smile on your face. Throughout this book, I use every (decent) DSP plug-in I can get my hands on for tutorials just to give you an idea what a difference it can make. In Table 7-6, take a look at products that do not come standard with any recording/editing software but are extras or add-ons.

Table 7-6 DSP Plug-ins

Product	Description	Suggested Retail	Compatibility	Mac	Windows
CD-Architect by Sonic Foundry	Master (and burn) Red Book Audio CD's. Capture and convert sound from Red Book Audio CD's.	$399	Sound Forge 4.0	No	Win95/NT
CyberSound by InVision Interactive	Reverb and other effects	$129	SoundEdit 16 Version 2 Adobe Premiere	System 7.1	No
DINR by Digidesign	Digital Intelligent Noise Reduction	$495	Sound Designer II (NUBUS) Pro Tools III TDM	System 7.1	No
D-VERB by Digidesign	Reverb for Pro Tools	$495	Pro Tools TDM	System 7.5	No
Hyperprism by Arboretum	23 Effects	$350/$750	Adobe Premiere Pro Tools TDM Audiosuite	System 7.5 PPC	No
The Liquifier for Pro Tools by Liquid Audio	Plug-in version of Liquifier Pro for Mac	$595	Audiosuite plug-in for Pro Tools 4.0	PPC	No
Native Power Pack by Waves	Trueverb, Q10 Paragraphic EQ, C1 Compressor Gate, WaveConvert, L1 Ultramaximizer, S1 Sterio Imager, IDR	$500	Bias, Cakewalk Pro Audio, Cubase VST, Sound Designer II (NUBUS), Sound Edit 16 v 2.4, Sound Forge 4.0	System 7.5	Win95/NT
QTools AX 1.0 by QSound	QExpander, QSYS AX, Q123 AX	$199	DirectX	No	Win95/NT
QSYS/TDM by QSound	Positional 3d Audio Processor	$199	Pro Tools III TDM	System 7.5	No
Sound Forge 4.0 Plug-In Pack by Sonic Foundry	Batch Converter Plug-in, Noise Reduction Plug-in, Spectrum Analysis Plug-in	$495	Sound Forge 4.0	No	Win95/NT

> **Note**
>
> At press time, Pro Tools 4 software was just released and many of the Audio Suite and TDM plug-ins had not been ported over to the Pro Tools 4 software. However, they will show up in tutorial chapters later in the book. There is absolutely no way to fit all the plug-ins available in this chapter (over 100 from Digidesign alone). Table 7-6 is a good start.

More stuff

You're not a musician; you've got limited experience in working with sound-based recording and editing applications, but you're a whiz with a computer. You want custom music and sound for your Web-based project and you're not afraid of the unknown. So, where do you go? You go to SmartSound for Multimedia from Sonic Desktop Software, and Tune Builder from Airworks—that's where! Both of these applications make it easy for the musically challenged to create a custom music track. Each has its own strengths and weaknesses, but both produce professional results. So, without any further confusion, let's take a tour!

■ SmartSound for Multimedia

The claim: Now, non-musicians can produce their own customized soundtracks using this new software program. And they sound great!

Wait a minute here, the last thing I and my fellow musicians need is someone else trying to put us out of business. We're still trying to recover from Karaoke pretty much eliminating the bread and butter gigs we had playing in the bars and lounges. I've never ignored progress before, so I guess we should see if the claim rings true.

The components

There are three main windows with SmartSound: the Controller, Sequence, and Block. If you're feeling as though you don't want to deal with the complexities of music editing, the Controller window is the way for you to go. You can custom create a music event using Maestro with no musical knowledge whatsoever. Your initial source for music is the library Audio Palette Volume 1, which is part of the SmartSound CD-ROM.

Specs and system requirements

SmartSound products run on both Mac OS and Windows machines (as everything well should). Table 7-7 shows the system requirements for installing and running SmartSound.

Table 7-7   SmartSound System Requirements

Computer	Operating System	Processor Speed	RAM	Disk Space	CD-ROM Drive	Soundcard	Monitor
Macintosh	Mac OS System 7 or better	68020 or better	4 MB	1 MB	Yes	n/a	Color
Windows	Windows 3.1 or 95	386 or better	4 MB	1 MB	Yes	8 or 16 bit	Color

Currently, SmartSound for Multimedia can export and import six different file formats:

- AIFF
- AU (NeXT)
- QuickTime
- Real Audio
- Sound Designer
- WAVE

The supported specs of these formats are listed in Table 7-8.

Table 7-8   Audio Specs

Sample Rate	44.1 K[*] 22 K 11 K
Bit Depth	16 bit 8 bit
File Type	Stereo Mono

[*]   To use Audio Pallette with 44.1 K sound files requires the purchase of a separate CD-ROM.

CD-ROM

In the Demo folder on the CD-ROM accompanying this book, you will find a demo version of SmartSound for Multimedia for both Mac and PC.

Setting up SmartSound for the Mac

This is easy. Simply copy the folder SmartSound for Multimedia to your hard drive. Even though you'll be running the application from your hard drive, leave the CD-ROM mounted as you'll need to access Audio Palette Volume 1. Be sure to set the preferences before starting.

Tutorial 7-1 Creating with Maestro

As I only have the Mac OS Version, that's where we're going to go in this tutorial. I have been assured by the big Kahuna at Sonic Desktop that the Mac and Windows versions operate identically. Running their demo (included on the CD-ROM with this book), it seems as though this claim is true.

Note

Using the demo version of SmartSound for Multimedia, you may follow along with many of the steps in this tutorial. However, there will be some different choices as our working copy is version 1.0 and the demo version is a later release.

1. Go to the folder SmartSound for Multimedia and double click the application. Select Maestro from the window, as shown in Figure 7-1. Figure 7-2 shows the preference settings for both sound quality and start up. Select Preferences from the Edit menu, and choose Best for sound quality as shown in Figure 7-2. Also be sure to assign a temporary drive for storage. In my case, I chose the Mac HD; in your case, it's up to you.

Figure 7-1
Select Maestro from the startup screen for SmartSound for Multimedia.

Figure 7-2
Set your sound quality to Best when setting up the preferences.

2. You will now be in the main screen of the Controller window (Figure 7-3), select Start Maestro.

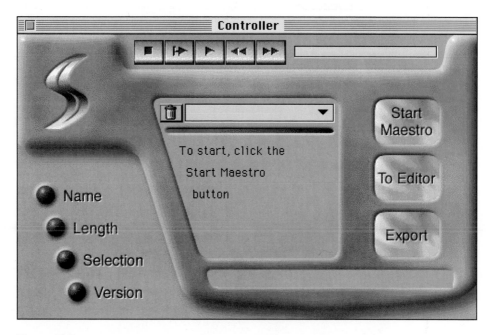

Figure 7-3
Select Start Maestro from the Controller window to get going.

3. Your first stop is the tips screen (Figure 7-4). For those of you whose musical experience is somewhat limited (or even non-existent), the tips window can point you in the right direction as to the what to use and the why as far as style. Select Presentations and click Next to go to the next step.

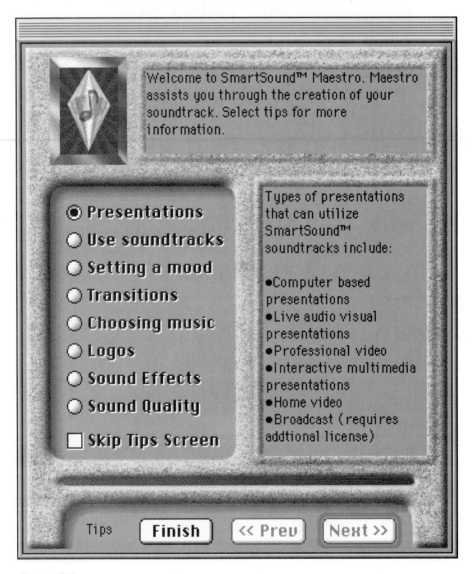

Welcome to SmartSound™ Maestro. Maestro assists you through the creation of your soundtrack. Select tips for more information.

- ⦿ **Presentations**
- ○ **Use soundtracks**
- ○ **Setting a mood**
- ○ **Transitions**
- ○ **Choosing music**
- ○ **Logos**
- ○ **Sound Effects**
- ○ **Sound Quality**
- ☐ **Skip Tips Screen**

Types of presentations that can utilize SmartSound™ soundtracks include:

- •Computer based presentations
- •Live audio visual presentations
- •Professional video
- •Interactive multimedia presentations
- •Home video
- •Broadcast (requires addtional license)

Tips   [**Finish**]   [**<< Prev**]   [**Next >>**]

Figure 7-4
Use the tips window to help choose the right musical style for your presentation.

4. In the window shown in Figure 7-5 (number 1 of 6), there are seven style choices available. For this tutorial, select Action/Modern and click Next to proceed.

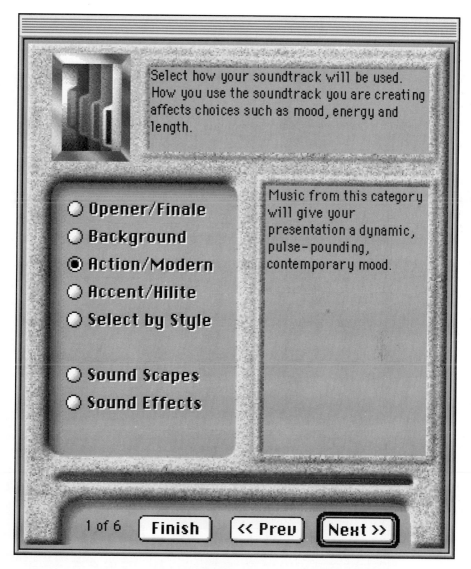

Figure 7-5
Select Action/Modern from the seven style choices.

5. In this next window (2 of 6), you have the option of using either a custom or preselected length for your musical sequence. As shown in Figure 7-6, I have chosen the length of my sequence to be 14.2 seconds. Do the same and click Next to proceed.

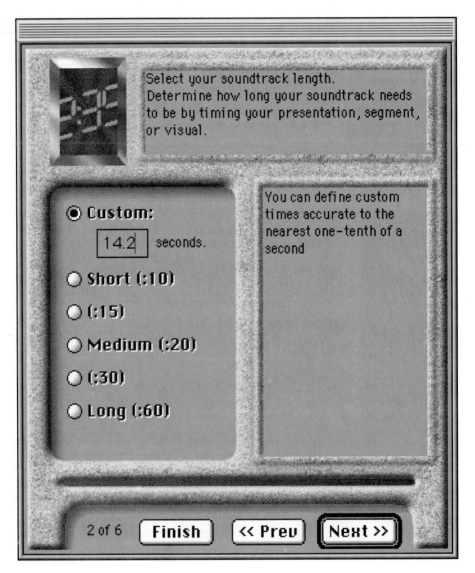

Figure 7-6
You can use preset or custom lengths for your sequences.

6. In this window (3 of 6), the task is to choose a musical style. In the case of this tutorial, choose Powerful (as shown in Figure 7-7) and click Next to proceed.

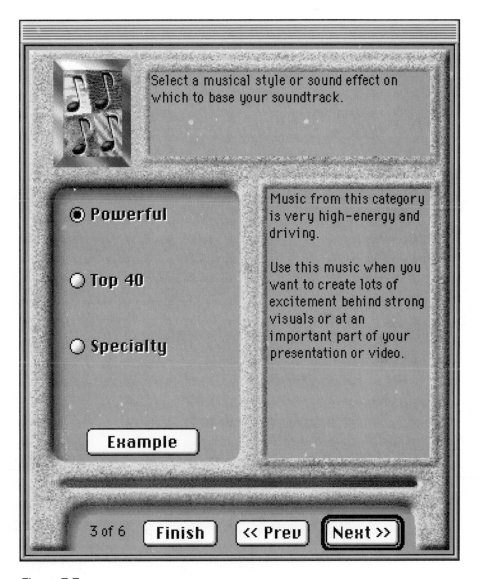

Figure 7-7
For a high energy musical style, choose Powerful.

7. In this window (4 of 6), the task is to the select the source file that the music will come from. Using Figure 7-8 as a reference, notice that there are three choices. For this tutorial, choose Gladiators and click Next to proceed.

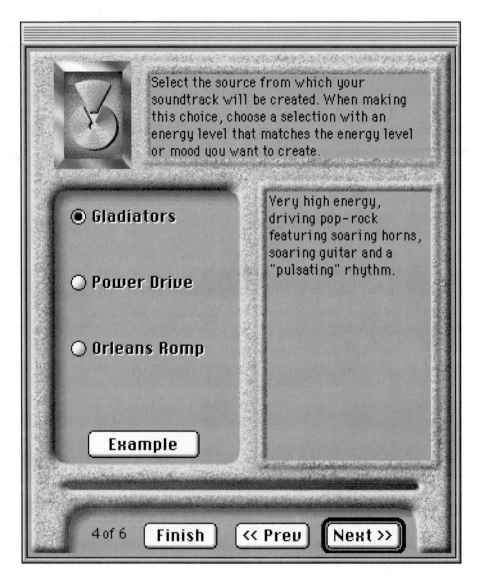

Figure 7-8
The combination of horns, guitar, and a driving beat makes Gladiators a good choice.

8. In the current window (5 of 6), you are offered four different variations (see Figure 7-9) of the same musical sequence. In some cases, the difference is subtle; in others, it's very obvious. You can click Preview to hear what each variation will sound like. Click Preview again to terminate playback. Sticking with this tutorial's theme of going over the speed limit, choose Kickoff and click Next to proceed.

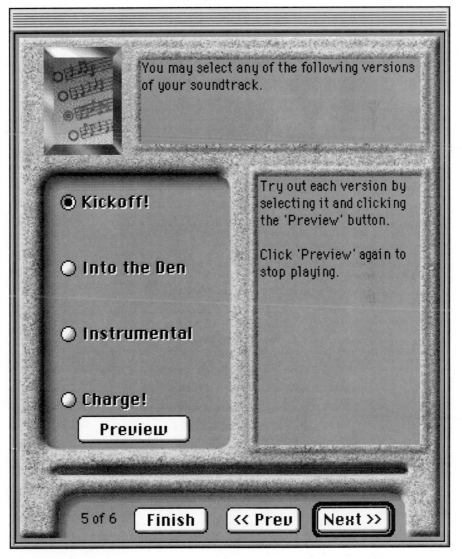

Figure 7-9
There are four available choices for variations of the same song.

9. Now comes the time to name the selection. In this case (see Figure 7-10), go with Example 7-1. Click Finish to find yourself back at the Controller window. In Figure 7-11, you can see that Example 7-1 is now present on the menu list. You can repeat the procedures in this tutorial and put together a number of different variations that can all reside on the menu list.

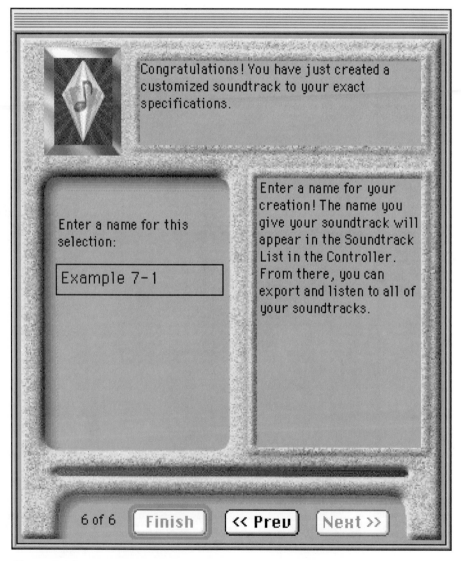

Figure 7-10
Name the selection in this screen.

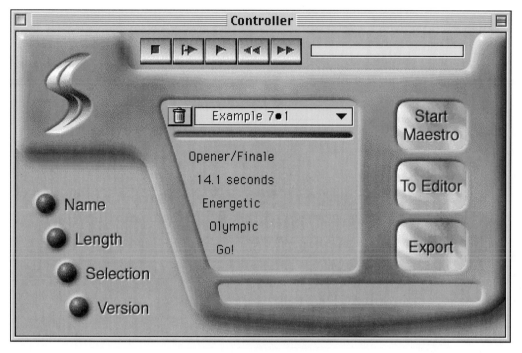

Figure 7-11
The menu list shows all the information about the current soundtrack.

10. It's now time to Export Example 7-1. Click on the Export button in the Controller Window. Click options and set the sample rate to 22K, the bit depth to 16, and the channel to stereo as shown in Figure 7-12. Name the file CH7EX1.AIF, select AIFF as the file type, and click export.

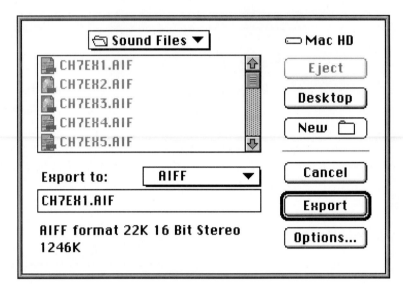

Figure 7-12
Set the attributes before exporting the sound file.

> **Note**
>
> Just a reminder that all tutorial examples in this book are saved on the CD-ROM as System 7 Sound and WAVE files. This permits you to review the tutorial sound files by simply double clicking the file regardless of platform.

▨ So is it true?

Does Sonic Desktop live up to their claims with SmartSound for Multimedia? In my opinion, it's a resounding affirmative. Even though I used version 1.0 (1.0 in any software can cause permanent injury to the unprepared), there were no problems that I couldn't find a way around (*occasional glitches* is actually a better way of describing them). These guys obviously put some serious thought into the way the different musical blocks were laid out. The variations and possibilities with just a few different tunes are pretty incredible. Audio Palette Volume 2 should be released before you read this and will have a suggested retail price of $69.95. For the 16-bit 44.1 kHz version of the Audio Palette CD-ROM, it's an additional (ouch!!) $99.95. Because sound files for Web delivery need to be sampled down to a lower resolution anyway, you're probably safe sticking with the 22 kHz version.

SmartSound for Multimedia is the ideal easy-to-use solution for the musically impaired who still have the urge to do a little hands-on creation. It's easy to create musical variations of the same theme. In some ways, this product reminds me of the Presentation Audio series from Network Music (Music Library kind of stuff), but with much more sophisticated software.

Let's look a little deeper

In the last tutorial, we only got our feet wet with the functions in SmartSound for Multimedia, so now let's take a quick look at a few of the other features. The Editor and Block windows are where you get to seriously mess with the mix of a sequence. But enough about theory; let's get our hands dirty.

Tutorial 7-2: Editing a sequence

I'm going to assume (rightly, I hope) that you already have SmartSound for Multimedia up and running.

1. Open the application SmartSound for Multimedia and click Editor. Both the Editor and Block windows will contain no data (see Figure 7-13).

Figure 7-13
The Editor and Block windows should be empty to start Tutorial 7-2.

2. Now it's time to add some content to the mix. Select Import from the File menu and from the CD-ROM SmartSound #1, select the file Gladiators 22k 16bit St (found in the sound files folder) as shown in Figure 7-14 and click Import. In Figure 7-15, you can now see the different blocks that comprise the sequence Gladiator in the Block window.

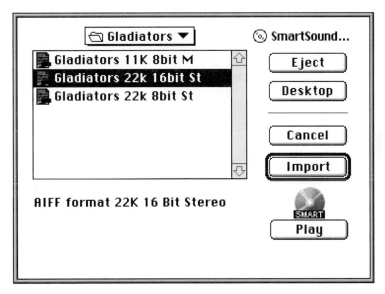

Figure 7-14
Select and Import the file Gladiators 22k 16bit St.

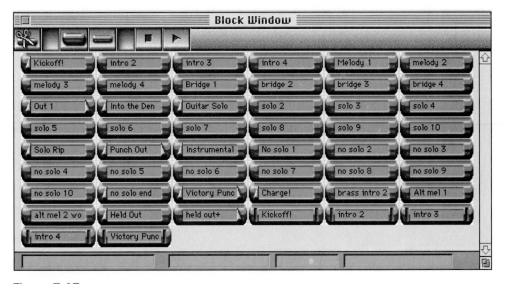

Figure 7-15
The different blocks of the sound file Gladiators.

3. Remember the tutorial file CH7EX1.AIF (the results of Tutorial 7-1)? This file is composed of five separate blocks that originated as part of the sound file Gladiators 22k 16bit St. Going through the same procedure as in Step 2, select and import the tutorial file CH7EX1.AIF (as shown in Figure 7-16). The five blocks that comprise tutorial sound file CH7EX1.AIF now reside in the Block window (shown in Figure 7-17). They are Kickoff, Intro 2, Intro 3, Intro 4, and Victory Punch.

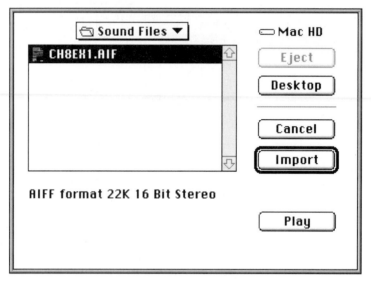

Figure 7-16
Import the tutorial file CH7EX1.AIF.

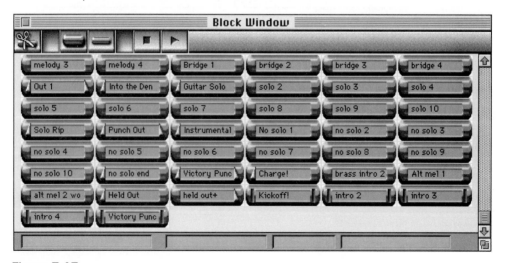

Figure 7-17
The components of both sound files reside in the Block window.

4. Select the five blocks that you just imported into the Block window and drag them to the Editor window (as shown in Figure 7-18). Now you have that rare opportunity to make a mess of something that sounds pretty good. I do it all the time, and it's great fun.

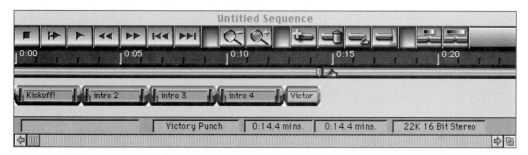

Figure 7-18
The components of both sound files reside in the Block window.

5. In the Editor window, you have the ability to rearrange the order of the sound blocks as well as delete or insert individual blocks from the Block window. This is a simple process that is as easy as drag and drop. You now need to remove the current ending. Select the block Victory Punch in the Editor and then select Cut from the Edit menu. In the Block window, select the block "No Solo End," drag it to the Editor and place it at the end of the sequence as shown in Figure 7-19. You now have the same musical sequence with a different ending. You can use this same process to replace any of the musical blocks in your sequence. Now you need to save this version of the sequence. Select Save Sequence As CH7EX2 from the File menu.

Figure 7-19
Drag the musical block No Solo End from the Block window and insert it into the sequence in the Editor window.

6. Because it is my job to come up with problems, I've found one. Fitting the musical block No Solo End into the space we've allotted has given us sort of a non-smooth ending and in fact it cuts off in the middle of the piece, sounding like a hack editing job. Listen to the tutorial file CH7EX2 to see what I mean. The solution is to select the block No Solo End (in the Editor) and then Select Smart End from the Sequence menu. Smart End will smooth things out and correct the problem. Save the new file as CH7EX3.

■ Tutorial 7-3: What about the Block window?

While I haven't even dug into the possibilities of using the editing features in the Block Window, I'm already sold on this system. Let's say you want to customize one of the individual blocks residing in the Block Window. No problem, as that's where we're going with this tutorial.

1. In Figure 7-20, look for the scissors in the upper left-hand corner of the window. This is the Block Snipper. Click on it once and you're ready to snip a musical block down to size.

Block
Snipper

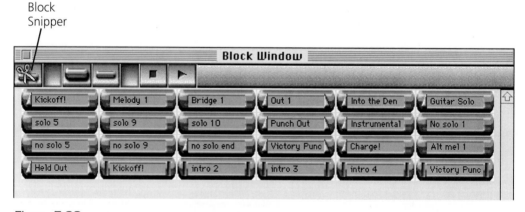

Figure 7-20
To activate the Block Snipper, click on the scissors icon in the top left corner
of the Block window.

2. The next step is to select and drag the block Punch Out into the Block Snipper (see Figure 7-21). Punch out is a great-sounding ending, but there's a little whump noise on the end of the file. All you need to do is snip that whump off the end and you're on the air.

Figure 7-21
Drag the block Punch Out into the Block Snipper for editing.

3. Where to snip? Press the Play button and you'll notice the offensive whump shows up about half a second into the playback of this short block. Using the marker and the Set Clip Out function, I've separated Punch Out+ into two separate blocks. Look at Figure 7-22 to see the clipped version of Punch Out+. The whump has left the building. Listen to the tutorial file CH7EX4.SND to hear the wump and CH7EX5.SND to hear the after.

Figure 7-22
The Block Snipper has trimmed the offensive whump from the file.

4. The Block now needs a new name. Double click on Make New Block (refer back to Figure 7-21) and you'll be able name the new block (see Figure 7-23). Name the new block "Punch Out New".

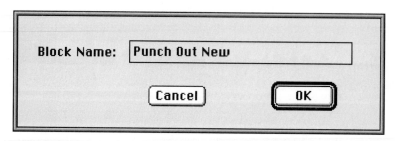

Figure 7-23
The Block Snipper has trimmed the offensive whump from the file.

The new block (Punch Out New) now resides in the Block Window with the other unedited Blocks. The only down side of this whumpless sound block is the smart features in the Editor Window will not work with it. A small price to pay for perfection, right?

In retrospect

SmartSound for Multimedia is an incredible tool for those of you who just have to do it yourself and lack the experience. At the time of writing this chapter, it was selling for $199, but it's my understanding that the price will go up as new features are added. I used version 1.0 for these tutorials and I can tell from the demo version (1.5) there are already a few changes in the screens and categories. This is a product I would recommend.

TuneBuilder from Airworks (a quick look)

On paper, TuneBuilder looks great. You simply choose a musical cue from one of the available music libraries, choose the length you'd like it to be (say 24 seconds), and through a process that defies explanation (at least to the layman) the song is automatically cut down to the proper length with professional sounding results. There's a bit of learning curve to deal with here but TuneBuilder works so well it's worth the extra effort. TuneBuilder is currently available as a Macintosh and a DOS application. However, the Windows 95 version will be available by the time you read this book.

Deadlines prevented me from putting a tutorial together using Tune-Builder but I did have enough time to run around the block with it a few times. I did my test drive with the Macintosh version and had no problems installing the application and getting it up and running. At first, I did have a bit of a problem understanding the interface and actually had to look at the manual. Once I realized TuneBuilder functioned more like a DOS application, it all made sense. Navigation in TuneBuilder will be greatly simplified once the Windows 95 version of it is released.

According to Airworks, around 25 percent of the available music libraries in North America have already been converted to work with TuneBuilder. This sheer volume of material will give multimedia and Web developers an almost unlimited source of musical content. If you work with production music and you're constantly under the gun to crank it out fast, TuneBuilder could be the way for you to go.

> **Web**
>
> For more information on TuneBuilder, go to www.airworks.com and take a look and a listen for yourself.

Summary

There's a lot of new gear out there, and as with the Web, the players seem to change on a weekly basis. Some have been major movers for quite a while, and there's the up-and-coming players as well. Use Table 7-9 to find out the latest product info from each of the hardware and software vendors I touched on in this chapter. Another online resource you might want to try for music hardware and software can be found at www.synthony.com, the Web site for Synthony Music (a keyboard/synthesizer and audio music store). I've found it a good place to start when comparing prices and features of music hardware and software.

Table 7-9   Contact Information

Company	Product Category	URL	Comments
AdB International	Hardware	http://www.adbdigital.com	Digital Audio Card
Airworks	Software	http://www.airworks.com	TuneBuilder
Antex	Hardware	http://www.antex.com	Digital Audio Card
Arboretum	Software	http://www.arboretum.com	TDM and Premiere Plug-in
Berkley Integrated Audio Software	Software	http://www.bias-inc.com	Recording/Editing Software
Cakewalk Music Software	Software	http://www.cakewalk.com	MIDI/Digital Audio sequencer
Creamware	Software/ Hardware	http://www.creamware.com	Recording/Editing Software
Digidesign	Software/ Hardware	http://www. digidesign.com	Recording/Editing Software and Hardware
Digital Audio Labs	Hardware	http://www.digitalaudio.com	Digital Audio Card
Emagic USA	Software	http://www.emagic.de	Recording/Editing Software
Innovative Quality Software	Software	http://www.iqsoft.com	Recording/Editing Software
InVision Interactive	Software	http://www.cybersound.com	SoundEdit and Premiere plug-ins
Korg	Hardware	http://www.korg.com	Digital Audio Card
Macromedia	Software	http://www.macromedia.com	Recording/Editing Software
Mark of the Unicorn Inc.	Software	http://www.motu.com	MIDI/Digital Audio sequencer
Metalithic	Software/ Hardware	http://www.metalithic.com	Recording/Editing Software and Hardware

Table 7-9   Contact Information *(continued)*

Company	Product Category	URL	Comments
Opcode	Software/ Hardware	`http://www.opcode.com`	MIDI/Digital Audio sequencer
QSound	Software	`http://www.qsound.ca`	3D audio plug-ins
Sonic Desktop	Software	`http://www.sonicdesktop.com`	Recording/Editing Software
Sonic Foundry	Software	`http://www.sfoundry.com`	Recording/Editing Software Audio Plug-ins
Steinberg North America	Software	`http://www.steinberg-us.com`	MIDI/Digital Audio sequencer Recording/Editing Software and Hardware
Turtle Beach	Hardware	`http://www.tbeach.com`	Digital Audio Card
Voyetra Technologies Inc.	Software	`http://www.voyetra.com`	MIDI/Digital Audio sequencer
Waves	Software	`http://www.waves.com`	Audio Plug-ins

Chapter 8

Recording and Editing Tutorials for the PC

In This Chapter

- Cool Edit 96
- Sound Forge 4.0
- Cool Edit Pro
- Native Power Pack from Waves

In this chapter, I'm going to focus on three different Windows sound applications. Cool Edit 96 is without a doubt the best bargain you can find for getting started in the world of sound for Interactive Multimedia and the Web. Sound Forge 4.0 is an easy-to-use feature-rich two-track professional sound recording and editing application that is used by entry-level and professional sound people alike. Brand new and about to create some serious waves is Cool Edit Pro. With 64 tracks (instead of 2), Cool Edit Pro is going to body slam a lot of the more expensive competition to the mat. The best way to tour each of these recording environments is through the use of simple tutorials, and in this chapter that's exactly what we're going to do. So . . .

without any further ado, let's take a trip into the world of Cool Edit 96 (from Syntrillium Software).

Cool Edit 96

Okay, so it's not 1996 anymore, but the latest version of this incredibly popular shareware is called Cool Edit 96, so live with it. For $50, you just can't go wrong and once you've tried it, you'll see what I mean. Many of the functions and features that I consider to be a necessity in (more expensive) commercially available software are standard here. There are a few things (such as the transport) that I wish were a little different, but all in all—Cool Edit rocks!

One of the features I sure like seeing that hasn't shown up with any regularity in Windows sound applications is (Digital) Capture CD Audio function. Fortunately, there's a simple way around this problem with Cool Edit, and in Tutorial 8-1 I show it to you. Before we dive into the first Cool Edit 96 tutorial, I'm going to render my humble opinion: Buy it! The feature-disabled version (that happens to be included on the CD-ROM that comes with this book) is great, but to access Reverb and some of the other really cool and necessary features, you need to have the full version.

Web

To find out the latest info on Cool Edit, go to the Syntrillium Software homepage at www.syntrillium.com.

File formats

Cool Edit more than covers the basics in this department. In my book, if you cover AIFF, AU, and WAVE, you can get the job done. There are a number of variations on the WAVE format that are supported and you can also convert and save an audio file as a RealAudio file. I'm wishing out loud that Syntrillium will include the QuickTime Movie format in the near future. Another new addition to the land of new and interesting formats is the support of the MPEG Layer I and II file format. While it's not actually in the application, it can be obtained free of charge from Syntrillium's home page.

What you need

To do the Cool Edit 96 tutorials in this chapter, there are a few components that are necessary, so read on.

- Cool Edit 96 (full version)
- A Windows 95/NT machine (486/33 or better) with CD-ROM player
- The Chapter 8 tutorial sound files (on the CD-ROM)

Tutorial 8-1: Recording CD audio

As I mentioned a couple of paragraphs back, it's currently not possible to do a digital capture and transfer of sound data from a Red Book audio CD. So, we break the rules and do it anyway (just not digitally). Because recording copyrighted material of any kind without the legal owner's permission is against the law (and in extremely bad taste), I will ask you to be careful during this next tutorial. Let's assume that you're going to accomplish this task using a commercially available sound effects CD that is licensed for this type of use. Because we are going to need a few sound effects for a couple of the future tutorials, there's no time like the present to capture and edit them. Just in case you don't have access to a SFX CD, any audio CD will do just fine for this tutorial. Just remember: If you're using copyrighted material, erase the file immediately after completing the tutorial. I'll make sure you have the SFX sound file you need (it's on the CD-ROM) for later use. So, let's get rolling!

1. Start the application Cool Edit 96 and select New from the File menu. At this point, the New Waveform window becomes active. Figure 8-1 shows the Cool Edit 96 main window.

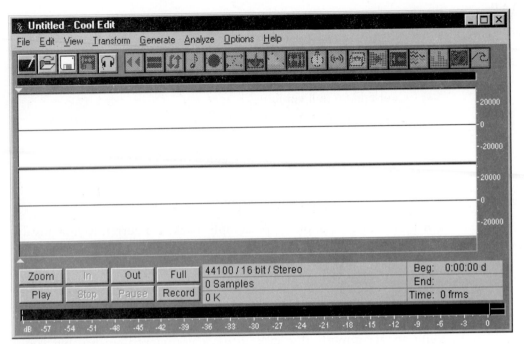

Figure 8-1
The main window in Cool Edit 96.

2. In the New Waveform window (Figure 8-2), set the sample rate to 44.1 kHz, the Channels to Stereo, and the resolution to 16 bit. Click OK when you have set these specs.

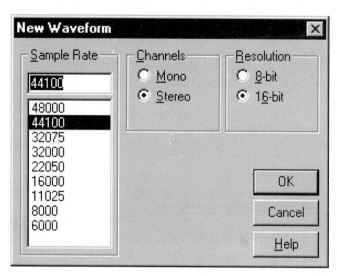

Figure 8-2
Set the recording attributes in the New Waveform window.

3. Insert the audio CD from which you wish to record in the CD-ROM drive of your computer. The Sound Effects CD I'm using for this tutorial is the Super Single Volume 1 (Hollywood Edge). In the case of this tutorial, it's okay to use any CD you wish. Select CD Player from the View menu. You will note the appearance of CD Player controls directly beneath the VU Level meters at the bottom of the window (see Figure 8-3).

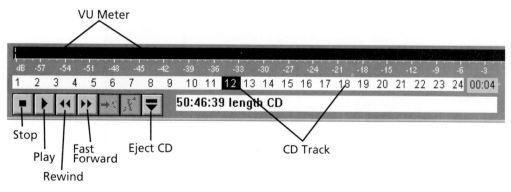

Figure 8-3
The CD Player controls in Cool Edit 96.

155

4. Press the Play/Pause button on the CD transport controls to begin playback of the audio CD. While the music is playing, select Monitor VU Level from the Option menu. You will now be able to preview the input record level. The optimum input level should be no higher than -3dB. Because you can't set the input level controls in Cool Edit 96, this leads us to Step 5 and Windows 95.

5. This next step will take us to the Volume Control window in Windows 95. Click the Start button on the Windows 95 task bar and select Run. Type sndvol32 in the entry field and click OK. Select Properties from the Option menu and click the Recording radio button. Check CD Audio as shown in Figure 8-4, then click OK. While watching the VU Levels on Cool Edit 96, adjust the record input (volume) level on the Windows 95 Recording Control dialog box (see Figure 8-5) until the peak input level is about -3 dB. Close the Recording Control dialog box after adjusting to the correct level.

Note

When trying to complete Step 5 in this tutorial, you might notice a slight difference in the Properties dialog box. The CD Audio check box may be called CD/Aux. If this is the case, check this box as the alternate to CD Audio.

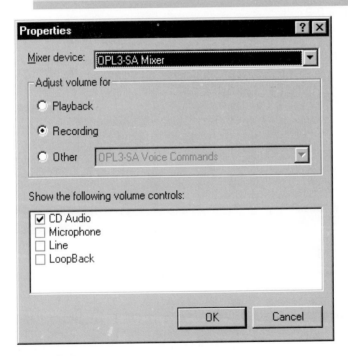

Figure 8-4
Select only the CD Audio level and click OK.

Figure 8-5
Adjust the record input (volume) level.

6. Okay, we're just about ready to give it a shot. Press the Stop button on the CD player transport controls and select the track from the CD that you want to record. Because we previously put Cool Edit in a preview mode to set the input levels, you need to go to the Transport control and click on the Stop button. You're now ready to proceed to the next step.

> **Note**
>
> Before enabling the record sequence, be sure you have already pre-selected the track you're going to record from the Audio CD (refer back to Figure 8-3).

7. The next step is to record your track. For this tutorial, choose a short snippet. In rapid succession, press the Record button on the Cool Edit Transport and then the Play button on the CD Transport controls. It's okay to have a little lead time on the back and the front of the recording, as you can trim it off later if needed. When the snippet of your track has been recorded, press the Stop buttons on both the Cool Edit and CD Transport controls. If everything goes as planned, you'll be staring at a short waveform on the Cool Edit screen. In this case, I've recorded Track 12 on my audio CD, which consists of a couple of quick automobile zip-bys.

8. As you can see in Figure 8-6, I've now got a couple of real short stereo sounds residing in the Edit window of Cool Edit. You should have something similar in your window. What you need to do now is trim off the excess blank audio from the front and the back of this sound file. Using your pointer and holding down the left mouse button, select the area of the sound file you wish to keep as shown in Figure 8-6. Select Trim from the Edit menu (or Ctrl + T) to trim away the unwanted sections of the audio file.

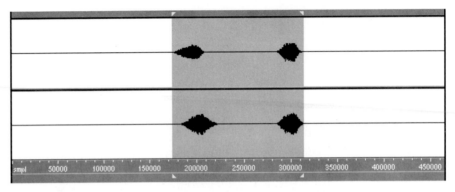

Figure 8-6
Select the area of the file you wish to keep and use the Trim control (Ctrl + T) to eliminate the rest.

9. Well, you're there! It's time to save your work. Select Save As from the File menu and name the file CH8EX1.WAV. Press Play on the Cool Edit 96 Transport controls to hear the results.

Recording CD audio is easy with Cool Edit and we've created the basic sound file that will be the heart of the next tutorial. Just to experiment, I tried duplicating the steps of Tutorial 8-1 using the CD player controls that are part of Windows 95 and it worked just fine.

Tutorial 8-2: Cool edit effects

There are a number of standard DSP effects that come with Cool Edit 96. Reverb, Chorus, Delay, and Flanging are just a few and there's even one called Brainwave Synchronizer (Can you say Heavens Gate? Sure you can). For those of you who didn't have the benefit of the SFX CD we used in Tutorial 8-1, you're in luck! I've saved the results as CH8EX1.WAV and you will find this file in the Chapter 8 Tutorial folder on the accompanying CD-ROM.

The SFX sound file is essentially two high-powered race cars zipping by at an excess (estimated) speed of 100 MPH. Being that I'm a forward-looking individual, I fully intend to show you how to turn the sound of these cars into space craft zipping by at thousands of miles per hour. So let's go do it!

1. Start the application Cool Edit 96. Select Open from the File menu and load the file CH8EX1.WAV from the CH8 tutorial folder on the CD-ROM accompanying this book.

2. The purpose of this exercise is to alter the nature of the original sound file using a Flanger. Select Delay Effects and then Flanger from the Transform menu, as shown in Figure 8-7.

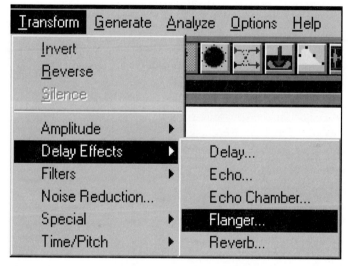

Figure 8-7
Select Delay Effects and Flanger under the Transform menu.

3. From the Flanger Presets (Figure 8-8), choose Sci-Fi 60's and click OK. This will give us the heavy flanged effect needed to create the right atmosphere. When the flanger conversion is done, press Play on the Cool Edit 96 Transport controls (or press the space bar) to hear the results of this step.

Tip

The lack of a preview feature in the effects section of Cool Edit 96 can be a pain if you want to do an A/B comparison of the audio file. Here's a simple solution. After you've applied the effect to the source audio (Flanger in this case), take a listen to it. Select Undo Flanger from the Edit menu to remove the effect from the source audio file. You can reapply the effect by repeating Steps 2 and 3 or by selecting Repeat Last Command from the Edit menu.

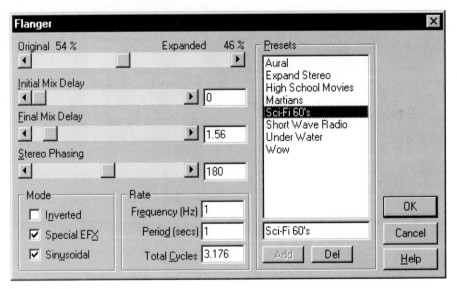

Figure 8-8
For the really heavy flanged effect needed, choose the preset Sci-Fi 60's.

4. Looking at Figure 8-9, notice that the Flange effect sort of squashed the waveform down just a little bit. You can bump up the level without adding distortion by using the Normalize feature. Select Amplitude and then Normalize from the Transform menu (see Figure 8-10). In this case, Normalize the file to 50% (see Figure 8-11). Make the change and click OK.

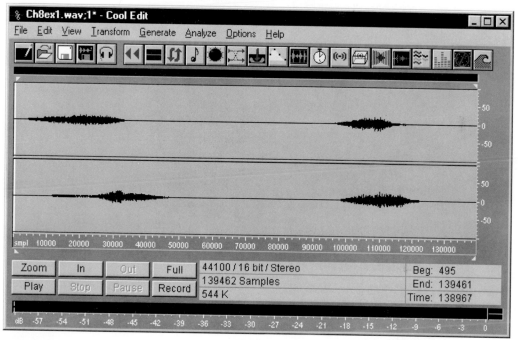

Figure 8-9
Adding the Flange effects lightly compresses the waveform.

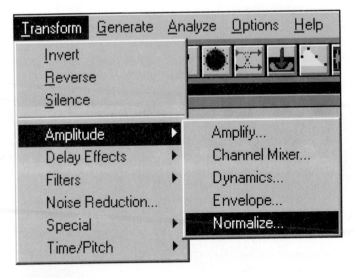

Figure 8-10
Under the Transform menu, select Amplitude and Normalize.

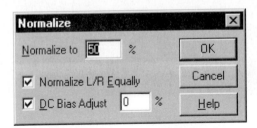

Figure 8-11
Set Normalize to 50% and click OK.

5. The last step in this not-too-rigorous process is to save your work. From the File menu, select Save As CH8EX2.WAV. Notice the visual difference in the Waveform (Figure 8-12) after Normalizing the file (refer back to Figure 8-9 for the before). When listening back to the file, you'll notice the audio level is somewhat higher and the Flange effect will be much more pronounced.

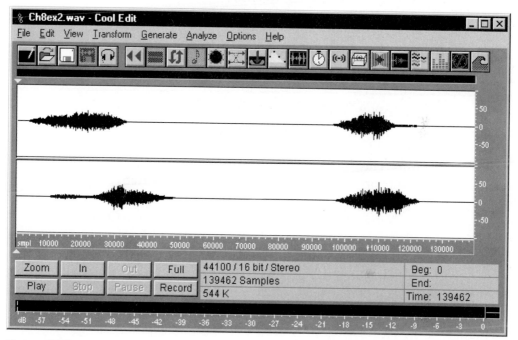

Figure 8-12
Notice how the Normalize effect raised the volume level of the Waveform.

How cool is it?

It's so cool there isn't even any real competition (in this price range) and if anyone asks, you're now an experienced sound designer after completing these first two tutorials. As you've probably noticed, there are a number of different DSP effects at your disposal with Cool Edit. While they sound pretty good, they're nowhere near the quality of professional-level audio plug-ins such as those available in the Native Power Pack from Waves. In fact, it's not possible to use third-party plug-ins with Cool Edit 96. Still, when you're the best in your class, it's all academic anyway.

For entry- to mid-level audio enthusiasts, you just can't go wrong with Cool Edit 96. There are a lot of little things I feel are missing—such as a preview function for the effects, for one—but again, what do you want for $50? If you're impressed with the feature-disabled version of this application from the CD-ROM with this book, give the registered version a try. I don't think you'll really like it; I think you'll love it!

Sound Forge 4.0

I hardly know where to start with this one. Sound Forge 4.0 has so many features and functions, I get lost in the possibilities. To me, this is the ultimate two-track (stereo) sound design tool on the Windows platform. One of the features that really puts Sound Forge 4.0 over the top is support for DirectX (formerly known as ActiveMovie) plug-ins. This gives you access to some really powerful plug-ins, such as the Waves Native Power Pack and QTools AX from QSound. You can record or import professional quality audio and create some stunning effects and music with the tools at your disposal. If there ever was an application suited for pre-mastering your audio for playback over the Web, Sound Forge 4.0 is it. There's nothing like starting the tour with a quick tutorial—so roll up your sleeves, and let's do it.

> **Web**
>
> To get the latest info on Sound Forge and related products, go to the Sonic Foundry homepage at www.sfoundry.com.

Tutorial 8-3: The loop

This tutorial is actually the first step in a series of several. The purpose of this tutorial is to create a sound file that can be set up as an ambient-sounding music loop. While silence is golden, there are numerous situations where a cool sounding piece of music repeating itself over and over again can bring many hours of pleasure (or pain) and fill out empty space (also known as dead air) on a Web site, kiosk, or other multimedia-type environment.

While in this case the loop won't be totally seamless, using the Fade In and Out process in Sound Forge, the transition should be a smooth one. The sound file we create in this tutorial (CH8EX3.WAV) is going to see a lot of life in this chapter—we'll use it to demonstrate in a number of different situations throughout.

What you need

For this tutorial, you need a few basic things to get rolling. Obviously to complete each step, a full working version of Sound Forge 4.0 is a necessity; however, the Demo version of Sound Forge will get you through many of the steps.

CD-ROM

In the Demo Software folder on the CD-ROM is a save-disabled demo version of Sound Forge 4.0. Also, the tutorial sound files for this chapter can be found in the Chapter 8 tutorial folder (on the CD-ROM).

- The application Sound Forge 4.0 (demo or full version)
- The tutorial sound file CH8EX3.WAV
- A Windows PC (minimum 486/33 running Win 3.1 or better)

■ Creating the loop

1. Start the application Sound Forge 4.0 and select Open CH8EX3.WAV from the File menu. Press the spacebar to start playback of the file (Figure 8-13). Close your eyes while listening and imagine something along the lines of watching the sun rise from over the horizon of a newly discovered planet. The main purpose of this tutorial is to take this file and create a smooth loop for playback from your home page.

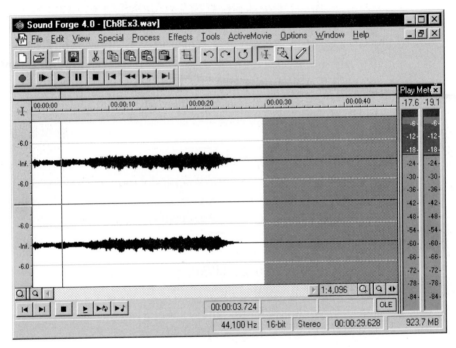

Figure 8-13
Press the spacebar to start playback of Tutorial file CH8EX3.WAV.

2. In this step, we're going to add a smooth fade in and fade out to the file. Select the last few seconds of the wave file (see Figure 8-14) by holding down the left mouse button and dragging over the target area. Under the Process menu, select Fade and Out as shown in Figure 8-15. The selected area now has a tapered fade to nothing.

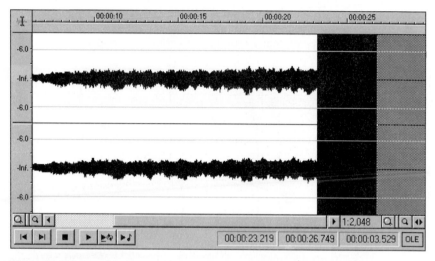

Figure 8-14
Select the area to be faded out by dragging the cursor while holding down the left mouse button.

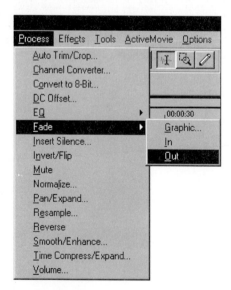

Figure 8-15
Under the Process menu, select Fade and then Out.

3. Now, if you're not the adventurous type, I'd say the easiest thing for you to do is to repeat Step 2 in the reverse doing a Fade In. Good thing you are the adventurous type. Select the first two seconds of the sound file using the same method you did in Step 2 and, under the Process Menu, choose Fade and Graphic. In Figure 8-16, you can view the Graphic Fade window. Not only are there preset fades to match most common situations, but you can create and save your own preset fades using the Graphic interface (however, that's a tutorial for another day and another book).

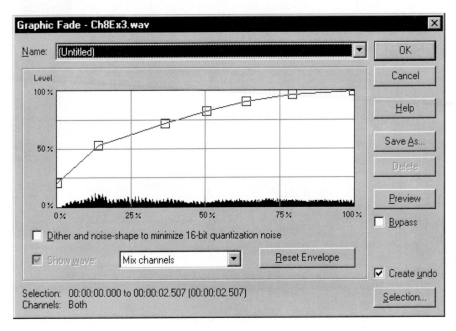

Figure 8-16
The Graphic Fade window enables you to create custom fade in or out presets.

4. Under the Name menu, select the preset -3 dB exponential fade in (shown in Figure 8-17). Before committing yourself to this fade in, click on the Preview button to hear what the fade in will sound like. Click Stop to end the preview. In this case, the fade-in preset does the job nicely, so all that's left to do is click OK.

Note

During the preview, you can change the fade envelope on the Graphic interface, creating a custom fade while listening to the results.

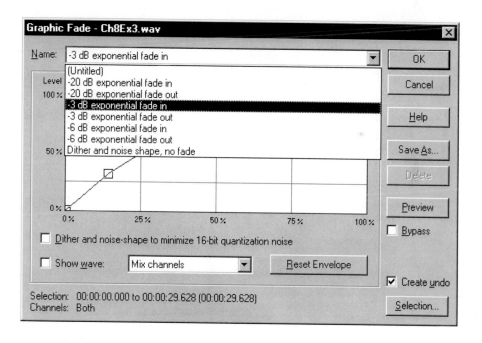

Figure 8-17
Select the preset -3 dB exponential fade in.

5. So, how do you loop the file? In the transport control directly below the Edit window (see Figure 8-18) is the Play Looped button. Press this button and it will repeat infinitely or until you press the Stop button. When ready, select File@(Save As CH8EX4.WAV.

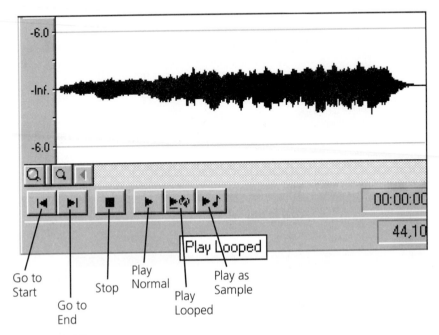

Figure 8-18
Press the Play Looped button to listen to how well the fade in and fade out work within the loop.

Tip

There is no way in Sound Forge (or any other sound editing application) to save this file so it will loop automatically. The actual loop command is set up in the application that is playing the file.

◼ And the verdict is...

Whether your sound file is going to loop or just play once, a smooth fade in and out is important. You can use such simple tricks to add some professional-type qualities to your sound files. As you experiment further with Sound Forge, you'll notice there are a lot of possibilities along these lines. While there's no way to cover them all in this book, the idea is pretty much the same and thanks to the multiple undo feature (found in the Edit menu), you can usually back out of any mistakes you could possibly make.

Flexibility is one of the strong points in Sound Forge and it's great to be able to use a preset effect as a template for creating a custom sound effect of your own. You might even want to go back to Step 3 of the last tutorial and experiment with creating your own custom fade in the Graphic Fade window. Simply use one of the preset fades as a starting point and take it from there.

Tutorial 8-4: Stereo imaging

There is no better way to beef up a music or sound file than to widen the stereo field. One of the components of the Native Power Pack (from Waves) is the S1-StereoImager. There are a number of subtle and not-so subtle effects you can achieve using the StereoImager. For this particular exercise, we're going to deal in width. This is sort of a mastering process and it seems that when the width increases, so does the clarity and warmth of the sound file. As you will see (and hear) as we run through this tutorial, the effect might seem somewhat subtle at first. In comparison, however, it's as though someone took a blanket off of your speakers. If you want a big sound, read on!

◼ What you need

This is a situation where you just aren't going to be able to do the tutorial with demo software and while I do apologize for that in advance, not everything in life is free. Still, what I'm going to do for you here is to make it possible to hear the results anyway. As you follow the tutorial, you will be asked to save the individual steps. You will find the results of each of these steps in the Chapter 8 tutorial folder on the CD-ROM. Simply click on the corresponding file and hear the results. So, let's get rolling! Here's what you need:

- The application Sound Forge 4.0 (full version)
- The Native Power Pack (from Waves)
- The tutorial sound file CH8EX4.WAV
- A Windows PC (minimum 486/33 running Windows 95 or NT)

Six steps to stereo imaging

1. Start the application Sound Forge 4.0 and select Open CH8EX4.WAV from the File menu. (You may remember this as our looped synthesizer ambient-type sound file from Tutorial 8-3). Select Waves S1-StereoImager from the ActiveMovie menu as shown in Figure 8-19.

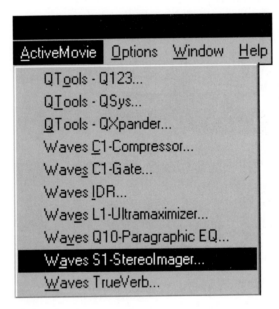

Figure 8-19
Select Waves S1-StereoImager from the ActiveMovie menu in Sound Forge.

Note

For those of you with a later version of Sound Forge 4.0, notice that ActiveMovie has been changed to DirectX. There is no difference in functionality, just Microsoft once again messing with your mind.

2. As you can see by Figure 8-20, you've opened the door. There are a number of controls that can alter and shape the sound of the stereo field, but the only one of real interest to you in this exercise is called Width. This is the controller that you use to widen the stereo field. Before adjusting the Width, though, you will want to preview the file. One of the really cool functions available in this plug-in is the preview, which lets you listen to and alter the sound file in real time. Click the Preview button to begin a looped playback of the sound file. Moving the Width slider is accomplished by placing the cursor on the slider and moving it up or down while holding the left mouse button down.. As you listen to the file, slowly move the Width slider up and stop when you achieve a width level of 2.75.

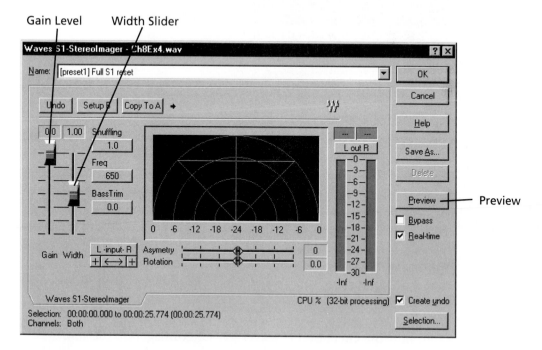

Figure 8-20
The Waves S1-StereoImager window.

3. At this point, we're into a pretty wide stereo field and there is a noticeable difference in the sound. To do an A/B comparison, check the Bypass box (directly below the Preview button) to bypass the stereo enhancement. As you toggle back and forth between the before and after, there will be a noticeable difference.

4. It helps to see as well as hear what you're doing when editing a sound file. Figure 8-21 gives you the graphic before and after of your manipulation of the stereo field. Click on the Setup button and it will toggle back and forth between the original setup and the edits you have made.

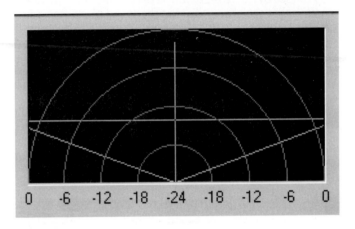

Figure 8-21
The before and after of the S1-StereoImager manipulation can be viewed in these two graphics.

5. It's time to make your move. Click OK and press the spacebar to have a listen.

6. If you're satisfied with the file, save it as CH8EX5.WAV.

Note

For those of you who wish to hear the before and after, here's what you do: Select and playback file CH8EX4.WAV to hear the before, and then playback the file CH8EX5.WAV to hear the effect of the Waves S1-StereoImager on the source audio file.

■ The bottom line

Subtle effects processing such as we just experienced in Tutorial 8-4 can give your sound and music files that slight edge that puts your work above the rest of the crowd. Whether your target vehicle for delivery is the Web or multimedia it doesn't matter; the bottom line is better sound. With DirectX (formerly known as ActiveMovie) plug-ins and the native editing capabilities in Sound Forge 4.0, there really isn't any close competition (for Windows) in this price range. If you work with multiple tracks or sound files, you might want to use an application with more than a two-track capability, but chances are you'll end up importing the results into Sound Forge for the final tweaks. If you're serious about music and sound design for the Web and multimedia, you'll want to add Sound Forge 4.0 to your arsenal to be competitive.

 Cool Edit Pro

In the interest of hanging out on the cutting edge, here's where you get what could quite possibly be your first look at Cool Edit Pro. So, how does 64 tracks sound? What about ActiveMovie (or DirectX, if you like) plug-in support? It all looks good on paper, and in fact even better in practice. For those of you who use Cool Edit 96, you will be familiar with how Cool Edit Pro is laid out and works (for the most part). So, instead of continuing to tell you how great it is, let's go use it!

Web

To find out the latest info on Cool Edit Pro, go to the Syntrillium Software homepage at www.syntrillium.com.

Tutorial 8-5: Multitrack mixing with Cool Edit Pro

What we're going to accomplish here is to take three separate WAVE files and bring them into the Multitrack environment of Cool Edit Pro. This tutorial will give you a basic idea of how to get around and edit the separate WAVE files, bring them into the multitrack environment, and mix them down into one stereo file. In this tutorial, we're taking the listener on a pleasant walk through the jungle—or at least it starts out that way. By the time you finish this tutorial, you'll know what I mean.

What you need

The following items are needed to complete this tutorial:

- Cool Edit Pro
- A Windows 95/NT capable PC
- Tutorial file CH8EX6 (roaring lion)
- Tutorial file CH8EX7 (music file)
- Tutorial file CH8EX8 (music file)

> **Note**
>
> Before we get started, let me explain the two environments in which we'll be working: the Waveform window and the Multitrack window. The Waveform window is very similar to the Cool Edit 96 environment. You can have as many as two tracks and this is where you would add effects and do the basic DSP Editing. In the Multitrack window, you can see all the tracks together (up to 64) and this is where we'll put together the final mix.

Steps to multitrack mixing

1. Start the Application Cool Edit Pro. We'll begin working in the Waveform window, so select Waveform from the View menu.

2. Select Open CH8EX6.WAV from the File menu (see Figure 8-22). Repeat the process with CH8EX7.WAV and CH8EX8.WAV.

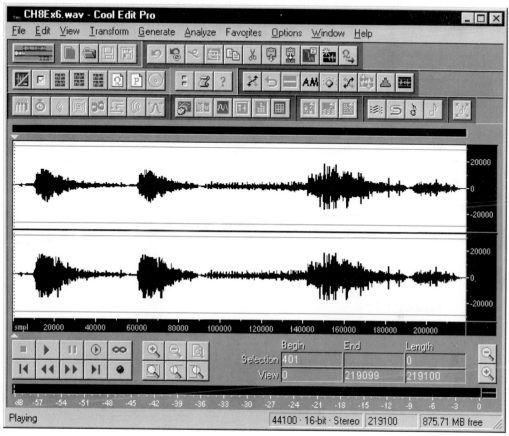

Figure 8-22
The Waveform View in Cool Edit Pro.

3. All three files can now be accessed in the Waveforms List window. To get there, select Waveforms List from the Window menu (see Figure 8-23). Select the three files simultaneously and click once on the Insert button. This will insert the three tutorial files into the Multitrack window. Click the Close button in the Waveforms List window when finished.

Figure 8-23
In the Waveform List window, select all three tutorial files and click once on the Insert button to place them in the Multitrack window.

4. Select Multitrack View from the View menu to get into the Multitrack window. You can see in Figure 8-24 that the three tutorial files now reside in the Multitrack window.

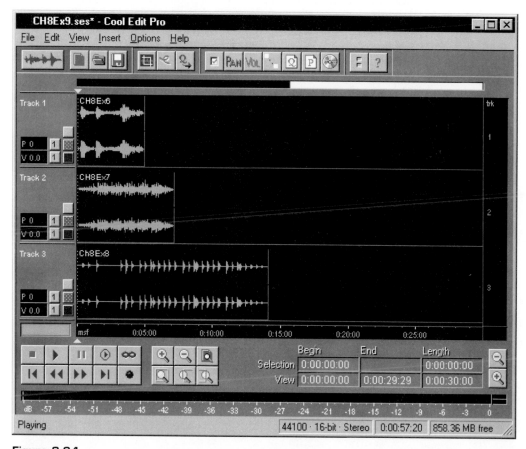

Figure 8-24
The three tutorial files now reside in the Multitrack window of Cool Edit Pro.

5. This next step involves getting the three sound files to line up in the proper order for playback. Ideally, they will be placed in the timeline to playback in the following order: music, sfx, and music. Track 3 (EX8) will be the first to playback and will remain in its current position. Track 1 (EX6), the roaring lion, will be the next in line, and finally Track 2 (EX7) will be the final component in the playback order. Moving the position of an audio file within a track in Cool Edit Pro is pretty simple. Select Track 1 by clicking on the WAVE. Holding down the right mouse button, drag the entire file so it's at a start position of about 12 seconds. Repeat the process with Track 2 and drag it so the start position is at about 13 seconds (see Figure 8-25 for reference). Remember, we're keeping Track 3 in its current position.

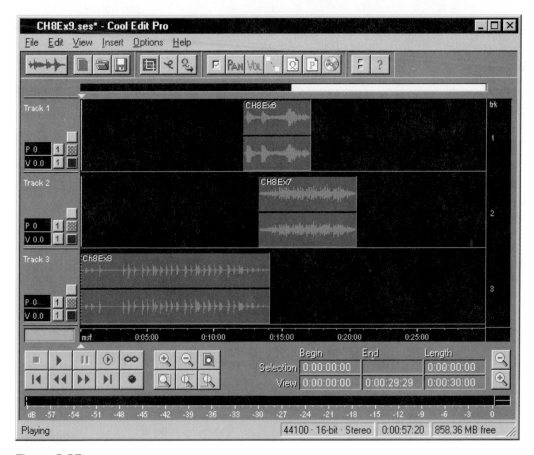

Figure 8-25
To move a WAVE file within a track, click on the file with the right mouse button and drag it to the proper position.

6. Press the spacebar to start playback and hear the results. It's possible you may want to position the three sound files a little differently than I did and that's fine. It all comes down to personal taste, so make the moves that work for you.

Now it's time to save the edits you performed in the Multitrack window; to do so, select Save Session As CH8EX9 from the File menu.

Note

Wondering what a Session is in the world of Cool Edit Pro? As you remember, we started this tutorial with three separate WAVE files. All three files now reside in the Multitrack window of Cool Edit Pro. You need to save these three files and the edits you've made in the Multitrack window as one piece of work. These three files and the edits are saved as a Session (as in Recording Session).

7. This is where you're going to take all three tracks and mix them down to one stereo pair. Use the command Control + A to select all three files that reside in the Multitrack window. Select Mix Down and then Selected Waves from the Edit menu. This converts the Multitrack session into a single stereo WAVE file as shown in Figure 8-26. Select Save As CH8EX10.WAV from the File menu.

To hear the results, press play on the transport controls (or press the spacebar).

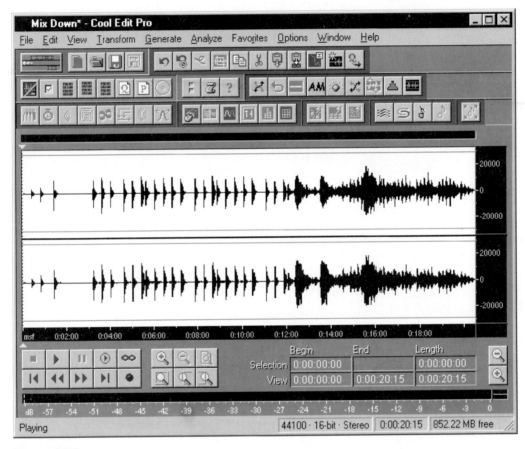

Figure 8-26
The selected audio from the multitrack session is converted to a stereo WAVE file during the mixdown.

Results

It works and it's easy to use. This is only one of the many possible uses for Cool Edit Pro. Musicians have traditionally used the multitrack cassette format for creating demos and work tapes. It sounded pretty bad, but was easy to use and not that expensive. If you've already got a decent PC, with the addition of Cool Edit Pro and a professional soundcard, you can create CD-quality music for about the same price as a good multitrack cassette deck and mixer.

New Features

There are a lot of new features in Cool Edit Pro, besides being able to record and playback up to 64 tracks. DirectX (formerly know as Active-Movie) plug-in support is by far my favorite and takes Cool Edit Pro to a higher level altogether. This gives the professional power user the option of turning this relatively inexpensive application (the suggested retail price was $399.00 at the time we went to press) into a high-end professional editing environment. Just to see if the DirectX plug-ins really worked, I tried out a few of the QSound and Waves plug-ins and they worked like a charm. Depending on your sound card, it is also possible to record up to eight tracks simultaneously.

The bottom line

Cool Edit Pro is definitely worth the price of admission. It has just about every feature you would need in a multitrack recording environment. What's really exciting here is you can start with a basic full-featured and inexpensive system and build it into a power-house recording and editing environment. The price point, 64 tracks, and DirectX plug-in compatibility gives Cool Edit Pro an edge over the nearest competition. When I started using it, I wasn't to sure if I liked it (you know, us Mac guys). But within 20 minutes, I was hooked. The bottom line is I'd buy it and you should too.

Sound In the World of Windows

When it comes right down to it, there are lots of pretty cool Windows sound applications coming down the pipeline. The three featured in this chapter each cover a certain block of the marketplace and were picked because of the old price/performance thing. Most of you reading this book aren't going to run out and spend 10 or 20K on recording software and hardware, but you might spend $50 or even $500 if the situation called for it. In most cases, the ActiveMovie plug-ins needed to take it to the next level cost more than the applications themselves, which will create a bit of a dilemma for the non-professional user. Still, if you're really serious about sound, you will find a way.

There's also been a rumor going around for some time that Sonic Foundry (the makers of Sound Forge 4.0) have a multitrack application under development. No one will of course confirm or deny that such a thing even exists, but I certainly won't be surprised to see it show up in the very near future.

When it comes down to it, I like Sound Forge and Cool Edit (96 and Pro) for different reasons. In the real world, you need full-featured applications that are easy to use and will get the job done with professional results. Between the three different products featured in this chapter, I was able to do just that. Visit the Web sites listed in Table 8-1 of the respective software companies to learn more about these products.

Table 8-1   Chapter 8 Featured Products

Company	URL
Sound Forge 4.0 by Sonic Foundry	`http://www.sfoundry.com`
CoolEdit 96 and Cool Edit Pro by Syntrillium Software	`http://www.syntrillium.com`

Chapter 9

Recording and Editing Tutorials for the Mac

 In This Chapter

- Sound Designer II
- SoundEdit 16 Version 2.04
- Peak
- Pro Tools 4.0

This chapter focuses on four different Mac-based applications. Some are improved versions of old standards, and one is even a brand new entry to the competition. The tutorials in this chapter will act as a guide through some of the basics of creating and editing sound with these Mac-based applications. Some of the applications have a more traditional background in developing sound for multimedia, while others are rooted in the music industry. It doesn't really matter—they all get the job done (and then some), just in a little different way. So, buckle up your seat belt and shoulder harness and let's get airborne.

Sound Designer II

If there was ever an application that fit the category "standard of the industry," Sound Designer II from Digidesign is it (from now on referred to as SD II). The intended uses of SD II include dialog editing, sound design, recording CD-quality audio tracks, and of course preparing sound for multimedia. One of the real strengths of SD II has been plug-ins such as DINR (Digital Intelligent Noise Reduction), also from Digidesign. Unfortunately, SD II plug-ins are not supported in the PCI version of SD II, causing much distress for those who have chosen to upgrade from NuBus-based Macs and PowerMacs to PCI. With the release of Pro Tools 4.0, Digidesign is (slowly) porting all of the SD II plug-ins over to the AudioSuite environment and is hoping to phase out SD II altogether. Still, there are quite a few recording studios that use SD II and plan to continue using it. When I need to do a quick minor fix on a sound file, you can bet I use SD II. So, let's go take a look.

> **Note**
>
> For more on AudioSuite, see the section on Pro Tools 4.0, later in this chapter.

SD II was one of the original file conversion utilities for those that have been doing Mac-based editing of audio files since the dark ages (the early 90's). Table 9-1 is a list of file formats supported by SD II.

Tutorials are the best way to guide you through the basic features and uses of an application, so let's get to it. Even if you don't have SD II, chances are you probably will run into it at some point. Using these tutorials as a guide, you can be up and running in a much shorter time span.

Table 9.1 SD II supported file formats

Supported File Formats	Description
AIFF	Audio Interchange File Format
Compressed	When saving a SD II file, it is possible to save it in a compressed format to conserve disk space.
Sound Designer	The original Sound Designer format (16 bit mono).
Sound Designer II	The recomended file format for use with Digidesign systems.
Sound Designer II Split Stereo	A SD II file where two mono files are treated as a split stereo pair.
snd Resource	The standard Macintosh sound resource format.
System 7 Sound	An updated version of the snd Resource that allows the sound file to operate independently of an application.
WAVE	The standard audio format for the Windows OS.

SDII system requirements

The system requirements for running SDII are:

- A NuBus-equipped 68030 (or better) Mac with a processor speed of 25 mHz (or faster) and 8 MB of RAM or a PCI Power Mac with 16 MB of RAM (32 MB is better)
- An Audiomedia (II or III) sound card or Pro Tools hardware
- System 7.1 or better running in the 32 bit mode
- A hard disk with an average access time of 18 ms or faster

Warning

Sound Designer II will frequently lock up and crash when playing a sound file from the same disk on which the application resides. Here's why: Audio (and video) are very memory-intensive and not only take up a large amount of disk space but require faster access time than say a text or graphics document. When running SD II (and many other audio applications) from the same drive as the source audio, quite often the drive can't process the information quickly enough and you get a crash. Any drive with a seek time of more than 12 ms will probably be too slow to handle playback of digital audio. The Iomega Jaz drive can handle audio playback without a hitch, but it's less expensive little brother—the Zip drive—is way too slow and can be used only as a storage medium.

Tutorial 9-1: Getting started with Sound Designer II

This first tutorial is intended to acquaint you with Sound Designer II and its interface.

■ What you need

There are a lot of different configurations that will work just fine with SD II. My rig for this series of tutorials reads like this:

- PowerMac 8500/120
- Digidesign Audiomedia III card (PCI)
- Seagate Barracuda 4.3 Gig AV Drive
- Mackie 1202 VLZ Mixer
- Alesis Monitor One Speakers
- Alesis RA-100 Reference Amplifier
- Sound Designer II (version 2.82)

◼ The nickel tour

1. Locate the SD II application on your desktop and open it. Select File@(Open CH9EX1.AIF.

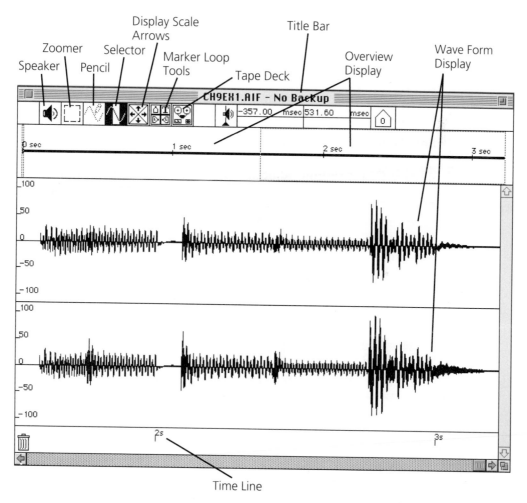

Figure 9.1
Tutorial file CH9EX1.AIF in the main window of SD II.

2. The playback controls in SD II may be just a little less intuitive and harder to find than most of you are used to. In the top left-hand corner of the Soundfile window, you will notice a row of little icons (refer back to Figure 9-1). The particular icon that needs your immediate attention is called Tape Deck. Click on the Tape Deck icon to enable the Hard Drive recording panel (Figure 9-2). You now have access to the Transport controls, record parameters, and Input Monitor. Press the Play button to initiate playback of tutorial file CH9EX1.AIF. Press Done to exit the Tape Deck controls.

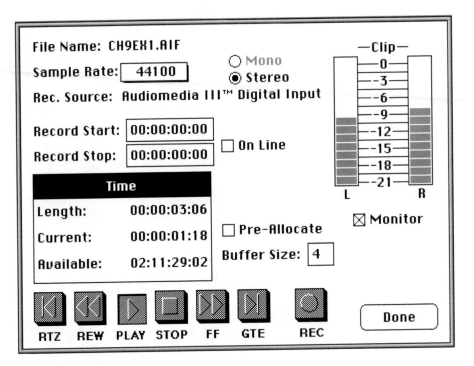

Figure 9.2
Press Play on the Transport controls to initiate playback of the tutorial sound file.

3. Audio playback can also be initiated from the Soundfile window. The Speaker button (refer back to the call outs in Figure 9-1) is the key to playing the tutorial file in the Soundfile window. Place the cursor on the Speaker button. Hold down the mouse button to begin playback and release the button to stop.

■ Don't touch that dial!

I always wanted to say that! Leave SD II and tutorial file CH9EX1.AIF up and running, as you'll be using them in Tutorial 9-2. The purpose for this first tutorial was to give a basic tour of the playback controls in SD II. The first time I opened the application (some years back,) it took me a minute to get my bearings and figure out how things worked and I thought I'd just save those of you just starting out the grief. So, let's jump to the next tutorial and check out a little DSP action!

Digital Signal Processing

Now we're going to take a little tour of the native DSP (Digital Signal Processing) functions in SD II. Table 9-2 gives you an overview and brief description of each function.

Table 9.2 DSP functions in Sound Designer II

Function	Description
Mix	Mix up to four separate stereo sound files into one.
Merge	Merge two files with a digital crossfade.
S R Convert	Use this DSP function to convert the sample rate of a soundfile.
Parametric EQ	Alter the EQ curve at a specific frequency.
Graphic EQ	Alter the overall EQ curve of the entire soundfile.
Dynamics	Use this function as a compressor/limiter, an expander, or a noise gate.
Frequency Analysis	A 3D display of the frequency spectrum of a sound file.
Time Comp/Exp	Time Compression and Expansion allows you to change the duration of a sound file without altering the pitch.
Pitch Shift	Adjust the pitch of a soundfile without changing the duration.

Editing sound in a virtual environment is what Tutorial 9-2 is all about. We're going to use the same tutorial soundfile CH9EX1.AIF and perform some DSP functions to it.

Tutorial 9-2: Using EQ via DSP

The most useful and powerful editing features in SD II are found in the DSP menu (found in the SD II menu bar). Trying to cover all the editing features in SD II would be a book in itself, so we'll just take a little side trip here and give you a taste of what can be accomplished. Using the Tutorial file CH9EX1.AIF, we're going to add a little EQ (Equalization) and beef up the overall sound.

If you followed along at the end of Tutorial 9-1, then the file CH9EX1.AIF is already open and you're ready to roll.

1. The purpose of this first step is to select the portion of the audio file that needs to be changed. Choose Select All (or command all) from the Edit menu to highlight the entire file in the Waveform display of the Soundfile window. Select Graphic EQ from the DSP menu. You should now see a five-band graphic Equalizer (Figure 9-3).

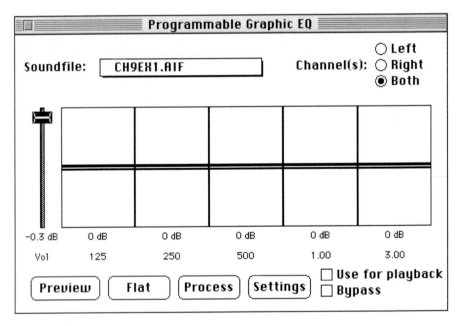

Figure 9.3
The Graphic EQ window and controls.

Note

If you are unfamiliar with what a graphic EQ is and how it works, reference the sidebar entitled "The Graphic EQ Made Easy," at the end of this tutorial.

2. There are five bands of EQ to work with and you have the option of selecting separate EQ settings for the left and right audio channels or the same EQ settings for both channels. For the sake of simplicity, the EQ changes we make will be for both channels. Click on the Preview button in the lower left-hand corner of the screen, which enables you to listen to a short preview of the sound file. This preview will repeat itself until you click the Preview button again to terminate playback. This is very helpful as you're now able to audition the EQ changes while you're making them, taking much of the guess work out of finding the setting you're happy with. You will notice a Volume fader on the left of the Graphic EQ window. You need to make a slight adjustment in the overall volume. Lower the volume level to -3 dB by dragging the volume fader down.

3. You can adjust the level of each of the five frequency bands by dragging the individual band faders up or down. This is best done while listening to the preview so you can hear the results playing back in real time. Starting from the left, slowly raise the setting to +6 dB as shown in Figure 9-4. Using Figure 9-4 as your point of reference, change the remaining EQ settings moving left to right. While you make these changes, you should notice how the sound file becomes more present and defined.

Warning

When raising the EQ sliders, remember you are raising the overall volume of that particular frequency. Make the changes a slow and gradual process so you won't blow out your speakers. It's also good to remember that no two sets of speakers sound the same and the EQ changes suggested in this tutorial may not bring about the same results with your speakers.

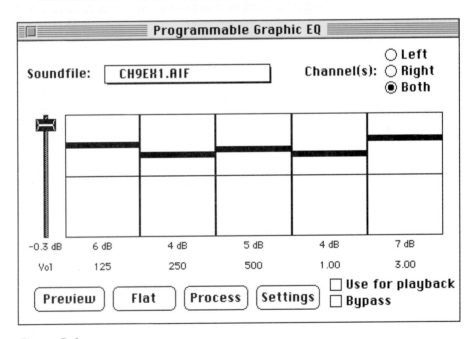

Figure 9.4
Change the EQ settings of the Soundfile CH9EX1.AIF.

4. Check the Bypass box in the bottom right-hand corner of the Graphic EQ window for an A/B comparison while previewing the tutorial soundfile. Here's an instance where personal taste (and your speakers) can enter into the equation. You don't necessarily need to use the EQ settings recommended in Figure 9-4. Experiment and you might find something you like better. When you've arrived at the settings that work best for you, click the Preview button again to stop the playback.

5. So far the original soundfile is unchanged. To save these changes to the original file, click the Process button. You will now be asked if you want to change the sound file. Click Yes and close the Graphic EQ window. The EQ settings have now been applied to the tutorial soundfile.

6. If you made all the right moves (and I know you did), you now have an improved version of the original tutorial sound file. To take a listen the easy way, position your cursor over the Speaker button (refer back to Figure 9-1 if you've forgotten) and hold down the mouse button. The file will stop playing when you let go of the mouse button or when it comes to the end (of the file).

7. You're loving how it sounds, but now it's time to save your work. Select Save As Copy from the File menu. Change the name of the sound file to CH9EX2.SND (see Figure 9-5) and change the file format to System 7 Sound. Click Save and you're done.

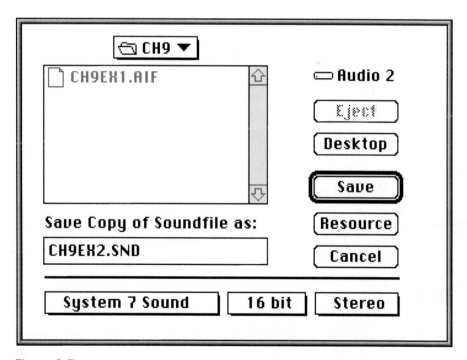

Figure 9.5
Save the edited sound file as CH9EX2.SND and change the file format to System 7 Sound.

■ The Graphic EQ Made Easy

For those of you who are completely unfamiliar with what a graphic EQ is and how it works, this is a highly simplified explanation. We'll use your home stereo as an example. Most stereos have a bass and a treble control that regulate the low-end frequencies (bass) and the high-end frequencies (treble). The graphic EQ works in the same way, but gives more options than just the low- or high-end controls. Notice back in Figure 9-3 that there are five control sliders. The slider on the far left is the bass control and the slider on the far right is your treble control. This leaves you with three other frequencies that you can adjust (low midrange, midrange, and high midrange). The more sliders on the graphic EQ, the greater control you have over the shaping of the overall quality of a soundfile. This is especially helpful when recording and editing original sound or music material.

Retrospect

I really had a chance to dig deeply into the functions of SD II and I'm telling you—I haven't even scratched the surface. I could write an entire book just about this application alone and probably not be able to cover it all. There are a number of very powerful DSP functions that can make SD II a great environment for the minor sound file tweaks needed in sound design or for pre-mastering music for an audio CD. Even though there may be no new releases of SD II, it's used so much by music industry professionals that I sort of felt it needed to be seen and heard. Again, many of us are sad that the PCI PowerMac version of SD II has no plug-in support, but I guess that's progress. One bad thing I did notice was the PCI version has a tendency to lock up and crash at a much higher frequency than I seem to remember when using SD II on a 680X0 Mac, but again I guess that's progress, too.

 ## SoundEdit 16 Version 2

If you're a Director user, then without a doubt you've at the very least come in contact with SoundEdit 16 from Macromedia. It is now part of the (Mac version) Director Multimedia Studio bundle (along with Deck

2.5). I initially made the mistake of ignoring Version 2 of this application after briefly working with the original and being less than impressed. Within five minutes of working with the latest release of SoundEdit 16, I was hooked. While the majority of my recording and editing work is done with Pro Tools, inevitably the files end up in SoundEdit 16 for the final tweaks before conversion to a Web audio format. For a look at a few other very usable features in SoundEdit 16, go to Chapters 3 "File Formats and Conversions" and 12 "Shockwave Audio" for even more tutorials.

SoundEdit 16 features

Here's just a few of the many features I think make SoundEdit 16 worth its weight in gold:

- Convert CD Audio
- Convert Shockwave Audio
- Convert to different bit depths
- Down Sample audio files
- Accept third-party DSP plug-ins (Xtras)
- Import and Export over 10 different file formats
- Edit audio within a QuickTime Movie
- PowerMac Native

This only touches on the basics, but hopefully you get the idea. Just the ability to digitally convert CD Audio (which I use all the time) and deal with the many different file formats is easily worth the price of admission. Take a look at Table 9-3 to see the specific file formats supported by SoundEdit 16.

Table 9.3 SoundEdit 16 (Version 2) supported file formats

Supported File Formats	Description
AIFF	Audio Interchange File Format
AU (Sun)	The standard Internet audio format
Instrument	A file format used by some Macintosh music applications
Quick Time Movie	Used by both Mac and PC for multimedia
RealAudio	Export only through a SoundEdit Xtra
Resource (snd)	The standard Macintosh sound resource format
Shockwave Audio	Export only through a SoundEdit Xtra
Sound Designer II	The recommended file format for use with Digidesign systems
SoundEdit format	An 8 bit file format used by early Macintosh applications
SoundEdit 16 format	An extension of the original SoundEdit format
System 7 Sound	Used mainly for System 7 beep sounds
WAVE	The standard audio format for the Windows OS

SoundEdit 16 system requirements

The system requirements for running SoundEdit 16 are as follows:

- 68030 Macintosh (or better) running System 7.1
- 15 MB free hard disk space and 8 MB of application RAM
- QuickTime 2.5
- A double-speed CD-ROM and a color monitor
- Hard disk with an average access time of less than 40ms

Unlike Sound Designer II, Sound Edit 16 requires no additional soundcard and can use the built-in sound capabilities of the Macintosh. I've also noticed I'm able to playback a sound file from the same drive as the application without crashing the computer (well, most of the time!). While recording source audio files with SoundEdit is possible, I tend to use it more for manipulation of already existing sound files. In Tutorial 9-3, we'll take two separate sound files and mix them down into one stereo file.

Tutorial 9-3: Combining and mixing sound files

In this little exercise, we're going to combine (or mix, as I would call it) a stereo sound effects (SFX) file and a stereo music file. Remember, you can use any file combination you want for your purpose, such as music and voiceover or voice and SFX. While it is possible to mix more than two stereo tracks together at a time, unless you have lots of RAM and a fast processor, you may experience a stutter in playback with five or six tracks running at the same time.

■ What you need

You've already seen the system requirements; here's the rest of what you'll need for this tutorial.

- ■ Tutorial sound files CH9EX3.SND and CH9EX4.SND.
- ■ SoundEdit 16 Version 2.04 (or better)
- ■ A properly configured Mac or PowerMac

CD-ROM

The tutorial sound files CH9EX3.SND and CH9EX4.SND can be found in the Chapter 9 tutorial folder on the CD-ROM.

■ Combine and mix

1. Open the application SoundEdit 16 (version 2). Select Open from the File menu, and choose the tutorial sound file CH9EX3.SND.

2. Now it's time to import the file you wish to mix with the file you have already opened. Select Import from the File menu, and choose the file CH9EX4.SND. Click on Import (see Figure 9-6).

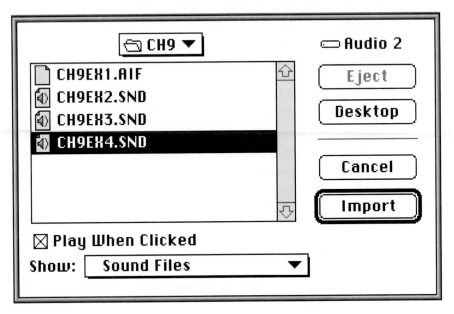

Figure 9.6
Import the tutorial sound file CH9EX4.SND into the file CH9EX3.SND.

3. You now have four audio tracks (two stereo pairs) residing in the Edit window. Chances are you can't see all four tracks at once. We'll fix that right now. Select Fit In Window from the View menu and all four tracks are now visible in the Edit window. (see Figure 9-7).

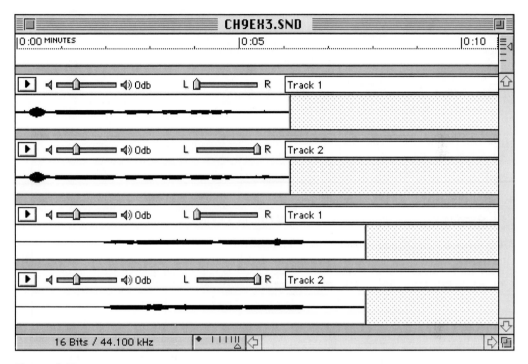

Figure 9.7
Under the View menu, the command Fit In Window enables all opened tracks to be visible at once.

4. For reference, you now need to rename each of the four tracks. To name or rename an audio track in Sound Edit 16, select the Track Name region with your cursor (see Figure 9-8) and enter the new name. Change Track 1 to SFX Left, Track 2 to SFX Right, Track 3 to Music Left, and Track 4 to Music Right (see Figure 9-8).

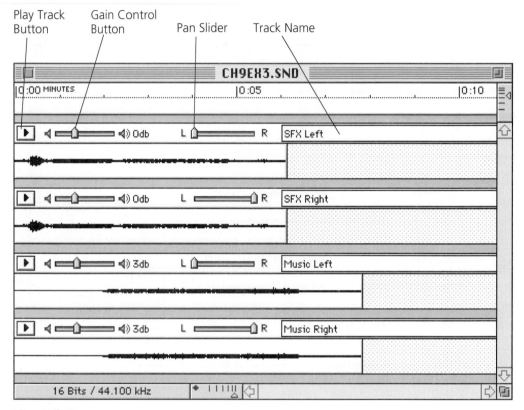

Figure 9.8
To change the track name, select the Track Name region with your cursor and enter the new name.

5. Now press the spacebar to initiate playback and take a listen to what you have. Tracks 1 and 2 are a sound effect, while 3 and 4 are a short music stinger. As you should notice, the music is drowned out by the sound effect. There are a number of ways to alter the volume on the music tracks, but for the sake of simplicity, we'll take the easiest route.

With the Gain controls, you can raise or lower the volume level of each individual track. In this situation, a minor adjustment is all that's needed. Raise the Gain controls by grabbing the Gain Control Slider and dragging it to the right on the Tracks labeled Music Right and Music Left to +3 dB (refer back to Figure 9-8). Press the spacebar to listen to the change. My word doesn't have to be the last one here—You can raise or lower the Gain controls on any of the four tracks to suit your individual taste.

6. Once you've achieved a good balance, it's time to mix the four tracks down to a stereo pair. Choose Select All from the Edit menu. All four tracks should now be highlighted. Now choose Mix from the Effects menu. You are presented with two options, the Simple Mixer and the Deluxe Mixer. Assuming you are totally in love with how the file sounds and all you need to do is convert it to a stereo (or mono) file, then the Simple Mixer is for you. Choose the Simple Mixer, Stereo, and New Document (refer to Figure 9-9); then click Mix. Without making any changes to your original file (it still exists), a new unnamed stereo file has been created. Press the space bar to initiate playback of the new file.

Figure 9.9
The Simple Mixer is so easy to use 9 out of 10 drummers get it right the first time!

7. Now all that's left to do is save your new file. Select Save As from the File menu and name this file CH9EX5.SND.

So far, so good

Using the Simple Mixer is an easy way to combine two or more separate audio files and mix them into a single stereo (or mono) file. Now it's time to get a little more advanced and work with one of my favorite plug-in tools: the Waves Native Power Pack.

Tutorial 9-4: Stereo enhancement

One of the things I really like about SoundEdit 16 is its support for a number of different audio effects plug-ins. There are a variety of standard plug-ins (Reverb, EQ, and Delay, to name a few) that come with SoundEdit, but the real strength comes from third-party developers. Cybersound from InVision Interactive is a set of reasonably priced entry-level plug-ins ($129) that are a step up from the basic plug-ins included in SoundEdit. I've been using them since their release and while I'm not totally knocked out by the results I've achieved, they definitely do the trick when it comes to processing a sound file.

The Native Power Pack from Waves is another story altogether. Not only is the sound quality good, but the entire set of plug-ins can be used in SoundEdit 16, Deck 2.5, Peak, and Studio Vision 3.5. There's also an Audiosuite version for Pro Tools 4.0 in the recently released Native Power Pack (NPP) version 2.3.

■ What you need

The following components are needed to complete this tutorial:

- ■ SoundEdit 16 (Version 2)
- ■ Native Power Pack by Waves
- ■ A properly configured Mac or PowerMac
- ■ Tutorial file CH9EX6.SND (on the CD-ROM)

■ Let's get wide!

As you've probably guessed by the title of this tutorial, we're going to take a stereo file and enhance it. The purpose of this exercise is to widen the music in the stereo field so it jumps out at you with a little more definition and clarity. While the difference between the before and after is somewhat subtle, you will definitely notice it.

1. Find and open the application SoundEdit 16. Select Open CH9EX6.SND from the File menu.

2. Choose Select All from the Edit menu to select the entire file (which is what you'll be processing).

3. Choose Waveshell from the Effects menu. You are now in the door. There are a number of Waves plug-ins that reside in the Waveshell and they are accessed in alphabetical order. The default window you see every time when entering the Waveshell is the C1-Compressor shown in Figure 9-10. Place the cursor on the Plug-ins Pulldown Menu, hold down the mouse button, and select for +S1 - Stereo Files Only.

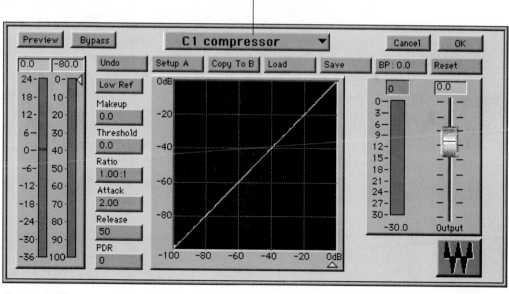

Figure 9.10
Place the cursor on the Plug-ins Pulldown Menu and hold down the mouse button to select the Waves plug-in module +S1 - Stereo Files Only.

4. You're now in the Waves +S1-Stereo Files plug-in module shown in Figure 9-11. Locate and click the Preview button (in the top left corner of the window). This initiates playback of a short loop of the target audio file several seconds long.

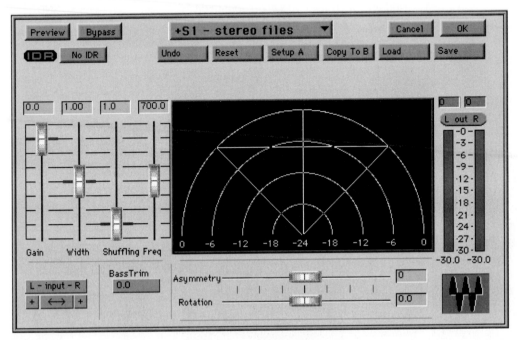

Figure 9.11
The Waves +S1 - Stereo Files plug-in module.

5. The main purpose of this tutorial is to widen the stereo field of the target audio file. Locate the Width control slider (to the left of the window). Drag the control up until the Width parameter control reads 2.75, as shown in Figure 9-12. You should notice a relatively subtle difference in the overall sound of the file as you raise the Width slider (remember the audio is still looping).

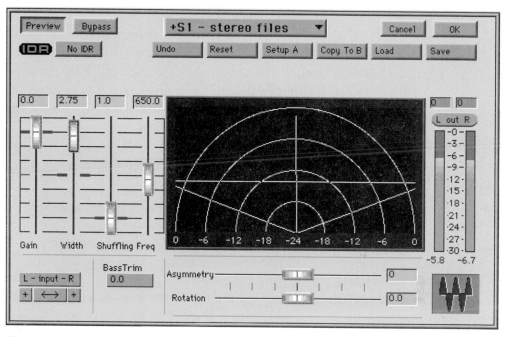

Figure 9.12
Drag the Width Control slider up until the width parameter control reads 2.75.

6. To do a simple A/B (before and after) comparison, click the Bypass button. This will bypass the stereo enhancement and let you hear the original source file. While this stereo enhancement is fairly subtle, you will really notice the difference when toggling back and forth using the Bypass button.

7. It's time to commit yourself to a wider, better-sounding audio file. Click the Preview button to terminate the preview loop. Now click OK.

8. Now that your file has been converted, press the space bar to initiate playback and take a listen to the entire audio file.

9. All that's left for you to do is save your work. Select Save As CH9EX7.SND from the File menu.

■ Is it really bigger?

The answer is a resounding YES! The +S1-Stereo Enhancer takes an audio file and enhances the overall stereo image in a variety of different ways. The sound seems to jump out at you and it's almost as though you're surrounded and in the middle of the music instead of just listening to it. If you're feeling adventurous, go back to Step 5 and try out a few of the other controls. Rotation changes the direction the sound is pointing. Asymmetry is also a very interesting effect, although I'm at a loss as to how to verbally describe the effect it has on the sound file. It's pretty cool though. Some of the greatest (and worst) inventions of mankind were discovered by accident. Be brave and experiment with the enhancer and all the other Waves Plug-ins as well.

■ Retrospect

I guess by now you've probably figured out that I really like SoundEdit 16. Each one of the four applications I've featured in this chapter are pretty cool and have their strengths and weaknesses and SoundEdit 16 is no exception. This is a great tool for the entry-level user, but it also has enough features (and expandability through plug-ins) to make it useful for just about anyone. As I (and the rest of the world) make the painful transition between Sound Designer II and Pro Tools 4.0, SoundEdit 16 is filling a lot of the gaps as a conversion utility and in a few other important areas as well. The price point and features make Sound Edit 16 a good all-around buy.

Peak 1.5 from BIAS

When I was doing the initial research for this book, I kept hearing about a new application for recording music and doing sound design called Peak. Of course, being overwhelmed with too much info, I forgot all about it until it came time to do this chapter. After checking out the demo software for Peak, I knew there was a spot or two for it in this book. Peak is for sure the new kid on the block, but I can already see that it's a strong contender and I promise you its found a permanent home in my arsenal of sound design tools.

Peak 1.5 features

Enough of my rambling—Let's take a look at a few of the features of Peak 1.5:

- Convert CD Audio
- Convert RealAudio 3.0 files
- Convert to different bit depths and sample rates
- Supports Adobe Premiere plug-ins
- Supports 7 different file formats, including Red Book audio
- Powerful native DSP functions
- Non-destructive editing with unlimited undo/redo
- Native for both 680X0 Mac and PowerMac

Peak 1.5 system requirements

The following are required to run Peak 1.5:

- 68030 Macintosh (or better) equipped with an Apple Sound Chip (ASC)
- System 7.1 or better
- 8 MB RAM on the 680X0 Macs
- 16 MB of RAM on Power Macs
- QuickTime 2.5 or later
- Hard disk with an average access time of less than 18 ms

Tutorial 9-5: Recording CD audio with Peak

So why record CD audio when it's probably easier just to import it? I'm glad you asked that question! I wanted to give you a chance to record something realtime in Peak without having to go through the hassle of hooking up a microphone, mixer, keyboard, or other device that you may or may not have. This way, you get to experience all the benefits of keeping it in-house (or at least in your computer). So let's get rolling.

■ What you need

The following items are needed to complete this tutorial:

- Peak (Version 1.5 or better)
- A standard audio CD
- A CD-ROM drive in your computer
- The application AppleCD Audio Player

Note

The application AppleCD Audio Player is a standard utility that is included as part of the Macintosh System 7 OS.

CD-ROM

You'll find a save–disabled demo version of Peak 1.5 on the CD-ROM. While you won't be able to complete all the tutorial steps using the demo version, it will help you get a good feel for the application all the same.

■ Let's get Peaked

1. Insert the audio CD in the CD drive of your Macintosh and open the application Peak.

2. Select Record from the Action menu. This opens the Record window (shown in Figure 9-13).

Figure 9.13
Use the Record window in Peak to change the audio settings.

3. Under Record Settings, change the source to Internal CD and make sure the Channels are set to Stereo. Also set the Bit-depth to 16 and the Sample Rate to 44.1 kHz. You now need to select the hard drive to which the audio you're about to record will be stored. From the Storage Disk drop-down list, I've selected the drive "Audio 2". You must now make a similar selection within your own system.

4. Now it's time to take a listen to the audio source we're about to record. Start the application AppleCD Audio Player. For the purpose of this tutorial, I'm using a Sound Effects CD and recording a track of a building blowing up. You can use an audio CD of your own choice for this tutorial.

CD-ROM

While the source audio for this tutorial originally came from the Hollywood Edge Super Single Volume 2, I've included before and after files on the CD-ROM for those of you who want to remain true to the sound and editing process. The files are CH9EX8.SND (raw file) and CH9EX9.SND (edited file).

5. Before starting the record process, you want to set the record level. Start the track you wish to record playing from the internal CD Player and make sure you've set the track to loop. You need to check the Monitor check box (directly below the level meters in the Record window of Peak) in order to hear what's being recorded. The next step is to set the Record level. Click the Level button in the lower right-hand corner of the Record window. Set the Level control by dragging it (see Figure 9-14) to match the input level of your source audio. Remember, if it's set too high, you will get distortion. For the purpose of this tutorial, I found a setting of 11 to be sufficient, so set the level at 11 and click OK.

Figure 9.14
Set the audio input level with the Level controls.

6. Now it's time to record. Back in Step 5, you put the AppleCD Audio Player in the loop mode while setting the levels and it still should be looping. When the track loops back to the beginning, click on the Start button in the bottom right-hand corner of the Record window to begin the recording process. Notice that once the recording process is enabled, you can monitor not only how much hard drive space is available but how much time has elapsed in the current record session.

7. When you've finished recording the source audio (around 30 seconds in this case), click Done (see Figure 9-15). You are asked to name the audio file. Call this file CH9EX8.SND. After naming the file, you are automatically sent back to the Record window. Click Cancel and move onto the editing phase of this process.

Figure 9.15
Click Done to terminate the record process.

8. Before we move to the editing portion of the show, let's take a quick look at the transport controls. To access the transport control, go to the Window pull-down menu and select Transport. The Peak Transport (Figure 9-16) is pretty straight forward with only four controls: Loop, Stop, Play, and Record. To rewind to the beginning of a file, simply click twice on the Stop button.

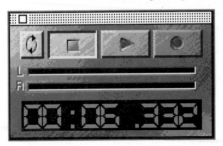

Figure 9.16
From left to right, Loop, Stop, Play, and Record are the four controls available in the Peak Transport.

9. You're now in the Audio Document window (shown in Figure 9-17). The sound file before you is essentially two versions of a building exploding. The decision you need to make is which of the two to keep. Press the spacebar (or the Play button) to begin playback and take a listen. Of the two explosions, I prefer the first one mainly because I like the sound of the falling debris in the aftermath, so for this tutorial choose the first explosion. The next step will be to trim the excess data.

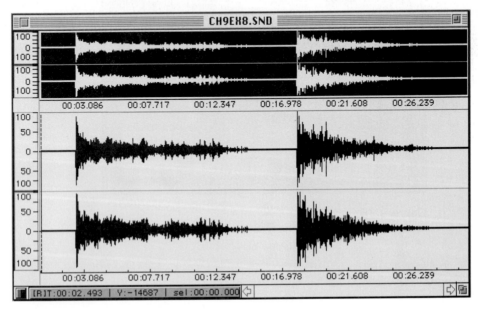

Figure 9.17
Tutorial file CH9EX8.SND in the Audio Document window.

10. One of the advantages of graphic editing is you can see the actual part of the file you want to remove while listening to it. In this case, we'll delete the section of the source audio file that contains the second explosion. To select the area to be deleted, place your pointer at the beginning of the section you want to delete and drag across it while holding the mouse button down. As shown in Figure 9-18, the area of the second explosion is now highlighted and ready for removal. Select Clear from the Edit menu. Repeat the entire process to trim the short few seconds of dead air from the front of the file as well. Now, press the space bar (or Play button on the Transport controls) to listen to the results.

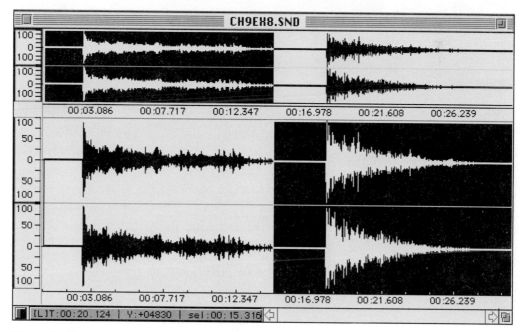

Figure 9.18
Select the area of the audio waveform to be deleted.

11. Now it's time to save your work. Before saving, make sure you change the file type to System 7 Sound. Select Save As CH9EX9.SND from the File menu and click Save. You can now see (and hear) a perfectly decent-sounding explosion (see Figure 9-19).

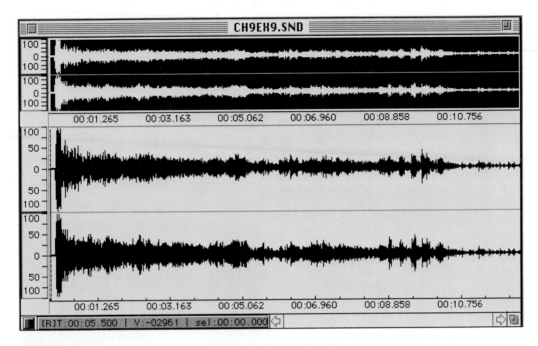

Figure 9.19
The results of your labor, a very explosive file CH9EX9.SND.

◼ A walk through the park

Recording and editing with Peak is pretty close to being a no-brainer. It's easy to use (as most Mac programs are) even for those who have little-to-no experience with sound and music. This is a very powerful sound design tool and while we barely scratched the surface in Tutorial 9-5, those of you who use Peak on a regular basis will really be amazed at the possibilities. I initially had a little problem with crashes when running demo versions of some of the third-party DSP plug-ins, but that was really the only problem I encountered. When you consider that Peak has been out slightly more than a year (at the time of going to press), that's pretty impressive. The bottom line is I would (and do) use Peak for many of the sound design jobs I do and am in fact looking forward to putting in more time with it. You can't ask for a better recommendation than that.

> **Note**
>
> You'll be seeing Peak again in Chapter 10, "Advanced Editing and Enhancing Tools," where we put it through the ringer using a very cool plug-in (also from BIAS) known as the SFX Machine.

Pro Tools 4.0

I don't mean this to sound like a commercial or anything, but I would be lost without Pro Tools. For those of you who have been hiding under a rock for the last seven or eight years, the various incarnations of Pro Tools (from Digidesign) have been the choice of the vast majority in the world of DAWs (digital audio work stations). There are a variety of options, starting with the software-only Pro Tools 4.0 DAE Powermix all the way up to a variety of configurations that include Pro Tools III hardware with the TDM (Time Division Multiplexing) bus. The release of Pro Tools 4.0 in March of 1997 has once again given Digidesign a pretty big edge over the closest competition.

As mentioned earlier, Digidesign plans to phase out their industry standard Sound Designer II software. This is kind of a bummer, as there are many very cool SD II plug-ins that many of us have come to rely upon in our work. This is where Audiosuite comes in. Audiosuite is Digidesign's new plug-in environment for Pro Tools 4.0. The plan is to convert all the Sound Designer II plug-ins to Audiosuite, giving the user a much more flexible environment for recording and editing sound in the form of Pro Tools 4.0. Granted, if you've got a large investment in Sound Designer II plug-ins, you will be unhappy. But, as I've said before, it's all in the name of progress.

Audiosuite is giving entry-level Pro Tools users an inexpensive option to the TDM plug-in environment. This is probably where I should explain the difference between Audiosuite and TDM. Using the TDM plug-in environment (with Pro Tools 4.0), the effects are applied in realtime. Essentially, you route the different audio signals from the tracks through the TDM Bus and then add the effects (such as reverb) to each track in realtime, just like you would with a tape deck and mixing board in analog recording. The DSP work is done by a NuBus or PCI card, called a *DSP Farm*, enabling the main processor of your computer to handle the more mundane tasks such as screen redraws. Your original source tracks stay unaffected and only the audio you are routing through the TDM Bus ends up with the effects as part of the track (which can be two or more tracks in Pro Tools, depending on your hardware). In Audiosuite, you merely select the area of audio you wish to change; choose the Audiosuite plug-in you wish to use; select, adjust, and preview the settings; then click Process. Using the main processor of your computer to add the effect to the selected area, the change is permanently added to the audio residing on your hard drive. This is what is known as *destructive editing*. To help you understand the difference between destructive and non-destructive editing, it's now time to take a little side trip to the following sidebar. I'll give some basic examples of how it works in the Pro Tools environment.

Destructive Editing Versus Non-Destructive Editing

Here's an example of non-destructive editing. In Pro Tools, when you record a source audio track, the entirety of what you originally record is permanently saved to the hard disk. Regardless of any edits you make to the tracks in Pro Tools, the original source material still resides on your hard drive. You can make changes on the playback portion of your track and while those are saved, the original file still sits in the background ready to be retrieved if needed. This has saved my butt more than a time or two when I accidentally (or on purpose) erased some material only to find at a later date that it was needed. With destructive editing, when you erase a file, it's gone forever.

Here's a simple real-life example of where non-destructive is a useful tool. When producing a voiceover session, I'll normally have the talent read the same take three different times to give me some variations in the performance come editing time. I then choose what I feel are the best parts from each sound bite and cut and paste the whole thing together. End of story (I wish). Of course, the client might not like the way the voice talent pronounced a certain word or even the tone of voice that was used. Even though I erased all the other source audio from the track, it's possible to go back and recover all of the original file, cut out a replacement phrase, and paste it in to replace the offending word (or words). With non-destructive editing, everyone ends up happy.

Tutorial 9-6: Recording in Pro Tools 4.0

This is going to be a simple little tutorial that will give you a taste of the basics of recording and editing in Pro Tools 4.0. In the real world, many of you won't be using the full-blown Pro Tools setup with all the hardware and expensive plug-ins, which is why I keep it simple here. You can perform this tutorial with the Pro Tools 4.0 software and a Power Macintosh sporting no additional hardware. Okay, you're gonna need 32 MB of RAM and while you can run on an 80 mHz machine, I'd recommend something in the neighborhood of 100 mHz to make sure things run more smoothly. I'm also using an Audiomedia III card to deal with my external inputs and outputs, although that's not necessary to do this tutorial.

In this tutorial, we'll be recording and editing a very short and simple mono voiceover track, which will in fact be one of the components of Tutorial 9-7. For those of you who don't have Pro Tools but wish to follow along all the same, each of the files is available to you on the CD-ROM accompanying this book so you can double click on the file and listen to the results of each step. In fact, those of you with a little initiative can assemble the components in another application (regardless of OS) and compare your results with mine.

> ### Note
>
> Some of the hardware components—such as a mixer, microphone, and speakers—may not be available to you, which could greatly vary the results of the actual recording process. Don't worry about it; use what you have. If you don't have any of these tools, simply load the corresponding tutorial file and work on the editing aspect. Every sound application is different and works better for some things than others. Much of what we try to accomplish in every tutorial is as much concept as it is learning to use the specific hardware and software. At the very least, follow the steps and double click the corresponding tutorial file to hear the results.

Recording hardware

I'm keeping it very simple here and using an inexpensive Audio-Technica Microphone running into a Mackie 1202 VLZ mixer. The audio outputs of the mixer are connected to the audio inputs of the PowerMac. I've turned off the speakers and am using a set of headphones to monitor the recording and playback of this voice session. This prevents the creation of an ugly-sounding feedback loop. If you are using a mixing board, I suggest you refer to the manual to make sure the connections and levels are set correctly for your system.

What you need

The following components are needed to complete this tutorial:

- Pro Tools 4.0 Software (DAE PowerMix)
- PowerMac with 32 MB of RAM running at 80 mHz
- Microphone
- Audio Mixer
- Headphones

The goal

This one's pretty simple. We'll record three takes of a two-sentence script. After deciding which part or parts of the performance is best, we'll edit it down to one take. If there's any problems with the source material, we'll fix it using an Audiosuite plug-in.

The steps

1. Start the application Pro Tools 4.0. Select New Audio Tracks from the File menu and create one new track (see Figure 9-20). Click OK.

Figure 9.20
Create one new track and click OK.

Note

Before we actually start recording, you need a script. So . . . here you go:

"Cutting Edge Web Audio by Ron Simpson. The only comprehensive up-to-date guide to creating sound and music for the Web. Anything else is just a book."

2. You're just about ready to record a take. I'm assuming your microphone and mixer are properly connected and ready to go. Click the Record Enable button (see Figure 9-21) on the Voiceover track and the Record button on the Transport to arm Pro Tools for recording. The Record process will not begin until you press the space bar or play button (on the Transport). You are now in sort of a record preview mode and can now test your microphone and monitor the input with the level meter. While you want to record as hot of a signal as possible, distortion will likely result if the level meter climbs up into the red. Adjust the level of your microphone until the peak level is in the yellow not quite hitting the red in the level meter.

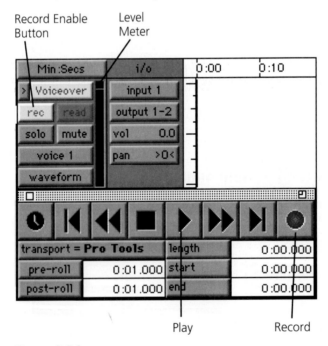

Record Enable Button

Level Meter

Play

Record

Figure 9.21
Click the Record Enable button on the Voiceover track and the Record button on the Transport arm Pro Tools for recording.

3. Okay, just to make sure you only have to do it once, record three separate takes of the script back to back. Press the space bar (or the Play button on the transport) to initiate the recording process. Read the script three times through and press the spacebar to stop recording.

4. Providing things went well, you should be viewing an almost identical scene to that shown in Figure 9-22. Press the space bar or Play button to start the playback and hear the results.

Note

Just in case recording the source audio material is not a possibility for you (no mic or mixer), you're in luck. In the Chapter 9 tutorial folder on the accompanying CD-ROM is a copy of my results from Step 3. The file is called CH9EX11.SND.

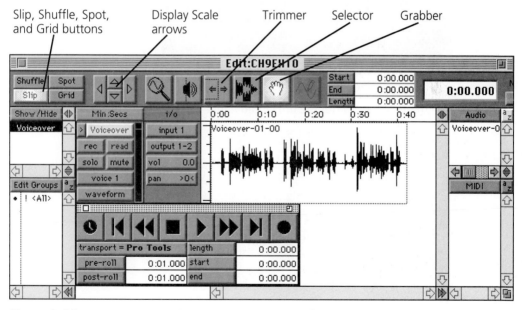

Figure 9.22
Press the Play button on the transport to hear the results of the recording that resides in the Edit Window of Pro Tools 4.0.

5. Okay, you've now got the source material and it's time to edit the three takes down to one performance. You'll use three tools to accomplish this task: the Trimmer, the Selector, and the Grabber. In short, they trim, select, and grab. By now you've listened to the source audio file and made your decision about what needs to go (as have I). My choice in this case is to keep the first take and dump the rest. To accomplish this task, use the Trimmer. Place the pointer on the Trimmer and click once to enable it. Your pointer is now the Trimmer. Place the Trimmer to the right of the audio file (see Figure 9-23) and simply hold down the mouse button and drag over the area you wish to trim (which trims the excess audio from the file). If you make a mistake, it's okay. With non-destructive editing, the entire source file is always there and you can use the Trimmer to just drag it back out. Start at the beginning of the waveform and repeat the process to trim the excess from the front of the file. Press the space bar to listen to the results and repeat if necessary.

Figure 9.23
Use the Trimmer to trim the unwanted audio from the voiceover track.

6. It's time to get a good look at the waveform in our sound file so we can do the final and more subtle edits. Currently, the waveform is a little too small (see Figure 9-24 to get a good look at it). The Display Scale Arrows are the answer. Click on the right arrow to expand the length of the waveform, which gives you a chance to read between the lines, so to speak. Two clicks on the right-hand arrow should expand the view of the waveform (see Figure 9-25) sufficiently.

Figure 9.24
The waveform on the voiceover track trimmed down to one take.

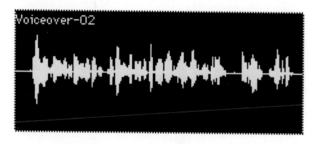

Figure 9.25
Two clicks of the right Display Scale Arrow expands the waveform on the voiceover track.

7. Just for the exercise, I've decided there's just not a long enough pause between the second and third sentence. To correct this, the Selector can be used to create two different files and the Grabber used to move them ever so slightly apart. First, make sure you click the Slip button to enable the Slip mode, then click on the Selector to enable it. Now, with the Selector, highlight the area you wish to delete (see Figure 9-26). Clear from the Edit menu to clear this section.

Note

Here is where we differentiate between the Shuffle mode and the Slip mode. In Figure 9-26, I've selected an area for deletion of data. In the Shuffle mode, when you delete the selected area, it will close up the gap, essentially putting the two files directly up against each other. In the Slip mode, it will simply leave a blank space.

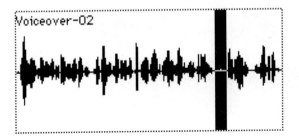

Figure 9.26
To create a separation within the file, highlight the area of the waveform to be deleted.

8. Time to make the big move. Select the Grabber and then double click (with the Grabber) on the smaller of the two audio files (Voiceover 3) shown in Figure 9-27. Remember when the Grabber is enabled, it becomes your cursor. The idea here is to create a slightly longer pause. Grab the selected audio and drag it (by holding down the mouse button) ever so gently to the right (a half second or so in real time). Deselect the audio (by double clicking outside of the selected audio) and then press Play to listen to the whole track. Repeat the process and adjust the gap using the Grabber until the pause between sentences suits your taste.

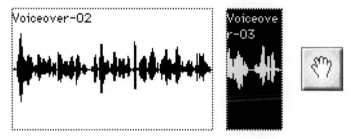

Figure 9.27
Use the Grabber to move the selected audio.

9.   With your voiceover now finished, Save from the File menu and let's move on.

What you're going to do next is take the edited file and move it out of Pro Tools for use in the next tutorial. Choose Select All from the Edit menu to select all the audio on the voiceover track. Select Bounce To Disk from the File menu. As shown in Figure 9-28, select Mono (as this isn't a Stereo file) and click Bounce. You'll be asked to give the file a name, so call it CH9EX12. Click Save. The file is automatically saved as a Sound Designer II file.

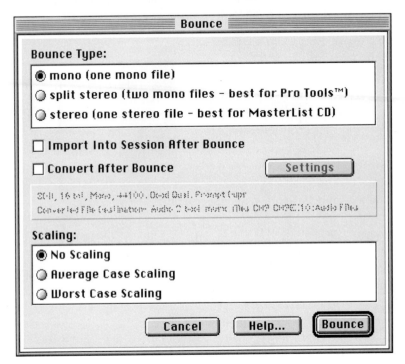

Figure 9.28
Bounce to Disk saves the selected audio as a Sound Designer II file.

■ Easy as . . .

Tutorial 9-6 gave you a small taste of what you can do with some of the basic tools available in Pro Tools 4.0. Now let's try something new.

Tutorial 9-7: Mixing multiple sound files

It's time to dig a little deeper into Pro Tools and do some work in the realm of multiple tracks. The plan is to import and mix 3 separate sound files into a Pro Tools session. The three components we'll use are the short voiceover file we created in the last tutorial, a short sound effect file, and a music file to help set the mood.

The files you need

All of the following files from previous tutorials are used in this tutorial:

- CH9EX12 (the voice)
- CH9EX13 (the Pro Tools Session)
- CH9EX14 (the SFX)
- CH9EX15 (the music)

■ The steps

1. Open the application Pro Tools 4.0. Open Session CH9EX13 from the File menu.

    Select Import Audio/Track from the File menu. Select the file CH9EX12 and click Add. Repeat this process with files CH9EX14 and CH9EX15.

    As you can see in Figure 9-29, the three files now reside in a window called Items Currently Chosen. You can preview any of the files by simply selecting it and pushing the Play button on the transport control. This is helpful if you're not exactly sure which file is what. Now that you have chosen the content to be imported into Pro Tools, click Done. In several seconds, all three files will reside in the Pro Tools session.

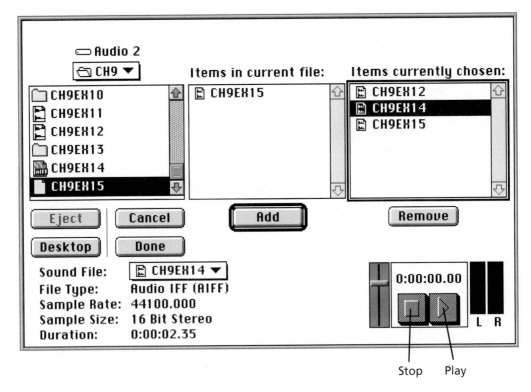

Figure 9.29
Move the files to be imported into the Items Currently Chosen window.

2. You now have a single (mono) voice track and two stereo tracks (SFX and Music) for a total of five tracks residing in the Edit window of the Pro Tools session CH9EX13. (see Figure 9-30).

Track Name

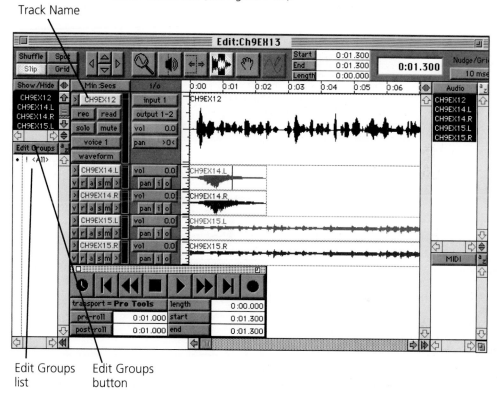

Edit Groups
list

Edit Groups
button

Figure 9.30
You now have a total of five tracks residing in Pro Tools Session CH9EX13.

Before going forward, however, it's a good idea to rename each of the five individual tracks to make things easier. This is done by double clicking on the Track Name (refer to Figure 9-30), which opens the Name dialog box. (see Figure 9-31). Enter the new name and click OK. Rename all five tracks using Table 9-4 as your reference.

Figure 9.31
After double clicking the track name in the Edit window of Pro Tools, enter the new track name and click OK.

Table 9.4 Tutorial 9-7 Track rename information

Track Name Before	Track Name After
CH9EX12	Voice
CH9EX14L	SFX.L
CH9EX14R	SFX.R
CH9EX15L	Music.L
CH9EX15R	Music.R

Note

One of the new features of Pro Tools 4.0 is the ability to resize the track view in the Edit window on a track-by-track basis. More tracks can now be visible in the Edit window and only the track that is currently being edited has to be in full view. Users of earlier versions of Pro Tools will love this new feature (I sure do!).

3. To streamline the editing process, we're going to group the SFX and Music tracks into individual groups of stereo pairs. First, select the tracks SFX.L and SFX.R by clicking on the light gray area (shown in Figure 9-32) while holding down the Shift key. Click the button Edit Groups and select New Groups. In the New Group window, change the name from Group 1 to SFX and select the Group Type: Edit and Mix (see Figure 9-33). Click OK. Repeat the process with the tracks Music.L and Music.R and name this group Music. Because the Voice track (1) is mono, there's no need for it to be part of a group.

Figure 9.32
Select the tracks SFX.L and SFX.R by clicking on the light gray area while holding down the shift key.

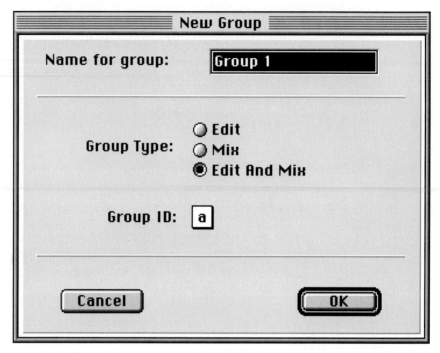

Figure 9.33
Name the Group and select Edit and Mix from the Group Type.

4. The next step is to place each of the individual sound files into the timeline where they will reside during playback. (We'll worry about the volume level later.) Use the Grabber to click and drag the Voice track (#1) so playback starts at 10 seconds. Select Group A (SFX) by clicking on it in the Edit Groups list (see Figure 9-34) and use the Grabber to drag the audio content on tracks SFX.L and SFX.R out to a start time of 25 seconds. Notice that, because the SFX files are grouped into a pair, if you drag one, the other will follow. Use Figure 9-35 as your reference to see where the Voice and SFX files should reside in the timeline.

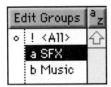

Figure 9.34
To enable the edit functions on both tracks to function simultaneously, select Edit Group A, SFX.

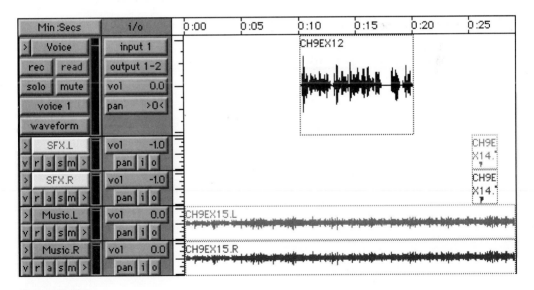

Figure 9.35
After moving the Voice and SFX files to their new start times, this should be your view in the Edit window.

5. The three sound components are now in the right position time-wise, but of course we now need to adjust the volume on each track. In the Edit Groups List, select Music.

6. Next, go to the Track Format Selector on the Music tracks. To change the Track view from Waveform to Volume, place the cursor on the volume button shown in Figure 9-36 and hold down the mouse button. This will give you access to a pulldown menu. From there, select Volume. As you can see, the Track view in the Edit window (Figure 9-37) has now changed from Waveform to Volume.

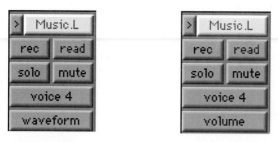

Figure 9.36
Click the Waveform button to select volume on the Music Track.

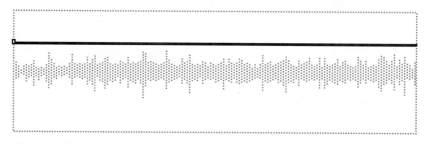

Figure 9.37
The Track view in the Window has now changed from Waveform to Volume in the selected track (or Group of Tracks).

7. In this next step, you need to use the Grabber to automate the necessary volume changes on the music tracks. Remember that because the music tracks are enabled as a group, any changes you make on one track will be made on both (this is a good thing in this situation).

When playing back the entire file, notice that the volume of the music is just too loud during the voiceover segment. The purpose of this step is to use the edit functions to automate a lowering of the volume during the voiceover and to create a fade out at the end of the piece. The Grabber tool enables the user to create breakpoints and then drag the volume level down or up as needed.

Using Figure 9-38 for reference, create six breakpoints by placing the Grabber on the graph line and clicking the mouse button once to create each breakpoint you wish to insert. Then, use the Grabber to drag the different breakpoints to create the volume changes needed, again using Figure 9-38 as your starting reference point. Essentially, the volume (on the music track) starts at 0 dB then goes to a quick fade (-7.2 dB) during the voiceover section. Immediately after the voiceover is finished, the volume is moved up to +1 dB, where it stays until going to another quick fade to nothing during the Jet flyby (SFX) sound.

You may hear things (or want to anyway) differently than I do. Experiment around with the volume change techniques in this step until you are pleased with the results. Use the Play control on the Transport or press the space bar to begin playback of the file.

Note

Volume changes may also be made manually on each Track (or Group) using the Volume Control shown in Figure 9-39.

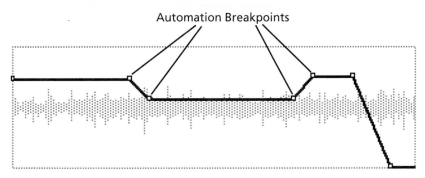

Figure 9.38
Use the Grabber to insert and drag the volume breakpoints.

8. The big picture will be more evident in Figure 9-39. You can now see how the file placement and automated volume changes fit into the Pro Tools session. Now it's time to crunch these five tracks down to two. Choose Select All from the Edit menu. All five tracks should now be selected. In Step 9 of Tutorial 9-6, we took a file and performed a Bounce To Disk. That's exactly what we're going to do here. The only difference is instead of bouncing it to a Mono file, select Stereo (one stereo file). (If you're confused, refer back to Figure 9-28). Select Bounce To Disk from the File menu and name the new file CH9EX16.

Volume Control

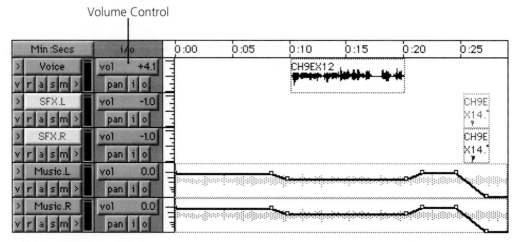

Figure 9.39
This overall view of the entire Edit window should give you a better idea of how the automated volume changes fit into the scheme of things.

◼ More tools

I know I've said this before, but I could probably do an 800-page book just on Pro Tools 4.0. The depth of this application is hard to communicate in even a complete chapter. In Chapter 10, "Advanced Editing and Enhancing Tools," we'll get into a couple of the Audiosuite plugins that have been recently released for Pro Tools and show you how they work and sound!

Life in the Fast Lane

I've always sort of liked living on the edge and as recently as some of these applications have been released, that's exactly what I've been doing in this chapter. Even though this chapter contains product-oriented tutorials, the concepts are just as important as the tutorial process itself. If you can figure out why something works a certain way, then it's possible to bend the rules a little bit and get similar results from less expensive and less complicated applications. Even though you can't complete many of the tutorials with the demo software included on the CD-ROM with this book, you can get a really good feel for how everything works and with the aural examples in the tutorial folder, you can hear the results.

Well, get ready and let's jump into the future of 3D sound, advanced noise reduction, and better reverb in Chapter 10!

Advanced Editing and Enhancing Tools

 In This Chapter

- SFX Machine from BIAS
- 3D plug-ins from QSound
- Hyperprism from Arboretum Systems
- The Ionizer from Arboretum Systems
- The Native Power Pack from Waves

I've probably started out more than one chapter saying "This one's my favorite," but I've got to admit—this really is the one. No matter how cool your recording and editing software is, it's the plug-ins that really give you the horsepower to make things happen. Here's a little of what you've got to look forward to.

With the tutorials in this chapter, we're going to bounce around indiscriminately between the Mac and Windows platforms. In some cases, the plug-ins are available for both platforms and in others they're either under development or something similar is available. Regardless, the concept and the ideas behind what you'll accomplish with the tutorials are just as important as the tutorials themselves. So without any further delay. . . .

SFX Machine

When I first saw the advertisement for the SFX Machine, I thought it looked kind of cool. But after trying the demo, I quickly realized that *kind of* cool was way off the mark. I can honestly say that I've never had so much fun with something I'm supposed to be using for work. The possibilities are endless for taking normal household sounds and turning them into sonic apparitions that would send even the bravest of souls screaming from the building.

Currently, SFX Machine is available as a Premiere plug-in and works only on a PowerPC Macintosh (or clone). The applications (besides Premiere) that it currently works with are BIAS Peak, Deck 2.5, and Vision (or Studio Vision) 3.5. Just for fun or my own curiosity, I recorded a short voiceover file and applied a few of the effects found in SFX Machine. Go take a listen to it and show a little mercy as it was my first try at it.

> **CD-ROM**
>
> You can find the results of my little experiment in the Chapter 10 tutorial as CH10EX1.

For those of you who listened, sorry about the Borg thing, but I just couldn't contain myself. Well, there's no time like the present for me to show you how easily even a novice can get professional results from SFX Machine—So get to it.

Tutorial 10-1: SFX Machine Basics

Nothing like being overwhelmed with possibilities, and that's what you're about to discover. There is a fairly large number of preset sound effects available to you, which is probably no surprise. It's the variations and random possibilities that make SFX Machine so interesting.

> **Note**
>
> If you're a Windows user, follow these results anyway and listen to the sound files that follow along with the different steps; you won't regret it.

▨ What you need

To complete this tutorial, you need the following:

- Peak 1.5
- SFX Machine
- PowerMac (with 16 MB minimum RAM)
- Tutorial file CH10EX2

> **CD-ROM**
>
> You're in luck in the demo department, as we've got save-disabled versions of both Peak 1.5 and SFX Machine on the CD-ROM accompanying this book. Also, the first tutorial file CH10EX2 resides there as well.

◼ Let's make some noise

1. Start the application Peak 1.5. Select Open CH10EX2 from the File menu and click Done. Because we're looking to process the entire sound file in this tutorial, select the entire track (Command All). Select SFX Machine from the Plug-ins menu to open the main SFX Machine window (see Figure 10-1).

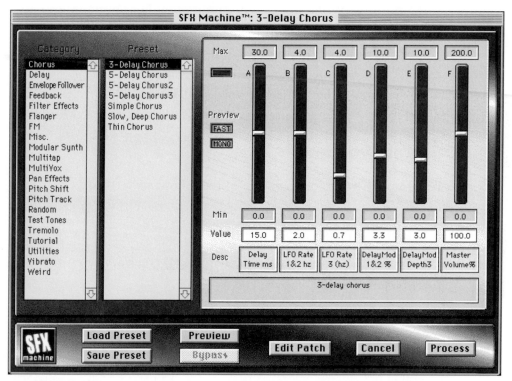

Figure 10-1
The main window of SFX Machine.

2. There are a number of preset choices for the user and I do encourage you to try all of them for no other reason than that it's pretty amusing. However, for this exercise, we're going where no man has gone before (except Captain Picard)—We're doing the Borg. Under Category, choose Pitch Shift (see Figure 10-2) and under Preset, select Munchkin Chorus. You're probably curious as to what this effect sounds like, so let's preview it. At the bottom of the page is a series of buttons (refer back to Figure 10-1). Click the Preview button to hear the Munchkin Chorus effect on the sound file, which will loop. Click the Bypass button to make an A/B comparison.

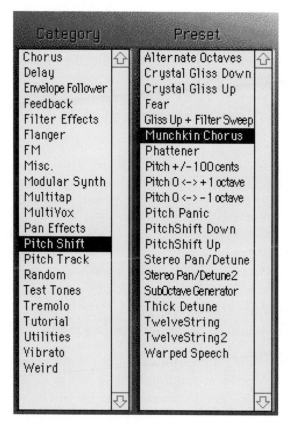

Figure 10-2
Choose the Category and Preset effect.

3. Okay, you're impressed and you totally love how it sounds, so click the Process button to complete the procedure. After a few moments, you have changed the original sound file. Select Undo from the Edit menu if you change your mind and want to back out of it.

■ More about SFX Machine

If you're not the adventurous type, that's okay. There are quite a few presets that cover all the bases and even a few that will take you where you don't even want to go. However, for those of you interested in conquering brave new worlds, the editing possibilities with SFX Machine are endless. Let's take a deeper look at the interface and I'll show you what I mean.

Sliders

Notice that whenever you call up a Preset in SFX Machine, a series of Sliders appears in the main window (see Figure 10-3). Depending on which type of preset you choose, there are a variety of different parameters available to you. To create a custom patch, I start with a preset that falls close in sound type to the category of what I'm looking for and use it as a template.

> **Note**
>
> Those of you not familiar with the term "patch," read on. Back in the old days of the original analog synthesizers, sounds were created by patching together the different modules with audio cables. Even as technology progressed to sliders, knobs, and beyond, the term *patch* remained as the unofficial term for synthesizer or signal processor programs.

While in the Preview mode, you can alter the parameters with the sliders and hear the results in realtime. This is a very effective way of making subtle (or not so subtle) changes to the preset you wish to alter. Still, this is only the tip of the iceberg when it comes to creating your own custom patch.

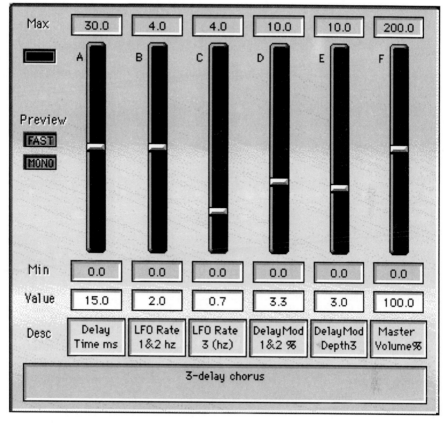

Figure 10-3
The Sliders can be used to alter some of the parameters of a Preset in SFX
Machine.

The Edit screen

Notice amongst all the buttons at the bottom of the main window (refer back to Figure 10-1) is one called Edit Patch. Click on the Edit Patch button and this puts you in the Edit Screen (Figure 10-4). You can see there are a number of modules (you can use as many as eight at one time) available. These modules are responsible for generating the process that creates the effects. Each module is identical and consists of four different sections (or blocks). These are the Source Block (1), the Process Block (2), the Modulation Block (3), and the Output Block (see

Figure 10-5). In the sidebar entitled "Edit Screen Modules," I offer a basic explanation as to the function of each block within a module.

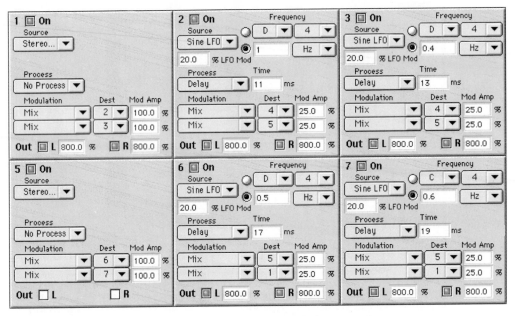

Figure 10-4
The Edit screen consists of eight different modules (six are shown here) that control the parameters that create the effects in SFX Machine.

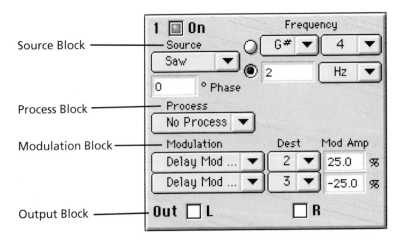

Figure 10-5
There are four sections in each module, the Source Block (1), the Process Block (2), the Modulation Block (3), and the Output Block.

Edit Screen Modules

There are eight separate Edit Screen modules and while each one is exactly the same, they can all be used differently (or not at all). In short, you are taking an audio signal and routing it through a number of different pathways used to create the final sound you hear. Each of the four sections in a module is responsible for a certain function.

1. **The Source Block**: The first step begins with a source signal that can come from the audio you have selected or from a generated waveform.
2. **The Process Block**: The next step involves adding Digital Signal Processing (DSP) to the source signal. This could be Delay or a variety of other types of DSP.
3. **The Modulation Block**: In this block, you set not only the destination of the signal (modules 1-8), but the type of modulation as well.
4. **The Output Block**: The final results of your signal manipulation can be routed to the left and (or) right outputs.

There are a number of variables, such as type of modulation or DSP and the levels themselves, not to mention the creative routing of signals through the different modules. You can also use as little as one or as many as eight of the modules at one time.

Randomize

One more very interesting feature is called Randomize. It's the old variation on a theme. Click the Randomize button and the machine will choose new settings for the Edit Modules creating something that you probably wouldn't have thought of in a million years. The idea is that you just might stumble onto something pretty unique. Sort of like going to Vegas, except in this case the odds of winning are more on your side. I gave it a try and while the results annoyed me more times than not, I did come up with some interesting sounds as a result. If you're patient, chances are you will too.

Creating and saving a patch

SFX Machine enables you to edit any of the Presets and then rename and save it as a custom patch. Simply edit any of the presets and then save it by clicking on the Save Preset button. You want to store the new patch in the SFX Machine Presets folder. If you do happen to stumble on something you've just got to have while using the Randomizer, you now have a way to keep it forever.

One last word

You are in luck even if you don't have Peak 1.5 or SFX Machine, as we're including save-disabled versions on the CD-ROM accompanying this book (look in the Demo Software folder). You can't save your experiments, but it's possible to load in a file and commit a number of sonic violations with SFX Machine. This is one plug-in I would not only recommend, but actually own. It has a number of uses that are both practical and fun. The way the modules in the Edit Screen are set up, a creative synthesizer programmer could really write some great patches. So use the demo and try it—You'll like it!

 QSound

Heading in another direction altogether is QSound. Creating a realistic 3D effect in a stereo field is not an easy task. Many plug-ins claim to be able to do just that, but for the most part the 3D effect is like drinking a Coca Cola that has lost its carbonation. The exception to the rule has been (and still is) QSound.

So, what exactly does QSound do? In layman's terms, with QSound technology it's possible to place sound beyond the capabilities of normal stereo. When listening to conventional stereo sound, you are limited by the physical placement of your speakers. As far as panning goes, it's pretty much a left/right listening experience. What we'll cover in this section is a series of comparatively inexpensive QSound plug-ins that do the job in a number of different ways. QSound plug-ins are available in different variations for both the Mac (Audiosuite and TDM plug-ins) and Windows.

Encode and decode?

I need to take you on a little side trip for just a moment. Let's say with something along the lines of Dolby Surround Sound, not only do you need to have the signal encoded but you need five to seven speakers and the Dolby decoding hardware for playback. This is an expensive process all the way around and let's face facts: The majority of the listening audience is not going to spend that kind of money, especially when it comes to multimedia and Web audio. With the QSound process, after encoding the audio file, no additional hardware is needed to decode the signal for playback.

QTools/AX version 1.0

It's time to take a look at three specific plug-ins available as DirectX (ActiveMovie) plug-ins.

Note

If you've been paying attention, you should notice there's been a reference to ActiveMovie or DirectX plug-ins. Microsoft keeps changing their collective mind about what this plug-in environment is called. Many applications currently call the DirectX plug-in ActiveMovie and I'm sure there will be some confusion about it for a while, but they are the same thing. In fact, at the time of going to press, there was another rumor going around that the name has been changed again. Go figure.

■ QX/AX

Known as the QXpander, this plug-in is used to widen the stereo field. The controls are pretty simple and, using the presets as a template, you are able to adjust and widen different audio files with ease. The effect is actually pretty stunning when compared side by side with an unprocessed audio file. The QXpander sort of picks up where the S1-

StereoImager (Waves Native Power Pack) plug-in stops and takes the listener to another realm altogether. As you can see in Figure 10-6, there are three sliders used to control the 3D effect in the QXpander. In Tutorial 10-2 (immediately following the QTools AX description), I'll take a test drive and show you how it works.

Figure 10-6
The QXpander enables the user to expand the width of an entire audio file beyond what is possible in normal stereo.

■ QSYS/AX

This plug-in enables the user to place a single mono sound outside of the normal listening range. Sometimes a picture is worth a thousand words, and this is one of those instances. In Figure 10-7, you can see just how the setting works with the pan position control. This enables you to place (and preview) a mono sound into a position well beyond the position of the user's speakers. This can be a very helpful effect in creating cool sound effects for a computer game. For music, the possibilities are endless.

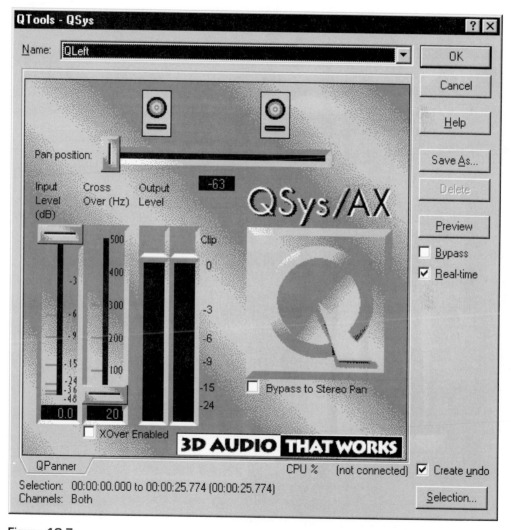

Figure 10-7
Use the pan position control to place a mono sound beyond the limited range of a stereo set of speakers.

■ Q123/AX

This plug-in is used to create a wide 3D image from a mono file. Q123 takes a mono signal and turns it into a stereo file that creates a simulated 3D stereo effect. The centering control (shown in Figure 10-8) is used to adjust the evident left/right balance, helping to create a more realistic-sounding stereo file.

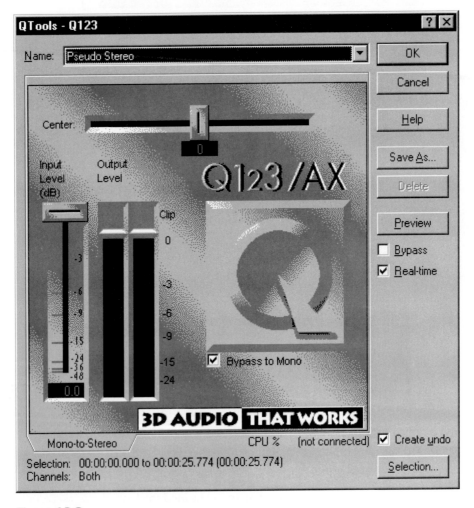

Figure 10-8
The centering control in Q123 is used to adjust the left/right balance, helping to create a more realistic-sounding 3D stereo file.

Tutorial 10-2: The QXpander

This is where you and I get to put the QSound process to the test. While I know it works, we both get to see—and more importantly, hear—just how well it works.

■ What you need

This is one of those situations where demo software isn't going to cut it. Those of you without access to full versions of the Sound Forge 4.0 and QTools/AX will just have to follow along and listen to the tutorial examples.

- ■ Sound Forge 4.0
- ■ QTools/AX 1.0 (or better)
- ■ A Windows 95 PC
- ■ Tutorial file CH10EX3.WAV (on the CD-ROM)

■ Coming at you in 3D stereo

1. Start the application Sound Forge 4.0. Select Open from the File menu. Load the tutorial file CH10EX3.WAV. Press the spacebar and listen to the soundfile. There is a fair amount of stereo interaction between the chimes making this file a perfect candidate for the QXpander. From the ActiveMovie menu, select QTools-QXpander.

> **Note**
>
> When editing a waveform (regardless of platform and application), use your eyes as well as your ears. You can sometimes actually see the pops, clicks, or other volume-related problems in the edit window. Learning to identify audio problems visually (as well as aurally) can sometimes speed up the repair process.

2. There are a number of basic presets that give the user a good starting template with which to work. We're going to start with the preset "Music" and use the three control sliders (see Figure 10-9) to adjust the QXpander parameters. The controller you need to be interested in for this exercise is the Input Level (far left). The QXpander process has a tendency to add gain (volume) to the source audiofile, so we're going to need to back off the input level just a little. First, however, it's important to actually hear what you're doing while editing, so we need to preview the QXpander process.

Go to the far right-hand side of the QXpander window, check the Real-time box (see Figure 10-10), and click the Preview button. This creates a realtime playback of the source audiofile, enabling you to preview the QXpander process.

Use the three sliders to make the necessary changes in realtime and immediately hear the results. In this case, back the Input Level down to -2.0 dB. If you want to hear the difference between the before and after, check either the Bypass or Bypass to Stereo box. You will be amazed.

Once you've made the proper adjustment, click OK to process the file.

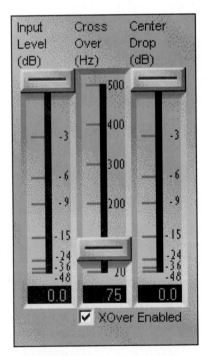

Figure 10-9
Adjust the QXpander parameters with these controls.

Figure 10-10
Check the Real-time box and click Preview to hear the QSound difference.

> **Tip**
>
> Always remember to check the Create undo box (refer back to Figure 10-10). It can save you from a fate worse than Manilow.

257

3. Now that your file has been QXpanded, press the spacebar (or the Play button on the transport) and listen. This file has gained presence, width, depth, and is sort of surrounding you all at the same time. It's as though you're in the bell tower instead of just outside of it.

Select Save As CH10EX4.WAV from the File menu and you're done.

More about QXpander

Hopefully, while you were in the QXpander edit window you did a little experimenting with some of the other control features as well. If not, here's a quick overview of what they do and how they work. Besides the Input Level control, there are two others: the Cross Over and Center Drop. The Cross Over allows some frequencies to bypass the QSound process. With a lower setting, the user will get more 3D processing in low-frequency range, while a higher setting will allow more low-frequency bypass. To use the Cross Over controls, be sure the XOver Enabled box is checked. The Center Control is used to set the level of the QSound process in content that is center panned in the stereo field. Essentially, this control helps maintain the mono qualities of a sound file that the user may not wish to process in 3D. For instance, the bass drum in a music file is normally panned center in the stereo field. Using the Center Control, it is possible to leave the bass drum largely unaffected while adding 3D characteristics to the rest of the file.

QX/TDM 2.0

For the Mac user that was sweating not having access to the QSound process, you can relax. QX/TDM 2.0 is an Audiosuite and TDM plug-in that works with the Pro Tools III hardware and with Pro Tools 4.0. As you can see in Figure 10-11, the controls are quite similar to those in Windows version with one exception: the addition of the Spread Control. At 0 dB, the width of the 3D field in the Spread control is at its widest. Backing it off down as low as -20 dB, you can bring the content on the sound file back into a more normal stereo field.

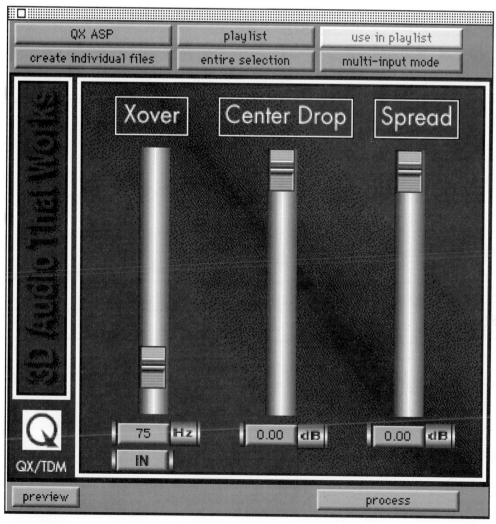

Figure 10-11
QX/TDM 2.0 is both an Audiosuite and TDM plug-in for Pro Tools.

Hyperprism

At the time of going to press, I was scrambling to find some Audiosuite plug-ins to stick into this chapter. While there were a number of Audiosuite plug-ins available, for the most part they were still so full of bugs my PowerMac threatened to go on strike if I even thought about installing them. There was, however, an exception: Hyperprism from Arboretum Systems. Not only is Hyperprism available as a set of Audiosuite plug-ins, but I was knocked out by the quality of the effects. Before we jump to the Audiosuite tutorial, go to Table 10-1 to get some basic information on the different flavors of Hyperprism that are available.

Hyperprism DX, a DirectX (formerly known as ActiveMovie) plug-in for Windows 95 sound applications, is also available.

Table 10-1   Hyperprism

Type	Description	Number of FX	MSRP
68K	Stand alone for the 680X0	29	$390
PPC	Stand alone application for the PowerMac	26	$380
VST	Cubase compatible	25	$350
MMP	Premiere compatible	25	$300
DAS	Pro Tools 4.0 Audiosuite plug-in	25	$390
TDM	Pro Tools TDM plug-in. NuBus and PCI (8–97)	23	$945
DX	DirectX Plug-in	25	$389

As I start playing with all the different versions of Hyperprism, it would be easy to go on a sidetrack for a couple of chapters and just do Hyperprism. There are so many creative possibilities with the stand-alone version of Hyperprism that I could get lost just trying to find a way to describe them. That, however, is probably another book and I need to focus on the current task at hand. So, what we're going to do now is check out a couple of the plug-ins via Audiosuite and Pro Tools 4.0.

Tutorial 10-3: Hyperprism Audiosuite and Pro Tools 4.0

Being one of those people who loved Pro Tools but couldn't afford to go the TDM route, I was excited about Audiosuite. After spending a little time with the Hyperprism Audiosuite plug-ins, I'm still excited and feel that it's well worth covering in this chapter. Many of the tutorials in this book can be covered using the demo software on the CD-ROM, but this is not one of them. If you don't have a licensed copy of this software, hang in there and follow the tutorial all the same. You will be able to listen to the before and after examples of each sound file used in this tutorial.

▓ What you need

Following is a list of the items needed to complete this tutorial:

- Pro Tools 4.0
- Hyperprism DAS (Digidesign Audiosuite)
- Tutorial file CH10EX6 (on the CD-ROM)
- PowerMac (or compatible) with 32 MB of RAM running System 7.5

■ Serious reverb

1. Open the application Pro Tools 4.0. Select New Session from the File menu and name the session CH10EX5. Select Import Audio/Track from the File menu. Select the file CH10EX6 and click Add. The sound file we'll be working on (see Figure 10-12) is a synthesizer emulation of a nylon string guitar. It was recorded fairly dry (very little reverb) and, while it sounds fine as is, this is a perfect opportunity to get it wet with one of the Hyperprism reverb plug-ins.

Edit Groups

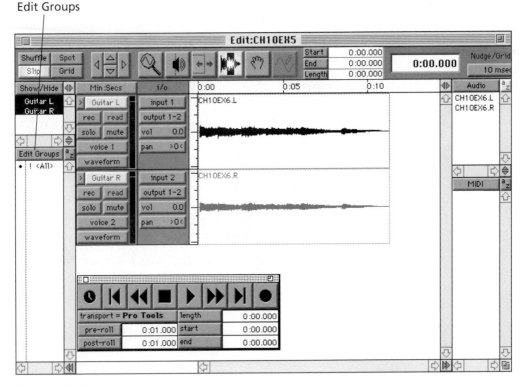

Figure 10-12
The Edit window of Pro Tools 4.0 with the tutorial file CH10EX6.

2. It's always a good idea to assign any stereo file that you plan to be editing to a Group. To get there, click the Edit Groups button and select New Group. Name this new group, which will consist of tracks one and two, Guitar. Under Group Type, select Edit and Mix (see Figure 10-13 for reference). Make sure your Group ID is set to A and then click OK.

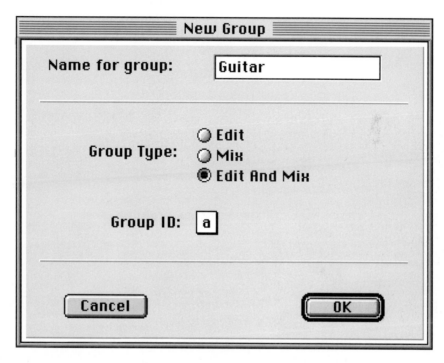

Figure 10-13
The Edit window of Pro Tools 4.0 with the tutorial file CH10EX6.

3. The next step in the chain of events is to select the tracks you wish to Edit. Choose Select All from the Edit menu. Both tracks will now be selected. Next, choose H-DAS Stereo Hall Reverb from the Audiosuite, which will put you in the Audiosuite main screen (shown in Figure 10-14). Click the Preview button (in the lower left-hand corner of the Audiosuite screen) to start a looping playback. In this instance, use the factory default settings for this reverb plug-in as the template and apply the effects real-time as you listen back.

Note

There are template plug-in settings available for each of the Hyperprism Audiosuite plug-ins. If you are unfamiliar with how a particular effect works, they can be a very good place to start.

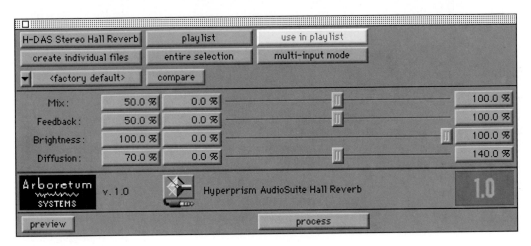

Figure 10-14
The factory default settings for the Hyperprism Stereo Hall Reverb.

4. The type of sound we're going for here is not too subtle and in fact is pretty wet. Imagine playing the guitar in a large room (say, the Grand Canyon) and you'll get the idea. As you listen to the preview, notice the default reverb sounds pretty good, but we're going for something more profound. As you can see in Figure 10-14, there are four sliders that control the reverb parameters. Using Figure 10-15 as your reference point, move the Mix slider to 70.18%, the Feedback slider to 70.18%, leave the Brightness slider where it is, and move the Diffusion slider to 30.18%.

At this point, you probably notice there is a considerable difference from the original. Click the compare button to go back and forth between the before and after. Use your own good judgment to make the final adjustments and click the process button. To return to the Edit window in Pro Tools, click the button in the top left-hand corner of the Audiosuite window.

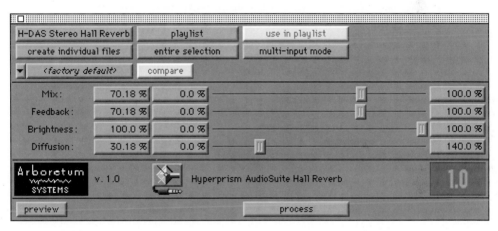

Figure 10-15
These custom Audiosuite reverb settings are achieved by following directions in Step 3.

5. Time to hear the results. Press the spacebar (or play in the Pro Tools transport) to listen to the source file with the reverb applied. I'll admit, it's a bit overdone but there's a reason for that. This is probably one of the best-sounding reverb plug-ins that I've ever heard and I wanted you to really experience it full-blast. To get an even better sense of the space created with this reverb plug-in, pan tracks one and two hard left and hard right respectively as shown in Figure 10-16. After you've finished, remember to save the session.

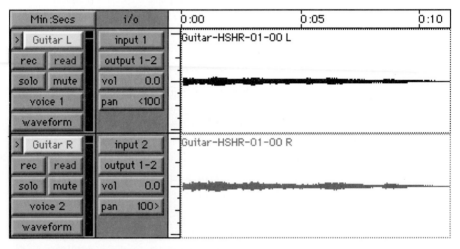

Figure 10-16
Pan the audio channels hard left and hard right on tracks one and two to enjoy a more profound effect from the stereo reverb.

For those of you who are dying to hear the results but don't have all the tools we used in this last tutorial, take a listen to tutorial file CH10EX7 for the results. For those of you who just completed the tutorial, let's backtrack for a moment. I'm hoping that you spent a little time playing with the four sliders that control the reverb parameters and checked out exactly what they do. If, by chance, you create an incredible reverb setting on your own, you can also save it for recall at a later date. By clicking the button directly to the left of the factory default setting in this Audiosuite plug-in, you can save or import different reverb settings.

So, how does it sound?

All the features in the world don't carry any weight if it doesn't sound good. Well, it just so happens that I'm very impressed and maybe even a little surprised with the sound quality of this reverb. If there are any products out there that can beat the price/performance ratio of the Hyperprism Audiosuite plug-ins then I'll buy them (and you should too). When it comes right down to it, after spending some time with the Hyperprism plug-ins, I wouldn't hesitate for a second to purchase them for myself.

More from Arboretum

Ionizer from Arboretum Systems is one of the most complex and cool audio tools I have stumbled upon. There is definitely a high learning curve here and to take advantage of the true potential of this audio tool you have to want to spend some time learning what makes Ionizer tick. At least at this time, Windows is not spoken here and you must have a PowerMac or Mac OS Compatible Power PC. Ionizer is available as a Premiere plug-in or as a stand-alone application via Arboretum's HyperEngine. During my initial usage of Ionizer, I found that Hyper-Engine was a somewhat more stable environment to work in (versus the Premiere plug-in environment).

How many bands of EQ?

Probably the one thing that really piqued my interest in Ionizer was the noise reduction capabilities. With a 512 band gated EQ (that's no misprint), you can pretty much isolate any extraneous sound and remove it from the mix. As you probably know by now, there are quite a few plug-ins that also do compression, expansion, noise reduction, and EQ, but none that I've seen have near the potential of Ionizer. One thing I would like to see in the near future is a wider variety of usable Ionizer presets. I think that having more preset templates to choose from would greatly reduce the time it takes for the uninitiated to figure out how this thing works. To find out more about Ionizer, go to the Arboretum Systems Web site listed at the end of this chapter.

Tutorial 10-4: Surfing the Waves

Excuse the pun, but sometimes I just can't help myself. For those of you who've been skipping around all over this book (versus reading it linearly), you have already noticed how much I use the Native Power Pack from Waves for just about everything. Well, I'm going for it again. I'm jumping back into Windows (95), Sound Forge 4.0, and taking you into the land of DirectX (ActiveMovie) plug-ins one more time with the Waves L-1 Ultramaximizer.

Allow me to use this tutorial to give you another simple example of subtle enhancement. Even when you've got a great-sounding WAVE file, there's always room for a little improvement.

■ What you need

The following items are needed to complete this tutorial:

- Sound Forge 4.0
- Waves L1-Ultramaximizer
- Windows 95 PC
- Tutorial File CH10EX8.WAV

> **Note**
>
> Even though Tutorial 10-4 is a Windows kind of thing, you can achieve pretty much identical results on the Mac with the +L1-UltMax plug-in.

Surfs Up!

1. Start the application Sound Forge 4.0 and choose Open CH10EX8.WAV from the File menu. Choose Waves L1-Ultramaximizer form the ActiveMovie menu to open the L1-Ultramaximizer main window (see Figure 10-17).

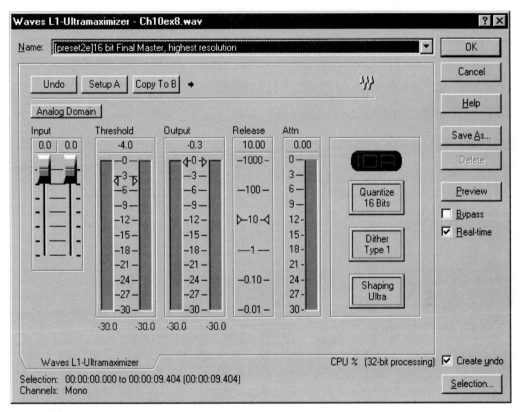

Figure 10-17
The Waves L1-Ultramaximizer main window.

2. The first task at hand in the main window is to choose the correct preset that will eventually enhance the source WAVE file. At the top of this window, click on Name and choose [preset2e] 16 bit Final Master, highest resolution (see Figure 10-18). This preset will enhance the quality of the WAVE file and give it more presence and clarity.

    Click the Preview button to hear what the enhanced file will sound like and check the Bypass for an A/B comparison (see Figure 10-19). I strongly recommend that you experiment with some of the Ultramaximizer controls just to get a feel for how they work. However, unless you come up with something that sounds better, go back to the [preset2e] and click OK when you're ready to convert the file.

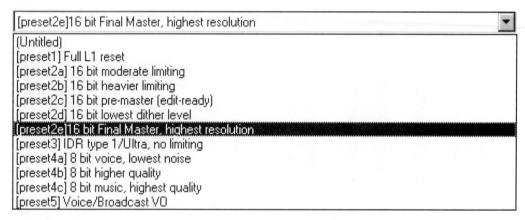

[preset2e]16 bit Final Master, highest resolution	▼

[Untitled]
[preset1] Full L1 reset
[preset2a] 16 bit moderate limiting
[preset2b] 16 bit heavier limiting
[preset2c] 16 bit pre-master (edit-ready)
[preset2d] 16 bit lowest dither level
[preset2e]16 bit Final Master, highest resolution
[preset3] IDR type 1/Ultra, no limiting
[preset4a] 8 bit voice, lowest noise
[preset4b] 8 bit higher quality
[preset4c] 8 bit music, highest quality
[preset5] Voice/Broadcast VO

Figure 10-18
Choose [preset2e] 16 bit Final Master, highest resolution to process the
WAVE file.

Figure 10-19
Click the Preview button to hear what the enhanced file will sound like and check the Bypass for an A/B comparison.

3. Elvis has entered the building. Use the spacebar (or click Play on the transport control) to listen back to the WAVE file. So, now it should have a more present sound, a more distinct sonic clarity, and just look more cutting edge (looks are important!). You might also notice the waveform (Figure 10-20) looks as though you added volume to it. Save the WAVE file as CH10EX9.WAV and along with Elvis you too can leave the building.

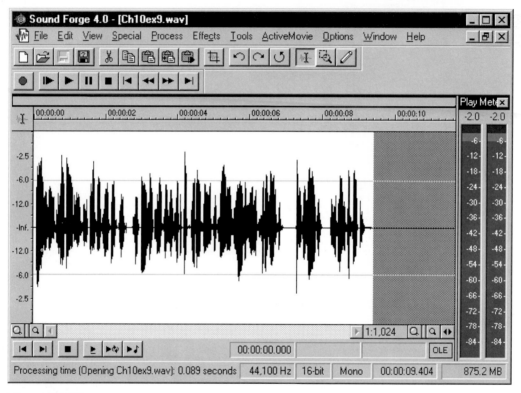

Figure 10-20
Not only does the waveform sound different after processing, it takes on a different look.

The Best of Enhancement

There are a number of different ways to enhance the sonic characteristics of a sound file. Whether it's QSound, a Waves Plug-in, or something as simple as the basic reverb that comes standard with Sound Forge, the possibilities are as interesting as you care to make them. This chapter was particularly fun for me as I got to dig into some new plug-ins that, up to this point, I'd only heard about. Some were fairly easy to figure out and others (especially Ionizer) I'm still learning. Not that long ago, just being able to put sound on your Web site was enough. Now, it's those of you who are willing to go the extra mile to be innovative not only with the content but with the extra enhancements that will get all the attention. Use the tutorials as a template and experiment to get your own settings for some of the incredible tools featured in this chapter. Chances are you may discover something totally by accident that could cause the world to sit up and take notice. It's been done before!

To find out more about each of the plug-ins featured in this chapter, go to your and my favorite resource, the Web.

Table 10-2   Advanced Tools on the Web

Product Name	URL
Hyperprism by Arboretum Systems	http://www.arboretum.com
Native Power Pack by Waves	http://www.waves.com
QTools/AX by QSound	http://www.qsound.com
SFX Machine by BIAS	http://www.bias-inc.com

Chapter 11

Real Audio

 In This Chapter

- The key players in this game
- Do you need a server? Get Real!
- Encoding tools and how to use them

RealAudio from RealNetworks (formerly Progressive Networks) has and will continue to set the standard for delivery of streaming audio over the Web. There are a number of different encoding tools available for RealAudio, and in the tutorial section of this chapter, we'll check out a few of them. To get a better idea where it's all going, you sometimes have to look at where it has been and we'll be doing a little of that, too. The setup and maintenance of servers is beyond the scope of this chapter (and this book), but when it applies, I will point you in the right direction (via the Web) all the same. For myself, and I'm sure for many of you as well, RealAudio was the first exposure to streaming audio on the Web and I'll never be the same because of it.

Web

Before you go any further, take a little detour to www.real.com and get the latest version of the RealPlayer (currently 5.0). It's free and all it takes is a little of your time. Not only will you be able to listen to streaming audio, but you can view streaming video and RealFlash animations with it as well.

Note

Right now it's possible to listen to sound on the Web in two different ways: download it or stream it. The old way was to download a file and then listen to it. Generally, you could go out to lunch, take the dog for a walk, and cook dinner while you were waiting for the file to download. In other words, it took a while. Then came *streaming audio*. The sound data is streamed to a plug-in/player that resides in your computer and after a brief (30-second or so) wait, you can listen to the audio as it's being downloaded. Very cool stuff.

The Player

The RealPlayer and RealPlayer Plus (5.0) is what makes it all happen (streaming audio, video, and animations) on the users end of things and there are several available options that make a good thing great. For the casual Web user, the RealPlayer (5.0) is free and will cover your basic RealAudio needs. However, once you've had a taste of the RealPlayer Plus (Figure 11-1), you'll never go back.

Figure 11-1
The RealPlayer Plus plays streaming audio, video, and animations.

Here's a few of the RealPlayer Plus features that make it worth the price of admission.

- PerfectPlay
- Scan and Preset RealAudio/RealVideo Locations
- Record

These features are overviewed in the following sections.

PerfectPlay

The PerfectPlay feature makes it possible for a faster download of media, providing higher quality audio and video than would be normally possible with a 28.8 modem. In the RealPlayer preferences (Figure 11-2), you can adjust the amount of buffer time. The larger the buffer, the better the quality of audio you can listen to and if you don't mind waiting a little longer than normal to start playback of the RealAudio file, you will be rewarded with better sound. With PerfectPlay, even if your Internet connection is relatively bad, you probably won't notice a degradation of quality in the sound or video.

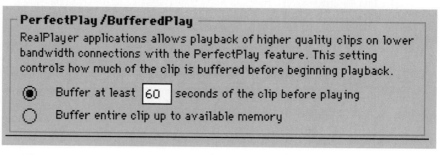

Figure 11-2
Adjust the buffer time for PerfectPlay in the RealPlayer Preferences.

Scan and Preset

The RealPlayer Plus (5.0) now has 40 available preset locations, enabling you to set, name, and recall each location at the push of a button. This is exactly like setting the radio in your car. Using the Scan function prompts the Player to scan live sites searching for RealAudio, RealVideo, and RealFlash content. In the Presets window of the RealPlayer Preferences (Figure 11-3), you can set and name the Presets as well as enter playback time for the scan feature.

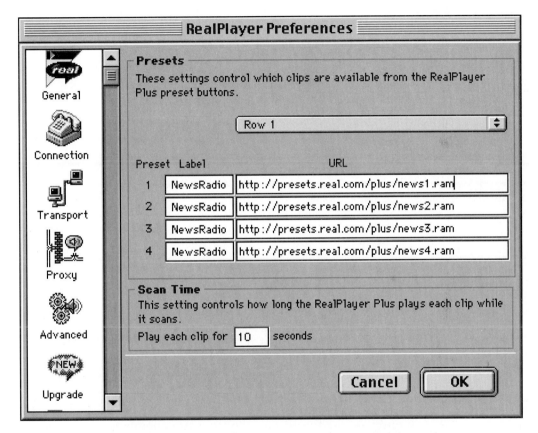

Figure 11-3
Name and set the URL Presets for the RealPlayer Plus in the Preference window.

Record

The Record feature of the RealPlayer Plus enables you to record content being streamed from a RealAudio or RealVideo site. However, when encoding a RealAudio file, it is possible to disable the Record feature for that particular file. The reason for this is obvious as it prevents unauthorized use of the performance.

Compatibility

Does your CPU and OS cut it? If you're running Windows 3.1 or a 68040 Mac and you want to experience RealAudio on the Web, your only option is the RealAudio Player 3.0. For those of you with Pentiums and PowerMacs, the RealPlayer and RealPlayer Plus 5.0 gives you audio, video, and animation in one easy-to-swallow package. Use Table 11-1 as a guide to make sure your operating system is compatible with RealAudio. As far as browsers are concerned, either Netscape Navigator 2.1 (or better) or Internet Explorer 3.0 (or better) will run the RealAudio plug-in.

Table 11-1 RealPlayer OS Compatibility

	68040 Mac (w/FPU)	Power Mac	Windows	Real Audio	Real Video	Real Flash	Cost
RealAudio Player 3.0	yes	yes	3.1, 95/NT	yes	no	no	free download
RealAudio Player Plus 3.0	yes	yes	3.1, 95/NT	yes	no	no	$30
RealPlayer 5.0	no	yes	95/NT	yes	yes	yes	free download
RealPlayer Plus 5.0	no	yes	95/NT	yes	yes	yes	$30

If you purchase the RealPlayer Plus, you are eligible for free upgrades so you'll always have the most current and best-performing version running on your system. A manual is also included (with the RealPlayer Plus) to make sure you get the most out of all of the added features. I'll tell you right now, I was apprehensive about paying anything for what I initially perceived as a slightly enhanced version of the free download. Within a few short minutes, though, my reservations were completely put aside. The convenience of PerfectPlay and Presets are well worth the financial inconvenience. In short: Go buy it!

RealMedia Architecture (RMA)

RealMedia Architecture is an extension of the RealAudio client/server system. Essentially, this means third parties can adapt their software to stream content through RealAudio servers. This opens the door to some very interesting possibilities, including streaming a MIDI file and an audio file in a synchronized performance. Which leads us to Real Time Streaming Protocol (RTSP).

Developed by RealNetworks and Netscape Communications, RTSP is a communications protocol for control and delivery of real-time media. It defines the connection between streaming media client/server software as well as a standard to stream multimedia content from multiple vendors. If RTSP is embraced by, say Macromedia, Liquid Audio, and a few of the other major players in streaming media, imagine the possibilities! Some of the current supporters of RTSP include Apple, IBM, and Sun Microsystems.

The RealNetworks Server

One way to get RealAudio to work at your site is to use the RealNetworks client/server architecture in which the client (your Web page) requests services from the server (i.e., the place where the streaming technology resides). The server, in turn, returns the requested service to the client. What this means is that a user at your Web page clicks the file he or she wants to hear and the RealPlayer launches, which then pulls the file from the server (located elsewhere) and streams it through to your site. This is made possible via the RealSystems server.

Not that long ago, the cost of putting up a RealSystems server was out of the range for the little guy—but no more. The entry-level RealNetworks Basic Server for RealAudio or RealVideo is now a free download. So, realistically, even I can afford and will in fact soon have my own RealSystems Server. And so can you.

While it is possible to stream RealAudio from your Web page without a RealAudio server, there are advantages such as PerfectPlay that are only available when the audio is streamed from a RealSystems server. One of the questions you need to ask yourself in setting up an entry-level RealSystems Server is whether you intend to broadcast live performances from your site or not. What kind of traffic you expect is also an indicator of how many live streams you will need. If you plan on doing a live net-cast of a radio station you just happen to own, you definitely want to go with a RealSystems Server Plus.

> **Web**
>
> Because of the constant changes in products and pricing, I'm going to send you to the RealNetworks homepage to see what's new in the world of RealNetworks Servers. Go to the RealNetworks home page at `www.real.com`.

RealAudio via Streaming HTTP

Another option that has recently become a reality is streaming a RealAudio file from your Web site using HTTP. This is cool and it's free! Essentially, you embed a RealAudio file in your Web page and it plays back without any server software. There are some limitations, including the loss of the Perfect Play feature. Still, for those who simply don't have the need for even an entry-level RealSystems Server, this is a wonderful option. In Chapter 17, "Embed Audio," I show you how to embed and playback a RealAudio file using streaming HTTP. It works, it's easy to accomplish, and again the price is right!

Downloadable RealAudio files

Downloading a RealAudio file is another way for visitors to your Web site to hear what you have to say. By making a direct link to the encoded RealAudio files in your HTML document, a file can be downloaded and played directly from the user's computer. Remember, though: This is not streaming audio, so it won't actually playback from your site. Tutorial 11-4 will walk you through the basics of playing a nonstreaming RealAudio file from your system.

Development Tools (Overview)

The tools are an important link in the chain. It's completely irrelevant (at least in this case) which platform you use for creating and converting RealAudio files, as there's something for everybody. For those of you who tend to have more time than money, Progressive Networks offers the RealAudio Encoder (Mac and Windows) as a free download (see Figure 11-4). In the tutorial section of this chapter, we'll encode a few RealAudio files using freeware, shareware, and commercial sound-editing software so you can see if you've really got to pay the big bucks for a good sound. Table 11-2 features sound recording and editing tools capable of converting a standard audio file into an RA file.

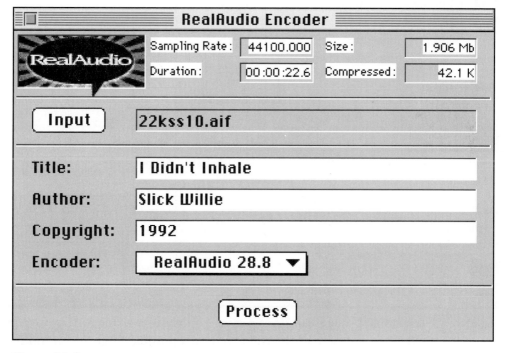

Figure 11-4
The RealAudio Encoder is a free download.

Table 11-2   RealAudio Development Tools

Product	OS	System Requirements	Plug-in Compatability	Price
Cool Edit 96 by Syntrillium	Windows 3.1/95	486/33	n/a	Shareware $50
Peak by BIAS	Mac OS 7.5	PowerMac	Adobe Premiere	$495
Peak LE by BIAS	Mac OS 7.5	PowerMac	n/a	$99
RealAudio Encoder (Mac) Real Networks	Mac OS 7.5	PowerMac	n/a	free download
RealAudio Encoder (Windows) Real Networks	Windows 95/NT	Pentium	n/a	free download
Real Encoder 5.0 Real Networks	Windows 95/NT	Pentium	n/a	free download
RealPublisher 5.0 Real Networks	Windows 95/NT	Pentium	n/a	$49.99
SoundEdit 16 Version 2 by Macromedia	Mac OS 7.1 or better	68040 25mHz PowerMac	SoundEdit 16 Xtras	$399 with Deck 2.5
SoundForge 4.0 by Sonic Foundry	Windows 3.1 95/NT	486/33	DirectX	$495

 Encoding a File

The encode process can be as easy as you want to make it. If you've got the time, patience, and the right tools, it's possible to go where no man (or woman) has gone before. Tutorials 11-1 through 11-3 feature three different programs that vary in cost and complexity of use. If your sound knowledge is limited and you're not all that adventurous, stick with the RealAudio Encoder. You won't get hurt, I promise. For the rest of you, roll up your sleeves and go get your hands dirty.

Tutorial 11-1: Using The RealAudio Encoder (Mac)

As I'm sure you'll agree, freeware is the way to go—whenever possible. Sure, you give up a lot of options (or do you?), but if it gets the job done, who cares? The RealAudio Encoder makes the encode process as easy as it's going to get. The Windows version of the Encoder is a little cooler and has more features than the Mac version, but the results end up being identical.

What you need

The following items are needed to complete this tutorial:

- The RealAudio Encoder
- Tutorial file CH11EX1.SND
- A PowerMac running System 7.5 or better

Web

The RealAudio Encoder (both Mac and PC) can be downloaded for free at www.realaudio.com.

CD-ROM

The tutorial audio file CH11EX1.SND can be found in the Chapter 11 tutorial folder on the accompanying CD-ROM.

◼ Steps to Encode

1. Start the application RealAudio Encoder. The main window of the RealAudio Encoder is shown in Figure 11-5.

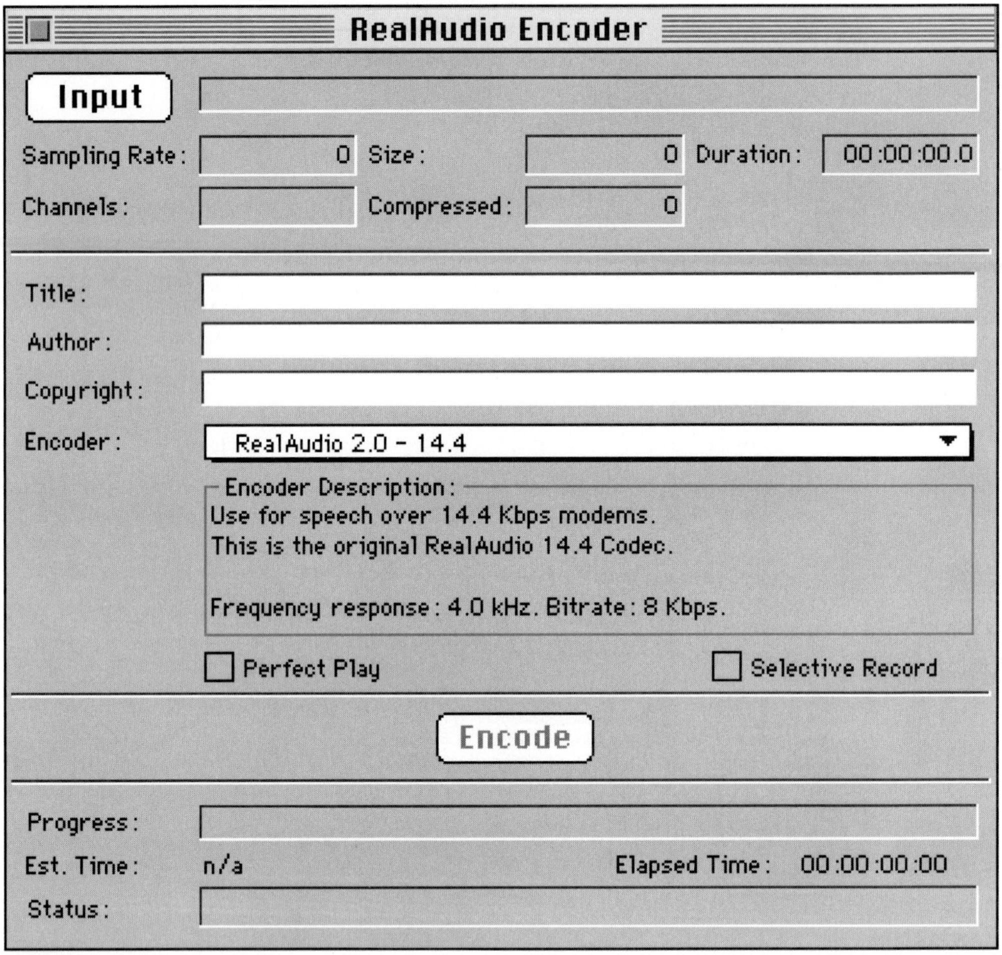

Figure 11-5
The main window of the RealAudio Encoder (Mac).

2. Click the Input button (in the top left-hand corner of the main window) and select the file you want to load (in this case, the tutorial file CH11EX1.SND).

3. Now it's time to enter the RealAudio Info. There are three fields: Title, Author, and Copyright. From the main window, enter the information as shown in Figure 11-6. This information shows up on the RealAudio Player when the file is playing. If you're using your own source audio, enter the information in the RealAudio Info that correlates to your project.

Title :	Pop Jazz
Author :	Ron Simpson
Copyright :	1997

Figure 11-6
File (or song) information is displayed on the RealAudio Player during playback.

4. From the Encoder options in the main window (see Figure 11-7), select the codec RealAudio 3.0—28.8 Mono, full response. Using this codec will ensure the highest sound quality possible for Mono playback using a 28.8 modem. While you're here, check the box Perfect Play. This enables listeners with a 14.4 modem connection to playback a 28.8 encoded RealAudio file.

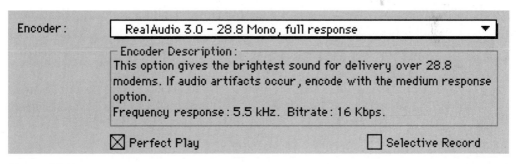

Encoder : RealAudio 3.0 - 28.8 Mono, full response ▼

─ Encoder Description :
This option gives the brightest sound for delivery over 28.8 modems. If audio artifacts occur, encode with the medium response option.
Frequency response : 5.5 kHz. Bitrate : 16 Kbps.

☒ Perfect Play   ☐ Selective Record

Figure 11-7
Select the codec RealAudio 3.0—28.8 Mono, full response and check the box Perfect Play.

5. I guess there's no reason to delay the inevitable, so click the Encode button (see Figure 11-8), choose the destination folder and name (CH11EX2.ra in this case), click Save, and in a few short seconds you have . . . RealAudio!

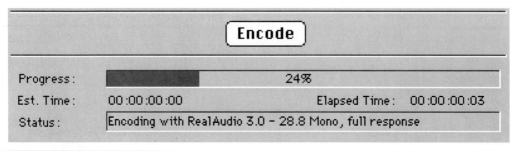

Figure 11-8
Click the Encode button to start the process.

■ Just Because It's Free . . .

Just because it's free, doesn't mean it doesn't work just fine; and this is certainly the case with the RealAudio Encoder. If the source audio doesn't require any in-depth editing or signal processing, then I would recommend using this freeware program without any hesitation. There is also a rudimentary cut-and-paste feature in the RealAudio Encoder. I would, however, recommend that you drop $50 and buy Cool Edit 96 (Windows users only) if you want to do anything more complex than encoding a file.

If you're interested in listening to the file you've just converted, jump to Tutorial 11-4 or just double-click the RealAudio file in question!

Tutorial 11-2: Converting audio to Real Audio (Windows)

Converting a standard WAVE file into a RealAudio 3.0 file is no difficult task, but at the same time it is a necessary one. There are certain steps—tricks, if you must—that optimize the sound files in such a way to make the listening experience a pleasant versus an annoying one. In the tradition of trying to keep it inexpensive, this tutorial is built around the most popular Windows audio shareware program in existence— Cool Edit 96.

What you need

The following items are needed to complete this tutorial:

- Cool Edit 96
- Tutorial file CH11EX1.WAV
- A Windows 95 Computer with a properly configured soundcard

CD-ROM

Cool Edit 96 (demo version) can be found in the demo software folder of the CD-ROM accompanying this book. The tutorial audio file CH11EX1.WAV can be found in the Chapter 11 tutorial folder on the CD-ROM.

Before you prepare a sound file for conversion, there are a few decisions you need to make. The sound quality of the source material is extremely important. For this tutorial, I'm using a 16-bit 22 kHz mono WAVE file from the CyberTunz clip music library. When you move past this tutorial and start encoding your own music and sound, avoid inferior sound sources such as standard audio cassettes and go more towards DAT, CD-ROM, or Audio CDs for your material. The results will be much better. Most Web users still connect at 28.8, so that is your target listening audience when you encode the WAVE file. Let's get started.

Note

The demo version of Cool Edit 96 is somewhat limited and you may not be able to complete all the tutorial steps with it. To unlock all the features of this Shareware program, go to the Syntrillium home page and get registered (no, it's not free; that's why it's called Shareware).

Converting in five easy steps

1. Start the application Cool Edit 96 and select Open from the File menu. Load the tutorial file CH11EX1.WAV. You now see the audio file in the Edit Waveform window shown Figure 11-9.

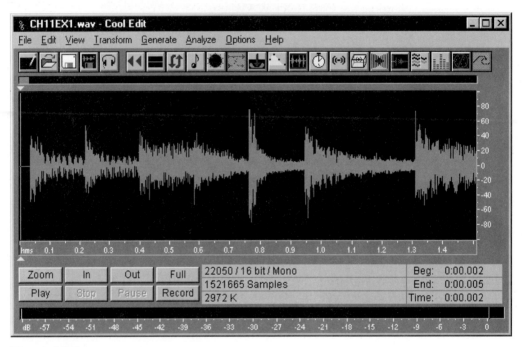

Figure 11-9
Tutorial file CH11EX1.WAV in CoolEdit 96.

Note

There are a number of preparatory steps that can be taken with a sound file before the encoding/conversion process takes place. The need depends heavily on the content of the source material. For more information on this subject, refer to sidebar called "Using Signal Processing to Prepare a File for RealAudio," later in this chapter.

2. Part of the RealAudio encode information includes title, artist, and copyright, which is displayed on the RealPlayer during playback. Select Info from the Cool Edit View menu. In the Wave Information window (Figure 11-10), enter the appropriate information. Click OK when finished.

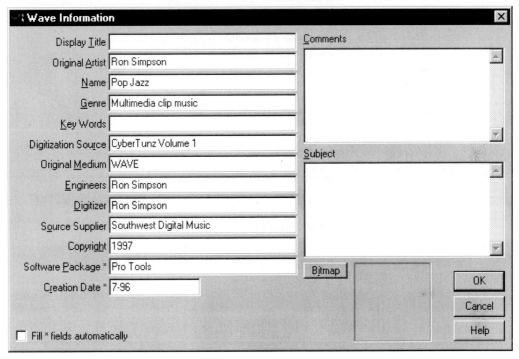

Figure 11-10
Enter the song information in the correct fields of the Wave Information window.

3. Select Save As from the File bar. Rename the file to CH11EX2.RA and select Save as type RealAudio 3.0 (Figure 11-11).

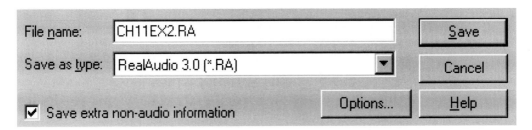

Figure 11-11
Rename the file to CH11EX2.RA and select Save as type RealAudio 3.0.

4.   Click the Options button. The RealAudio Options window opens. Select Music and RealAudio 3.0 - 28.8 Mono full response (see Figure 11-12) and click OK.

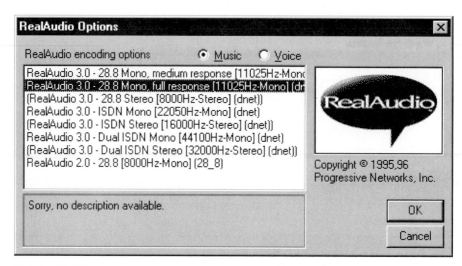

Figure 11-12
Select Music and RealAudio 3.0 - 28.8 Mono full response as your choices in the RealAudio Options window.

5.   You are now back in the Save Waveform window. Click Save and in a few seconds (Figure 11-13) you have a RealAudio 3.0 file.

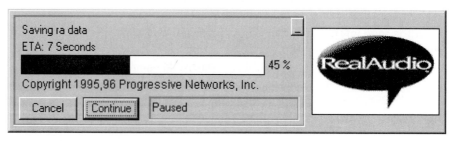

Figure 11-13
Saving and encoding a RealAudio file.

Using Signal Processing to Prepare a File for RealAudio

On occasion, you may have a sound file that has been recorded under less-than-optimum conditions. In other words, there's a bunch of sonic garbage mixed in with your content. When playing this file back at a high resolution, you probably won't notice the background noise all that much. However, when you down sample and convert the file to the RealAudio (or any other compressed) format, the unwanted background noise could take on a life of its own and might even jump out at you like a poodle in heat. Here are a few potential problems that can occur when a file is encoded and an overview of how to deal with them.

1. DC Offset can occur when a file is digitized. This is generally caused by the improper grounding of a sound card. It can cause a low-end rumble in a converted file that can at the very least drive you (and anyone else listening) crazy. In some editors, the correction of DC Offset is automatic, while with others it's a manual process. Check the documentation of your editor and sound card for more information on this subject.

2. The Noise Gate is used to eliminate the unwanted background noise that becomes noticeable in the blank spots (or dead air) in a recording. In short, you set the gate to open when there's music or voice action and to close when you desire silence.

3. Audio Compression/Limiting is essentially used to put a ceiling on the audio signal. It is favorable (especially for an encoded file) to have the audio as loud as possible. By giving the signal a ceiling, it allows you to bring the overall volume up, making the quiet passages louder. This will help to mask any artifacts that might show up at a quieter volume.

4. EQ (Equalization) is used to boost or cut certain frequencies. An example would be if the Bass is booming too loudly on your stereo, you would simply turn it down (the Bass) until you like what you hear. Using a graphic or parametric EQ, it is possible to isolate and adjust a wider range of frequencies than just Bass or Treble.

Table 11-3 shows you which programs offer the Signal Processing features mentioned in the preceding sidebar.

Table 11-3 Signal Processing Compatibility Table

Product	Correct DC Offset	Noise Gate	Compressor Limiter	EQ
CoolEdit 96	no	yes	yes	yes
Peak	third-party plug-in	third-party plug-in	third-party plug-in	third-party plug-in
Peak LE	no	no	no	no
SoundEdit 16 Version 2	third-party plug-in	yes	yes	yes
SoundForge 4.0	yes	yes	yes	yes

Tutorial 11-3: Converting Audio to Real Audio (Mac)

Converting an AIFF (or SND, in the case of this tutorial) into a RealAudio 3.0 file is a walk through the park using Peak from BIAS. Peak is a very powerful sound design tool and gives you a multitude of editing options that are not available with a simple conversion program. Depending on the quality and content of the sound files you wish to encode as a RealAudio 3.0 file, Signal Processing may be required to help optimize the file before conversion. See the sidebar entitled "Using Signal Processing to Prepare a File for RealAudio" for reference on this subject.

What you need

The following items are needed to complete this tutorial:

- Peak by BIAS
- Tutorial file CH11EX3.SND
- A Macintosh (68030 or 68040) or Power Macintosh with an Apple Sound Chip

CD-ROM

A demo version of Peak can be found in the demo software folder of the CD-ROM accompanying this book. The tutorial audio file CH11EX3.SND can be found in the Chapter 11 tutorial folder on the CD-ROM.

Note

The demo version of Peak is save-disabled, making it somewhat limited and you will not be able to complete all the steps in Tutorial 11-3 with it.

Mac conversion

The tutorial file is a 16-bit 22 kHz mono file and our target listening audience (the majority of them anyway) use 28.8 modems. So enough already—let's get started!

1. Start the application Peak and open the tutorial file CH11EX3.SND. You are asked to Convert (instead of open) the file, as shown in Figure 11-14. Click Convert to load the file and then click Done when finished. The Audio Document window opens, as shown in Figure 11-15.

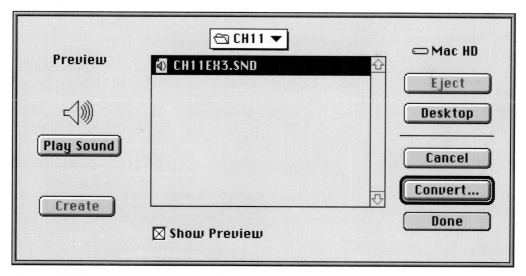

Figure 11-14
Click Convert to load the tutorial file CH11EX3.SND.

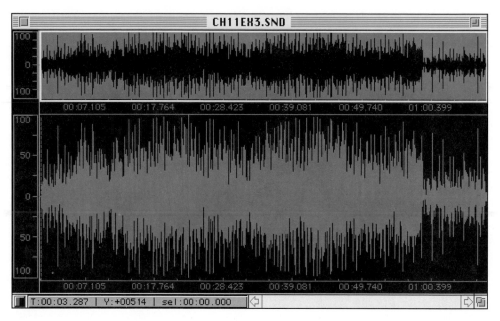

Figure 11-15
The Audio Document window in Peak.

2. Select Save As from the File menu and name the file (to be encoded) CH11EX4.RA. Under File Type, select RealAudio 3.0 (see Figure 11-16). The Real Audio Encoder window opens.

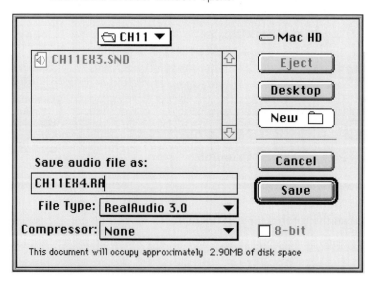

Figure 11-16
Select the File Type Real Audio 3.0.

3. The RealAudio Encoder shown in Figure 11-17 is the utility that enables you to enter the proper information to be encoded in the RA file. For Source, choose Music and for Encoder, choose RealAudio 3.0 28.8 Mono Full Response. Enter the Title, Author, and Copyright information. This is displayed during playback on the RealAudio Player.

Refer to sidebar entitled "More RealAudio Encoder Options," for information on the other options in the RealAudio Encoder. When finished, click OK.

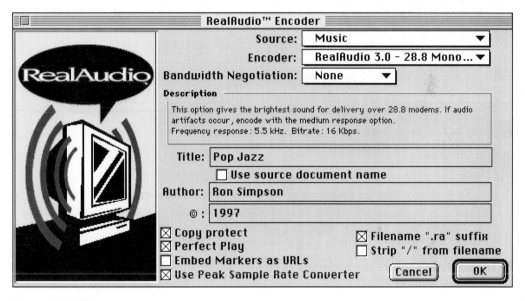

Figure 11-17
The RealAudio Encoder is integrated into Peak.

4. Click Save. Two things happen now. First, your sound file is downsampled to a lower resolution; second, it is converted into a RealAudio file. This is an undoable process as you can't alter or edit the converted file in any way, and neither can anyone else.

More RealAudio Encoder Options

When using Peak to convert an audio file to the RealAudio format, you have an expanded number of options that are not available in the freeware version of the RealAudio Encoder. Following is a brief description of each of these options.

1. **Copy Protect** creates a RealAudio file that can be played but not recorded.
2. **Perfect Play** enables a user with a 14.4 modem to playback a file encoded at 28.8.
3. **Embed Markers as URLs** gives you the option of synchronizing Web pages with Audio.
4. **Use Peak Sample Rate Converter** gives you the option to use the higher-quality Sample Rate Converter available in Peak.
5. **Filename .ra suffix.** Unlike Windows and DOS files, Mac files don't normally have the .wav or, in this case, .ra at the end of the file. This feature simply adds it to the end of the RealAudio file.
6. **Strip"/" from filename.** To prevent the confusion of a file being mistaken as a URL (this goes back to option number 3 of this sidebar), this function eliminates the potential problem before it happens.

Tutorial 11-4: Testing a RealAudio File

The next logical progression, as you've probably figured out, is to listen to the RealAudio file you've just encoded. This of course will not be possible unless you have already installed the RealAudio 3.0 Player or the newer RealPlayer 4.0. Fortunately, I have faith in the fact that you took my advice at the beginning of this chapter and installed the necessary browser and plug-in. If not, do so now. This tutorial is for both the Mac and the Windows OS and, while the RealPlayer for each system looks slightly different, there is very little difference in function and performance.

In Tutorials 11-1 through 11-3, we encoded the same basic music file as a RealAudio file. Is there any difference in sound between the freeware, shareware, and the commercial sound editing software? This is where you get to be the judge.

What you need

The following items are needed to complete this tutorial:

- RealAudio File Tutorial Files CH11EX2.ra, CH11EX3.ra, CH11EX4.ra.
- The RealPlayer

> **CD-ROM**
>
> Just in case you didn't participate in either Tutorial 11-1, 11-2, or 11-3 and need a RealAudio file, you're in luck. In the Chapter 11 Tutorial folder on the CD-ROM accompanying this book there reside the RealAudio files you need for Tutorial 11-4.

Get Real!

1. The easiest way to initiate playback of a RealAudio file is to simply double-click the file. Go to the Chapter 11 tutorial file folder on the CD-ROM with this book and double-click the file CH11EX2.ra. The RealPlayer (shown in Figure 11-18) opens and begins playback immediately.

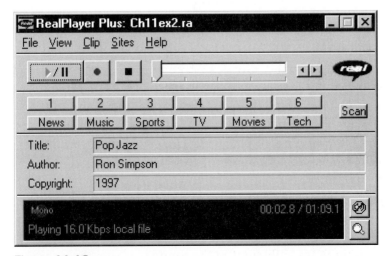

Figure 11-18
Double-click a RealAudio File to initiate playback.

2. The RealPlayer is now up and running, giving you the option of loading and listening to other RealAudio files. Select Open File from the File menu on the RealPlayer (Figure 11-19). Go to the Chapter 11 Tutorial folder and select a RealAudio file for playback.

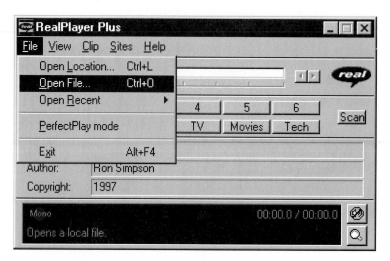

Figure 11-19
Use the RealPlayer Plus to open and play a local file.

▓ Now that you've listened

It's time to make some comparisons. Obviously, the first one is between the source WAVE or SND file and the encoded RealAudio file. The original file had a size of 1.4 MB and the RealAudio encoding process crunched it down to 149 K. That's close to 10 percent of the original size, which is pretty incredible when you think about it.

Now, the second comparison is obviously the sound. A lot of the sparkle of the original file is gone. The crisp definition of the cymbals has been mucked up a bit and the flute has lost a lot of clarity. With all the pitfalls and short comings of streaming audio at 28.8, it still sounds a whole lot better than dead air and that's the bottom line.

Here's another something to consider. In the three encoding tutorials in this chapter, we used three different programs to encode the same file. So, is there any difference in the sound between these three applications? At first I was sure there was. There were some subtle differences for sure.

Here's where you get to let your ears be the judge. Using the RealAudio Player, play each of the tutorial RA files back to back. Table 11-4 gives you the basic info on where each file came from.

Table 11-4   Tutorial File Comparison Table

Tutorial #	Application	RA File Name	OS
11-1	RealAudio Encoder	CH11EX2.ra	Mac
11-2	Cool Edit 96	CH11EX3.ra	Windows 95
11-3	Peak	CH11EX4.ra	Mac

Okay, by now you've listened and hopefully formed an opinion. I have, too. If your source files are of a good quality, the free RealAudio Encoder will do the job just fine. The differences between the files are so subtle, I'm not sure if they're imagined or real. Life is like that sometimes.

 # RealSystem 5.0

Just as I was about to turn in this chapter to my editor, the RealSystem 5.0 products were released. Curiosity (as always) got the best of me and I thought it wouldn't kill me to take a look and listen to what was available. The long promised RealAudio Xtra (plug-in) for SoundEdit 16 was just one really nice surprise as well as a RealAudio Premiere plug-in. Another really cool addition to the whole package is the integration of Macromedia Flash into the mix. RealFlash enables the user to synchronize audio to the Flash animations. Will it ever stop?

One of the tools I just got my hands on is RealPublisher 5.0. This Windows (95/NT) application enables the user to create and publish RealAudio and RealVideo to the Web. With a few easy steps you can load a WAVE file, covert it to RealAudio, and automatically create a Web page in HTML that is audio-enabled. If that wasn't enough, Real Publisher shows the user how to take their newly created media-enriched Web page and upload it to a Web server or RealServer. RealPublisher is so cool and easy to use that I'd feel extremely guilty if I didn't take you on a test drive. So let's check it out.

Tutorial 11-5: RealPublisher 5.0

For those of you who want to embed RealAudio (and or video) into a Web page and get it up on the Web with little to no hassle, this is the tool for you.

■ What you need

The following items are needed to complete this tutorial:

- ■ RealPublisher 5.0
- ■ Tutorial file CH11EX1.WAV
- ■ Netscape Communicator or Internet Explorer 4.0
- ■ A Windows 95 Computer with a properly configured soundcard

Got to be Real

1. Start the application RealPublisher 5.0. You're now in the main RealPublisher window shown Figure 11-20.

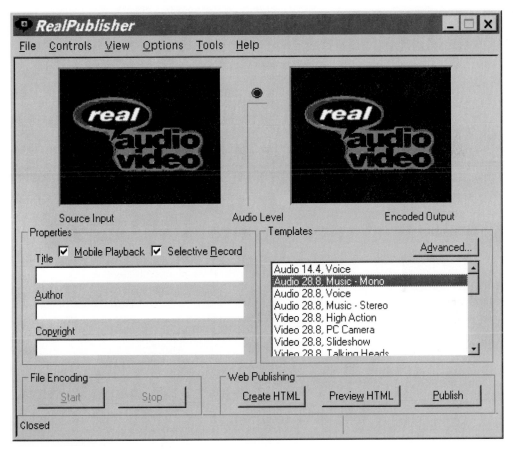

Figure 11-20
The main Window in RealPublisher.

2. Select Open Session from the File menu and then Add (tutorial file) CH11EX3.WAV from the Source menu. Under Destination, check the RealMedia File box and click Save As, naming this new file test1 as shown in Figure 11-21. Click OK when finished.

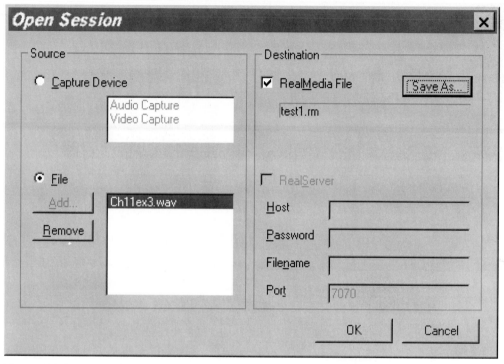

Figure 11-21
Select the source audio file and save it as test1.

3. For this next step, enter the Title, Author, and Copyright information in the appropriate Properties fields, as shown in Figure 11-22.

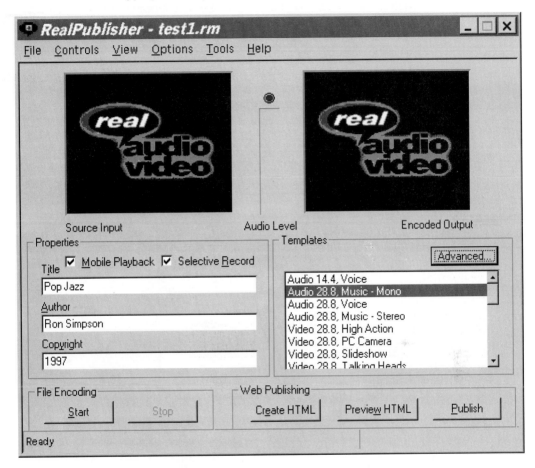

Figure 11-22
Under Properties enter the Title, Author, and Copyright information.

> **Note**
>
> Notice the two boxes at the top of the Properties window, Mobile Playback and Selective Record. Mobile Playback enables a RealAudio file to be downloaded to a portable device. This would be an alternative way to listen to an audiobook. Selective Record (if enabled) enables the owners of the PlayerPlus to record the streaming media to their local hard drive for playback at a later time.

4. In the Templates field (refer back to Figure 11-22), select Audio 28.8, Music - Mono as the Codec and click on Advanced. In the Advanced Settings window, you have a number of options to optimize the encoding of the RealAudio file. As shown in Figure 11-23 select 16Kbps Music - High Response. This gives you the highest quality in a Mono RealAudio file while still being able to deliver at 28.8. Click Save and Close.

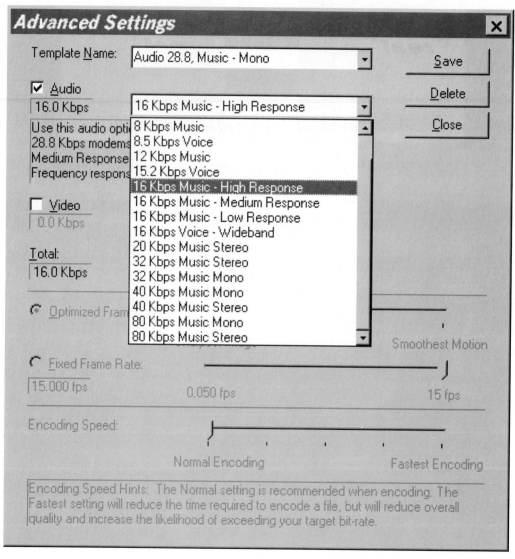

Figure 11-23
In the Advanced Settings window choose 16Kbps Music - High Response.

5. Now it's time to encode the target audio file. Under File Encoding (shown in Figure 11-24), click on Start and the file will be encoded with the settings used in Step 4.

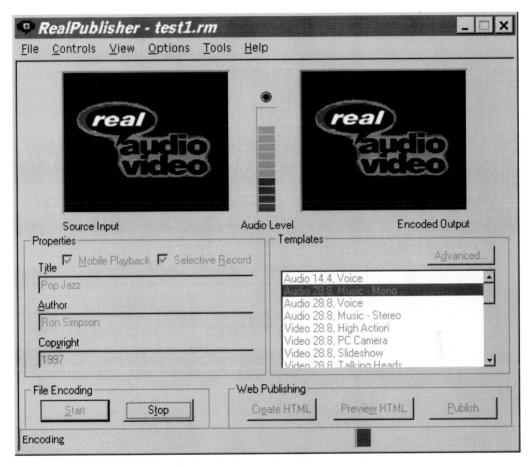

Figure 11-24
Under File Encoding, click Start to encode the target audio file.

6. Now we're ready to turn this RealAudio file into a Web page. In the Web Publishing field (refer back to Figure 11-24), click Create HTML. This activates the HTML Generation Wizard shown in Figure 11-25. Click Next to proceed.

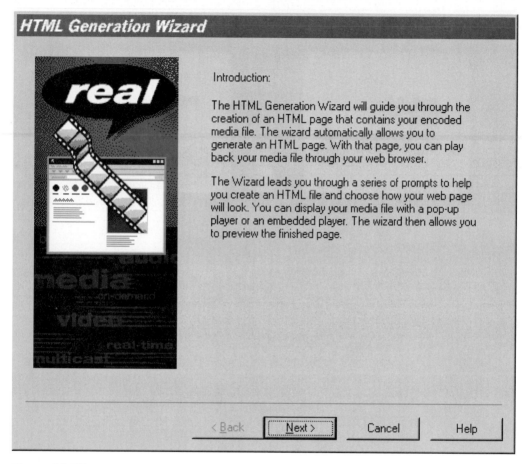

Figure 11-25
The RealPublisher HTML Generation Wizard.

7. In this step, you're going to choose the RealAudio (media) file you just encoded. The choice is the file test1.rm as shown in Figure 11-26. Click Next to proceed.

Figure 11-26
Choose the file test1.rm and click Next.

8. Playback method is where you get to choose the type of player you wish to use. The Embedded Player resides on your page permanently while the Pop-up Player shows up when you click on the link on your page. For our purposes, choose the Embedded Player (as shown in Figure 11-27) and click Next to proceed.

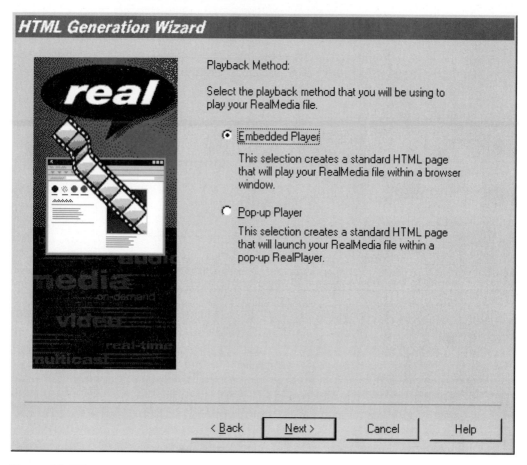

Figure 11-27
Choose the Embedded Player and click Next.

9. The next window is the Player Control Layout. Of the six different RealPlayer types (see Figure 11-28) you can go with, choose Standard Player. I'll leave it up to your discretion whether to check the Auto Start box (I didn't). Click Next to proceed.

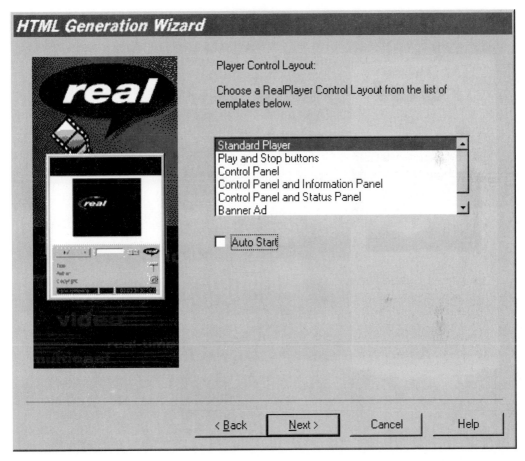

Figure 11-28
Choose the Standard Player and click Next.

10. In the next window is where you enter a caption that can reside either above or below the RealPlayer. Under Caption, enter "Cutting Edge Web Audio" and click the Place caption above embedded player radio button, as shown in Figure 11-29. Click Next to proceed.

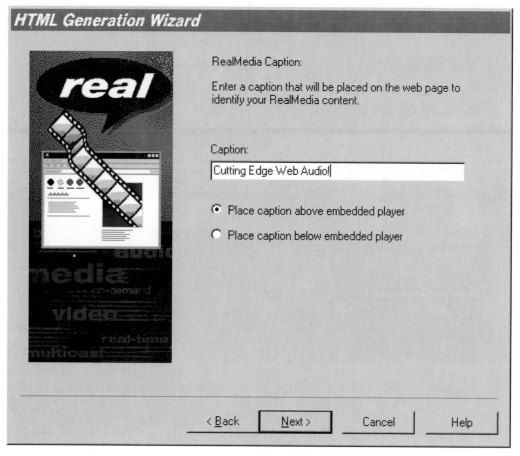

Figure 11-29
Under Caption, enter "Cutting Edge Web Audio" and choose Place caption above embedded player.

11. This next step is to enter the full path and name of the file. If you've made no changes from Step 7 it should already be there (see Figure 11-30). If not, enter the correct information and click Next to proceed.

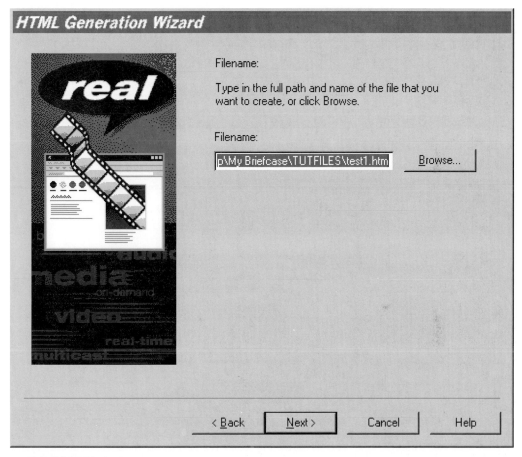

Figure 11-30
If you've made no changes from Step 7, the full path and name of the file will already be in place.

12. Click Preview HTML. Your browser will then start up and the results (shown in Figure 11-31) will be at your fingertips. Press play and take a listen. If you're pleased with the results, close the new window in your Browser and click Finish in RealPublisher.

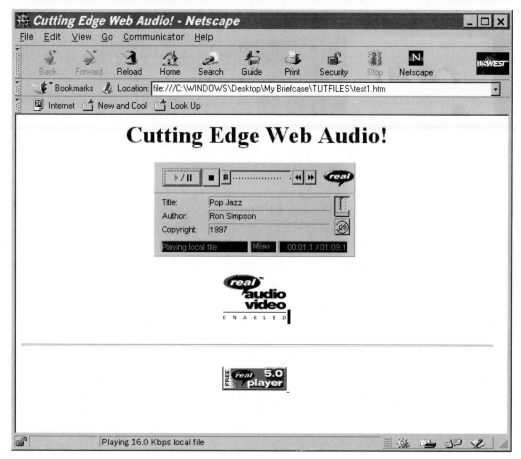

Figure 11-31
Click Preview HTML and take a look and a listen to the results.

Wow!

This little exercise was as much of a tour as a tutorial. If you don't have RealPublisher, this is an excellent opportunity to see just how it works. RealPublisher is easy to use and as you can see (and hear) the results are great. Using the Publish feature of RealPublisher you can also upload your work in a few easy steps (although that is beyond the scope of this book). This is a tool that I would highly recommend if you're not all that familiar with HTML and getting content onto the Web. It's quick, easy, and inexpensive, and those are my three favorite words. How could you ask for more?

RealAudio in Retrospect

I've gotta say it: RealNetworks has opened the doors to some absolutely incredible possibilities for the delivery of streaming media over the Web. Listening to an archived interview with your favorite band or a live radio broadcast from your old hometown (from the other side of the country) is just too cool. As with Liquid Audio and Shockwave Audio, RealAudio is an absolutely great way for an unknown band to get discovered and even heard by millions of people worldwide. And how about the RealPlayer! Audio, video, and animation streaming at you—over the Web, no less. Granted, as we stand on the brink of a DVD player in every home and Digital Television looming in the not-too-distant future, the quality of delivery of streaming media over the Web is not exactly cutting edge. So what!?! This is like having hundreds of thousands of cable channels that give you what you want when you want it. Hang in there; we won't be traveling by covered wagon all that much longer.

One last thought on Real Time Streaming Protocol: Currently, the exact specifications of RTSP are still up in the air. While the media is making a lot of noise about the many companies embracing RTSP as the new standard, at this time it's still a wait-and-see situation. Even though it's still a little fuzzy out there, if everyone embraces the same standards for delivery of streaming media, we'll all come out winners.

Half the battle is getting there first and without a doubt RealNetworks seems to always be standing at the front of the line. When it comes down to it, I love a good race!

Web

The RealNetworks home page is an incredible resource for the latest information about RealAudio and all the different components that make it tick. Go to `www.real.com`.

Chapter 12

Shockwave Audio

In This Chapter

- Learning about Shockwave Audio
- SoundEdit 16
- Creating and auditioning SWA files

Macromedia's Shockwave technology first burst onto the Web scene in '95, and has since become the unofficial standard for delivering true multimedia and interactivity via the Internet. Shockwave introduced the possibility of including interactive graphics, sounds, and animations to otherwise static Web sites, but without the huge file sizes associated with these types of files. It only made sense that the Shockwave technology would be refined and applied to audio delivery, and with the evolution of Shockwave Audio (SWA), your Web site can now benefit from streaming audio with impressive compression rates and even more impressive sound quality.

In this chapter, we'll take a look at just what Shockwave Audio means to Web developers and walk through several tutorials for optimizing playback of SWA files with some simple sound-editing tricks, file conversion processes, and an introduction to some cool extras that make more advanced techniques possible for higher-quality sound.

What Is Shockwave Audio?

At last, you've gathered up the nerve to ask the big question: What is Shockwave Audio (SWA)? In short, SWA is a streaming audio format that enables playback of compressed "Shocked" audio files over the Web. Shockwave Audio is scaleable, enabling you to choose the level of quality for playback depending on the modem speed of your target audience. Initially, if you weren't a Macromedia Director programmer, you were out of luck if you wanted to create a SWA file for Web playback. Fortunately for me (and for many of you), with the new SoundEdit 16 Streaming Audio Toolkit, it is possible to do the SWA thing on your Web site and be Director-impaired all at the same time.

Use Table 12-1 to determine the bit rate and modem speed of your target audience. More kbps means less compression and better sound quality.

Table 12-1 Shockwave Audio Data Rates

Bit Rate	Modem Speed of Target Audience	Stereo
8Kbps	14.4	no
16Kbps	28.8	no
32Kbps 56Kbps	ISDN	no yes
64Kbps 128Kbps	T1	yes yes

How Does SWA Work?

One of the advantages of playing back a SWA file from your Web site is that Director acts as your server (through the Shockwave plug-in). Using a Director movie configured as a SWA player, it is possible to play multiple sound files back one at a time in the order the user chooses. There are limitations, though. Currently, you can't fast forward or rewind a SWA file; but you can pause. In the future (don't ask me exactly when), this situation will be rectified.

Once the SWA player is loaded to your Web page, playback is almost instantaneous. There is usually a 5- to 10-second delay while the buffer loads and then you're on the air.

What Do I Need to Get Going with SWA?

To get this show on the road, the first component needed is the (most current) Shockwave plug-in for Netscape Navigator 4.0 (or Internet Explorer 4.0). This is both free and easily available for download.

> **Web**
>
> Get the Shockwave plug-in at `www.macromedia.com/shockwave/`.

> **Note**
>
> While it is possible to play a SWA file back from Netscape Navigator 2.02, please . . . use 3.0 or later; otherwise I won't get any sleep worrying about you and the bugs crawling around on your desktop.

You're telling yourself, "I want to get Shocked on the Web!" Well, Table 12-2 tells you if the components in your system are compatible with the Shockwave Browser Plug-in.

Table 12-2 Shockwave/Browser Playback Compatibility Table

The Browsers	Macintosh		Windows
Internet Explorer 3.0	Power PC	68K	Win95, Windows NT 4.0
Netscape Navigator 3.0	Power PC*	68K†	Windows 3.1, Win95, Windows NT 4.0
America Online 3.0	no		no

* Mac OS 7.5.1 or newer is required for the Power Macintosh

† Mac OS 7.1.2 or newer is required for the 68K Macintosh. Minimum requirement is a machine with a 68040 CPU running at 25mHz (with an FPU).

> **Note**
>
> AOL and Web audio is a possibility if you use a special version of Internet Explorer that is downloadable with the most current version of AOL. The Web browser that is part of the standard AOL software does not support SWA.

 # Creating and Auditioning a Shockwave Audio File

Nothing like getting right to the heart of the chapter. The best way for the non-Director initiated to prepare, convert, and embed a SWA file is to start with SoundEdit 16. In our first tutorial, we take a WAV file and convert it into a SWA file using SoundEdit 16.

> **Note**
>
> Stop! If you have not installed the Shockwave Browser Plug-in, do it now. See Table 12-2 to be sure your Browser is compatible with Shockwave.

Tutorial 12-1: SoundEdit 16, converting WAVE to SWA

There are a number of sound editing tricks that can help to prepare a sound file for optimum playback as a SWA file. We cover the basics in this tutorial and get into the advanced editing topics a little later in this chapter. For those of you using the demo version of SoundEdit 16, it will not be possible to complete many of the steps in this tutorial. For some reason, Macromedia just won't give away full working versions of SoundEdit 16. Go figure.

■ What you need

Here are the other components you will need to accomplish this task:

- SoundEdit 16 version 2.04 or better.
- Tutorial File CH12EX1.WAV
- Macintosh Power PC
- SWA Export Xtra
- SWA Settings (SE16) Xtra

CD-ROM

You will find a save-disabled demo version of SoundEdit 16 (Mac) in the Demo Software (DEMOSOFT) folder on the CD-ROM accompanying this book. The tutorial file CH12EX1.WAV and the two SWA Xtras (Export and Settings) are located in the Chapter 12 tutorial file on the CD-ROM.

Note

The SWA Export Xtra and The SWA Settings Xtra must be placed in the SoundEdit 16 Xtras folder before you start Tutorial 12-1.

Shocking, Isn't It?

1. Open SoundEdit 16 and choose Open CH12EX1.WAV from the File menu (shown in Figure 12-1).

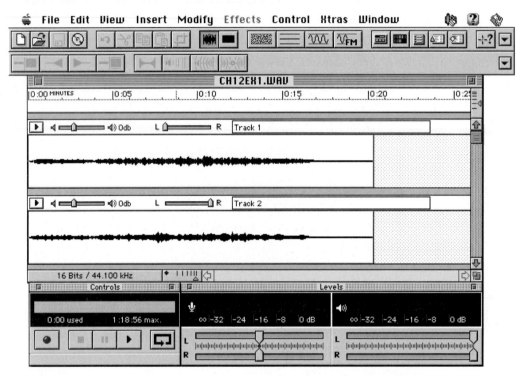

Figure 12-1
File CH12EX1.WAV should look like this in the main screen of SoundEdit 16.

2. Down sampling is a fact of life when preparing a sound file for playback on the Web. In this case, the source file is 16-bit 44kHz stereo. Macromedia strongly suggests converting 44kHz files to 22kHz, and who are we to argue. Select Sound Format from the Modify menu. Using the controls shown in Figure 12-2, I've set the sample rate to 22.050kHz and have elected to use the Boost Highs option. Also, notice I have kept the sample size at 16 bits. Click OK to proceed.

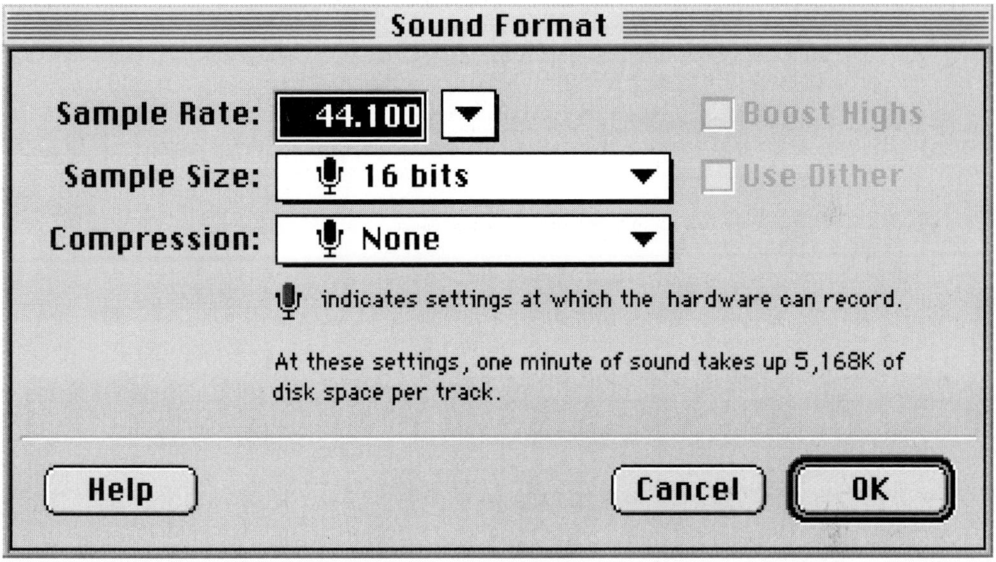

Sound Format

Sample Rate: **44.100** ▼   ☐ Boost Highs

Sample Size: 🎤 16 bits ▼   ☐ Use Dither

Compression: 🎤 None ▼

🎤 indicates settings at which the hardware can record.

At these settings, one minute of sound takes up 5,168K of disk space per track.

(Help)   (Cancel) (OK)

Figure 12-2
When preparing a sound file for export to the .SWA format, it is recommended the sample rate be set at 22.050kHz.

3. Compressing a sound file and playing it back at a lower resolution does alter the overall sound quality. In certain frequencies, an annoying harshness can appear out of nowhere. Adjusting the EQ on the file is the solution. Choose Select All from the Edit menu, and then select Equalizer from the Effects menu. In Figure 12-3, notice that all seven sliders are set to zero. Using Table 12-3 and Figure 12-4 as a reference, reset the EQ. It may take some experimentation to find the EQ settings that work best for your SWA files. After making your choice, click the Equalize button.

Note

The EQ settings in Table 12-3 are a good starting point but are not necessarily the optimum settings. Practice with the EQ to find the settings you prefer.

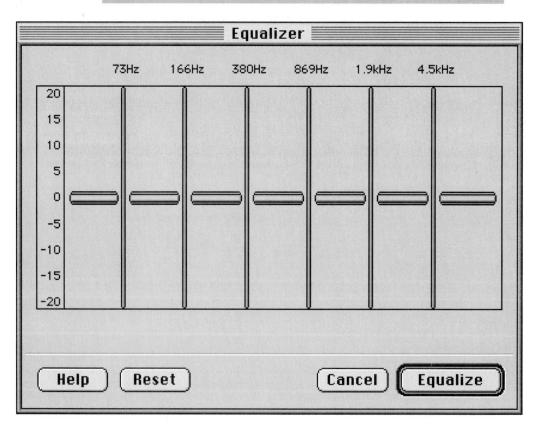

Figure 12-3
The Equalizer window before changing the settings.

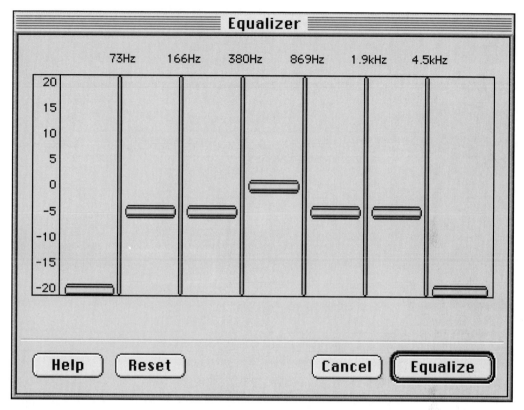

Figure 12-4
These EQ settings are recommended by Macromedia in preparing a sound file for export as a SWA file.

Table 12-3 EQ Settings

EQ settings	1	2	3	4	5	6	7
Before	0	0	0	0	0	0	0
After	–20	–5	–5	0	–5	–5	–20

There are seven control handles on the Equalization function of SoundEdit 16. Starting from left to right, use the settings in the After row from Table 12-3 as the point of reference for setting your EQ.

4. The purpose of this step is to Normalize the track (or tracks) in question. Choose Select All from the Edit menu and then choose Normalize from the Effects menu. This effect will boost the signal (on the destination track) to the maximum possible without causing clipping or distortion. For our purpose, set the effect to between 90 and 95 percent of the maximum and click Normalize (see Figure 12-5).

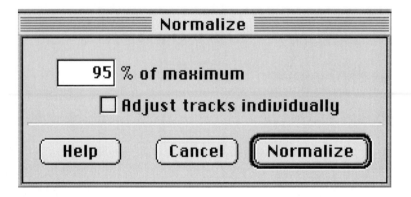

Figure 12-5
The Normalize function (or effect) is used to boost the entire signal to a level just short of distortion.

5. As the final step in preparing a file for export to SWA, choose *Shockwave for Audio Settings* from the Xtras menu. Because our target listening audience (in this case) uses 28.8 modems, the bit-rate selected is 16kbps (shown in Figure 12-6). After selecting the correct bit rate, click OK.

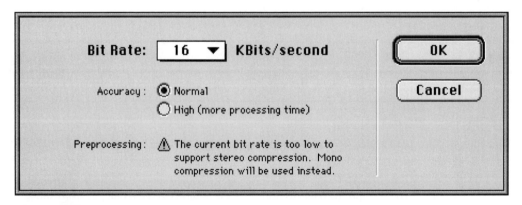

Figure 12-6
The final step in preparing a file for conversion to SWA is the Shockwave For Audio Settings in the Xtras menu.

6. To export the file CH12EX1.WAV, select Export from the File menu. If the bit rate on your sound file is less than 32Kbps, the SWA Export Xtra will automatically convert the file from Stereo to Mono. Name the new file CH12EX1.swa and make sure the Export Type is set to SWA File (see Figure 12-7). Click Save.

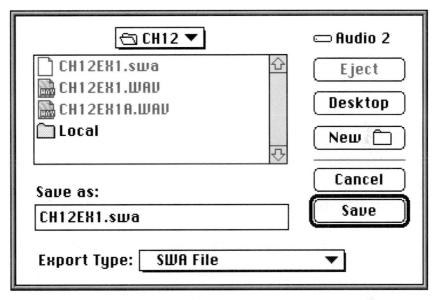

Figure 12-7
Name the new file CH12EX1.swa and make sure the Export Type is set to SWA File.

Once a SWA file is converted, the parameters are set in stone. You can't open and edit a SWA file after the conversion/export process. The settings used in this tutorial are merely a starting point and, because each music and sound file has different sonic characteristics, the optimum settings will vary. Experiment and use your own ears to discover what works best for you.

Tutorial 12-2: Auditioning a SWA file (Mac)

You've gone through the grueling process of preparing your first SWA file and now you want to hear it. Neither a bad idea, nor an unreasonable one. In the next tutorial, you'll learn how to audition SWA streaming audio files from your hard drive.

■ What you need

Here are the components you will need to accomplish this task:

- Netscape Navigator 3.0 (or better)
- The file folder named Local found in the Chapter 12 Tutorial folder
- A properly installed Shockwave Plug-in

> **CD-ROM**
>
> The files needed to complete this tutorial all reside in the folder named Local found on the CD-ROM accompanying this book.

■ Psst! Take a listen . . .

1. On the CD-ROM accompanying this book, locate the Chapter 12 tutorial folder and open it. Inside, locate the folder named Local (see Figure 12-8). Copy this folder to your hard drive.

Note

Note that the files local.dcr, local.htm, and local.swa should reside in this folder.

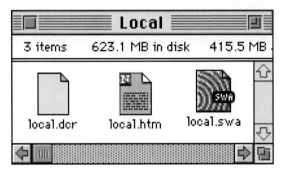

Figure 12-8
Be sure to copy the file folder Local to your hard drive.

2. Open your Netscape folder and drag and drop the file local.htm (shown in Figure 12-9) onto the Netscape Icon. Netscape will launch but you will not go online.

local.htm   Netscape Navigator™ 3.0

Figure 12-9
Drag and drop the file local.htm onto the Netscape Icon.

3. You should now be staring at a Director movie (shown in Figure 12-10) that has the look (and the feel) of a CD-Player. There are three basic controls (left to right): Stop, Play/Pause, and Volume (up and down). Press play, sit back, and listen.

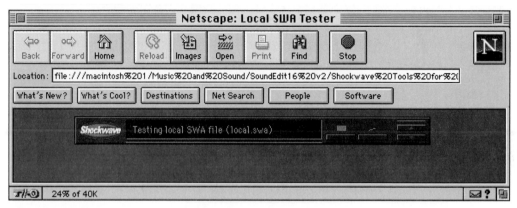

Figure 12-10
Click the Shockwave button as an alternative way to start playback of the .SWA test file.

4. Now let's take a listen to the CH12EX1.WAV file that we converted to a SWA file. Move the converted file (CH12EX1.swa) from the CD-ROM into the Local folder, as shown in Figure 12-11.

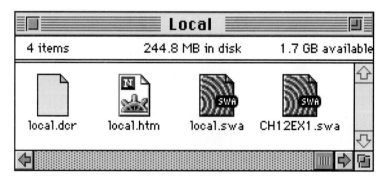

Figure 12-11
Move the file CH12EX1.swa export into the Local file folder.

5. Rename the file local.swa as local1.swa and rename the file CH12EX1.swa as local.swa as shown in Figure 12-12. This is necessary in order to playback the converted file from Tutorial 12-1.

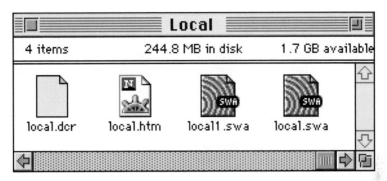

Figure 12-12
Rename the file local.swa as local1.swa and rename the file CH12EX1.swa as local.swa.

6. Now repeat Steps 2 and 3 for playback and you will hear the SWA file we converted in Tutorial 12-1.

Congratulations! You have successfully been Shocked!

Tutorial 12-3: Batch file conversions for the Mac

This is about as simple as it can get—the old drag and drop method. First, there are a few things that you must have to pull this off. I'm rightfully assuming that you SoundEdit 16 users have upgraded to at least version 2.04. If not, go to the folder MISCSOFT on the Mac portion of the CD-ROM and find "SoundEdit16 v2.0.4 Update.sea." Everything you need to upgrade SoundEdit 16 to version 2.04 can be found there.

■ What you need

Here are the other components you need to accomplish this task:

■ SoundEdit 16 version 2.04 or better.
■ Tutorial File CH12EX1.SND, CH12EX2.SND, and CH12EX3.SND

■ Macintosh Power PC

■ SWAtomator Droplet

CD-ROM

The SWAtomator Droplet is a component of SoundEdit 16 Shockwave Developer Tools for SoundEdit 16 (see the MISCSOFT folder on the CD-ROM that accompanies this book). The SWAtomator Droplet can also be found in the Chapter 12 Tutorial folder.

■ Converting by the batch

1. The first and most important component is the SWAtomator Droplet shown in Figure 12-13. Make sure this component is in the same folder as SoundEdit 16 (version 2.04).

Figure 12-13
Make sure the SWAtomator Droplet resides in the same folder as SoundEdit 16.

Note

Make sure the levels window in SoundEdit 16 is closed before proceeding to Step 2.

2. Select and drag the three tutorial files (found in the Chapter 12 Tutorial folder) and place them on the SWAtomator Droplet (shown in Figure 12-14). You will be asked "Where is SoundEdit 16 version 2?" Even if it is residing right beside the SWAtomator, as you can see in Figure 12-15, it will still ask you this question. Don't argue (I did and it didn't work); simply open the application.

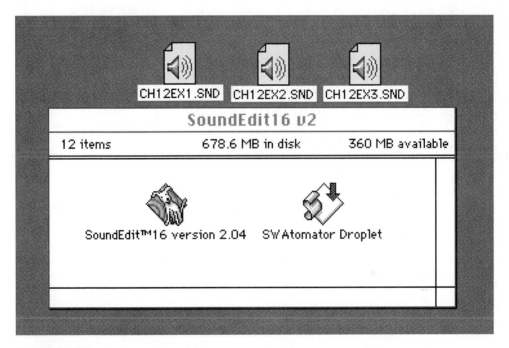

Figure 12-14
SoundEdit 16 opens to complete the batch conversion and then automatically close itself when the process is completed.

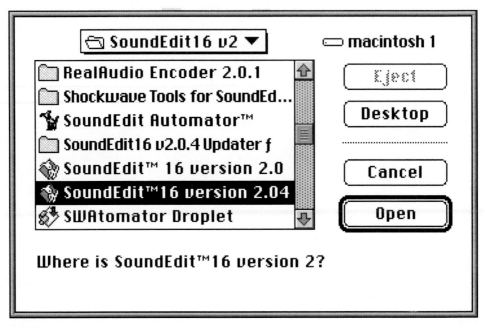

Figure 12-15
When asked "Where is SoundEdit 16 version 2," open the application.

3. The SWAtomator automatically exports and converts the files into SWA files (Figure 12-16).

Figure 12-16
This automated procedure converts the files one at a time.

Tutorial 12-3 was so much of a no brainer; I almost didn't do it, but then again you just never know. It's easy to forget that which is easy for some could be very confusing to others.

Some Advanced SoundEdit 16 Stuff

Remember Tutorial 12-1? Well, if you don't mind dropping a few extra bucks, you can pretty much bypass the first five steps of that tutorial with possibly even superior results. Using an Xtra called AudioTrack from Waves, you can prepare a sound file for conversion into a .SWA file using the presets in the AudioTrack Setup Library. To make this Xtra work, I installed AudioTrack (following the directions, no less) and placed the Setup Libraries file folder in the SoundEdit 16 file folder. Then I was ready to start rolling.

Tutorial 12-4: Using AudioTrack

1. Start the application SoundEdit 16 and select Open CH12EX4.SND from the File menu.

   CD-ROM

   File CH12EX4.SND is located in the Chapter 12 Tutorial folder on the CD-ROM.

2. Choose Select All from the Edit menu, and choose Waveshell from the Effects menu.
3. Select Audio Track Stereo. You will see the screen shown in Figure 12-17.

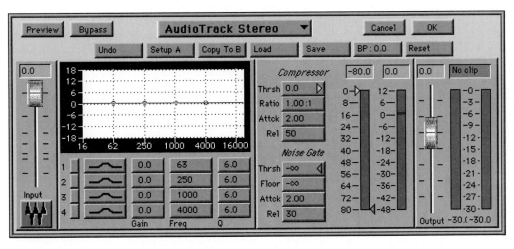

Figure 12-17
The main window of AudioTrack in the reset position.

4. Click the Load button, and select Shockwave Audio Setups from the Setup File menu. Because the target audience is the 28.8 modem crowd and the sound file is music, choose the preset 16K Music. In the main screen of Audio Track (Figure 12-18) are the settings for the preset 16K music. Use the preview feature to audition and then do the minor adjustments to tweak this sound file to your personal liking. It is also possible to save any preset that you create in Audio Track.

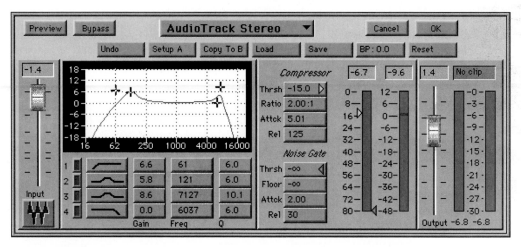

Figure 12-18
Using the preset 16K Music in the Shockwave Audio Setups is a good way to prepare an audio file for conversion to a .SWA file. Note the difference between these settings and those in Figure 12-17.

5. Click OK and the file is ready to export. You can do this by either dropping the file on the SWAtomator droplet or selecting Export from the File menu (refer back to Tutorial 12-1, Step 6).

For both convenience and better control over your preconversion sound file, I strongly recommend AudioTrack. I like having all the bells and whistles, and once you learn how to use these more complex tools, the extra control you're able to achieve will greatly enhance the end product—your sound.

More SoundEdit 16 Xtras

In my travels, I've stumbled onto some really cool tools that work well with SoundEdit 16. My hands-down favorite is the Native Power Pack from Waves. Not only is this set available as a plug-in (or Xtra, if you must) for the SoundEdit 16, but also for a number of other Mac-based software products. To make it even better, the same plug-ins are available and work with a number of Windows products, including Sound Forge 4.0 and Cakewalk. Let's say you're not very experienced in audio processing. Many of the sound processing plug-ins have presets that can be used as templates for your own custom sounds. We dive head-first into all of these plug-ins in tutorials throughout the book, but for now Table 12-4 offers just a quick look.

Table 12-4   Native Power Pack (Waves)

Product	Description	Preset Library	Mac	Windows	Stereo
Trueverb	Virtual room and reverb Processor	yes	yes	yes	yes
L1 Ultramaximizer	Digital Limiter	yes	yes	yes	
S1 Stereo Limiter	4 Stereo Image Modifiers	yes	yes	yes	
Q10 ParaGraphic EQ	Use 1 to 10 bands of Parametric EQ	yes	yes	yes	yes
C1 Compressor Gate	Compressor, Gate and Expander	yes	yes	yes	yes
WaveConvert	Multimedia Batch File Processor		yes	yes	yes

Another very reasonably priced effects Xtra for SoundEdit 16 is Cybersound FX from InVision Interactive. While these plug-ins are not as sophisticated as the products from Waves, they are very usable and a step above the effects that are included in SoundEdit 16.

Tutorial 12-5: Windows—Xtra Convert WAV to SWA

I really didn't want you Windows users to feel left out and think that the Mac was the only tool available for intense preconversion tweakage of SWA files, so after this tutorial, I'll be able to sleep a little better. However, I'll warn you in advance that I am Director-impaired and am not responsible for anything that may happen to you (or me) beyond the use and conversion of sound files. Many of the preconversion (to SWA) steps found in Tutorial 12-1 can be duplicated for Windows users using Sound Forge 4.0 or even the handy little shareware program CoolEdit 96.

Remember, your SWA file will automatically be converted to a mono file unless your bit rate is 56Kbps or higher (see Table 12-1 for reference). It's also a good idea to convert 44kHz sound files down to 22kHz before doing the SWA conversion.

What You Need

Here are the basics of what you'll need to do Tutorial 12-5:

- Macromedia Director 5 (Windows 95/NT)
- Director Convert .WAV to SWA Xtra
- Tutorial file: CH12EX05.WAV

CD-ROM

Item 2 can be found in the tutorial folder for Chapter 12 (Windows) and Item 3 in the Windows Plug-ins folder on the accompanying CD-ROM. Sorry, but we can't do anything about Item 1; you're on your own for that.

■ Doing the Windows thing

1. In Windows 95 (or NT), open the application Director 5 (shown in Figure 12-19).

Figure 12-19
The Toolbar for Director 5.

2. Choose Convert WAV to SWA from the Xtras menu (shown in Figure 12-20).

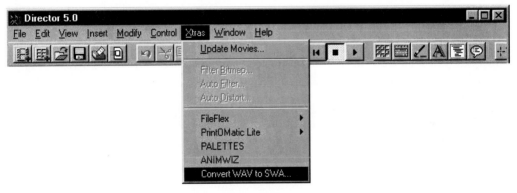

Figure 12-20
Choose Convert WAV to SWA from the Xtras menu.

3. As shown in Figure 12-21, click the Add Files button, select the tutorial file CH12EX05.WAV, and click Open. This places the file (or files) into the target folder.

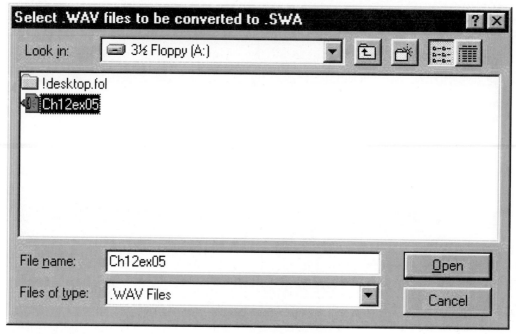

Figure 12-21
Select the Add Files button to load the tutorial WAV file.

4. Under Compression Settings (Figure 12-22), choose the proper bit rate (16kbps in this case as the target audience is 28.8 modems). Under accuracy, choose High.

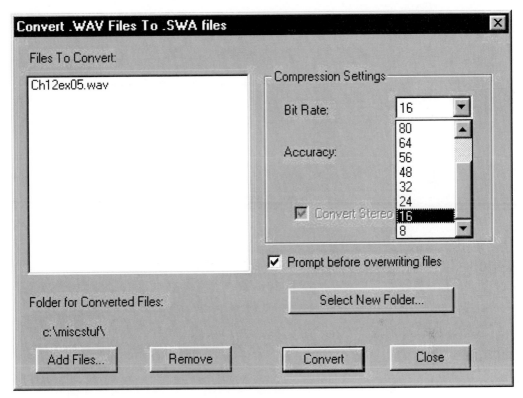

Figure 12-22
Choose the proper bit rate for the target audience.

5. Choose Select New Folder shown in Figure 12-22 and click the Select Folder button shown in Figure 12-23.

Note

At the time of going to press, the Director Convert .WAV to SWA Xtra did not offer a Save As option. The file retains the same name after conversion. As a safety measure, make sure your target folder is different from the one with your source WAVE files. This will prevent an unplanned overwrite of your source audio file.

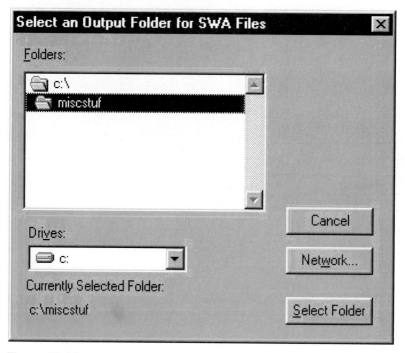

Figure 12-23
Select the destination folder.

6. Click the Convert button (see Figure 12-24) and, after the conversion, close the window and quit Director.

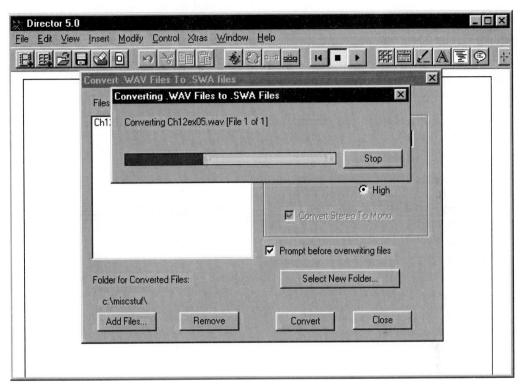

Figure 12-24
Click Convert to complete the conversion process.

One Last Look

You may be curious as to where to find all the Xtras and applications I've talked about in this chapter. Table 12-5 will answer all those questions for you (and many more!).

Table 12-5 Products and where to find them.

Product	Mac 68K	Windows	URL
Cybersound FX by InVision Interactive	68K Power PC	no	http://www.invision
Director 5 by Macromedia	68K Power PC	Windows 3.1 Win95/NT	http://www.macromedia.com
Shockwave by Macromedia	68K Power PC	Win95/NT	http://www.macromedia.com/shockwave/
SoundEdit 16 by Macromedia	68K Power PC	no	http://www.macromedia.com
AudioTrack by Waves	68K Power PC	no	http://www.waves.com
Native Power Pack by Waves	68K Power PC	Windows 3.1 Win95/NT	http://www.waves.com

One Last Thought

In the world of streaming audio, Macromedia's Shockwave Audio is, without a doubt, one of the major players. Like all of the streaming audio formats, SWA is still in its infancy and the best is yet to come. There are a lot of content developers using Director and, with the release of Director 6, you can bet that we will see more and more innovative content-rich Web sites. Shockwave Audio is one of the components that will transform the Web experience into an explosion of color and sound. Using the information and the tools featured in this chapter as a starting point, you can go out there and set the new standards for sound on the Web.

Liquid Audio

 In This Chapter

The first time I heard Web music via the Liquid MusicPlayer, I was completely stunned. It wasn't just that it sounded better than anything else I'd heard over the Web (at least at 28.8); it was how smoothly the Liquid MusicPlayer worked. No hiccups or annoying breaks in the sound stream. Considering that the PowerMac version was in alpha at the time, the fact that it worked at all was amazing in itself. Part of what makes this rather small compressed data stream sound good is the encoding process. Liquid Audio licensed and optimized technology from Dolby Labs for playback over the Web, giving the Liquid Music-Player a definite sonic edge over the competition. Oh I forgot, Liquid Audio doesn't have any competition!

I know what you're thinking, what about Real Audio? Well, we're talking apples and oranges here. The Liquid Audio plan is to be a one-stop solution for online music retailers and record companies. Now, not only will you be able to purchase a CD after previewing it (you can do that now), but you will also be able to purchase and download a single song as well. That's right—preview it, download it, and even burn it directly to a CD. The tracking system that is part of the Liquid Audio Server makes sure everyone from the Record Company and Publisher all the way down to the Artist gets paid. Someone was bound to do it eventually, but it looks as though Liquid Audio is going to change the face of the recording industry as we know it. Who knows—the artist might even actually get a little control over his or her work for a change.

 ## The Liquid MusicPlayer

I'll be as objective as I can be in this situation—I love the Liquid MusicPlayer! At first look, it seems to be just another audio player (Figure 13-1) with standard playback controls. Click on View and a whole new world opens before your eyes. Not only can you listen to the music, but all sorts of options present themselves to you as well. The lyrics, the liner notes, and the cover art are accessible at the click of a button. All this while you're listening to the music, which can be paused, fast forwarded, or stopped and started again without any glitches. This is streaming audio at its finest. If you like the music you're listening to, simply click the Order CD button and buy it. Even better—How about purchasing a song (or songs) online, downloading it to your computer, and burning it to an audio CD for playback. Just imagine the impact this is going to have on the music business. Talented artists who can't get shelf space in the record stores or radio airplay will finally be able to get worldwide exposure and sales because of the Liquid MusicPlayer. Where do I sign up?

Figure 13-1
With the Liquid Music Player, it's possible to play streaming as well as local audio files.

Web

Before you proceed, go download the latest version of the Liquid MusicPlayer. Go to http://www.liquidaudio.com.

The LiquidMusic Server

To stream Liquid Audio files to the masses via the Web, the only server solution at the time of going to press is the LiquidMusic Server. There is, however, a more affordable Windows NT solution under development, although there are no details about price or features currently available. Because the scope of this book does not include dealing with servers, here's a brief overview of the LiquidMusic Server and some of its features.

The Liquid MusicServer is able to provide any number of music streams from UNIX or Intel platforms. The audio streams are Dolby encoded, scaleable, and deliverable at six different data rates. Some of the features of the Liquid MusicServer include royalty tracking and reporting as well as copyright protection for the musical content. Secure transactions for online music retailers are just part of what the Liquid Music-Server has to offer.

Table 13-1 shows the six possible data rates for Web and Liquid MusicPlayer playback. It is possible to use the Liquid MusicPlayer as a stand-alone audio player. Purchasing and downloading CD-quality LA1 files for personal playback is not only possible, but could very well become the new standard of the recording industry via the Web.

Table 13-1 Scalable Data Rates

Data Rates	Mono	Stereo	Downloadable Audio Files
14.4	yes	no	no
28.8	yes	yes	no
ISDN 1	yes	yes	yes
ISDN 2	yes	yes	yes
Dolby Digital	yes	yes	yes
Linear PCM	yes	yes	yes

Development Tools

It doesn't matter whether you develop with a Mac or Windows machine; Liquid Audio has got the development tools that will cover your needs. The Liquifier Pro for Windows 95 and Liquifier for Pro Tools (AudioSuite plug-in) for the Mac both do the job with equal results. Probably the best thing to do is to dive in head-first with a tour and a few tutorials with the Liquifier Pro, followed directly with a look and comparison of the Pro Tools 4/Audiosuite plug-in.

The Liquifier Pro

There's a few things we need to run through before starting the Liquifier Pro tour and tutorials. The Task buttons of the Liquifier Pro are set up in such a way to step you through the logical order of the production process. The following sidebar, "The Liquifier Pro Task Buttons," gives you a brief overview of each of the six Panes and where they fit into the plan. I'm going to warn you in advance—The Liquifier is too cool.

The Liquifier Pro Task Buttons

This is an overview of each of the specific functions related to each Task. Using the tutorial in this chapter, you will go in-depth with the functions and practical uses within each Window.

1. **Media**: In the Media Pane, you can input the general recording information, including the lyrics and copyright info. Remember reading the liner notes on a record or CD? The same type of information is input here.

2. **Record**: The Record Pane is used to record audio through the sound card of your PC or to convert audio from a Red Book Audio CD.

3. **Edit**: The Edit Pane is where the audio file is prepared before encoding. There are basic editing features (cut, paste, copy, and delete, to name a few) as well as transport controls.

4. **Preview**: In the Preview Pane, you can compress the audio at different rates and settings and hear a Preview of what the general public will hear when the file is uploaded to the Web.

5. **Print**: The Print Pane takes all the parameters that were set in the Preview Pane and saves the file to disk as a LA1 (Liquid Audio) file.

6. **Publish**: The Publish Pane is used to send the Liquid Audio file to the Liquid Audio MusicServer.

CD-ROM

We have lucked out here! At the last minute, I was able to get my hands on an evaluation version of the Liquifier Pro. This can be found in the demo software folder on the CD-ROM that accompanies this book. However, for those of you using the Liquifier demo, some of the functions performed in the next tutorial will not be available to you.

Assuming that you have installed Liquifier Pro, we can get rolling.

Warning

Pentium alert! If you are not running a Windows 95 machine with a 100 mHz Pentium processor (or faster), you will be left out in the cold when trying to use Liquifier Pro. Cutting Edge means upgrade!!!!

■ Touring the Media pane

The Media pane is the data entry gateway to the 21st Century version of the album cover and liner notes. All this information is accessible to anyone listening to a song using the Liquid Audio Player. Even those of us who are poor starving musicians can create the illusion of success with a minimum of effort. There are eight different tabs in the Media pane, enabling the user to enter more information than I really would want anyone to know about me or any of my songs. Table 13-1 contains a brief description of each tab. Figure 13-2 shows the Recording tab and gives you an idea of just how simple it truly is to enter the info about your song in the Media pane.

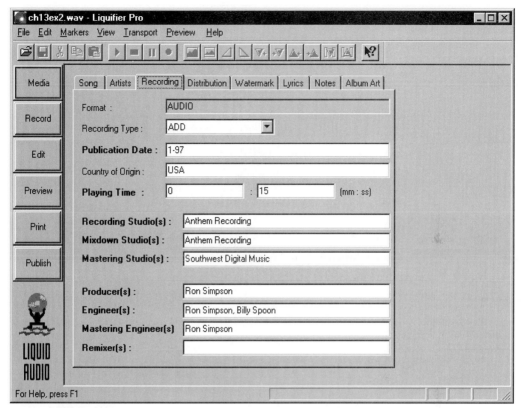

Figure 13-2
The Recording tab in the Media pane has 13 separate fields of information.

Table 13-2 The Media Pane

Media Pane Tabs	Description	No. of fields
Song	This tab includes Song Title, Album Title, and UPC Code.	10
Artists	This tab contains fields for everything from "Main Artist" to "Conductor."	7
Recording	The 13 fields that appear in this tab include Recording Studio, Engineers, and Country of Origin (see Figure 13-2).	13
Distribution	The Record Label, Publisher, and Performing/Mechanical rights agencies can be entered in this field.	4
Watermark	The Watermark tab is not currently supported in the early release version of Liquifier Pro. (We're currently at 1.0).	5

Table 13-2 The Media Pane *(continued)*

Media Pane Tabs	Description	No. of fields
Lyrics	I like this one. It's now possible to find out just what the real lyrics were to "Louie Louie."	1
Notes	This is where the artist can thank his (or her) ex for the heartbreak that made this torturously haunting song possible.	1
Album Art	The user can import a GIF file of the album cover art to be displayed with the song on the Liquid Audio Player.	2

Entering information in the Media pane is very simple. The information can be saved separately or as part of the audio file. Either way, the information is saved as a LA1 file.

▓ Touring the Record pane

The second component of Liquifier Pro is the Record pane. There are two main windows in the Record pane: CD Import and Wave Record.

CD Import

First, the good news: CD Import enables you to digitally import audio from an audio CD. Now for the bad news: Not every CD-ROM player will allow this to happen—It's a Windows driver and 32-bit addressing problem. So depending on your version of the Liquifier and Windows 95/NT and the CD-ROM driver in your system, it may or may not work. Figure 13-3 shows the CD Import window. Note that with the exception of Record Options (Figure 13-4,) all functions and controls for CD Import are available in the main (CD Import) window. Simply select a Track, click the Import button, and you're there. It doesn't get much easier than that.

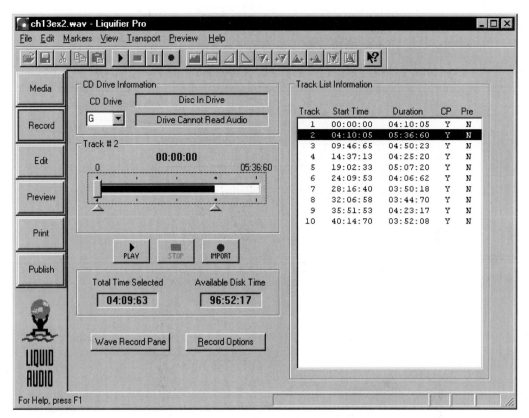

Figure 13-3
The CD Import main window.

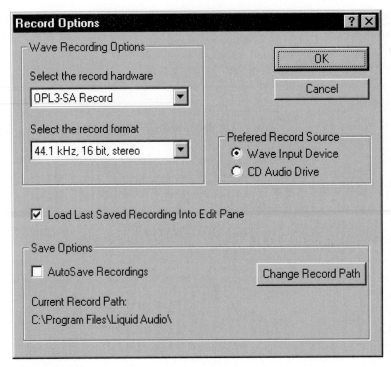

Figure 13-4
Set the Record Options for either the CD Import or Wave Record pane.

Wave Record

Just in case you might need to bring your music in via the sound card, the Record pane includes a basic WAVE recorder. There are very few options here (see Figure 13-5), although you can adjust and monitor the input levels. Basically, about all you can do here is to record and save a WAVE file.

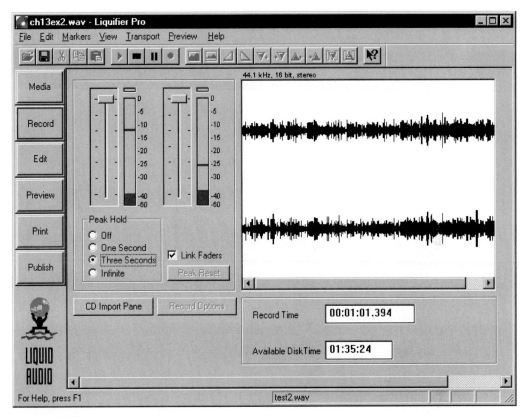

Figure 13-5
Adjust and monitor audio input in the Wave Record window.

The features in the Record pane are basic and to the point. For those who have no other recording software, it will get the job done and convert or record your audio into the WAVE files you need to move to the Edit pane, which is the subject of our first tutorial in this chapter.

Tutorial 13-1: The Edit pane

The Edit pane in Liquifier Pro offers basic WAVE editing functions as well as a few tricks of its own. Whether you use the Record pane to create your WAVE files or use another program such as Sound Forge 4.0, the Edit pane is one more step on your road to rockin' out on the Web.

■ What you need

The following components are needed to complete this tutorial:

- Liquifier Pro Software (or demo)
- A Windows 95computer using a Pentium processor
- Tutorial file ch13ex1.wav

CD-ROM

The demo version of the Liquifier Pro can be found in the Demo folder on the CD-ROM that accompanies this book. Tutorial file ch13ex1.wav is located in the Chapter 13 tutorial file.

Note

With the demo version of Liquifier Pro, you will not be able to access all of the functions of the full working copy. Some of the tutorial steps may not be possible as a result.

■ A Liquifying experience

At this point, I'm hoping you have installed the application Liquifier Pro to your hard drive. If not, do it now and let's get started.

1. Start the application Liquifer Pro. You should see the Edit window shown in Figure 13-6 on your screen. Until you load a WAVE file, it's going to look pretty gray and lonely in there. In the left side of the Liquifer Pro main screen, notice a series of six buttons (the Task Buttons). See the sidebar entitled "The Liquifier Pro Task Buttons," earlier in this chapter for a brief explanation of each.

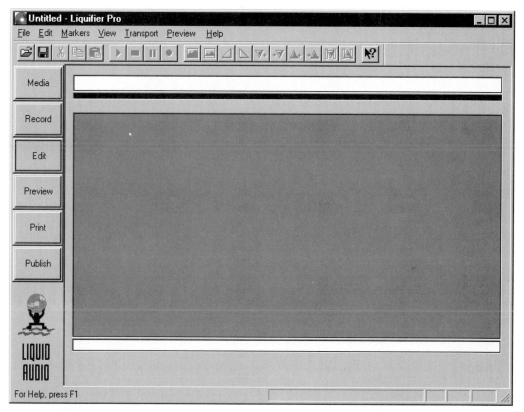

Figure 13-6
The Edit Window in Liquifier Pro.

2. Select Open from the File menu and open the file ch13ex1.wav (from the Chapter 13 tutorial folder on the CD-ROM). A stereo WAVE file should now reside in the Edit window (see Figure 13-7). Listen to the file by selecting play from the transport controls (see Figure 13-8). You may also start or pause playback with the spacebar.

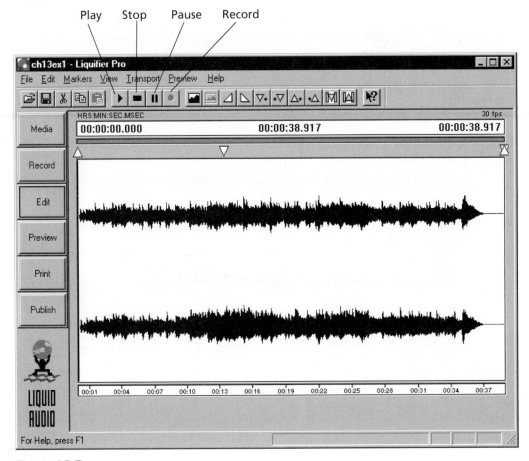

Figure 13-7
File ch13ex1.wav in the Edit window.

3. The Crop feature can be very useful in trimming off excess time and space from a WAVE file. Notice at the tail end of the file (refer back to Figure 13-7) there is a blank space about one second in duration. Not only does it eat up disk space, but unsightly background noise could reside there as well. After previewing the file, highlight the portion of the (WAVE) file you wish to keep. In Figure 13-8, note the gray area on the tail of the file, which is now set for elimination. There are several ways to accomplish this task (cut, delete, or crop). For this tutorial, select Crop from the Edit menu to complete the task.

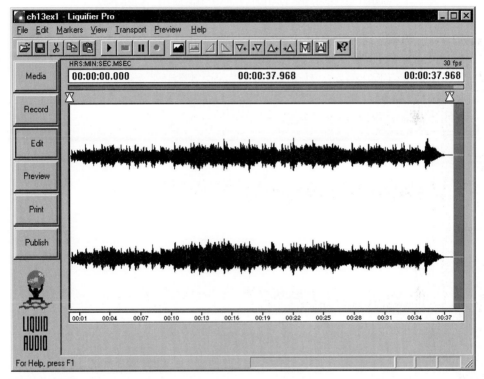

Figure 13-8
Highlight the area of the WAVE file you wish to keep. In this case, the goal is to trim one second off the tail (note that area is gray).

> **Note**
>
> Setting the Song (or Clip) Markers gives the user a way to edit the source WAVE file in a non-destructive way. The original file remains the same and only the data that is stored in RAM is affected. This gives the user the option of creating different versions without changing the original file. The user can also set an adjustable (non-destructive) fade in or out at the beginning or end of a Clip or Song.

4. Setting Clip Markers enables you to create a short song (or alternative mix, if you like) within a song. Choose Select Clip from the Markers menu. For this step, you want to select the first 15 seconds of the audio file, as shown in Figure 13-9. Place the cursor at the beginning of the file (in the Edit window) and, while holding down the left mouse button, drag the cursor across the screen until you reach the 15 second mark, then release the mouse button. Note the unselected audio is masked in gray. Choose Clip Mark Out from the Markers menu. The Markers are now set.

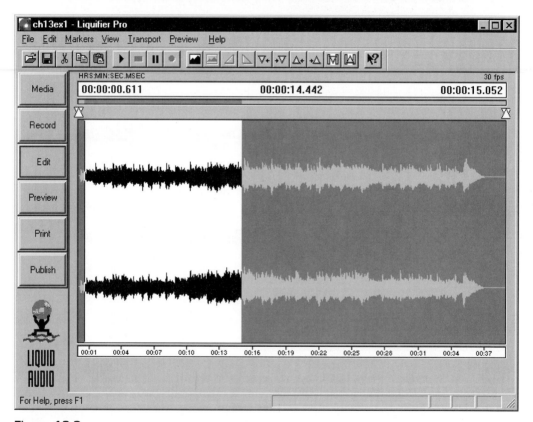

Figure 13-9
Highlight the first 15 seconds of the tutorial file then choose Select Clip from the Markers menu.

5. When playing back the file (go ahead, try it), notice that the ending is a little abrupt. The Fade In/Out feature will clear that up. Select Set Fade Length from the Markers menu. Under Clip Fade Times, select a Fade In Duration of one second and a Fade Out Duration of two seconds (see Figure 13-10). Click Apply and OK. Now all that's left to do is to insert the Fade Command. From the Markers menu, select Fade In and Fade Out. Now play the file. Notice a smooth transitional fade at the beginning and ending of the song.

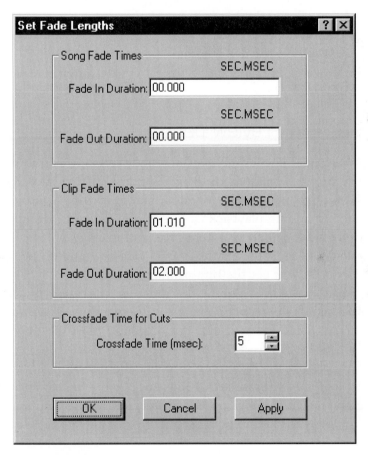

Figure 13-10
Set the Fade In and Out duration times.

■ More Edit pane tips

Remember the file you have just created is not saved. It still resides in the RAM memory waiting for you to move to the next step, the Preview Pane. You might want to repeat Steps 4 and 5 using the Song Markers in place of the Clip Markers. Doing this enables you to set up two different musical pieces (a Clip and a Song) with a separate Fade In and Out for each. Under the Markers menu are the commands Select Clip and Select Song. This feature enables you to toggle back and forth between the Clip and Song. In the Preview Pane, it is possible to save both of these musical events as separate LA1 (Liquid Audio) files.

Tutorial 13-2: The Preview pane

Hopefully, you heeded my warning and have not closed out the Clip (and or Song) data from the Edit Window as they are an important part of this next tutorial. Obviously, before moving a sound file to the Web for streaming playback, it has to be converted, compressed, and generally crunched down into a small and manageable size. There's no way to avoid it; some of the sound data is going to be tossed out. Here's where you get the opportunity to listen to what is going to be heard back over the Web at the different streaming data rates. This tutorial takes you through the process and shows you some of the options available for attaining the optimum playback of your Liquid Audio files.

For this tutorial, I'm continuing to use the file from Tutorial 13-1 as we'd left it after the last step. I repeated Steps 4 and 5, creating both a Song and a Clip, giving me two (three actually, if you count the raw WAVE file) separate mixes to convert to a Liquid Audio file.

1. From the Task buttons, select Preview. The Preview Pane, shown in Figure 13-11, should now be active on your screen.

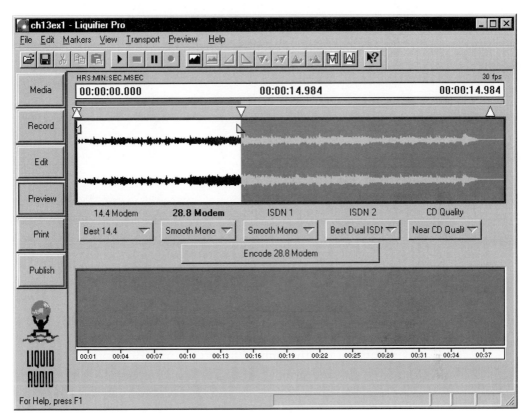

Figure 13-11
The Liquifier Pro Preview pane.

2. The next step is to encode the Clip to one of the five available LA1 data rates. Notice in the center of the Preview Pane there are five choices in regard to data rate. As shown in Figure 13-12, select 28.8. In this case, there are four preset options; select Bright Stereo 28.8.

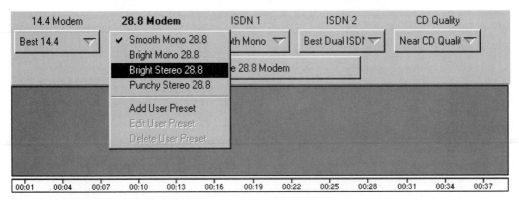

Figure 13-12
Select the data rate 28.8 modem and the preset Bright Stereo 28.8.

Note

Creating your own encoding presets is an option we will explore at the end of this tutorial.

---

3.   Click on the button Encode 28.8 Modem. There are now two separate windows containing the before and after WAVE data (see Figure 13-13). To listen back and compare the before and after, simply click on the region you wish to hear and it will become active. In this case, select the encoded file (the bottom one of the two) and press Play. Toggle back and forth to compare the difference by clicking in the region you wish to listen to and then pressing play.

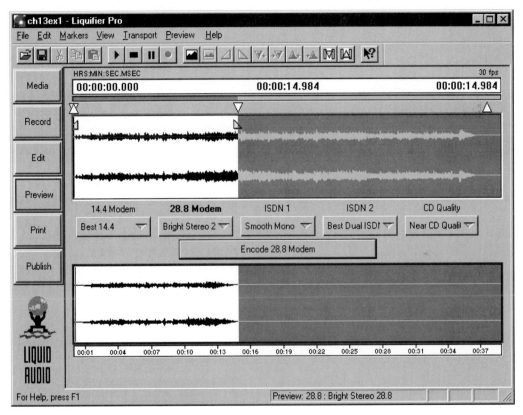

Figure 13-13
Click the region you wish to listen to for a preview of the pre and post encode audio files.

◼ More Preview pains

Assuming you like the sound of the converted file, then you're ready to move onto the next step, the Print Pane. I tried all the options (28.8) from Smooth Mono to Punchy Stereo and actually thought the Smooth Mono sounded better. It is possible to create and save your own user presets, so I experimented a little bit. Using Smooth Mono as my template, I set out to create my own Smooth Stereo file. The results were ugly and I went back to the preset Bright Stereo 28.8. Figure 13-14 shows the five basic components used in creating the encode presets. The Equalizer and Dynamics are where the user can make the most significant changes to the sound. The best thing you can do is experiment and maybe by luck or maybe by skill (or a combination of the two), you'll come up with an encode preset that changes sound on the Web as we currently know it. Let's move on to the next tutorial and print this puppy!

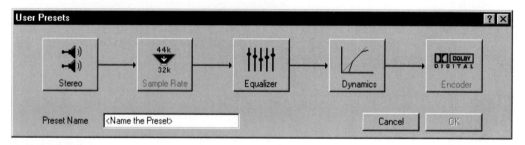

Figure 13-14
These are the five basic components that can be used in creating the encode presets in the Liquifier Pro.

Tutorial 13-3: The Print pane

At last, the time has come to actually save the your work as an LA1 file. As with the other steps in the Liquifier, this one is a walk through the park. It is possible to encode an LA1 file at five different data rates. You can also choose between Clip and Song or Clip only. What I particularly like is you can encode all 5 data rates into one LA1 file. Yet another well thought-out feature of the Liquifier. Enough of my rambling; let's get this thing saved.

1. You're now going to continue with the file you were working with in the Preview pane. Select Print from the task buttons. You now should see the main screen of the Print pane (Figure 13-15).

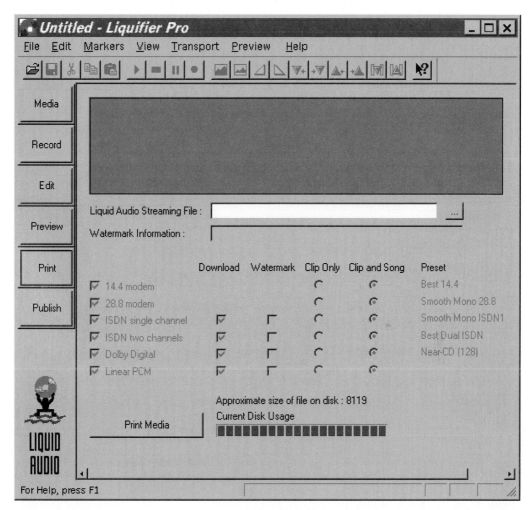

Figure 13-15
The Print pane is the last stop in turning your music into a Liquid Audio file.

2. Here is where it gets cool. Using Figure 13-16 for reference, select all six data rates, check Downloadable, and select Clip and Song. All of the information you have selected will be converted and saved into one Liquid Audio file. Sort of a six-in-one scaleable streaming audio solution.

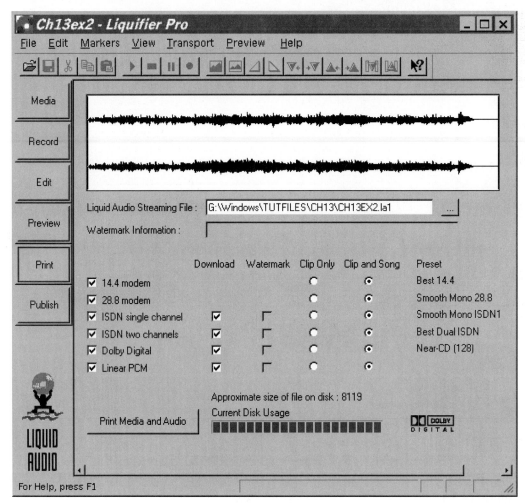

Figure 13-16
All six data rates can be incorporated into one Liquid Audio file.

> **Note**
>
> Check Downloadable only if you wish users to be able to download your file. Because the demo version of the Liquifier Pro is for evaluation only, it is not possible to complete all the steps in this tutorial as shown.

3. Name the file and select the destination (in this case, ch13ex2.la1). Click on the button Print Media and Audio found in the lower left-hand corner of the Print pane (refer back to Figure 13-16 if you can't find the button). This saves any information you may have entered in the Media pane as well as the WAVE file and the steps from the Edit and Preview pane (as an LA1 file).

That was easy. You now have a rather large LA1 file. All the information including cover art (if you loaded any into the Media pane) resides on your file. If you have no cover art, one is supplied for you in the form of a default Liquid Audio logo. Now, the last step is to move to the Publish pane.

The Publish pane

The Publish pane is the last step in getting your Liquid Audio file up on the Web. At this time, I don't have an account with a Liquid Audio server, so walking you through a tutorial of the process is not an option. Still, that's okay because it does work and like all the other steps in the Liquifier, the Publish process is simple and easy to understand and execute.

To upload your LA1 files (see Figure 13-17), you enter the server name, port number, and password, then choose the file (or files) you wish to upload, select the Publish button and the process is underway. That's it!

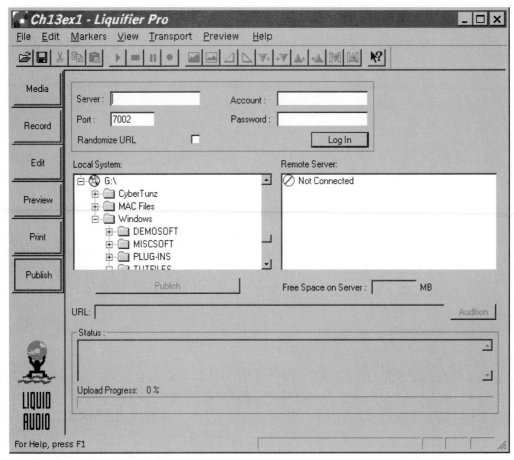

Figure 13-17
The Publish pane is the last stop in the process. To upload your LA1 files, enter
the server name, port number, and password, then choose the file (or files)
you wish to upload. Then it's simply a matter of clicking the publish button.

Note

At the time of going to press Liquid Audio announced the
addition of a Batch Pane to the Liquifier Pro.

Tutorial 13-4: Testing a LA1 file

Like me, you're probably wondering what this file we've been working on sounds and looks like now that it's been converted. Regardless of whether you're running a PowerMac or Windows machine, you can use the Liquid Music Player to play a Liquid Audio file without going online.

▓ What you need

The following components are needed to complete this tutorial:

- ▓ The Liquid Audio Player
- ▓ The file ch13ex2.la1

Web

Just in case you haven't already downloaded the latest version of the Liquid Audio Player, do it now. Go to: `http://www.liquidaudio.com` and follow the instructions.

▦ Let's go!

1. Find and open the Liquid Audio Player. Note that there is currently no media information residing in the player (see Figure 13-18). Open the file ch13ex2.la1.

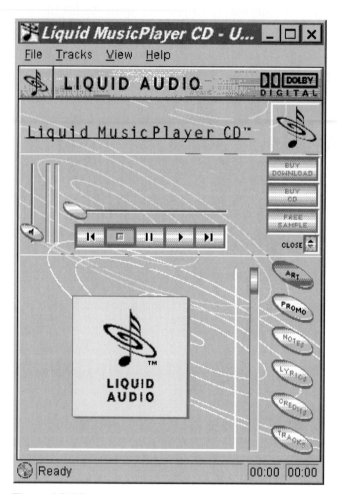

Figure 13-18
The Liquid Audio Player with no Media or Audio.

Note

After installing the Liquid Music Player for the first time, you may need to set your preferences for playback. In the case of both the PowerMac and Windows 95 versions, you can find the preferences under the File menu. The instructions are self-explanatory.

2. By clicking on the buttons Art, Info, Notes, Lyrics, and Credits (on the Liquid Music Player) you are able to check out the cover art and other relevant information about the recording artist while the music is playing.(Figure 13-19). Press play and take a listen.

Figure 13-19
The Liquid MusicPlayer with the tutorial file ch13ex2.la1 up and running.

▨ What did I learn?

The Liquifier Pro is way too easy to use. For a company that has been in existence for about 24 months (at the time of going to press), this is an incredibly well thought-out product. There may be some changes in the Liquifier by the time you read this but in the fast-paced world of Web audio that's no surprise. If some of the screens look a little different on the demo version of the Liquifier Pro that comes with the CD-ROM it's because I was able to obtain a later release version at the last minute. The edit features in the Liquifier are very basic and I recommend using something more powerful if your music needs anything other than a little basic editing. Still, if all you're looking for is just to transfer your tunes, then this package is more than adequate to get your music ready for the Web.

Liquid Audio for Pro Tools

That's right, my brothers and sisters in the land of the PowerMac, we have not been abandoned (at least not by Liquid Audio)! The Liquifier for Pro Tools (4.0) is in the building. The Liquifier Audiosuite Plug-in for Pro Tools is a scaled-down version of the Liquifier Pro, consisting of the Liquify Pane (Figure 13-20) and the Media. The functions of the Preview and Print panes in the Liquifier Pro are all condensed down into the Liquify Pane for this Pro Tools Plug-in, while Record and Edit are handled in Pro Tools itself. You probably notice that the look of the Liquify and Media panes is a bit different in this AudioSuite plug-in; however, anyone even slightly familiar with the Liquifier Pro will have no problem accomplishing the task at hand. The advantage here (over the Liquifier Pro) is the superior recording and editing environment of Pro Tools. The more options the better!

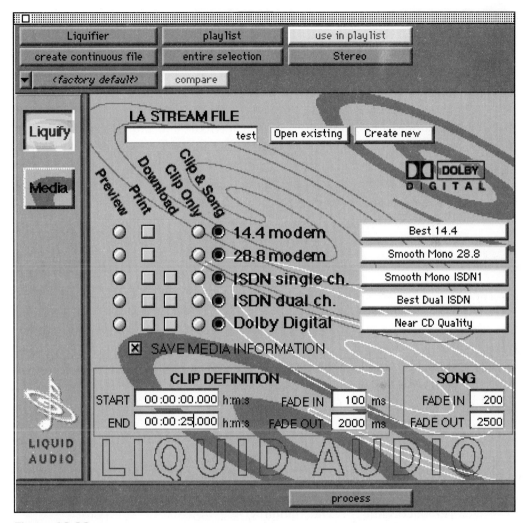

Figure 13-20
The Liquify pane in this Pro Tools plug-in combines may of the functions of
the Preview and Print panes in the Liquifier Pro.

Real Media and Liquid Audio

Just when I was thinking about what will happen when Real Audio and Liquid Audio meet in battle, I see a press release about them joining forces. Another corporate merger? Hardly; but possibly a meeting of the minds, which is much better. RealNetworks is taking a stab at creating a streaming audio protocol with Real Media and Liquid Audio is one of many companies that looks to be jumping on the Real Media bandwagon. To see how it's going to work and how it might effect your plans for sound on the Web, go to Chapter 11, "Real Audio," for the lowdown. Also at the very last minute Microsoft and Liquid Audio are partnering up as well. Who'd have figured that one?

The Bottom Line

Does it work well and does it sound good? Yes! Every musician and independent producer that has been looking for a way to bring product to market while bypassing the traditional channels will find their saving grace in Liquid Audio. The Liquifier Pro works like a charm and the LA Player is great (and free). You can bet that as soon as I'm done with this book, I'll be putting my own music package together and getting it up on a Liquid Audio Server for the world to hear. I guess that means I'm giving Liquid Audio a thumbs up!

Table 13-3   Liquid Audio Products

Product Name	Description	Cost
Liquid MusicPlayer	Power Mac System 7.5 Windows 95 (Pentium)	free (download)
Liquifier Pro	Windows 95 (Pentium)	$995.00
Liquifier Pro Tools	Audio Suite Plug-in for Pro Tools 4.0	$595.00
Liquid MusicServer	The Liquid Audio Server	$5K to $20K

Table 13-4 Liquid Audio Resources on the Web

Company or Organization	Description	URL
E_Mod	online music retailer	`http://www.e-mod.com`
IUMA (Internet Underground Music Archive)	alternative online music retailerLiquid MusicServer enabled site.	`http://www.iuma.com`
Liquid Audio	download free Liquid MusicPlayer	`http://www.liquidaudio.com`
Music Boulevard	online music retailer	`http://www.musicblvd.com`
Music 411	online music retailer	`http://www.music411.com`
911 Entertainment	online music retailer	`http://www.911entertainment.com`

Beatnik!

 In This Chapter

My first impressions of a real live Beatnik (a pre-hippie character back in the early 60's) was shock, then amazement, and finally wonder. My first sonic exposure to the Beatnik Web Music System was not all that different. What knocked me out (in the Beatnik demo) was not only the good sound but the relatively small file size and the Beatnik Editor itself. This chapter offers a basic guide through the development tools used in creating music and sound with Beatnik.

There was a point where I battled internally with myself about where and how to present this chapter. Did Beatnik deserve its own chapter or was it just more MIDI on the Web? By the time I completed the first tutorial in this chapter, there was no doubt—Beatnik is a powerful Web audio tool. There are still a few sound quality issues that I have, especially in regards to the stock General MIDI Beatnik sound set, but I'll

address those as we go. Figure 14-1 shows the splash screen when you
open Beatnik.

Figure 14-1
The splash screen of Beatnik from Headspace.

Web

To get the full feel and sound of just what Beatnik is, go to:
`http://www.headspace.com/beatnik` and download
the Beatnik Demo. While you're there, download and install
the Beatnik plug-in. At the time of going to press, you could
only get full and proper use of the Beatnik plug-in by Using
Netscape Navigator 3.0 or better. It's a Java thing.

What It Is and Isn't

Listening to the Beatnik demo (PowerMac only at this time), you are given the impression that Beatnik is *the* complete solution for high-quality audio on the Web and in fact the demo knocked me out. However, my impression after importing (and playing back) a Standard MIDI file into the Beatnik Editor was a little foggy. Like real life, the only way to find out for sure is to dig in and take a test drive. So, let's go see what we can find out.

Tutorial 14-1: MIDI to Beatnik

In this first tutorial, we take a General MIDI file and optimize it to reach the maximum sonic potential available using Banks 1 and 2 in the Beatnik Editor. While there are some great editing features in the Beatnik Editor, it is not a sequencer. Fortunately, using the feature "Link To Sequencer" it is possible to use the Headspace Audio Engine in the Beatnik Editor as an external MIDI module. Headspace recommends (as do I) Vision 3.0 (or better) from Opcode.

For this tutorial, I created a short General MIDI sequence (CH14TUT1.MID) using a Yamaha MU50 sound module (or Tone Generator, as Yamaha likes to call them) and Vision 3.0 from Opcode.

> **Note**
>
> When creating a sequence and using the Headspace Audio Engine (in the Beatnik Editor) as the playback synthesizer, you may notice a considerable MIDI delay. It is best to use a different General MIDI synthesizer (or module) to create the content if precise timing is important to you (and it should be).

■ What you need

To create this tutorial, I used a number of specific components (both hardware and software) that are listed as follows:

- Apple PowerMac 8500/120
- Studio Vision 3.08
- Studio 4 MIDI Interface
- Yamaha MU50 (Tone Generator)
- The Beatnik Editor
- Tutorial MIDI file CH14TUT1.MID

CD-ROM

The MIDI file CH14TUT1.MID can be found on the CD-ROM in the Chapter 14 tutorial file.

Web

At the time of going to press, a beta version of the Beatnik Editor was available as a free download at `http://www.headspace.com/beatnik`.

■ The steps

Just in case you only have some or even none of these components, don't worry—You can listen to the results by playing back the file CH14TUT1.MID.

1. Start the application Beatnik Editor. You are asked to "Get A Session File." Click on New and name the Session EX1.

   So what exactly is a Session? The Beatnik Editor calls the environment in which you work and edit a Session. This makes sense as we're allegedly working in a musical environment. Refer to Figure 14-2 for a look at the Real Time Window in the Beatnik Editor.

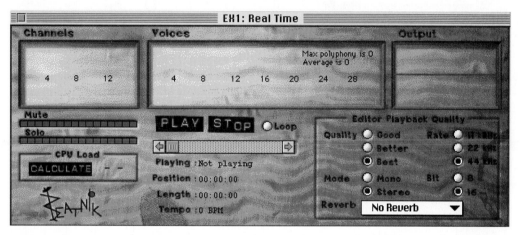

Figure 14-2
The Real Time Window of the Beatnik Editor.

2. Open your sequencer (Vision or Studio Vision 3.0 or better) and load (or import) the file CH14TUT1.MID. This particular sequence uses three separate tracks and MIDI channels as shown in Figure 14-3. Using a sequence featuring piano, bass, and ride cymbal will give you a good idea of the overall sound quality of the General MIDI sound set.

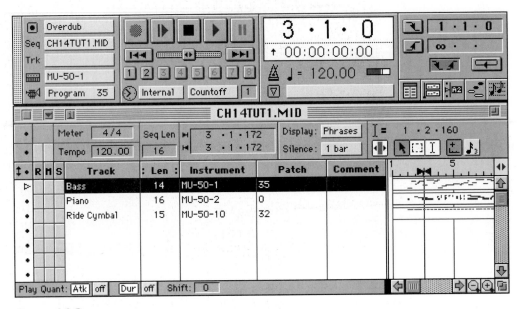

Figure 14-3
File CH14TUT1.MID in Vision 3.0.

3. Go back to the Beatnik Editor and select Link To Sequencer from the File menu. You are given two different options, OMS or the Apple MIDI Manager. In this case, OMS is the choice to make (see Figure 14-4).

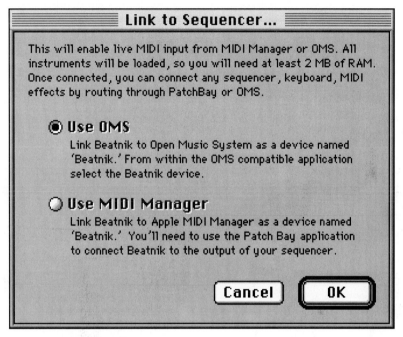

Figure 14-4
When linking the Beatnik Editor to a sequencer, choose between OMS and Apple's MIDI Manager. In this instance, choose OMS.

Note

OMS (Open Music System) is Opcode's way for the Mac to deal with assigning and routing MIDI information.

4. Currently, the Beatnik instruments do not reside in the sequencer's (Vision) Instrument set up. To preview and edit this sequence using the General MIDI sound set residing in the Beatnik Editor, you need to add three instruments to the MIDI Instruments in Vision. Select Instruments (or Option I) from the Windows menu. Access the Instrument Window Menu (click the button shown in Figure 14-5) and choose New Instrument to add three new Beatnik Instruments to the setup. You need to select an individual MIDI channel for playback of each instrument. Use Figure 14-5 as your reference for these settings. After adding the Beatnik instruments to the Vision instruments setup, you can audition and edit the sequence using the Headspace Audio Playback engine as the General MIDI sound source.

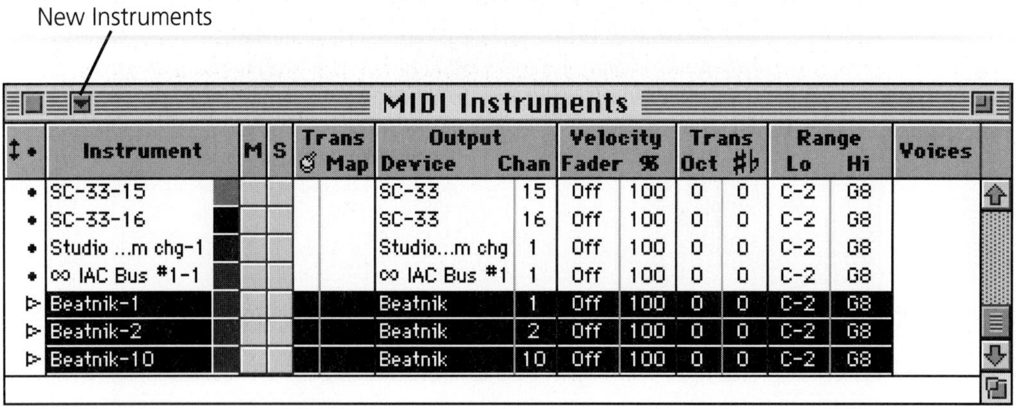

New Instruments

‡ •	Instrument	M	S	Trans ♂ Map	Output Device	Chan	Velocity Fader %	Trans Oct ♯♭	Range Lo	Hi	Voices
•	SC-33-15				SC-33	15	Off	100	0 0	C-2	G8	
•	SC-33-16				SC-33	16	Off	100	0 0	C-2	G8	
•	Studio ...m chg-1				Studio...m chg	1	Off	100	0 0	C-2	G8	
•	∞ IAC Bus #1-1				∞ IAC Bus #1	1	Off	100	0 0	C-2	G8	
▷	Beatnik-1				Beatnik	1	Off	100	0 0	C-2	G8	
▷	Beatnik-2				Beatnik	2	Off	100	0 0	C-2	G8	
▷	Beatnik-10				Beatnik	10	Off	100	0 0	C-2	G8	

Figure 14-5
Click the Instrument Window Menu button and select New Instrument.

5. The next step is to edit the example sequence and optimize it for export to the Beatnik Editor. I've made two copies of the original sequence and have made a few minor changes so we can look and listen to the difference. CH14TUT2.MID will use the General MIDI sound set (from Bank 1) and CH14TUT3.MID will use the Special Instruments sound set (Bank 2) for playback. To keep it simple, I changed only the Instrument Patch #, Volume, and Reverb Depth using the Event Editor in Vision (shown in Figure 14-6). Refer to Table 14-1 for the basic info on each of the three sequences.

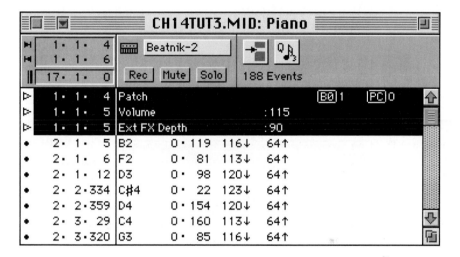

Figure 14-6
In Step 5, The Event Editor in Vision is being used to change the Volume, Patch #'s, and Reverb depth of each sequence.

6. The next step is to Export each of the MIDI files and place them in the Beatnik Editor Folder (see Figure 14-7). Select Export As MIDI File from the File menu. Name the MIDI file, check the Multitrack box, and click Export. When completed, close the application Vision.

Figure 14-7
Export the tutorial MIDI files to the Beatnik Editor Folder.

7. You are now ready to go to work in the Beatnik Editor. Select Import from the File menu and import the files CH14TUT1.MID, CH14TUT2.MID, and CH14TUT3.MID. When finished, select Songs Window (or use Command 4) from the Windows menu. All three MIDI files should now reside in the Songs Window, as shown in Figure 14-8. To playback any of these sequences, simply double click on the file in the Sound Window and you have noise.

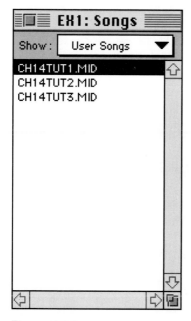

Figure 14-8
Simply double click on a file in the Songs Window to start playback in the Beatnik Editor.

8. You now have three minor variations of the same sequence loaded into the Songs Window. Click each of them to initiate playback and see if you notice a difference. The differences are very subtle, such as the level of Reverb and a slightly different piano and bass patch in each version of the sequence. In the bottom right-hand corner of the Realtime Window (see Figure 14-9), are the settings for Editor Playback Quality. This is where the user (that's you and me) gets to play with the sound quality of a file for preview in the Beatnik Editor. As you can see in Figure 14-9, you can change the bit rate and sample depth as well as the overall sound quality. Experiment with the different settings and see what you come up with. In the next tutorial (14-2), we will convert these imported MIDI files into the real thing, RMF files. Remember to leave the Beatnik Editor up and running to continue on to the next tutorial. But first . . .

Figure 14-9
The Editor Playback Quality controls are found in the Real Time Window.

Table 14-1 Sequence stats for tutorial sound files

Track Name	Sound Source	Bank #	Patch #	Reverb Depth	Volume	Instrument Name
Sequence Stats: CH14TUT1.MID						
Bass	MU50	1	35	0	100	Fretless Bass
Piano	MU50	1	0	64	100	Grand Piano
Ride Cymbal	MU50	1	32	90	110	Jazz Kit
Sequence Stats: CH14TUT2.MID						
Bass	Beatnik	1	32	0	100	Acoustic Bass
Piano	Beatnik	1	0	80	100	Piano
Ride Cymbal	Beatnik	1	0	90	110	GM Percussion
Sequence Stats: CH14TUT3.MID						
Bass	Beatnik	2	35	0	100	Fretlass Bass
Piano	Beatnik	2	0	90	100	Grand Piano
Ride Cymbal	Beatnik	2	32	90	110	GM Percussion

▨ But first ... Groovoids

I sort of stumbled onto the Groovoids by accident the first time I went into the Songs Window. You have three choices from the pull-down menu in the Songs Window: All, User Songs, and Groovoids. All is obvious, User Songs fit into the category of the MIDI files we imported into the Beatnik Editor in Tutorial 14-1, and then there's the Groovoids, which I'll now explain.

Groovoids can be used as button sounds, stingers, or as short musical interludes. Some of the Groovoids are musical and loop flawlessly, while others fall more into the sound effects category. Then there are others that sort of defy category. You can audition any one of the 50 different Groovoids that are built into the Beatnik Editor by highlighting your choice and double clicking on it in the Songs Window (see Figure 14-10). I really feel that Groovoids are a cool addition to the whole Beatnik package and will come in handy to the user who has little to no musical abilities but still wants some custom music and sound.

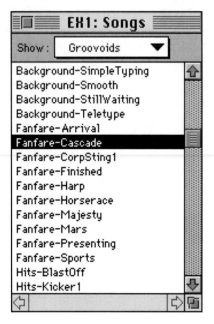

Figure 14-10
For playback, double click on any Groovoid in the Songs Window of the Beatnik Editor.

Web

For the most up-to-date info on Beatnik and Groovoids, go to: `http://www.headspace.com/beatnik/`

CD-ROM

Just a reminder—All the files needed to do each of the tutorials can be found on the CD-ROM accompanying this book. Look in the tutorial file folder that corresponds to the chapter you're working on.

Tutorial 14-2: Converting to RMF

Rich Music Format (RMF) was created by Headspace as a way to combine MIDI and audio samples into one format. In this tutorial, you will take one of the MIDI files you imported into the Beatnik Editor in Tutorial 14-1 and walk through the process of converting it into an RMF file.

■ What you need

Tutorial 14-2 is sort of a continuation of 14-1. Here's a list of what you need to continue.

- Beatnik Session file EX2
- Apple PowerMac (or clone)
- Vision or Studio Vision 3.0 or better
- Mac compatible MIDI Interface
- The Beatnik Editor

RMF, here we come!

1. Open the Beatnik Editor and load the session EX2. Go to the Songs Window and under User Songs select the Song CH14TUT2.MID.In the Real Time Window of the Beatnik Editor, take notice of the Loop button (directly to the right of Play and Stop). Clicking on the loop button causes the file to loop continuously during playback. This can be helpful when making adjustments to the Editor Playback controls.

    Press Play to audition the file CH14TUT2.MID in the Beatnik Editor. Some of you (the less adventurous) may be unfamiliar with the settings that control the Editor Playback Quality (please refer to Figure 14-11). With the Beatnik Editor, you can set the Sample Rate, Bit Depth, Overall Sound Quality, Reverb Type, and choose between Mono or Stereo. This can be done in real time during playback of a song in the Beatnik Editor. Unless you are using custom samples that take up a large amount of space, always use the highest settings available. This ensures that the end user will have a more pleasant listening experience.

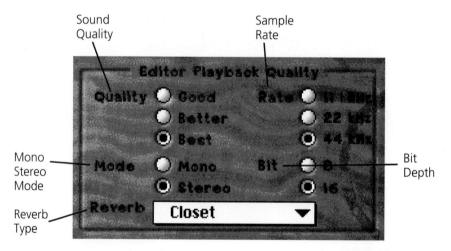

Figure 14-11
Adjust the file attributes in the Editor Playback Quality window located in the Realtime Window of the Beatnik Editor.

2. In this step, we deal with previewing the different Reverb types in the Editor Playback Quality section of the Real Time (refer back to Figure 14-11). If you remember, we set the Reverb depth in the MIDI file during Tutorial 14-1, Step 5. The rate of Reverb depth is set in stone at this point, but the Reverb type is not. In Table 14-2 is a list of the eight possible Reverb settings available in the Beatnik Editor. In this instance, choose Closet as your reverb type; it has a more subtle effect than Cavern. To access a menu with the different types

of Reverb, click on the arrow next to the Reverb type in the Editor Playback Quality Window. This enables you to access the Reverb Type pulldown menu. If you're not already listening to the song while making the changes in Editor Playback Quality, then press Play to preview the effect it has.

Note

Once you've exported a file to RMF, it can't be opened or changed. Be sure you are happy with *all* aspects of the sound file before you export it to RMF.

3. One of the advantages of saving your music and sound to the RMF format is that it can't be opened or altered in any way. You can embed all copyright and licensing info in the RMF file, making theft and unauthorized reuse of your sound file a moot point. From the Windows menu, select Songs Window and then CH14TUT2.MID. Now select Copyright (command Y) from the Song menu. This is where you enter the song title, composers name, copyright date, performer, and any other information you feel is relevant. This data will be permanently encoded into the RMF file after the conversion. Refer to Figure 14-12 as an example of what type of information to input. Click OK when finished.

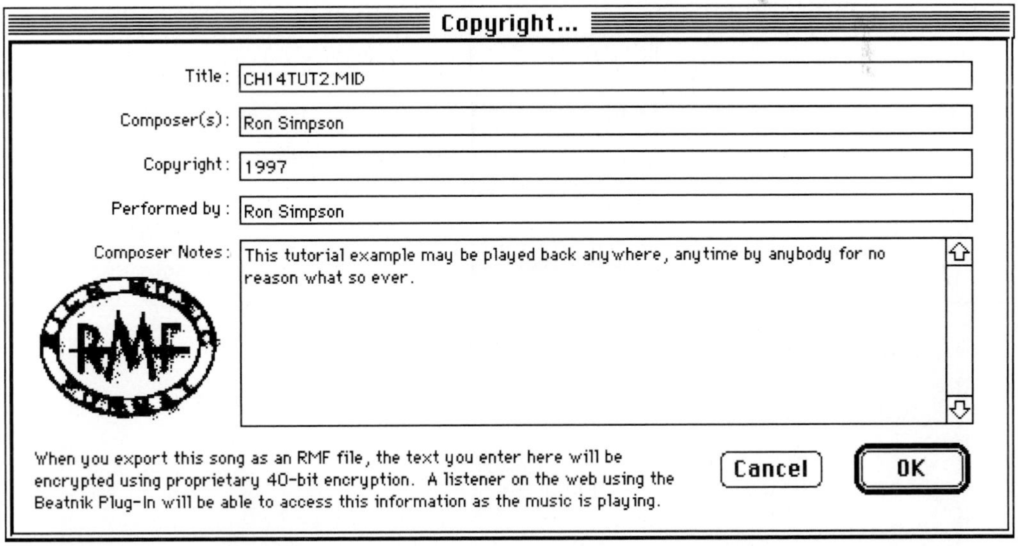

```
╔══════════════════ Copyright... ══════════════════╗
║                                                    ║
║        Title: │CH14TUT2.MID                      │ ║
║                                                    ║
║  Composer(s): │Ron Simpson                       │ ║
║                                                    ║
║    Copyright: │1997                              │ ║
║                                                    ║
║ Performed by: │Ron Simpson                       │ ║
║                                                    ║
║ Composer Notes: │This tutorial example may be    │⇧║
║     _____      │played back anywhere, anytime by│ ║
║    /RMF \       │anybody for no reason what so   │ ║
║   |      |      │ever.                           │ ║
║    \____/       │                                │⇩║
║                                                    ║
║ When you export this song as an RMF file, the text you enter here will be  ║
║ encrypted using proprietary 40-bit encryption. A listener on the web using the  ┌─────────┐ ┌────────┐ ║
║ Beatnik Plug-In will be able to access this information as the music is playing.  │ Cancel │ │   OK   │ ║
║                                                    └─────────┘ └────────┘ ║
╚════════════════════════════════════════════════════╝
```

Figure 14-12
The Copyright information is unalterably embedded in the RMF file upon export.

4. **Song Settings**: This is the last step before actually exporting the file. Select Song Settings from the Song menu. Using Figure 14-13 for reference, notice you have three different settings: Reverb Type, Tempo, and Volume Gain.

The *Reverb* settings are the same as those in the Editor Playback Quality section of the Real Time Window with a couple of minor exceptions. Small Footprint and Variable are not included and a setting called Default Reverb is present. My only explanation for this at present is I'm working with the first Beta release of the Beatnik Editor. (In other words, when in doubt, blame it on the Beta!). See Table 14-2 for a list of the Reverb settings.

The *Tempo* setting is easy. This feature is used to speed up or slow down your sequence. There is currently no undo for this feature so once you make the adjustment you live with it. I suggest you have several different copies of your sequence in the Songs Window just in case.

If the musical event is a little (or a lot) too soft or loud, the *Volume Gain* setting is your one last chance to make things right before export. For this tutorial, don't mess with the Tempo or Volume Gain (unless you're feeling rebellious or just really want to) and make sure the Reverb is set to Closet. Click OK when finished.

Note

I thought I should remind you that as this book goes to press the Beatnik Editor is still in Beta and some of the quirks that are in the version used for this tutorial may no longer exist. There could be minor changes such as reverb types in the release version.

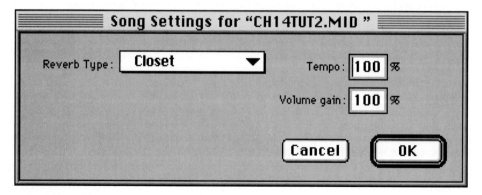

Figure 14-13
Adjust the Reverb, Tempo, and Volume Gain in the Song Settings Window.

5. **Export RMF**: The moment of reckoning has arrived. It's time to turn all this sweat, grief, and anger (on my part anyway) into an RMF file. Select Export RMF from the File menu. In Figure 14-14, notice that all the different instruments that are part of the musical sequence are up for one last review. This gives you one last chance to eliminate a possible mistake. (Where did that crash cymbal come from?) In this case, click the All button and then click OK. The results are CH14TUT2.rmf.

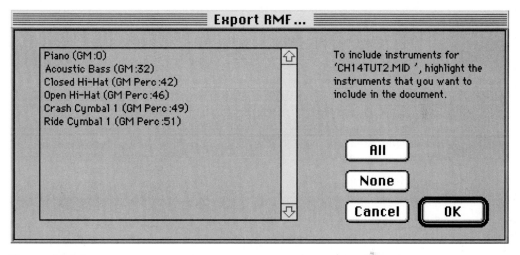

Figure 14-14
The final step is to export file CH14TUT2.MID to RMF.

Table 14-2 Reverb Settings in the Realtime Window

#	Reverb Type
1	No Reverb
2	Closet
3	Garage
4	Acoustic Lab
5	Dungeon
6	Cavern
7	Small Footprint
8	Variable

◼ You are there

There are a lot of variables and possibilities when preparing a file in the Beatnik Editor for export to the RMF. The purpose of these tutorials is to give you a feel for how things work. Then it's up to you to create something different and unique using the tools that are available, which in this case would be the Beatnik Editor. With all its strengths and shortcomings combined, the Beatnik Editor is something fairly unique as it was designed for one purpose: creating sound for the Web. So, let's continue and look at a few more features of the Beatnik Editor.

Tutorial 14-3: Importing an audio file

The ability to Import, Edit, and assign an audio file is one of the features that makes Beatnik not just another MIDI on the Web technology. Unfortunately at the time of going to press, all that was available to me was a Beta version of the Beatnik Editor and currently there is no way to audition many of the sample editing functions. This is a pain, but have no fear. In the first commercially released version of the Beatnik Editor 1.0, you will be able to audition sounds during editing using either the keyboard window (see Figure 14-15) or while linked to a MIDI sequencer. The good news is I can take you through the process and give you a brief tour of the features. I've been assured by the folks at Headspace that the public release version of the Beatnik Editor will be up and running before you even get a chance to read this book. So let's get rolling.

Figure 14-15
The Keyboard Window in the Beatnik Editor can be used to audition the different instruments.

■ What you need

Here's a short list of what you need to do this tutorial.

- ■ Beatnik Session EX3
- ■ Tutorial sound file newsteps2

> **CD-ROM**
>
> The files for Tutorial 14–3 can be found in the Chapter 14 Tutorial folder on the CD-ROM.

■ Steps to import

1. In the Beatnik Editor, select Session EX3 from the File menu. Next, Import the file newsteps2 (the audio file found on the CD-ROM accompanying this book). Select Samples Window from the Window menu. Note the AIFF newsteps2 will now reside in the Samples Window (refer to Figure 14-16).

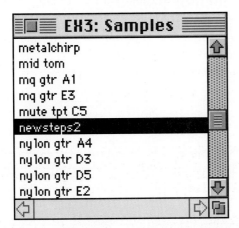

Figure 14-16
The AIFF newsteps2 now resides in the Samples Window.

2. **Sample Settings**: In the Samples Window (select Samples Window from the Window menu), double click on the sample newsteps2 or select Sample Settings from the Sample menu; this gets you to the Sample Settings Window shown in Figure 14-17. The attributes of the file are displayed in this window and you can change the sample name as well. The loop function is pretty rudimentary and it's best to do your looping in another editor. Press Play to audition the file newsteps2. As you can see in Figure 14-17, the sample newsteps2 is a 16-bit 22.050 K mono file.

Note

The file newsteps2 is set to loop seamlessly. Content-wise, it is a Robot taking four rather loud stomping footsteps.

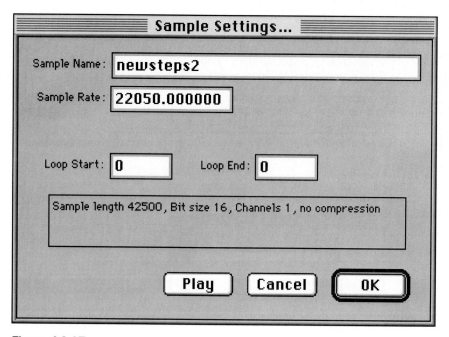

Figure 14-17
The Sample Settings Window.

3. **Compression**: There are four options for compression of your samples (see Figure 14-18). I chose None as the sample was relatively small in file size. If you were going to playback this (or any other) sample via the Web, your best bet for compression would be IMA 4:1. While this doesn't shrink the playback size of a file, it can reduce storage and download by around 75 percent. That will speed things up considerably.

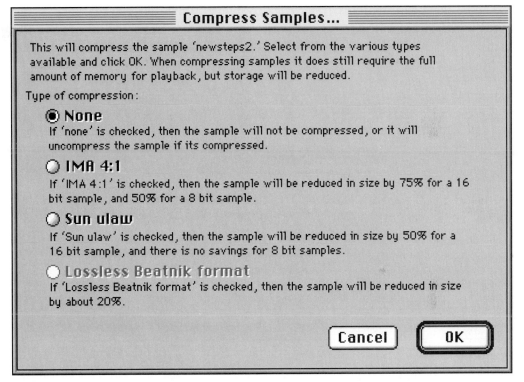

Figure 14-18
Compressing a sample reduces the storage (but not playback) size of a sample.

Importing an audio file is by no means a difficult task. It's what you do with the file once you get it into the Editor that really counts. Because of the limitations of this early beta version of the Beatnik Editor, it's not really possible to do a tutorial that can really show off the editing capabilities in the Instruments Window. However, there's nothing here to stop me from giving you a tour.

Touring the Instrument Window

In the Instrument Window, you have access to potentially three different banks of up to 128 different instruments (per bank), plus as many as 128 percussion sounds in each bank of percussion sounds. Any sound can be auditioned by highlighting the instrument and using the keyboard window (refer back to Figure 14-15) for playback.

■ **Bank 1GM Instruments :** This is a set of 128 General MIDI sounds with a Bank of General MIDI percussion (see Figure 14-19).

Figure 14-19
Bank 1 of the Instruments Window in the Beatnik Editor.

■ **Bank 2 Special Instruments:** Bank 2 consists of 128 custom instruments (and a percussion bank) created by Headspace for the use and abuse of the those in possession of the Beatnik Editor.

■ **Bank 3 User Instruments:** Bank 3 has room for 128 Instruments and a full percussion bank as well. This is where you can take existing instruments and edit them to your own tastes or create new ones with audio samples that the user can Import into the Beatnik Editor.

I guess now's as good a time as any to take a look into the editing features available to us in the Instrument Window.

1. Just to make it interesting (for me anyway), I copied the patch Tremelo
Electric Piano (#5) from the Special Instruments Bank. When copying a
patch in preparation to move it to another location, you are asked if you
want to include the samples in your instrument copies (see Figure 14-20).
Because the sample source of my instrument already resides within the
Beatnik Editor, in this case the answer is no. I then pasted Tremelo Electric
Piano into location #0 of (User) Bank 3.

Figure 14-20
When copying an Instrument, you have the option of copying the
Instrument Samples as well.

2. **The Keymap Window**: This is the first stop in building a custom musical instrument from the samples that reside in the Beatnik Editor. By selecting individual samples and linking them to zones (see Figure 14-21), you can create a custom musical instrument. I'm using the Tremelo Electric Piano (currently in Bank 3 Location #0) as the example.

> **Note**
>
> Move any musical instrument you wish to edit to one of the user locations in Bank 3.

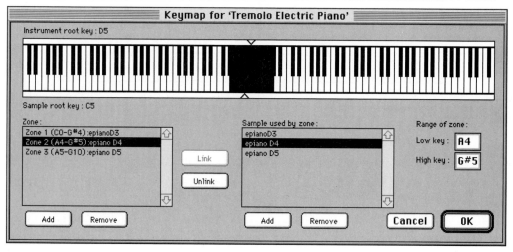

Figure 14-21
Use the Keymap Window to add samples and link them into zones.

3. **Modulation:** One of the great aspects of the Beatnik Editor is the ability to assign synthesizer-type controls to an instrument. Selecting Modulation under the Instruments pull-down menu permits you to use Low Frequency Oscillators (LFOs) to reshape the sound of your custom Instrument. In the Modulation Window, there is a choice of six different LFO Types, Six Wave Shapes, and the option of using preset or custom envelope types (see Figure 14-22).

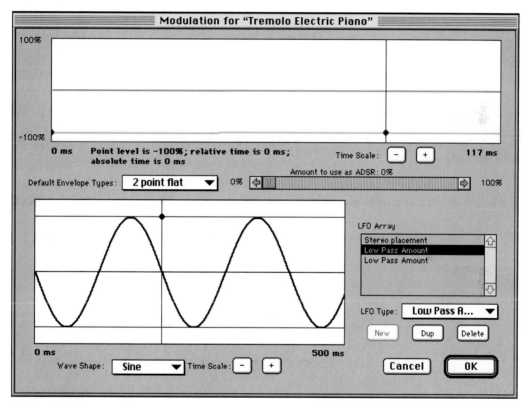

Figure 14-22
The Beatnik Editor allows the use of LFOs to shape the sound of individual instruments.

4. **Volume:** This feature enables the user to create or modify an instrument's volume envelope (see Figure 14-23). There are preset envelopes or you can create one from scratch. New Instruments have no volume envelope therefore one must be created.

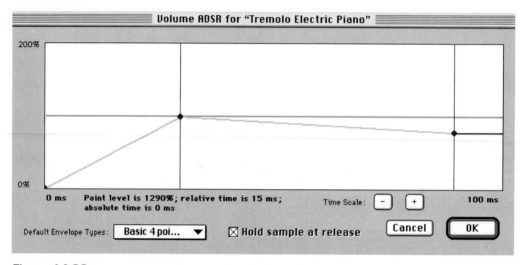

Figure 14-23
Select Volume from the Instruments pulldown menu to create or modify an instrument's volume envelope.

5. **Instrument Settings:** There are five different options available to the user under Instrument Settings (Figure 14-24).

a. Factor sample frequency for pitch allows the user to enable (or disable) the Sample Rate parameter for the samples used in the selected instrument.

b. Play at sampled frequency is used to enable (or disable) transposition of a sample within a Key map.

c. Disable waveform looping is used to turn off the loop information in a sample.

d. Default reverb is off completely disables any reverb parameters regardless of the settings sent by any controllers (including MIDI).

e. Stereo Pan Placement controls the placement of the instrument with the Stereo field.

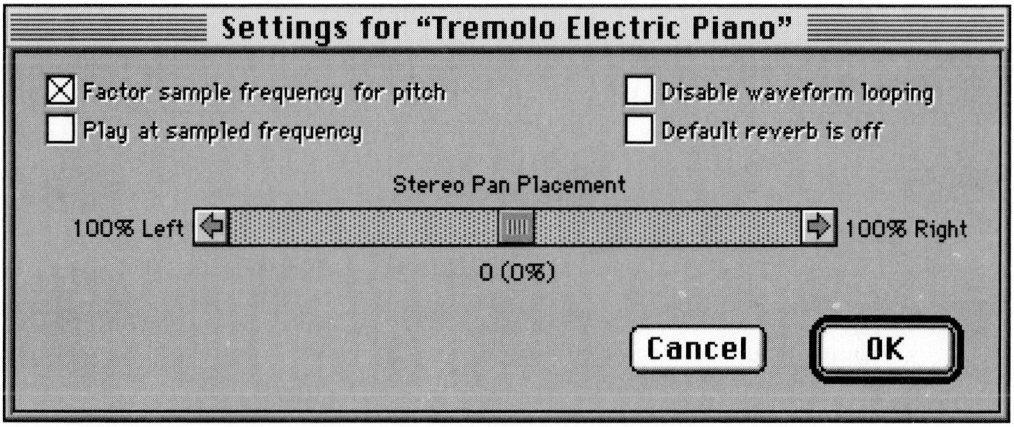

Figure 14-24
The Instrument Settings offers five options for configuring your instrument.

The Bottom Line

So after getting a chance to run the Beatnik Editor through the wringer, what do I think? It has the potential to be a seriously powerful tool in the hands of someone willing to take the time to learn it inside and out. Granted the limitations of this early Beta release version made many of the more powerful functions more of a pain in the butt than most of us would be willing to deal with, but again these issues will be cleared up in the first commercial release of the Beatnik Editor. The MIDI delay experienced when trying to use the Beatnik Music System as an external MIDI sound source was really annoying, but not quite as bad the QuickTime Musical Instruments and, even though the Power Mac is my preferred weapon of choice, it seems that the release of a Windows version of the Beatnik Editor is not too far in the future.

In the real world of audio, the overall sound quality coming out of the Beatnik Web Music System is not going to set the world on fire. No matter how many cool edit parameters are available, you still have to go back to the overall sound quality of the source samples and the standard Beatnik sound set is not that great. If you were to put the Beatnik Web Music System head to head against a decent General MIDI module or sound card (say a Roland Sound Canvas), Beatnik would be the loser in overall sound quality. Music over the Web is, however, quite a different story. The potential to create and playback unique music with Beatnik is there and there is no doubt in my mind you will hear some pretty cool stuff in the very near future.

Here's where I get a little confused. I just went back and played the Beatnik Demo that I originally downloaded off the Web and took a really close listen to it. The sound quality was great! In fact, it was as though I was listening to two different sound sets altogether. Well, because you can load custom samples into the Beatnik Editor, just maybe the sample quality for the demo was a little (or a lot) higher than that of the standard Beatnik sound set. I don't know for sure and I doubt anyone would tell me or you if that was the case. You take a listen and decide for yourself.

Let's look at file size for a moment. Allegedly an RMF file is supposed to be quite small therefore downloadable in the fraction of a second, right? The Standard MIDI File used in tutorial example 14-1 was 17k in size when it was exported. The same file as an RMF file was 182k when exported from the Beatnik Editor. That's a lot of fat to pick up a long the way for 12 bars of music.

Java and Headspace

And so it goes. . . The Headspace Audio Engine has been licensed to JavaSoft and will be included as part of the Java Sound API in the release of the Java Virtual Machine. Although the specifications for the Java Sound API had yet to be released at the time of going to press, I got a little preview and you will be blown away. Whether you use the Beatnik Editor or some futuristic yet-to-be-announced development tool for creating your Web audio, it's going to be interesting for sure.

And We're Outta Here...

I'm going to admit it, I'm just not sure. I've been going through a love/hate relationship with the Beatnik Editor from the beginning. For instance, the acoustic piano sounds were probably some of my least favorite I've ever heard. The piano sounds fine for quick attack percussive playing, but if you sustain a chord for even a few seconds it takes on an accordion-like quality that I and everyone else I played it for found distasteful. On the other hand, if you create the music using the Beatnik Editor as your sound source and work around the limitations, the results can be pretty cool.

Okay, right here and now is where I stick up for Beatnik. Your sound is only going to be as good as the samples used to create the instruments. Because the sound files reside on the user's Browser Plug-in, adding custom samples will just mean anyone using your RMF files will first have to download your custom samples. This takes time and most people just won't bother with it. Oh well.

When it comes right down to it, I like Beatnik way more than I don't. Listening to demos of the Headspace RMF collections, I've got to say the music sounds pretty good. The estimated price (and this is subject to change) of the first commercially available release of the Beatnik Editor is going to be in the area of $100. So the big question, would I buy it? Yes.

Chapter 15

QuickTime

In This Chapter

- What's new with QuickTime 3.0 audio?
- Options with QuickTime Musical Instruments
- Creating and editing QuickTime Movies
- Combining audio and MIDI into QuickTime

QuickTime is a complete multi-platform multimedia software architecture created by Apple Computers. Multimedia developers and content creators use the architecture to store, edit, and play multimedia content (that is, synchronized graphics, sound, video, text, and music – or any combination thereof) in applications and for Internet delivery. It even includes components that enable the addition of virtual reality and 3D media into a QuickTime movie. (It's important to note that, even though a QuickTime file may not necessarily contain video, it is called a QuickTime movie, regardless of content.) Users with the QuickTime plug-in installed on their machines can view QuickTime movies on the Web.

While the majority of the audio development tools for QuickTime are still Mac-based, this is bound to change in the very near future. Until then, I guess the rest of you will have to suffer. SoundEdit 16 is a very popular, easy-to-use program that gives you the option to import, edit, and export sound in a QuickTime Movie. Studio Vision Pro (3.5) and its baby brother Vision (3.5) from Opcode are powerful and flexible MIDI sequencers that just happen to be audio-enabled as well. With either of these Vision products, you can import and export audio and MIDI in the QuickTime Movie format. The tutorial section of this chapter features both SoundEdit 16 and Vision doing what they do best and doing it in QuickTime.

> **Note**
>
> A complete discussion of the entire QuickTime architecture (which includes QuickTime, QuickTime VR, and QuickDraw 3D) would be far beyond the scope of this book, so this chapter's discussion is focused primarily on the QuickTime Musical Architecture.

QuickTime 3.0

At the time this book goes to press, the release of QuickTime 3.0 for the Mac and Windows (that's right—Windows) looms just around the corner (Q1 of 98). Probably the biggest news as far as we're concerned in the world of audio is a level playing field between the two platforms. One of the problems I've run into working with the current version of QuickTime tends to revolve around the playback of MIDI within a QuickTime Movie. The QuickTime Musical Architecture makes MIDI playback on the PowerMac (through a QuickTime Movie) a pretty decent experience, but listening to the same file on the PC can be a downright disturbing experience. QuickTime 3.0 will change all that. Regardless of where you create your sound and music file, playback will be globally indistinguishable. I like that and so will you.

The audio formats supported by QuickTime 3.0 are as follows:

- AIFF
- AU

- MIDI
- MPEG Layer 2
- Sound Designer II
- WAVE

There have been a considerable number of changes in QuickTime 3.0 to make it a well-rounded multimedia software architecture, but because the scope of this book is audio, we'll confine our discussion to the music architecture. I'm glad that the QuickTime Music Architecture has finally arrived with an equal footing in the world of Windows.

> **Note**
>
> Just as we were about to go to press, Apple released more information about QuickTime 3.0 including adding the Roland Sound Canvas sound set (GM GS) to QuickTime 3.0. This will greatly improve the sound quality of the QuickTime Musical Instruments for both the Macintosh and Windows platform.

MIDI and QuickTime Musical Instruments

One method of music delivery over the Web that hasn't been quite as constrained by the bandwidth problem has been MIDI (Musical Instrument Digital Interface). A MIDI file can be quite small in comparison to even a low-resolution, highly compressed audio file. Consistent playback quality of MIDI files over the Web (or anywhere else) has been a problem that Apple has addressed with QuickTime Musical Instruments (QTMI). QTMI is, in essence, a software-based General MIDI synthesizer that is part of QuickTime (2.1 or better). This enables a consistent-sounding playback of MIDI files with no external hardware.

Options are always nice, and it is also possible to assign the MIDI playback to other software (or hardware) synthesizers. The QuickTime settings in the Control Panels (see Figure 15-1) of the Macintosh enable you to assign playback to another hopefully higher-quality MIDI instrument.

In my case, I've assigned playback of MIDI to a Yamaha MU50, which is a General MIDI-compatible external synthesizer module. The reason for using an external synthesizer in my case is not only superior sound quality, but the fact that an internal software synthesizer cuts into to the processing power of the PowerMac 8500/120 I use.

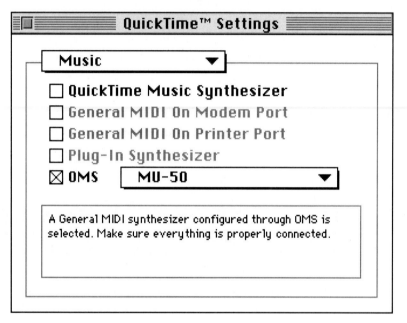

Figure 15-1
In the QuickTime preferences, select an alternative MIDI sound source for higher-quality playback.

Another different option comes from InVision Interactive: the Cyber-Sound Studio. I bypassed the hardware in this package (MIDI interface and keyboard) and went straight to the CyberSynth, which is quite similar to the QuickTime Musical Instruments, except that it offers a variety of different sound sets and a better overall quality of sound. The downside is the CyberSynth in the CyberSound Studio package eats up hard drive space like you wouldn't believe. I would recommend this package for the home hobbyist with a desire to create and edit MIDI-based music that has a small budget. Where else are you going to get a MIDI Interface and Keyboard plus a soft synth with some decent sounds all for under a hundred bucks? Just make sure you've got lots of extra drive space!

MPEG Audio

Apple recently released an MPEG extension for QuickTime (2.5 or better), making it possible to playback MPEG Layer 2 audio over the Web. Head to head against a WAVE file of similar size, an MPEG audio file does have better sound quality. So far (anyway), MPEG as an audio source for playback over the Web has not gained the popular following of RealAudio or Shockwave Audio. This is probably due to marketing and the brand name recognition factor as well as the extremely high cost of MPEG server software. Still, it's good that Apple has had the foresight to make MPEG audio accessible in QuickTime. MPEG may just be the future of high-quality audio over the Web. I guess we'll have to wait and see.

The MPEG extension for QuickTime is a free download, so go check it out. For more information on the state of MPEG audio on the Web, go to Chapter 18, "Advanced Topics."

> **Web**
>
> Download the MPEG extension at `http://www.quicktime.apple.com`.

Tutorials and Tools

Finding the right audio development tool for your project is important. With the release of QuickTime 3.0, both the Mac and the PC will stand head to head—dead even in the playing field. The software developers on the audio side of the Windows community have largely ignored the QuickTime Movie format altogether (still hoping the Mac will just go away). Once someone on the other side of the fence gets a clue, then developing sound and music for QuickTime will no longer be the exclusive domain of the Mac.

The two applications we'll be using in the tutorial section of this chapter are SoundEdit 16 (Version 2) from Macromedia and Studio Vision Pro 3.5 from Opcode. They are both Mac OS applications that I've used pretty extensively, so I know they work. Again, the only thing that prevents me or anyone else from using Windows applications for creating sound content for QuickTime is the lack of QuickTime support from Developers. Let's get to it!

Before we get started

In the first two tutorials, we use SoundEdit 16 Version 2 from Macromedia. There's a little setup you need to do in the Preferences. From the main menu of SoundEdit 16, select Preferences from the File menu. Now it's time to select and set the sound file preferences. In the first three tutorials, we'll be dealing with 16-bit 22 kHz mono files, so you need to set the Document preferences to correspond with these settings. If in doubt, use Figure 15-2 as your reference.

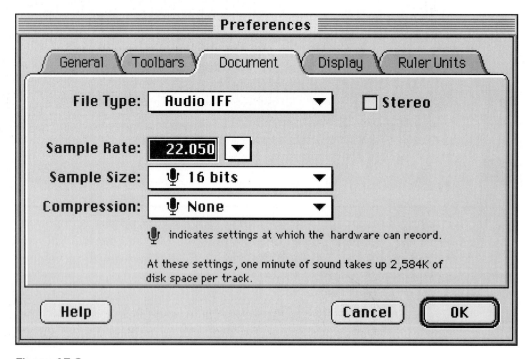

Figure 15-2
Set the audio preferences in SoundEdit 16 before starting the first tutorial.

Tutorial 15-1: Creating a QuickTime audio file

Using SoundEdit 16 (Version 2) from Macromedia is probably the easiest way to record, edit, and convert an audio file into a QuickTime Movie. In this first tutorial, that's exactly what we'll do.

Note

Don't let this movie thing confuse you, as a QuickTime file is called a *Movie* whether or not there is actually a movie (in the traditional sense) embedded in the file.

▓ What you need

The following items are needed to complete this tutorial:

- ▓ SoundEdit 16 Version 2
- ▓ CH15EX1.SND (tutorial sound file)
- ▓ 68030 Macintosh (or better) with a CD-ROM drive
- ▓ QuickTime 2.1 or better

CD-ROM

The tutorial sound file CH15EX1.SND can be found in the Chapter 15 tutorial folder on the CD-ROM accompanying this book.

Note

The demo version of SoundEdit 16 (found on the CD-ROM with this book) cannot be used to perform Tutorial 15-1. It is save-disabled and does not allow the user to save or convert files.

Time to create

1. Start the application SoundEdit 16 and load the file CH15EX1.SND (see Figure 15-3).

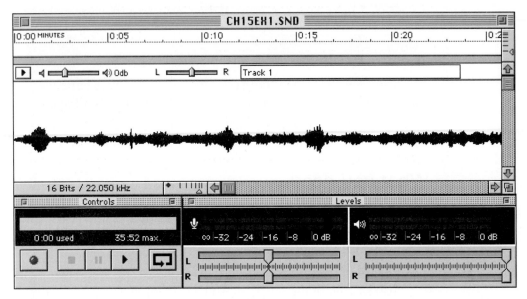

Figure 15-3
The tutorial file CH15EX1.SND in the edit window of SoundEdit 16.

2. Choose Save As from the File menu. Change the file name to CH15EX2.MOV and the file format to QuickTime Movie (as shown in Figure 15-4). Click Save. The view is now changed from that of a waveform to that of a QuickTime movie.

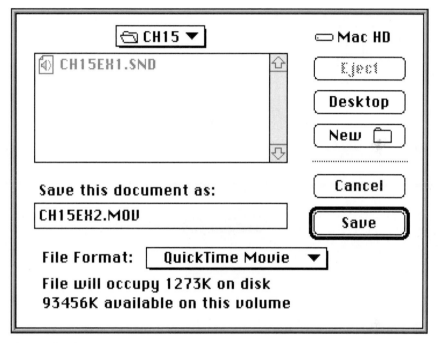

Figure 15-4
In Step 2, rename the file and change the format to QuickTime Movie.

3. In this step, we give the individual soundtrack its own name within the QuickTime movie. Click the Info button (shown in Figure 15-5) and the Soundtrack Information window opens (see Figure 15-6). In the Title field, rename the track "Ancient Voices". Click OK.

Figure 15-5
Click the Info button to access the Soundtrack Information window.

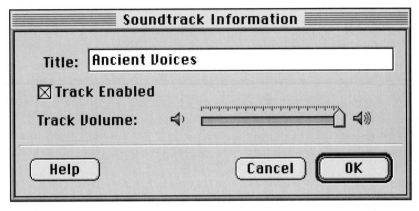

Figure 15-6
Rename the track, set the volume level, and enable or disable the track in
the Soundtrack Information window.

> **Note**
>
> Note that in the Soundtrack Information window are the
> controls for individual track volume and the track enable/
> disable box.

4. There are four basic playback controls in a Quicktime movie (see Figure 15-
   7).Press Play to listen to the QuickTime movie file you've just created.
   Assuming you have finished working with the file, choose Save (or
   Command S) from the File menu in SoundEdit 16 to save the file.

Figure 15-7
Press the Play button to listen to the QuickTime Movie file.

■ Kind of cool

That was easy and hopefully fun. You might have noticed the Edit and
New buttons in the QuickTime Movie (refer back to Figure 15-5).
You may have even clicked on them to see what would happen. Well,
in Tutorial 15-2, we're going to explore just what you can (and can't)
do within a QuickTime Movie file in regards to audio.

Tutorial 15-2: Editing a file within QuickTime

Let's pick up where we left off in the last tutorial (15-1). This time, we
take the QuickTime Movie (audio file or whatever you want to call it)
and add another track within it.

> **CD-ROM**
>
> The tutorial files CH15EX2.MOV and Ch15EX3.SND can
> be found in the Chapter 15 tutorial folder on the CD-ROM.

1. Open the QuickTime Movie file CH15EX2.MOV (in SoundEdit 16). Click the
    Edit button. While still in the QuickTime Movie, you are now able to edit in
    the SoundEdit 16 environment (see Figure 15-8).

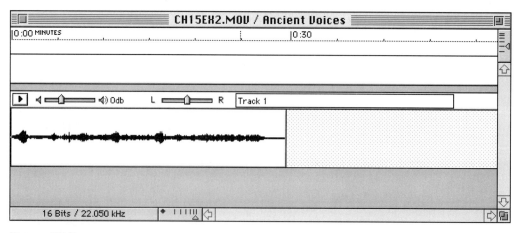

Figure 15-8
While in a QuickTime Movie, you can now edit in SoundEdit 16.

2. In this step, we Import an audio file into the music track Ancient Voices. I sort of felt the need for some ambient background noise to enhance the mood of the music and chose a 40-second sound file of Jungle noises. From the SoundEdit 16 Menu bar, choose Import from the File menu and select the file CH15EX3.SND. Notice in Figure 15-9 that there are now two files residing in the Sound Window.

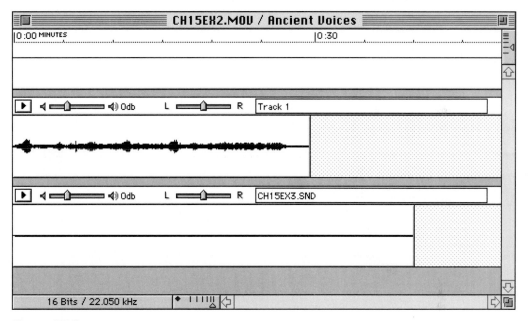

Figure 15-9
The file CH15EX3 has been Imported into the Sound Window of Ancient Voices.

3. The best way to explain the reason for this next step is to have you listen to these two sound files simultaneously. Engage playback with the spacebar on your keyboard. Notice that the music (on track 1) is overpowering the ambient sound (on track 2) considerably. While there are a number of ways to adjust the level of sound between the two tracks, let's go with the easiest and most logical way—the individual gain controls on each track. Using the example shown in Figure 15-10, select and lower the gain control on the music track (Track 1) to -3 db and raise the gain control on the ambient sound track (CH15EX3) to +6 db. Always remember that your personal taste (and hearing loss???) may be different than mine, so if you so choose, adjust the gain controls to what you hear.

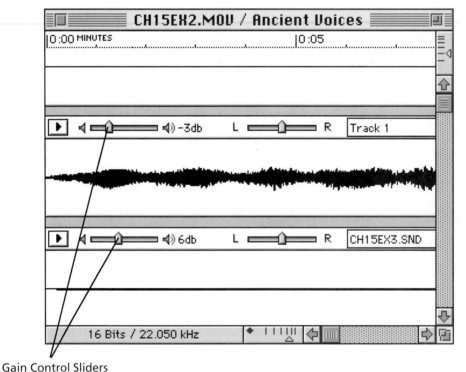

Gain Control Sliders

Figure 15-10
Adjust the volume on the individuals tracks with the gain control sliders.

4. The next task is to adjust the length of these two files. As you should have noticed, the ambient track is slightly longer than the music track. We could simply trim the length off of the ambient file and be done with it but... not this time. Instead, center the music track to set up a little ambiance for before and after the music. Select Track One by double clicking on it in the Sound Window. By holding down the option button, the cursor now becomes a hand. Using Figure 15-11 for reference, drag Track One to a central position in regards to Track Two.

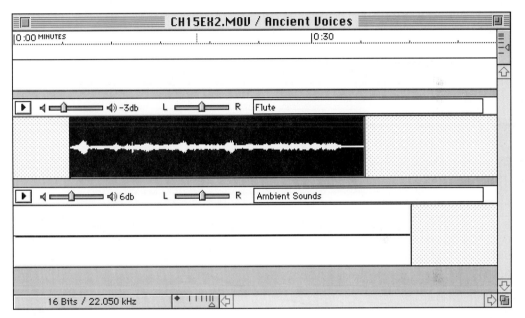

Figure 15-11
Drag Track One to a central position in regards to Track Two.

5. The start and finish of this track would feel a lot better if they were smoothed out a bit, so it's time to introduce you to the Fade In/Fade Out feature in SoundEdit 16. Using the cursor, select (highlight) the first four or five seconds of the ambient track (Track Two). From the Effects toolbar (shown in Figure 15-12), click Fade In. The Fade In window (see Figure 15-13) opens. There are three preset options available for a Fade In (slow, medium, and fast), or you can create your own. For the sake of this tutorial, select Slow. Click the Fade button to create the Fade In.

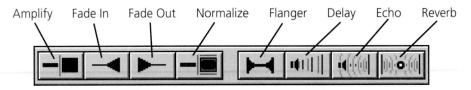

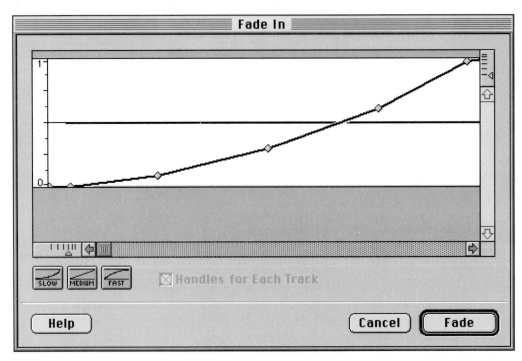

Figure 15-12
Choose Fade In from the Effects Tool Bar.

Figure 15-13
In the Fade In window, you can choose one of three presets or create a custom fade in.

6. On Track Two, select (highlight) the area from 33 to 40 seconds. Click the Fade OutIn button on the Effects toolbar (refer to Figure 15-12). To create a fade out, the process mirrors that in Step 5. Select the preset Slow and click the Fade button. Now, there is a smooth and gradual fade in and out on the ambient track that helps to set up the music. Test your fades by playing it back (tap the spacebar). We've made all these changes to the original file, so before we move on I guess you'd better save them. Choose Save Movie Soundtrack from the File menu on the main menu bar.

7. Close the Edit Window (Command W will do it). Even though you've saved the new version into the Soundtrack (Ancient Voices), it has yet to be saved as a QuickTime Movie file. Choose Save As from the File menu bar and rename the movie CH15EX4.MOV. As shown in Figure 15-14, also choose the options Make Movie Self-Contained and put an X in the box labeled Playable On Non-Apple Computers. Take a deep breath and click Save.

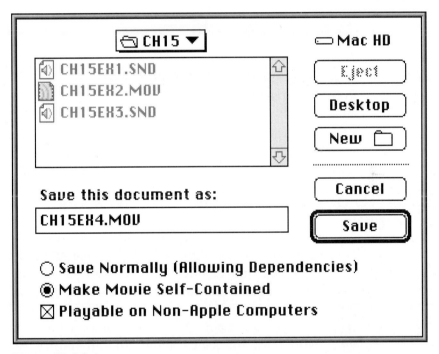

Figure 15-14
Rename the Movie, choose the option Make Movie Self-Contained, and put an X in the box Playable On Non-Apple Computers before clicking Save.

427

The New button?

One edit feature in the QuickTime Movie we have yet to address is the New button. What does it do? For our purposes, it essentially makes it possible to add new sound files to the movie. While this is a wonderful feature, it probably makes more sense (in our situation, for sure) to import the sound files in one at a time (like we did in Tutorial 15-2) and deal with the editing and internal mixing of everything inside of one file. This gives you easier control of the overall mix as well as the start and stop times. While it is possible to do this either way, repeating or slightly modifying the steps in Tutorial 15-2 will save time, effort, and more than likely give you superior results.

> **Note**
>
> The bit and sample rate set in the Preferences will remain true even to files you Import. In the case of Tutorial 15-2, even if you were to import a 16-bit 44 kHz file, it would automatically be converted to 16-bit 22 kHz because of the Preference settings.

Tutorial 15-3: Using the QuickTime Musical Instruments

One of the absolute coolest features of QuickTime (2.1 or better) is the QuickTime Musical Instruments. This software-based General MIDI synthesizer can playback a Standard MIDI File (SMF) without any additional hardware in a Mac or a Windows machine. Vision (and Studio Vision Pro) 3.5 from Opcode combines a full-featured MIDI sequencer with tracks of digital audio. In this tutorial, we work in Studio Vision Pro 3.5 and turn a General MIDI sequence into a QuickTime Movie. But first, we need to take a look at OMS.

OMS

OMS, what's that all about? Well, Opcode created OMS (Open Music System) to open up lines of communication between MIDI software and hardware. Using OMS as the brains behind the operation, your music software (sequencing and otherwise) can identify the synthesizers, drum machines, and other various MIDI devices that reside in your music and computer setup. The OMS Setup application is used to create a Studio Setup document (see Figure 15-15) where all the relevant MIDI information in your system is stored. Detailed information for each individual MIDI device (see Figure 15-16) is entered and stored within the document providing the proper setup and connection information to all OMS-compatible applications. Vision and Studio Vision

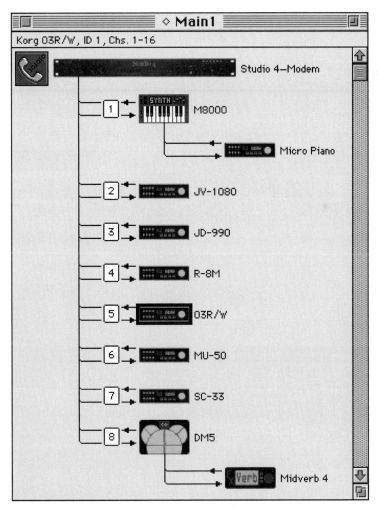

Figure 15-15
The Studio Setup document in OMS.

Pro 3.5 are among a few of the MIDI sequencing software packages that rely on OMS to keep things organized.

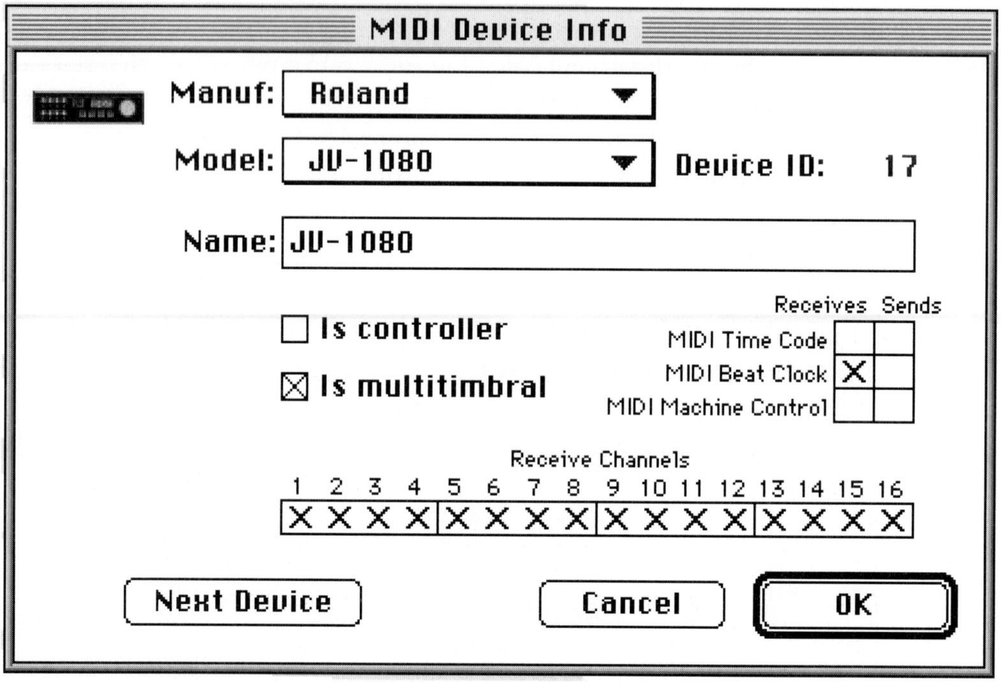

Figure 15-16
The MIDI Device Dialog Box in a OMS Studio Setup document.

What you need

The following items are needed to complete this tutorial:

- Studio Vision Pro 3.5
- MIDI file CH15EX5.MID
- A PowerMac running System 7.5 (or better)
- Quicktime 2.1 (preferably 2.5) or better

CD-ROM

In the Chapter 15 tutorial folder on the CD-ROM accompanying this book, you will find the MIDI file CH15EX5.MID.

▧ QTMI

1. Start the application Studio Vision Pro 3.5. Choose Open from the File menu and select the MIDI file CH15EX5.MID. Use the space bar (or transport controls) to start playback from the beginning of the sequence. This particular MIDI sequence is about 50 seconds in length. As you can see in Figure 15-17, there are four instrument tracks and two drum tracks. You might also note that the instrument you're listening to for playback happens to be the QuickTime Musical Instruments.

Note

Both Vision 3.5 and Studio Vision Pro 3.5 have some incredibly powerful editing features. While composing, playing, and arranging music is beyond the scope of this book, I still recommend experimentation using the MIDI files supplied in the Tutorial folder of this chapter on the accompanying CD-ROM.

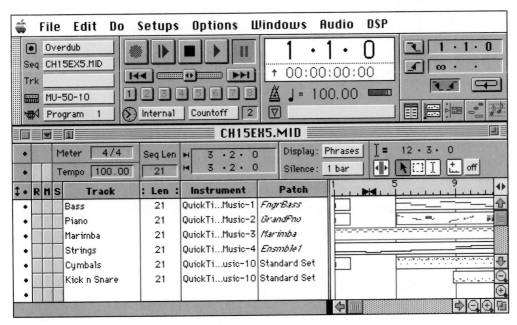

Figure 15-17
The tutorial file CH15EX5.MID in Studio Vision Pro 3.5.

2. Okay, you've listened to the MIDI file and if you're experienced in editing a MIDI file in Vision, you may have even made a few changes of your own to the file. It's time to turn this little gem into a QuickTime Movie. Select Export as QuickTime Movie from the File menu., The Export as QuickTime Movie window, shown in Figure 15-18, opens. In this case, you want select Create new movie and the Export MIDI box (we'll deal with exporting audio in Tutorial 15-4). Click OK. You are asked to name the new movie file (see Figure 15-19); name it CH15EX6.MOV and click Save.

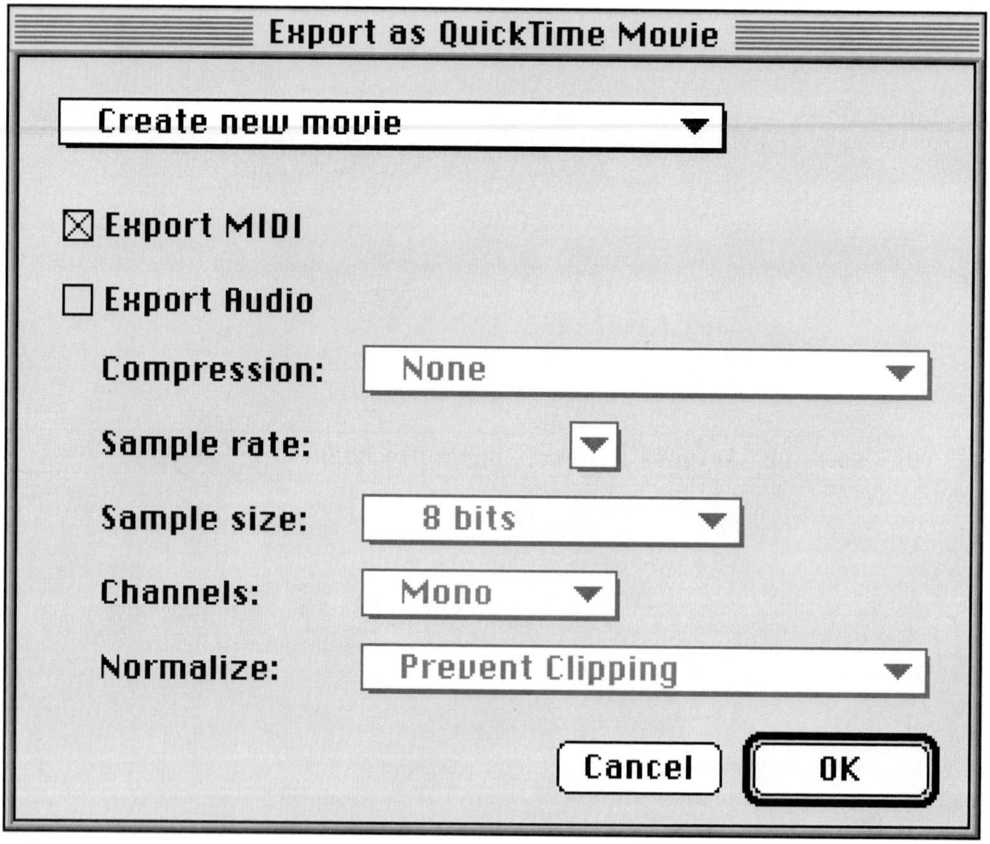

Figure 15-18
Set the attributes for exporting the MIDI file as a QuickTime Movie.

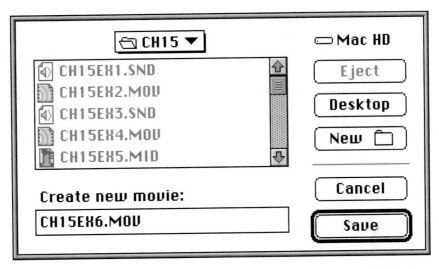

Figure 15-19
Name the QuickTime Movie CH15EX6.MOV.

3. Now it's time to give the QuickTime Movie a try on its own. Double click on the file CH15EX6.MOV. As shown in Figure 15-20, a compact little QuickTime Movie shows up on your desktop. Press the Play button to start (or pause) playback. You now have a music file that plays as a QuickTime Movie on QuickTime-enabled Mac or a Windows machine.

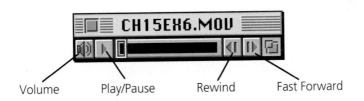

Figure 15-20
Start playback by pressing the spacebar and listen to the QuickTime Musical Instruments.

■ A few more thoughts

I realize that not all of you are going to go out and pop the dollars necessary for Studio Vision Pro (or even Vision), but that's okay. You can still download the latest version of QuickTime from the Web and follow all the steps in this last tutorial. Sometimes it's just as important to understand the concepts of creation (even if they seem simple), regardless of which platform or tools you use.

In Tutorial 15-4, we'll mix audio and MIDI together and then save them into a QuickTime Movie. So one more time, Let's Rock!

Tutorial 15-4: Saving Audio and MIDI into QuickTime

Combining MIDI and an Audio file into QuickTime and saving them as a stand-alone QuickTime Movie is the exercise in this tutorial. To give it an interesting twist, we're going to import the audio from a standard audio CD. Chances are you won't have many of the components in this tutorial, but I've got a solution to every problem. You can use an audio CD of your choice or simply import the file CH15EX8.AIF (more on that during the tutorial).

> **Warning**
>
> When using the QuickTime Musical Instruments in Studio Vision Pro (3.5), there is sometimes a bit of a conflict between the DAE (Digidesign Audio Engine) and the Apple Sound Manager. This is unfortunately unavoidable and can cause a couple of unscheduled crashes. The moral of this story is: Save after every step.

■ What you need

Don't even make me remind you to have Vision 3.5 (or Studio Vision Pro 3.5) and QuickTime 2.5 installed in your computer.

- CH15EX5.MID
- The Hollywood Edge Super Single Volume 1.
- CH15EX8.AIF (this file is optional)

CD-ROM

The tutorial file CH15EX5.MID can be found in the Chapter 15 Tutorial folder on the CD-ROM. The other files in Tutorial 15-4 are there simply for reference.

The steps

1. Start the application Vision 3.5 and load the file CH15EX5.MID. In the Track window (see Figure 15-21), name Track 7 "SFX," and enable the Record button on the SFX track by clicking on it once. This is the track where the soon-to-be imported audio will reside.

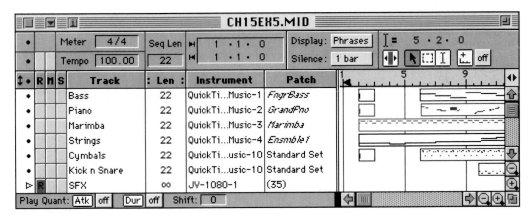

Figure 15-21
Name Track 7 "SFX" and enable the record button.

2. What we're going to do here is to Import our source audio from a Red Book audio CD, in this case the Super Single Volume One from The Hollywood Edge. Choose Import Audio Using QuickTime from the File menu. You are now able to select a track from the audio CD (see Figure 15-22) for conversion. In this case, I chose #51, which contains ambient traffic noise. After making your selection, click Convert and the Save dialog box opens.

CD-ROM

For those of you who wish to bypass Steps 2 and 3, simply Import the audio file CH15EX8.AIF found in the Chapter 13 Tutorial folder on the accompanying CD-ROM.

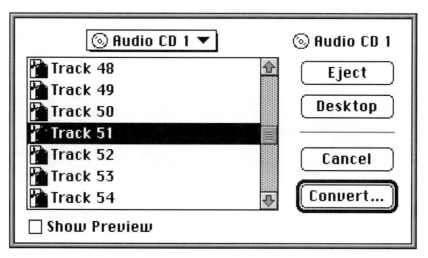

Figure 15-22
Choose the CD audio track to convert.

3. The Save dialog box (Figure 15-23) is where you name the converted file and save it. Let's call it CH15EX8.AIF. Notice in Figure 15-23 a button called Options . . .; Click on it and find your bad self in a very important space—Audio CD Import Options, as shown in Figure 15-24. (This window is a dead ringer in looks and function for the Import CD Xtra in SoundEdit 16.) Time for us to make a few adjustments. Set the Sample rate to 44.1 kHz, the bit rate to 16, and select Mono. Leave the Audio Selection area as it is. Click OK to get back into the previous window and click Save. The CD audio is now converted and imported as a QuickTime Movie file, and you are returned to the main Vision window.

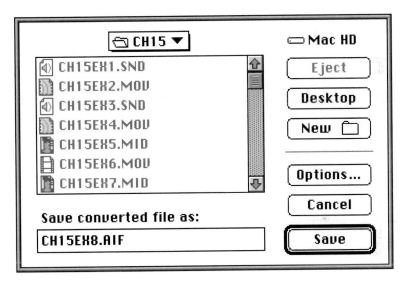

Figure 15-23
Name the audio file CH15EX8.AIF and click the Options button.

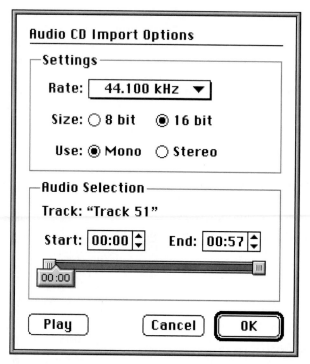

Figure 15-24
Set the Audio CD Import Options before converting the file from CD audio.

Note

The Audio Selection feature in the Audio CD Import Options window is very useful for previewing all or part of the file you wish to convert.

4. Use the spacebar or the Play button in the transport to start playback and listen to the mixture of MIDI and digital audio. For my taste, the digital audio track is just a little too soft in volume, so let's go fix it.

Your area of interest is the new audio Track "SFX" (see Figure 15-25). This is where the imported audio now resides within Vision. Directly to the right of the Track window is the Edit Track window. Double click on the audio waveform in the Edit Track window and the selected waveform (shown in Figure 15-26) is ready for editing.

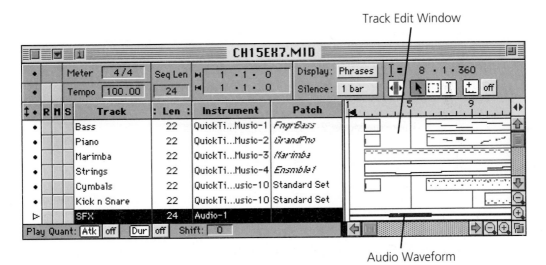

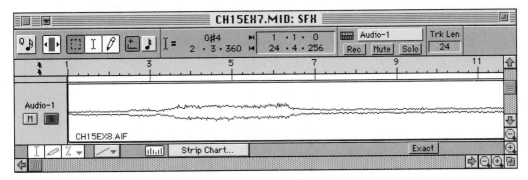

Figure 15-25
The digital audio imported from the CD is now residing on the SFX Track (7). Select the audio for editing by double clicking the the audio waveform in the Track Edit window.

Figure 15-26
The target audio is now selected and ready for editing.

439

Choose Modify Notes from Vision's main Do menu. You are now going to scale the velocity of the selected track to 150% of it's original volume as shown in Figure 15-27. This will give you a 50% overall increase of the original volume. Change the settings and click OK. Before proceeding, go to the File menu and select Save As. Rename this hybrid MIDI/audio file CH15EX7.MID.

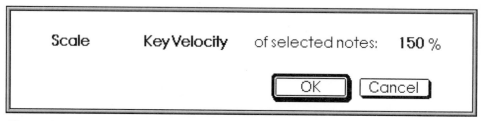

Figure 15-27
Scale the velocity of the selected track to 150% of it's original value.

5. Okay, it's time to take this hybrid MIDI/audio sequence and turn it into a QuickTime Movie. Choose Export as QuickTime Movie from Vision's main File menu. As shown in Figure 15-28, the Export as QuickTime Movie window is now active. Starting at the top, select Create new movie and check the Export MIDI/Export Audio boxes. Because audio takes up too much space, we're going to make sure this file is small. Choose IMA 4:1 in the Compression field; 11,025 in the Sample rate field; 8 bits in the Sample size field; Mono in the Channels field; and Prevent Clipping in the Normalize field. Click OK after you've selected these settings and the Save dialog box opens.

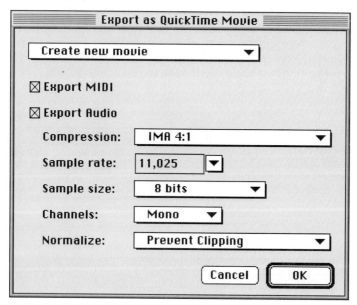

Figure 15-28
Set the attributes for the audio portion of the QuickTime Movie.

6. Well, we're just about to the end of the creation portion of this tutorial. In the Save dialog box, name the new movie CH15EX9.MOV (see Figure 15-29) and click Save. Stand up and stretch because it will take a minute to convert the audio and MIDI file. When the process is completed, quit Vision.

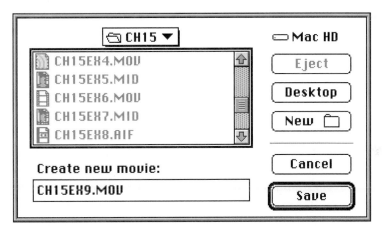

Figure 15-29
Save the new movie as CH15EX9.MOV.

7. Now it's time to hear what this puppy sounds like as a QuickTime Movie (it should be the same). Remember, we compressed and down-sampled the audio track considerably. The original audio track was 4.8 MB in size before the conversion. The new movie is 363K, which is considerably smaller. Find the file CH15EX9.MOV and double click on it. You should now see the QuickTime Movie and player shown in Figure 15-30. Start playback with the Play button or the spacebar. You should now be hearing your new QuickTime Movie.

Figure 15-30
Playback the QuickTime Movie CH15EX9.MOV by pressing the Play button on the transport or the spacebar on your keyboard.

Options are good

It's nice to know that there are options when creating audio content and Vision is full of them. The audio side of Studio Vision Pro can use Premiere plug-ins. As an example, our old friend the Native Power Pack from Waves works with Studio Vision Pro. If you have Pro Tools III hardware with TDM (Time Division Multiplexing), you can now have as many as 64 audio tracks in addition to an almost unlimited number of MIDI tracks. I wish there was more time and space to really get into Vision as it is by far my most favorite MIDI-based sequencer, and I really am impressed with all the improvements and new features that have shown up in version 3.5. Opcode created the first MIDI/ digital audio sequencer and everyone else has been playing catch-up ever since. Adding the ability to create and edit a QuickTime Movie in Vision is just another feather in Opcode's cap.

Another feature we haven't discussed is the ability to import MIDI and audio from an existing QuickTime Movie. You can edit, rerecord, and even add more content and ship it right back to the original movie. This is opening up some interesting possibilities and I, for one, look forward to exploring this function a lot deeper.

 The Future of QuickTime Audio

Where's it all going? Equality in the cross-platform compatibility issue seems to have taken on a larger priority at Apple—at least as far as QuickTime is concerned. This equality between platforms is going to open up some cool possibilities for developing sound and music content using Apple's QuickTime Music Architecture. It's also still too early to really see what kind of impact MPEG audio is going to have on the Web and within QuickTime Movies in general. Whether QuickTime is really going to take off among Windows developers is also a bit of a mystery (maybe if Microsoft buys Apple and . . . ?). I guess I'll just keep my fingers crossed and see what happens!

Table 15-1 Where to find it on the Web

Company	Products	URL
Apple Computers	QuickTime	`http://www.quicktime.apple.com`
Opcode	Vision 3.5 Studio Vision Pro 3.5 OMS	`http://www.opcode.com`
InVision Interactive	CyberSound	`http://www.cybersound.com`

Chapter **16**

MIDI On The Web

 In this Chapter

- The Yamaha MIDPlug
- Crescendo from Live Update
- Microsoft's New (MIDI) Development Tools
- The Internet Music Kit
- MIDI resources on the Web

Without a doubt, MIDI (Musical Instrument Digital Interface) is the easiest hassle-free solution for getting sound on your Web site. The small size of a MIDI file and the fact that almost every computer running the Mac or Windows OS is capable of playing back a MIDI file in one way or another makes it the most reasonable place to start. The software synthesizer (QuickTime Musical Instruments and the Yamaha MIDPlug, for instance) is becoming more and more commonplace in today's computers. With the faster-than-lightning PowerMacs and MMX Pentiums becoming the rule rather than the exception, a dedicated piece of MIDI hardware is not always needed for high-quality playback of MIDI files. In this chapter, I'll drag you kicking and screaming through all the options and make sure you know where to download every plug-in needed to experience playback of high- (and even low-) quality MIDI over the Web.

 Playback: MIDI Browser Plug-Ins

Regardless of which platform or operating system you use, there are enough MIDIfied options for Web playback to shake a stick at. Table 16-1 details a few of them.

Table 16-1   MIDI Browser Plug-ins

Product	Cost	Compatible Browser	Mac OS	Windows	Sound Source	Streaming MIDI	URL
QuickTime Musical Instruments ★★★★ by Apple	Free	Netscape Internet Explorer			Soft Synth on Browser Plug-in	n/a	http://www.quicktime.apple.com
Beatnik★ by Headspace	Free	Netscape 3.0 ★★	PowerMac only		Soft Synth on Browser Plug-in	no	http://www.headspace.com/beatnik
Crescendo by Live Update	Free	Netscape 2.0 Internet Explorer 2.0	System 7 QuickTime 2.1		SoundCard (Windows) QuickTime Musical Instruments (Mac)		http://www.liveupdate.com
Crescendo Plus by Live Update	$19.95	Netscape 2.0 Internet Explorer 2.0	System 7 QuickTime 2.1		SoundCard (Windows) QuickTime Musical Instruments (Mac)	yes	http://www.liveupdate.com
Crescendo Plus Webmaster Edition by Live Update	$49.95	Netscape 2.0 Internet Explorer 2.0	System 7 QuickTime 2.1		SoundCard (Windows) QuickTime Musical Instruments (Mac)	yes	http://www.liveupdate.com
Live Audio by Netscape	★★★	Netscape 2.0	yes	yes	SoundCard (Windows) QuickTime Musical Instruments (Mac)		http://www.netscape.com

Table 16-1   MIDI Browser Plug-ins *(continued)*

Product	Cost	Compatible Browser	Mac OS	Windows	Sound Source	Streaming MIDI	URL
MIDPlug by Yamaha	Free	Netscape 2.0 Internet Explorer 2.0	PowerMac only System 7.5	Pentium only	Soft Synth on Browser Plug-in		`http:// www.ysba.com`

* The Beatnik Music System is just unique enough to warrant its own Chapter. For all the details, see Chapter 14 "Beatnik!"

** Beatnik was only partially functional in Internet Explorer 3.0. However, Java compatibility problems with Beatnik are expected to be fixed in IE 4.0.

*** The Live Audio plug-in is a standard default MIDI plug-in that is part of Netscape Navigator/Communicator.

**** QuickTime Musical Instruments is a component of QuickTime 2.1 or better. QuickTime 3.0 is scheduled for release in Q1 of 1998.

Live Update

Probably the best-known MIDI browser plug-in has got to be Crescendo from Live Update. I guess three million downloads would give you sort of a dominant presence in the marketplace. Currently, there are three versions of the Crescendo plug-in commercially available (see Table 16-1). So how does it work? Pretty well and depending on which version you have it's also capable of almost instantaneous playback. Crescendo Plus uses streaming MIDI so even while graphics and text are loading, the user is able to listen to (and control) the music. Even though a MIDI file is very small in comparison to an audio file, it can still take a moment to load and I, for one, am into instantaneous gratification.

Crescendo Plus has all the obvious controls (Fast Forward, Rewind, and so forth) and a few other options such as the ability to save the MIDI file you're currently listening to and to set the file to loop endlessly. It's nice to give the user the choice for a change. How many times have you gone to a site and been slammed by a loud obnoxious and possibly poorly performed MIDI file, with no way to shut it off or at least lower the volume without leaving the vicinity? Probably more times than not.

The sound source for MIDI playback with Crescendo resides on the user's computer. Depending on the platform OS combination, the results could be very mixed. After some silent moments (read the installation instructions, it'll save you time), I was able to get both my PowerMac and Windows machines to run Crescendo Plus without any problems. My

MIDI sound source on the PowerMac was QuickTime Musical Instruments (the Software Synthesizer that's part of the QuickTime 2.5 browser plug-in), while my Windows 95 machine uses a comparable Yamaha Software Synthesizer in place of the traditional hardware. With Crescendo, the user always has the option as to the MIDI playback engine.

Note

The many options for improving sound quality with QuickTime Musical Instruments are covered in Chapter 15, "QuickTime."

Crescendo for RealMedia

Imagine the possibilities with the combination of streaming audio and streaming MIDI at the same time. With Crescendo for the Real Media Architecture, another interesting possibility has been thrown into the equation of Web sound. Synchronizing RealAudio and MIDI together for playback over the Web might just create a strange and abstractly creative subculture of Internet music artists. The fact that Live Update was forward thinking enough to be one of the first to jump on the Real Media bandwagon shows they may have a few other surprises for us all to look forward to.

Note

Get the latest free version of Crescendo by taking a trip to `http://www.liveupdate.com`, or go to the DEMO-SOFT folder on the CD-ROM accompanying this book.

The Yamaha MIDPlug

It's free! It sounds great! It gives you many of the control options of the Yamaha XG synthesizers! What more do you need to know? The MIDPlug is a Netscape Navigator/Communicator plug-in with a MIDI software synthesizer that is GM compatible. So far so good, right? The downside is that the main processor of your computer is doing all the work here, so if there's any graphic-intensive action happening on the MIDPlug-enhanced site that you're visiting, you better be running a fast computer. Fortunately if you're reading this book, you probably are.

> **Note**
>
> The XG format (from Yamaha) is an extended version of General MIDI that offers three effects per channel, as well as a larger and more diverse set of sounds while still remaining compatible to GM.

Now to the good stuff. The MIDPlug is cross-platform and, from what I can tell, it works equally well with machines running the Mac and Windows operating systems. So how does it sound? I sure like it, and compared to some of the music I've heard over the Web via streaming audio, the soft synth in the MIDPlug has a far superior sound quality. There's also a hot-rodded version that was built to take advantage of Intel's MMX technology, the S-YXG50C. Full XG compatibility and playback at a CD-quality sample rate of 44.1 kHz makes S-YXG50C the current King of the Hill in this category. Of course, you never know what the future's going to bring. At this time, there is no set price or plans to distribute the S-YXG50C. To get the latest version of the MIDPlug and see what's new in XG land, go to `http://www.ysba.com` (see Figure 16-1) and tell 'em I sent you.

Figure 16-1
Download the MIDPlug and find out what's new with XG all at the same
time.

WebTracks

Like Crescendo, WebTracks is a multi-platform MIDI playback plug-in
for the Internet Explorer and Netscape browsers. Also, like Crescendo,
the MIDI playback engine resides on the user's computer. Instead of
boring you with the details, I'm going to send you to Tutorial 16-1
(later in this chapter) where you can take an in-depth tour of The
Internet Music Kit from Wildcat Canyon.

> **Web**
>
> The WebTracks browser plug-in is available as a free
> download at `http://www.wildcat.com`.

More MIDI Plug-ins

LiveAudio is a multi-talented browser plug-in that ships as part of
Netscape Navigator/Communicator. In regards to dealing with MIDI
and Web sites, it will playback (by default) using whatever MIDI sound
source is available on your computer. In Chapter 2, "The Browsers,"
we take an in-depth tour of the native sound capabilities of the latest
release versions of Netscape Navigator/Communicator and Internet
Explorer. Beatnik is more than a MIDI plug-in—and yet it isn't. While
it probably fits somewhere into this Chapter, the best place to learn the
whole story is Chapter 14, "Beatnik."

Web

Regardless, go download the Beatnik Plug-in at `http://www.headspace.com/beatnik/`.

The Software Synthesizer

The Software Synthesizer (or soft synth) is probably the answer to the inconsistent playback sound quality of MIDI files over the Web (and elsewhere, for that matter). For instance, if I as a composer were to put together a great sounding sequence using a Roland Sound Canvas (MIDI module) as the sound source and you were to listen back using a Sound Blaster 16 card, the difference would be ugly. The Distorted Guitar patch that was dripping with too much reverb and squealing with delight on the Roland, would be a dry and nasty sounding jolt back to reality.

There are a number of options for soft synth playback over the Web, including the Yamaha MIDPlug, Apples QuickTime Musical Instruments, the recently released software version of the Roland Sound Canvas, and a few others as well. Live Update also has plans for a Wave Table synthesizer version of Crescendo in the very near future. Some of the features are astounding and may change the way music is composed and performed over the Web. I'd tell you more, but if I did they'd have to kill me.

Note

In Chapter 15, "QuickTime" I go into the many options and possibilities available to beef up, alter, and break the rules using QuickTime Musical Instruments.

You can bet that as processor speed gets faster (an almost weekly occurrence as of late) that software synthesizers with incredibly high-quality custom sound sets will become the rule rather than the exception. The ability to instruct a browser to load the custom sounds to match the MIDI sequence before allowing playback could even become a reality. Finally, musicians will be able to say "Listen to it as I played it or not at all."

What about Microsoft?

At times I find it hard to figure out exactly what Microsoft is up to, but as far as MIDI is concerned, it's getting interesting. Note the following three products that are currently brewing in the Great Northwest:

■ The Microsoft Interactive Music Control

■ The Microsoft Synthesizer

■ Microsoft Music Producer

The Microsoft Interactive Music Control is an ActiveX control used to combine MIDI and WAVE technologies. This control will make it possible to have music respond to user interaction with a Web page. Imagine having music follow you around instead of just running in the background.

> **Note**
>
> Microsoft Interactive Music control is currently available for machines running Windows 95/NT using Internet Explorer 3.0 or better.

The playback engine for the Microsoft Interactive Music control is an optional add on, the Microsoft Synthesizer. Using software wavetable synthesis and a specially commissioned Roland Sound Canvas Set, the Microsoft Synthesizer is GM (General MIDI) and GS compatible. Like the software synthesizer in the Yamaha MIDPlug, the Microsoft Synthesizer uses the processing power of the computer's processor to playback the synth sounds.

> **Note**
>
> The GS format is an extended version of General MIDI that, while remaining true to GM specifications, enhances the experience with enhanced features. One of my favorite features is separate reverb and chorus for each of the 16 MIDI channels.

Last but not least is Microsoft Music Producer. I unfortunately got to the MMP site too late to get a beta version to experiment with, but was able to get a run down on the basics all the same. This is definitely a computer program for the non-musician. The user is able to choose from a number of preset options and then use them to create a song. Some of the available parameters for creating a song include style, personality, and motif. I'll be honest: I'm not a fan of these "let the computer insert a little soul into your music"-type programs, but this one looks like it would be really fun to work with. It also looks to be considerably more powerful and interactive than Roland's DoReMiX, which is featured in Tutorial 16-1.

Microsoft is putting a lot of time and effort into creating tools that will make MIDI on the Web an interesting interactive experience. One can only imagine what they're working on behind closed doors. You can bet I'll be standing at the door knocking loudly; hopefully, you will be too.

The Internet Music Kit

For those of you who are inexperienced with both HTML and MIDI music, Wildcat Canyon Software has a low-cost, one-stop easy solution for you. The Internet Music Kit is a Windows (3.1 and 95)-only development tool that walks the user through the process with three relatively simple steps. In Tutorial 16-1, we will make the journey together.

Because the IMK is geared toward beginners, this tutorial is going to be done in such a way as to leave little to no mystery. The cool thing about it is even the Web audio power user (by bypassing the DoReMiX section of the tutorial) can find this program extremely useful. Converting a MIDI file and embedding it into your Web page just doesn't get any easier than this.

Tutorial 16-1: The Internet Music Kit

To perform the functions in this tutorial, you need:

- 486 or faster computer
- Windows 3.1 or 95
- 8 MB RAM
- 5 MB Hard Disk Space

■ Windows compatible sound card

■ CD-ROM Drive

There are a number of different options one can use in regards to step one and the Internet Music Kit (see Figure 16-2). At least for the first part of the tutorial, we're going to keep it simple and color inside of the lines.

Figure 16-2
Create, Convert, and Embed in nothing flat!

1. **Creating Music:** Start the application Internet Music Kit. In the main IMK screen, select the first option: (1) Create Music. There are three options from which to choose (see Figure 16-3). For this tutorial, choose Launch DoReMiX.

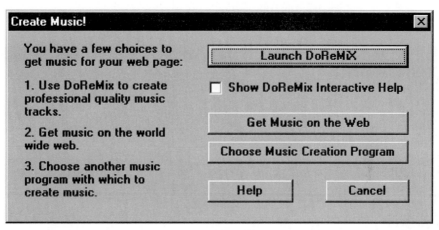

Figure 16-3
In this first step, choose Launch DoReMiX.

Note

DoReMiX enables you to insert a series of preset musical phrases into a grid. Each phrase is available in a series of styles and variations. With other adjustments such as tempo, it is easy for someone with no musical experience to create a custom soundtrack.

The first thing you notice upon launching DoReMiX is the empty Grid Window staring you in the face (Figure 16-4). Directly above the grid are nine icons. Eight of them represent a different musical instrument and phrase (the ninth is the eraser). The idea is to drag a number of musical phrases into the grid to create a custom musical event.

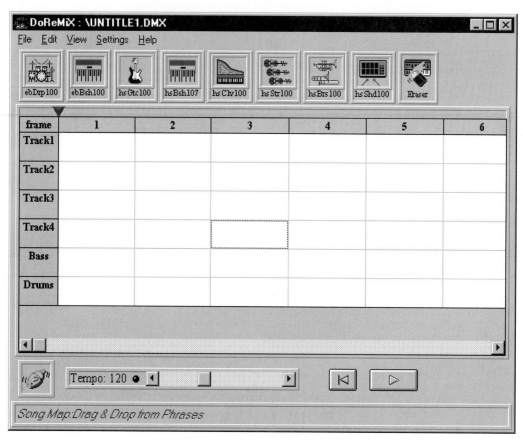

Figure 16-4
The main screen in DoReMiX.

2. To choose a musical style, select *phrase* from the Settings menu (shown in Figure 16-5). You have six basic style choices; for this tutorial, choose *house* and click OK. You can also set the tempo in the Settings window. For this tutorial, leave the tempo at its default setting of 120.

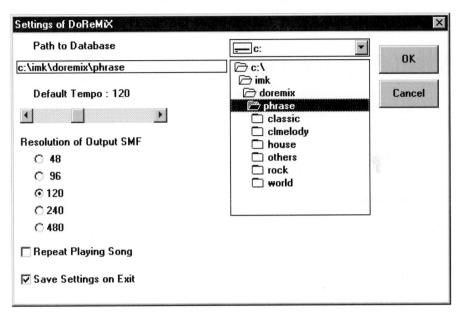

Figure 16-5
You can set the Tempo and Choose between six different musical styles in the Settings window.

Table 16-2 lists each of the Musical Phrases that may be used to create a custom song in DoReMiX. In addition to the six different musical styles, there are also a number of variations of each musical phrase. There are over 600 possible variations to choose from in creating a MIDI-based song using DoReMiX.

Table 16-2 DoReMiX Musical Phrases

Instrument	Description
Drums Phrase	Acoustic and Electric Drums and Percussion
Bass Phrase	Acoustic, Electric and Synthesized Bass
Guitar Phrase	Acoustic and Electric Guitar
Synth Phrase	Various Synthesizers
Keys Phrase	Piano, Organ and Clavinet
Strings Phrase	Orchestral Instruments
Wind Phrase	Brass and Woodwind Type Instruments
Others Phrase	Musical and Sound Effects

3. **Building a song:** Employing the drag-and-drop method, select a musical phrase and while holding down the left mouse button, drag and drop the phrase into a spot on the grid. Using Figure 16-6 for reference, match the placement of the different phrases. Press the Play button to hear your new song.

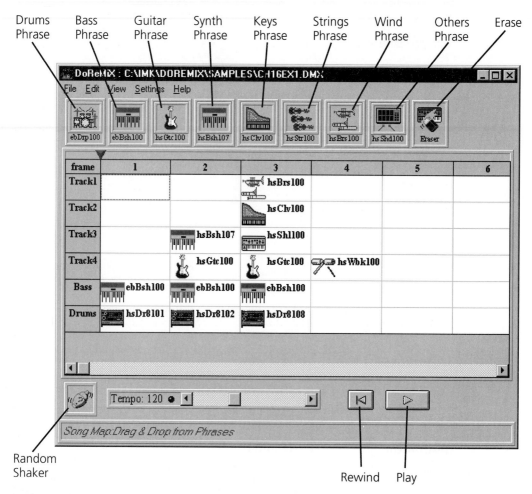

Figure 16-6
Drag and Drop musical phrases into the DoReMiX grid to create a song.

4. **Variations on a Phrase:** In this step, you can alter the nature of each phrase by changing both the music and the instrument type. To access these options:

a. Right mouse click the phrase you wish to alter in the grid. A drop-down list presents you with a number of new phrase selections (see Figure 16-7).

b. Double click on the desired selection The new phrase replaces the old phrase in the grid.

You can create a rather large number of variations by using this method with any of the phrases in your grid.

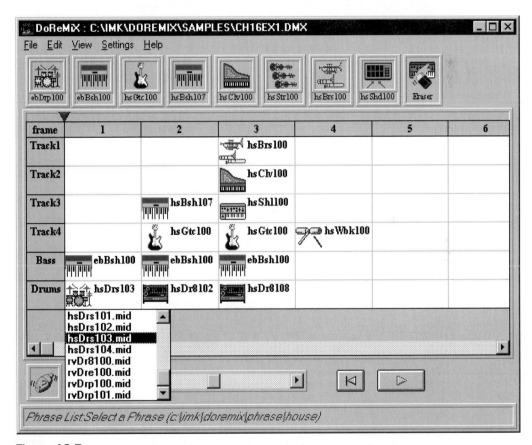

Figure 16-7
Variations of each musical phrase can be accessed with a single right mouse click within a frame.

5. **Random Musicality:** Letting DoReMiX choose to make its own contribution to the musical event is a very real possibility. In the bottom left-hand corner of the screen (refer back to Figure 16-6), notice a little Shaker with a question mark on it. If you select a frame location within the grid and double click on the Shaker icon, a series of random musical phrases will appear on the different tracks within the frame location. You can also drag and drop the Shaker icon to a grid location for even more random results. Compare Figure 16-7 (before) with Figure 16-8 (after) and note the random shuffling of the phrases. Now the big question: Can a computer develop musical taste? Select a grid location, double click on the Shaker icon, and you be the judge.

CD-ROM

In the Chapter 16 tutorial file are two Standard MIDI files (CH16EX1.MID & CH16EX2.MID). These are the before (Step 4) and after (Step 5) examples created in DoReMiX. Listening to these files will give you an idea of the typical results using this program.

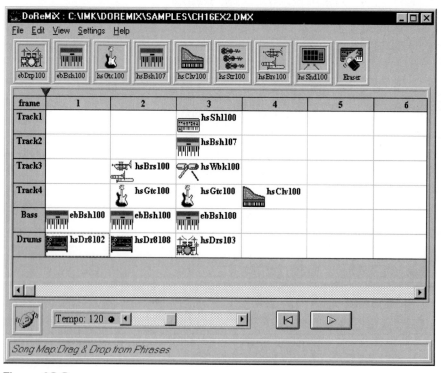

Figure 16-8
Use the Random Shaker to create a Random Musical Frame.

6. **Export as SMF:** The last step of the DoReMiX process is to take a .DMX file and export it as a Standard MIDI File. To do so:

a. Select Save SMF from the File menu. This takes the file currently loaded into DoReMiX (see Figure 16-9) and saves it as a Standard MIDI File.

b. Select Exit from the File menu and quit the application DoReMiX.

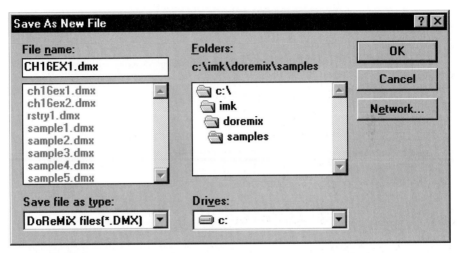

Figure 16-9
Export and save the .DMX file as a SMF.

Note

A Standard MIDI File (SMF) allows MIDI sequence information to be shared by different computers and sequence programs.

7. **Convert Music:** Now it's time to head back into the Internet Music Kit. The task before us is to convert a SMF to the Web Tracks Format. Referring back to Figure 16-2, we want to proceed to the second option, Convert Music.

a. In the main window of the Internet Music Kit, select (2) Convert Music.

b. Choose the MIDI file you wish to convert (in this case, CH16EX3.MID). Notice that the file plays as you contemplate the decision, giving you a last chance to change your mind.

c. Select 'Convert This File' (as shown in Figure 16-10).

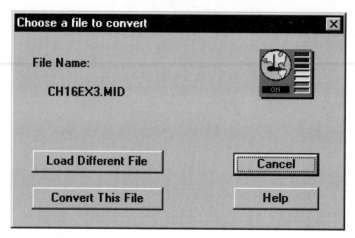

Figure 16-10
The MIDI file CH16EX3.MID will be converted into the Web Tracks format (.WTX).

8. **Embed Music:** How sweet it is! In just moments (through a process so simple, even I can do it), we'll move through the quick and painless process.

In the main window of Internet Music Kit, select the third option (3) Embed Music.

a. Your first step, Choose web page, is shown in Figure 16-11. CH16EX4.HTM is the choice in this case. Click on Next.

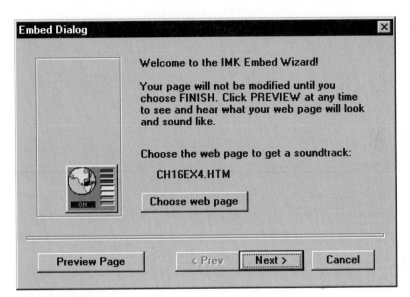

Figure 16-11
Choose the Web page to receive a soundtrack.

> **Note**
>
> Click on Preview Page at any time to see how the page looks and sounds with the current settings.

b. Choose a Web Tracks file (see Figure 16-12): File CH16EX1.WTX is the file of choice. You also have the option of looping the sound file or not. Loop it and click Next to proceed.

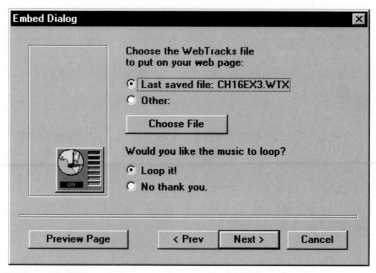

Figure 16-12
Select the Web Tracks file to put on your Web page.

c. Choose a style for music control (see Figure 16-13): My choice was obvious, Floating. It's always nice to be able to move the Icon around the page. Choose Floating and click Next to proceed.

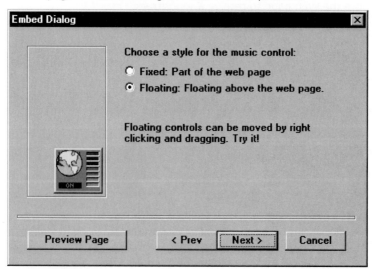

Figure 16-13
Set the music control to Floating.

d. Position Level Meter (Figure 16-14): There are five options in this step. Placing the level meter at the bottom of the page may cause a delay in starting the music. The choice in this case is yours, make your selection and click Next to proceed.

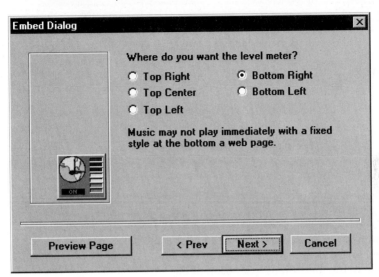

Figure 16-14
Position the level meter on your Web page.

e. Setting the logo: I've chosen to show it all. Choose Globe and Level Meter, as well as Show Status (see Figure 16-15). Click Next to proceed.

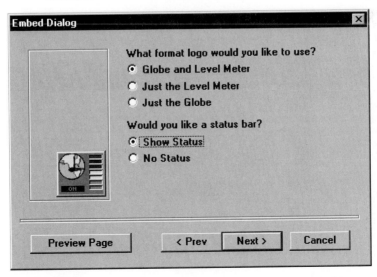

Figure 16-15
Set the format and status bar for the Logo.

f. Choose Location (Figure 16-16): Choose the location to upload your Web page. Make your selection and click Next to proceed.

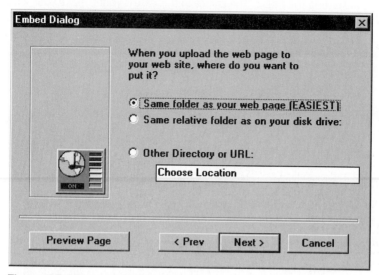

Figure 16-16
Choose the location for your Web page.

g. You're there! Click Finish (as shown in Figure 16-17) and the process is complete. The Web page and the music file will need to be uploaded to your server.

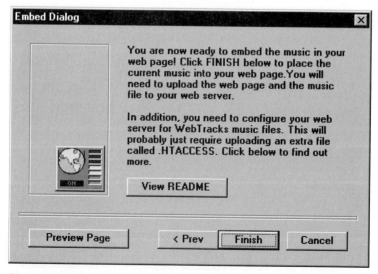

Figure 16-17
Click Finish to embed the .WTX music file on your Web page.

▨ I can hear it!

If you've followed these very easy-to-understand steps, your results should resemble Figure 16-18. You should probably also know that your Web server needs to be configured for WebTracks music files. In most cases, this requires uploading an extra file called .HTACCESS.

> **Note**
>
> The information needed to configure your Web server to playback WebTracks files is in the Chapter 16 tutorial folder as a text file (CH16CNFG.txt). Everything you need to know about uploading the file called .HTACCESS is in this file.

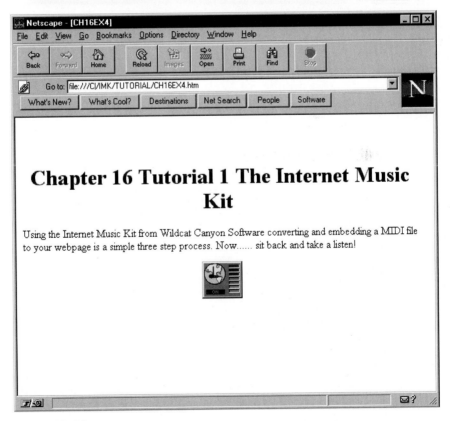

Figure 16-18
What a concept!

■ The bottom line

When I first saw this inexpensive MIDI on the Web package ($30 to $40 street price), I was thinking "What's the catch?" Well. . . there really isn't one! If you plan on using the WebTracks technology on a commercial site, however, there is a licensing fee. Depending on the size of the site and a few other variable factors, the average monthly rate charged by Wildcat Canyon seems to run in the area of $30. A small price to pay for the privilege of having an audio-enhanced site. Another bonus was the actual download time for the WebTracks plug-in: less than two minutes. If that isn't enough, there is also an upgrade path for those of you who feel the need for a more powerful current version of Roland's DoReMiX. When it comes right down to it, I would buy this product without so much as a second thought.

MIDI Resources on the Web

There are a number of Web sites that offer everything from free MIDI files to very expensive professionally composed MIDI-based song libraries. I also found when going to one site there are often links to 20 or so others. Use Table 16-3 as a place to begin and—happy hunting.

Table 16-3   MIDI Clip Music (Commercial)

Company or Site Name	Description	URL
The Complete MIDI File Directory	Links to other MIDI-related sites.	`http://www.flexfx.com/search.html`
Keyboard Magazine	MIDI files for playback as well as lots of cool links to other sites.	`http://www.keyboardmag.com`
Live Update	Home page for the Crescendo MIDI plug-in. Links to other MIDI sites and commercially available music libraries.	`http://www.liveupdate.com/proddes.html`
Microsoft	Download and information about the Microsoft Interactive Music control, which offers dynamic musical accompaniment for Web pages.	`http://www.microsoft.com/music`

Table 16-3   MIDI Clip Music (Commercial) *(continued)*

Company or Site Name	Description	URL
The MIDI Farm	This is one of the most comprehensive Web-based resources for MIDI out there.	`http://www.midifarm.com/`
Standard MIDI Files On The Net	List of sites containing MIDI files, and other information about MIDI.	`http://www.aitech.ac.jp/ ~ckelly/midi/`
MIDI File Central	The files on this site are free but distribution may push the limits of International Copyright law.	`http://www.tst- medhat.com/midi/`
MIDI Space	Reasonably priced original music libraries.	`http:// www.webproducers.com/ midispace/`
Music and Computers	Magazine geared toward anyone of any level interested in using the computer to play, compose, or record music.	`http://www.music-and- computers.com`
Opcode	Music software company, creators of OMS (Open Music System). Site contains products, news, downloads, and more.	`http://www.opcode.com`
Yamaha	Free examples of XG MIDI files.	`http://yamahaxg.ysba.com/ xg_free_midi_index.html`

■ One Last Thought

I really used to think that listening to MIDI files with anything other than high-end (and expensive) MIDI hardware was a complete waste of time. I've since been converted, and as I jump from site to site listening to the creative possibilities unfold before me, I look forward to joining into the creative process myself. MIDI is probably the least complicated solution to the current bandwidth problem and with the many software synthesizers that are beginning to pop up (in browser plug-ins), sound on the Web is going to keep getting better.

Part 3

Back to the Future

This part of the book will give you a look at the how to embed your music and sound in a Web page as well as a brief look at the future. I'll show you the basic how-to of the embed process using MIDI, QuickTime, RealAudio, and Shockwave Audio. For those of you who have a bit of apprehension in dealing with HTML, have no fear; there is an easy way to deal with it and I'll show you how it works in Chapter 17. What lies just over the horizon in Web audio and where is it going? In Chapter 18, we'll take a look so you can be ready for the future before it arrives. What more can you ask for?

Embed Audio

In This Chapter

- Embed a MIDI file
- Embed a QuickTime Movie
- Embed a RealAudio File
- Embed a Shockwave Audio File
- Netscape Communicator
- Claris Home Page 2.0

If you've been good students and have done most of your homework, you're probably wondering when we were going to get around to embedding a few of the music files we've created in this book into a real live Web page. You're there! While creating, editing, converting, and generally manipulating sound files is a veritable walk through the park for me, HTML itself was a bit of a mystery to me. After a few brief pointers from a Web-savvy friend (thanks Marisa!), I'm now ready to show you how easy it is to slap a sound file to your Web page and make some noise.

> **Note**
>
> HTML is an intricate markup language that requires skill and practice to fully understand. You won't learn HTML from this chapter. If you really want to get serious with HTML, pick up one of the many books dedicated to the subject. What you will learn in this chapter is enough HTML wizardry to enable you to embed sound files into your Web pages.

Embed a MIDI File

I figured it would be easiest to start with the lowest common denominator, our old friend the MIDI file. Whether you have a Mac or Windows machine, you should be able to play a MIDI file back with some degree of success. For Mac users, if you haven't yet installed QuickTime 2.5 or better, you might want to go do it. This way, you'll be able to playback a MIDI file without hardware via QuickTime Musical Instruments.

Tutorial 17-1: Embedding MIDI the easy way

For this first tutorial, we'll take the easy route and use the intuitive interface and magic guidance of Netscape Communicator to embed our sample MIDI file into a sample Web page, both of which can be found on the CD-ROM accompanying this book.

> **Note**
>
> While I am doing Tutorials 17-1 and 17-2 using a PowerMac, I also duplicated the procedures using Windows 95. Other than the slight difference in the look of the Mac and Windows screens, there was no difference in functions or results between the two machines. Some of the commands are slightly different but the difference is easy to understand.

▧ What you need

The following items are needed to complete this tutorial:

- ▧ Tutorial Folder CH17EX1 (the contents)
- ▧ Netscape Communicator
- ▧ Crescendo MIDI Plug-in
- ▧ Macintosh running System 7.1 (or better) or a Windows 95/NT PC

CD-ROM

All the tutorial files for this chapter can be found in the Chapter 17 tutorial folder on the CD-ROM accompanying this book.

Web

For the latest and greatest version of the Crescendo MIDI plug-in for Mac or Windows, go to `http://www.liveupdate.com`.

▓ Let's embed

1. Open up the tutorial folder CH17EX1. Double click on the file CH17EX1. This launches Netscape Communicator without signing you on-line. Select Open from the File menu, and then Page in Composer. You should now be looking at the ready-to-edit test/demo Web page shown in Figure 17-1.

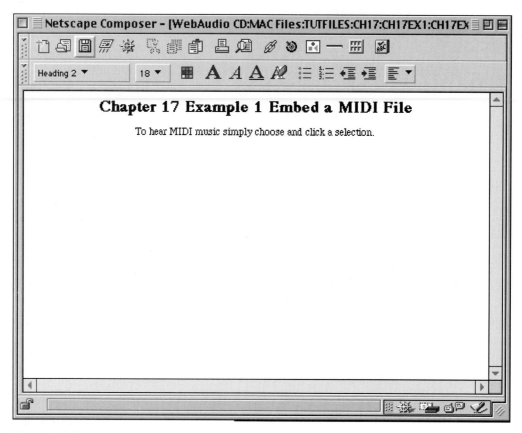

Figure 17-1
While this page doesn't look like much, it'll at least sound great once you embed a MIDI file!

2. In this next step, we're going to link a MIDI file to the tutorial page. Notice that in the file folder CH17EX1 there are two files: CH17EX1 and a MIDI file midtest1.mid. These must both be in this file folder for this tutorial to work. Select Link from the Insert menu. The Format dialog box opens with the Link tab active. Using Figure 17-2 as a reference, enter MIDI File 1 under Linked source and midtest1.mid under Linked to. Click OK when finished. Before you can playback the MIDI file, you need to save the HTML file and click the Browse icon to exit the Edit mode.

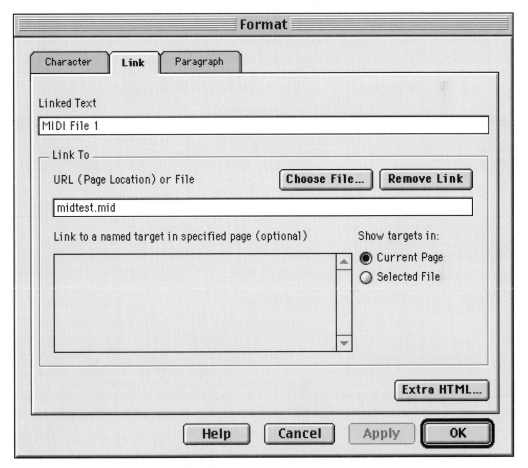

Figure 17-2
Under Linked text, enter MIDI File 1 and under Link To, enter midtest1.mid.

3. Okay, we're ready to see if this puppy works. Click on the link MIDI File 1 (see Figure 17-3). The next thing that should (and will) happen is the plug-in that you've assigned to handle MIDI playback from your browser becomes active and playback of the target MIDI file begins. In this case, I'm using Crescendo (MIDI plug-in from Live Update) as my default MIDI browser plug-in. Crescendo works equally well with either the Mac or Windows operating system. You can control the playback with tape transport type controls (see Figure 17-4). Like it or not, you're hearing music at this point.

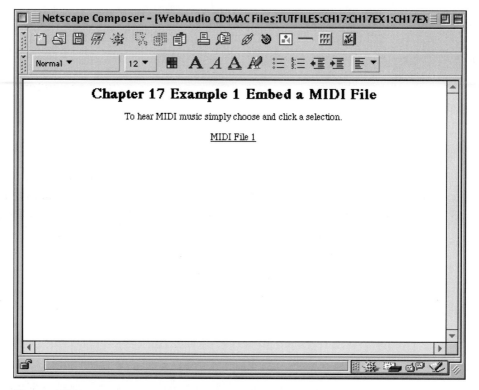

Figure 17-3
Click the link MIDI File 1 to initiate playback.

Figure 17-4
Crescendo is the default browser plug-in for MIDI in this instance.

▩ Wow!?!

This is kind of an experience for me, as I've always had the Webmaster in question handle the actual embed and encode stuff. It's simple, it's easy, and it works. To add playback of multiple MIDI files, add more MIDI files to the folder and repeat Step 2, making sure each link corresponds with a matching MIDI file. I tried it and it was easy and cool.

Like me, you're probably a little curious about the actual HTML code that makes this musical experience happen, so I guess that's probably the next step in the process. In Tutorial 17-2, we use another multi-platform editing tool, Claris Home Page 2.0, to accomplish the task of adding code to our sample Web page. Essentially, instead of letting the editor write the code, you'll do it.

Tutorial 17-2: Embed a MIDI file 2

The difference between Tutorial 17-1 and this tutorial is that you're going to write the code that will embed the file into the page from scratch and place it in the document manually. There is a low-cost alternative to using Claris Home Page and I'll get to that at the end of this tutorial.

▩ What you need

The following items are needed to complete this tutorial:

- ▩ Tutorial Folder CH17EX1 (the contents)
- ▩ Claris Home Page 2.0
- ▩ Macintosh running System 7.1 (or better) or a Windows 95/NT PC

▦ Doing some coding

1. Open the application Claris Home Page 2.0 and load the file CH17EX1. Select Edit HTML from the File menu. Figure 17-5 shows all the current HTML code residing on the tutorial Web page.

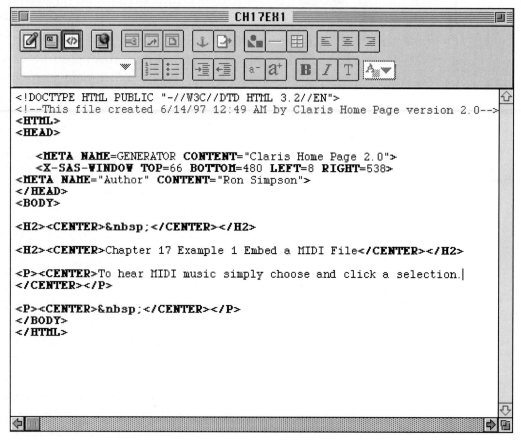

```
<!DOCTYPE HTML PUBLIC "-//W3C//DTD HTML 3.2//EN">
<!--This file created 6/14/97 12:49 AM by Claris Home Page version 2.0-->
<HTML>
<HEAD>

    <META NAME=GENERATOR CONTENT="Claris Home Page 2.0">
    <X-SAS-WINDOW TOP=66 BOTTOM=480 LEFT=8 RIGHT=538>
<META NAME="Author" CONTENT="Ron Simpson">
</HEAD>
<BODY>

<H2><CENTER> </CENTER></H2>

<H2><CENTER>Chapter 17 Example 1 Embed a MIDI File</CENTER></H2>

<P><CENTER>To hear MIDI music simply choose and click a selection.|
</CENTER></P>

<P><CENTER> </CENTER></P>
</BODY>
</HTML>
```

Figure 17-5
The Edit HTML window in Claris Home Page 2.0.

2. What we're going to do here is insert a line of code that will accomplish the exact same task performed in Tutorial 17-1. Using Figure 17-6 for reference as to where, insert the following line of code:

```
<CENTER><P><A HREF="midtest1.mid">MIDI File 1</A> </P></CENTER>
```

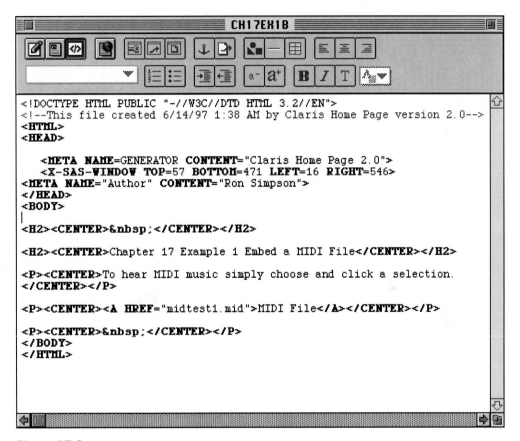

Figure 17-6
The <A HREF>...</A> tags are what enable you to embed the MIDI file into the Web document.

3. Select Save As from the File menu and rename this file CH17EX1B. Now it's time to preview the file and see if it really works. Click on the Preview in Browser icon (see Figure 17-7) and the tutorial Web page opens in Netscape Communicator. Click on MIDI File 1 to initiate playback.

Review

Figure 17-7
Click on the Preview in Browser icon to open the tutorial Web page in Netscape Communicator.

■ Easy stuff

The thought of writing HTML code used to scare the you know what out of me, and in some cases still does. Fortunately, something as simple as embedding a MIDI file to a Web page is not real tough if someone (me, for instance) shows you the basics. As you can see by the first couple of tutorials in this chapter, getting a MIDI file to your Web page is way easier than writing and recording the music. The big question is: Are you having fun yet? I am!

But What If I Don't Have an HTML Editor?

For those of you with a limited budget and lots of ambition, you can bypass Claris Home Page and Netscape Communicator completely. Real HTML writers typically use a simple word processing program, such as Word Pad (Windows) or Simple Text (Mac), to write their HTML code. It's very simple, really: write the code and content in the word processor, and save it with the HTML (rather than the .txt, .doc, or whatever) extension.

The magic to embedding an audio file into your page lies in the <A HREF>...</A> *embed* tags, as follows:

```
<A HREF="midtest1.mid">MIDI File 1</A>
```

Translated into English, this code instructs the browser to play the file named `midtest1.mid` when the user clicks on the text `MIDI File 1` (refer back to Figure 7-3 to see what this line looks like in a browser). And it's as simple as that.

The complete source code for the page shown in Figure 7-3 is saved as a text file (CH17EX1C.TXT) in the Tutorial Folder CH17EX1. You can open it in any word processor, play with the HTML, and save it as an HTML file to view it in your browser.

Embed a QuickTime Movie

Apple's QuickTime movie format is a pretty decent cross-platform solution for dealing with audio for multimedia or the Web. The impending release of QuickTime 3.0 will bring total equality between the platforms in both performance and development, which is long overdue. For this section, we again take the approach of showing you the easy way and the not-so-easy way of embedding QuickTime Movies into your Web pages.

Tutorial 17-3: Let Communicator do it

In this tutorial, we'll take the easy route and let Netscape Communicator do all the work of embedding a QuickTime movie into the sample Web page. Because we did the MIDI stuff on a PowerMac, we'll do the tutorials in this section in Windows 95, just to keep you on your toes. Remember you can duplicate this tutorial on the Mac as well.

Note

This tutorial can be done with equal results using Netscape Navigator Gold for Mac or Windows. There are some minor differences (between the Mac and Windows versions of Communicator) but if you read all the tutorials in this chapter, you will have no problems navigating around them.

What you need

The following items are needed to complete this tutorial:

- Tutorial Folder CH17EX2 (the contents)
- Netscape Communicator
- Windows 95/NT PC or a Macintosh running System 7.1 (or better)
- QuickTime 2.1 or better

CD-ROM

All the tutorial folders for this Chapter can be found in the Chapter 17 tutorial folder on the CD-ROM.

Web

For the latest version of QuickTime for both the Mac and Windows go to: `http://www.apple.com/quicktime/`

Steppin' out

1. Copy the tutorial folder CH17EX2 to your hard drive, open the file folder CH17EX2, and double click on the file CH17EX2.html. This launches Netscape Communicator without going online. Select Edit Page from the File menu and you are ready to edit the tutorial Web page shown in Figure 17-8.

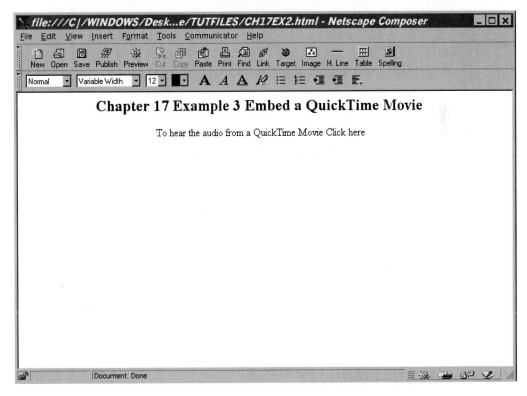

Figure 17-8
Edit Page in Netscape Communicator enables the user to insert and alter content without any knowledge of HTML.

2. Select Link from the toolbar (or Control + Shift + L). Using Figure 17-9 as your reference, enter Audio 1 under Link source and CH17EX2.mov under Link to. This function creates the HTML code that links the QuickTime movie file to your Web page. Click Preview (in the tool bar) and you are asked if you want to save the file. Select a destination and click Yes.

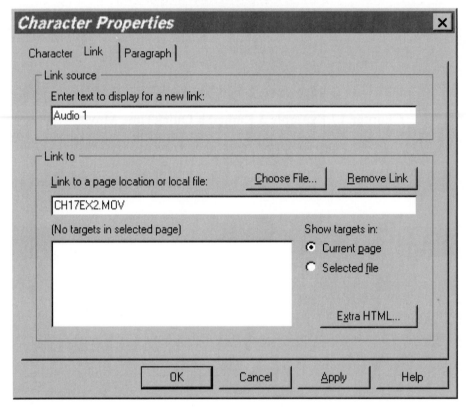

Figure 17-9
Enter "Audio 1" under Link source and "CH17EX2" under Link to.

3. This is so easy, it probably should be illegal. Looking at the example Web page (Figure 17-10), you see the link (in blue, no less) Audio 1. To playback the linked QuickTime Movie file, simply click on Audio 1. Press the Play control on the QuickTime Movie player (Figure 17-11) to hear the audio file.

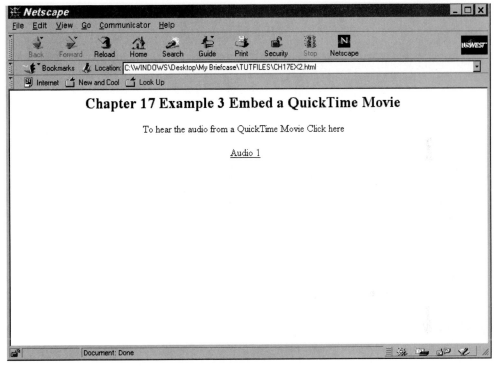

Figure 17-10
Click Audio 1 to initiate playback of the QuickTime movie file.

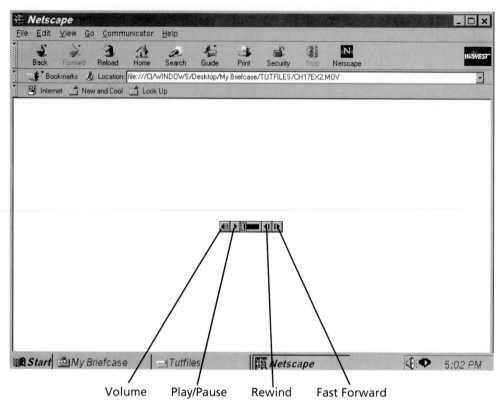

Figure 17-11
Press play to hear the audio in this test file.

Now what?

Like I said before, QuickTime is a good way to play audio and video on hardware using both the Mac and Windows operating systems. I tried this procedure using both my PowerMac and Pentium, and the entire process went so easily and smoothly I still can't get over it.

Well, as we did in the MIDI embed tutorials, we shall do with Quick-Time as well—Write our own code.

Tutorial 17-4: Embed A QuickTime Movie 2— The coding sessions

Just to keep you on your toes, we're going to write a very simple line of HTML code. Claris Home Page is a multi-platform solution for creating and editing Web pages for those of us with little to no HTML experience. All the steps in this tutorial can be duplicated on the Mac (or PowerMac) using the same software. You will get the same results.

> **Note**
>
> You can embed just about any kind of audio file (including a QuickTime Movie file) into a Web page using the <A HREF>...</A> HTML tags. Refer back to the sidebar entitled "But What If I Don't Have an HTML Editor?" previously in this chapter for information on embedding files using true HTML instead of the Claris Home Page editor.

▧ What you need

You need the following items to complete this tutorial:

- ▧ Tutorial Folder CH17EX2 (the contents)
- ▧ Netscape Communicator
- ▧ Windows 95/NT PC or a Macintosh running System 7.1 (or better)
- ▧ QuickTime 2.1 or better

Doing lines of code

1. Copy the tutorial folder CH17EX2 to your hard drive. Open the application Claris Home Page 2.0 and load the file CH17EX2.html. Select Edit HTML Source from the Window menu (or Shift + Control + L). In the resulting Edit window should appear all the current HTML code that resides in the tutorial example (Figure 17-12).

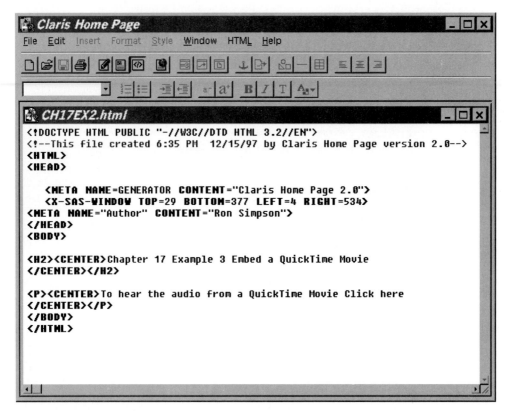

Figure 17-12
The HTML code for the tutorial example CH17EX2.html.

2. In Figure 17-13, I've highlighted the line of code you need to manually insert, which is:

```
<P><CENTER><A HREF="CH17EX2.MOV">Audio 1</A></CENTER></P>
```

After entering the HTML code, select Save As from the File menu and save this tutorial file to a folder on your local harddrive. This results in the page shown back in Figure 7-10.

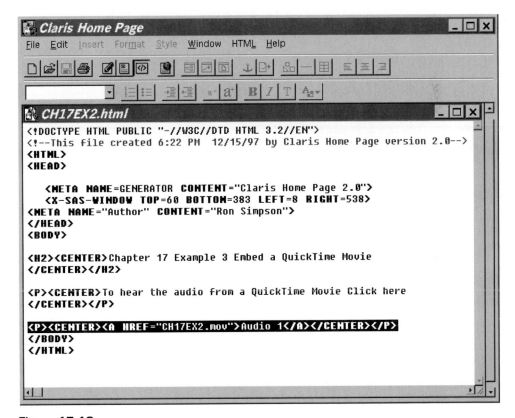

Figure 17-13
Insert this highlighted line of HTML code into this location to accomplish Step 2.

3. Now it's time to see if this works as well as letting an editor generate the code for you. Select Preview Page from the Window menu. In the tool bar of Claris Home Page, click the icon "Preview in Browser" (see Figure 17-14). This opens up Netscape Navigator without going online and enables you to test the playback of the QuickTime movie. Before trying to test your link, be sure that the file CH17EX2.MOV resides in the same folder as the file CH17EX2.HTML. Click Audio 1, press play on the QuickTime movie transport, and providing you followed all the steps correctly, you've got music!

Preview in Browser

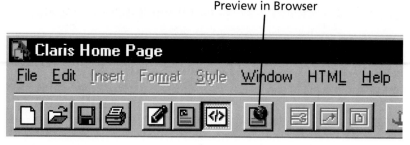

Figure 17-14
Click the icon Preview in Browser to test the results in Netscape Navigator.

■ One last thought

It's okay to let the editor generate the code and do all the work for you. Still, I get curious as to the how and why, and I'm sure many of you do, too. In the process of creating these tutorials, I've learned enough about HTML to spot little bugs and just understand the general principals behind how it works. I'm sure there will be many of you out there who are extremely familiar with writing HTML, but there's probably also a lot of you whose main gig is content creation and you might have bypassed the code stuff up until now. I do expect to find a lot more sound-enhanced Web sites in the coming weeks, months, and years. I hope that most of them belong to readers of this book.

Tutorial 17-5: Embed RealAudio

For those of you who are like me and probably aren't going to go out and purchase a RealAudio Server right off the bat, then this tutorial is for you! With RealAudio 3.0 (and beyond), you can playback RealAudio files from your site via streaming HTTP. Okay, so there are some limitations, but what do you want—It's free! For those of you who aren't going to be taking multiple simultaneous hits on your site, and are just doing RealAudio for fun, this is the ticket.

■ What you need

The following items are needed to complete this tutorial:

- Tutorial folder CH17EX3 (the contents)
- Netscape Communicator
- PowerMac running System 7.5 or PC with Win95
- RealAudio plug-in (installed)

CD-ROM

The folder CH17EX3 (and its contents) can be found in the Chapter 17 Tutorial folder on the CD-ROM.

Web

Because of licensing restrictions, we were not able to include a version of the RealPlayer on this CD-ROM. However go to `http://www.real.com` and download (for free no less) the latest version of the RealPlayer (currently 5.0).

▧ Let's get real

While we'll be doing this tutorial using Windows 95, every step can be duplicated on a Mac or PowerMac with the same results.

1. Copy the tutorial folder CH17EX3 to your hard drive. Open the folder and double click on the file CH17EX3A.htm. This launches Netscape Communicator and opens the RealAudio tutorial Web page. Select Edit Page from the File menu and you're in the Edit Window of Netscape Composer, as shown in Figure 17-15.

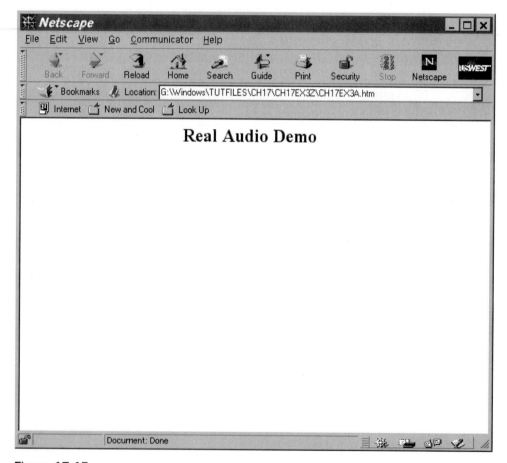

Figure 17-15
The Real Audio tutorial Web page in the Edit window of Netscape Composer.

2. Select Link from the Toolbar (or Control + Shift + L). Under Link source, enter "Get Real Now!" and under Link to, enter the file name CH17EX3B.RA as shown in Figure 17-16. Click OK.

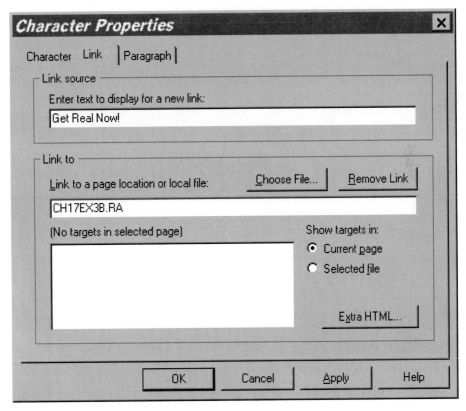

Figure 17-16
Under Link source enter "Get Real Now!" and under Link to enter the file name CH17EX3B.RA.

3. Click Save then leave the Edit window by clicking the View In Browser icon in the Navigator control bar. The tutorial Web page now has a link called "Get Real Now!" (see Figure 17-17) and by clicking on the link, you can do just that. Press Play on the transport of the RealPlayer (shown in Figure 17-18) to playback the tutorial file as a RealAudio file.

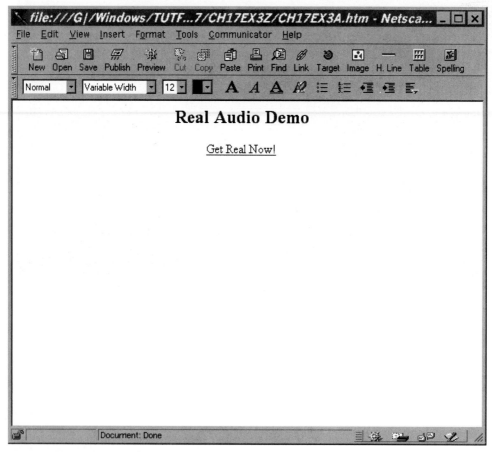

Figure 17-17
Click the link "Get Real Now!" to initiate playback of the RealAudio file.

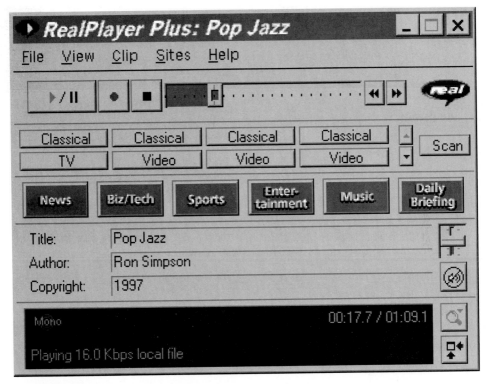

Figure 17-18
Use the RealPlayerPlus to playback the tutorial RealAudio file.

How real do you want it?

I found the RealAudio embed process to be a quick and painless one. To really take advantage of RealAudio technology, you need to use a RealAudio Server, but because that subject is definitely worth a book in itself, we'll leave it to someone else. You now have the basic ammunition needed to embed and playback RealAudio from a Web page. For more on RealNetworks and RealAudio, go to Chapter 11, "Real Audio." Now that you know what it's like to get Real, I guess it's time to get Shocked!

Tutorial 17-6: Embed Shockwave Audio

I'm going to warn you up front: If you're not familiar with Macromedia Director, this could get a little tricky. In an effort not to lose you in this one, I've prepared all the components in advance, and while we won't be writing any HTML code on this one, at the end of the tutorial I'll point you in the right direction. As always, I ran this tutorial on both my PowerMac and Pentium just to make sure they worked. We'll be doing this tutorial itself using Netscape Communicator and a PowerMac 8500/120 running System 7.5.

What you need

The following items are needed to complete this tutorial:

- Tutorial Folder CH17EX4 (the contents)
- Netscape Communicator
- PowerMac (or clone) running System 7.5
- Shockwave Audio Plug-in

CD-ROM

The components for this tutorial can be found in the Tutorial folder (Chapter 17) of the CD-ROM that accompanies this book. The latest Shockwave plug-ins (at the time of going to press) are also on the CD-ROM in the Plug-ins folder under Shockwave.

◼ Shocking stuff

1. There are four main components in the tutorial folder (CH17EX4) that you need to do this tutorial (see Figure 17-19). They are the Director movie that is the SWA player (CH17EX4.dcr), the main Web page (CH17EX4.htm), the SWA file (CH17EX4.swa), and the page we're going to be linking to (CH17EX4A.htm). These files need to stay in this folder and reside on a local drive for this tutorial to work. To make it easy, copy tutorial folder CH17EX4 to your hard drive. Double click the file CH17EX4.htm, which opens Netscape Communicator. Select Edit Page from the File menu.

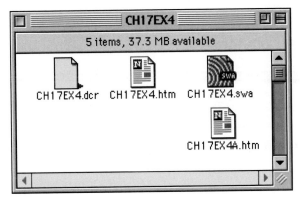

Figure 17-19
These are the four files you need to complete Tutorial 7-6.

2. You're now in the edit mode of Netscape Composer. What you'll be doing in this step is setting up a link between this page and the page where the embed codes for the SWA player reside. Select Link from the Insert menu. Using Figure 17-20 for reference, under Link source type "Click Here To Get Shocked!" Under Link to, click Choose File and select the file CH17EX4A.htm. When finished, click OK and then Save.

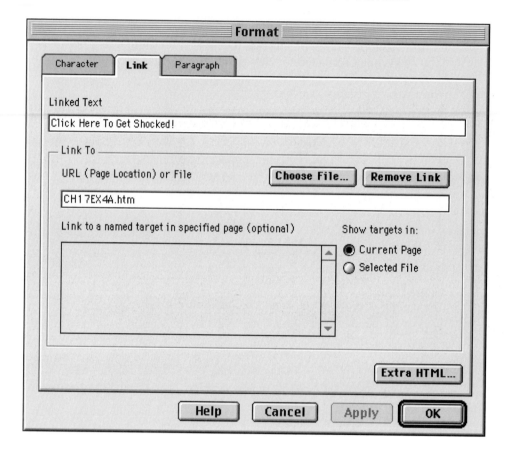

Figure 17-20
Under Link text, type "Click Here To Get Shocked" then under Link to click the Choose file button and finally select the file CH17EX4A.htm.

3. Click View in Navigator from the tool bar. We're now ready to see if this thing works. In Figure 17-21 is our main page (CH17EX4.htm). Select "Click Here To Get Shocked." This will link you to the SWA player (see Figure 17-22). Press Play on the SWA transport or click on the Shockwave logo to initiate playback. While you currently can't rewind an SWA file, you can pause or restart the file.

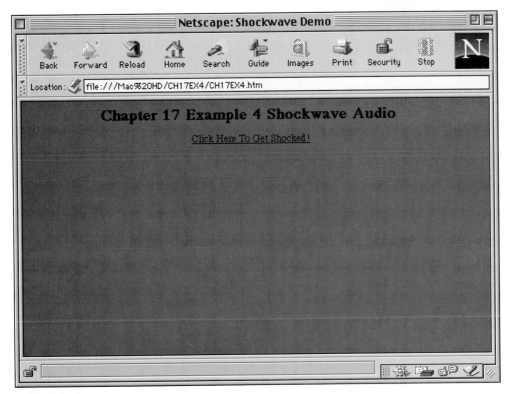

Figure 17-21
Click on the Link "Click Here To Get Shocked."

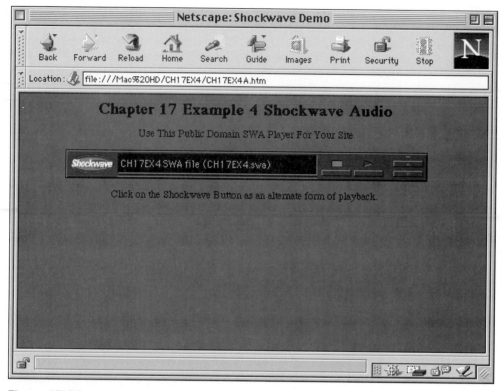

Figure 17-22
Press play or click the Shockwave logo to initiate playback of the SWA file.

Okay, it works; now what?

I knew you were going to ask it, so I beat you to the punch. We need to step back and look at the HTML code in the file CH17EX4A.htm. When dealing with SWA, you are also dealing with the SWA player, which is a quirky little Director Movie. It's all actually pretty simple but this is a situation where you can't use your editor to generate the embed tags. There's two solutions: Learn Director (maybe later on that one), or make a few minor tweaks to the current code. Just for your dining and dancing pleasure, I put a text file (CH17EX4B.txt) that contains all the HTML code from the file CH17EX4A.htm. You can open it in SimpleText or as a TXT file in a Windows word processor (see Figure 17-23).

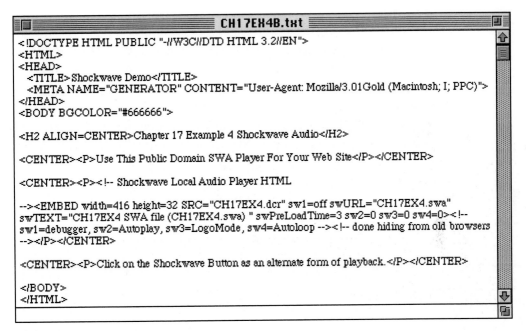

```
CH17EH4B.txt
<!DOCTYPE HTML PUBLIC "-//W3C//DTD HTML 3.2//EN">
<HTML>
<HEAD>
  <TITLE>Shockwave Demo</TITLE>
  <META NAME="GENERATOR" CONTENT="User-Agent: Mozilla/3.01Gold (Macintosh; I; PPC)">
</HEAD>
<BODY BGCOLOR="#666666">

<H2 ALIGN=CENTER>Chapter 17 Example 4 Shockwave Audio</H2>

<CENTER><P>Use This Public Domain SWA Player For Your Web Site</P></CENTER>

<CENTER><P><!-- Shockwave Local Audio Player HTML

--><EMBED width=416 height=32 SRC="CH17EX4.dcr" sw1=off swURL="CH17EX4.swa"
swTEXT="CH17EX4 SWA file (CH17EX4.swa) " swPreLoadTime=3 sw2=0 sw3=0 sw4=0><!--
sw1=debugger, sw2=Autoplay, sw3=LogoMode, sw4=Autoloop --><!-- done hiding from old browsers
--></P></CENTER>

<CENTER><P>Click on the Shockwave Button as an alternate form of playback.</P></CENTER>

</BODY>
</HTML>
```

Figure 17-23
The HTML code from the fileCH17EX4A.htm.

How I went about altering the little batch of code that you see in Figure 17-23 was to replace the original file SWA names with the ones I wanted to play back. If you look at the corresponding file names in the tutorial file folder (CH17EX4) and match them to the corresponding chunks of HTML code shown in Figure 17-23, you can get an easy idea of how to make this little SWA player bend to your will. Another really cool little tip that was tossed in my direction was the fact that you can save a text file with an .HTML extension and open it into your browser; if you've written the right code, your Web page displays. To check it out, load the Text file in the tutorial folder (CH17EX4B.txt) into your word processor, save it with the .HTML extension, and open it in Netscape Navigator and see what you get. While there's probably a good portion of you that already know this, chances are there are many more who don't.

One last shock

Because of the fact that no special server is needed for Web playback, Shockwave Audio is probably the least expensive way to get your sound and music out to the masses via streaming audio. With a little time, it's not too difficult to figure out the ins and outs of tweaking the code to make the SWA player we used in this last tutorial play your music and sound for all the world to hear. My take on this is if I can figure it out, so can you!

The Fear of Embed

Some of you may have come into this chapter with a slight apprehension and possibly even fearing the unknown (HTML, for instance). Although there are a number of variations depending on your level of experience with HTML, you at least now have the basics needed to get the sound out there. If you learned as much from reading this chapter as I did from writing it, then my work is done.

Chapter 18

The Future

 In This Chapter

The one constant thing about technology and the Web is change. It's like you take a nap and wake up to a whole new world, and this seems to happen every day. Staying on the cutting edge isn't easy because today's cutting edge might just end up being tomorrow's old news. While the main focus of this book is content creation of audio for the Web, there's a lot of interesting little side canyons that you—the reader—probably need to travel. There are also a few things that are sort of in the process of happening, even as I write this, that have yet to define themselves. So, what this chapter comes down to is stuff that is significant, on the verge of breaking out, or information I simply couldn't decide where to put in the rest of the book. While I wanted to call this chapter "More Stuff," I just didn't think that name would fly with the powers that be, so I've resigned to call it "The Future" instead, and that's where we should be looking.

 MPEG Audio

I battled with myself internally about whether MPEG audio should be covered in a chapter on its own, part of a chapter, or just a paragraph. For now, I'm taking the middle ground, but I'm also betting that in the not-too-distant future, MPEG audio may be the principal delivery system for high-quality streaming and downloadable audio on the Web. This will most likely come about through the widespread use of cable modems and the personal satellite dish. As we get wired for speed, the industry will probably move toward one high-quality codec as a standard, and don't be surprised if it's MPEG.

What is MPEG?

Named after the Motion Pictures Experts Group, MPEG is a data compression scheme for digital audio and video. One of the reasons you can get such a high-quality sound compressed into such a small space is through perpetual coding. Frequencies that are beyond the level of human hearing are trashed, making the file size smaller and allegedly you won't be able to hear the difference. There is sort of a debate about that, but we're not going there today.

For those of us that have been following all the emerging technologies for streaming audio on the Web and waiting for one to stand out a head above the rest, it's sort of been a mystery why MPEG hasn't gotten much mention in the popular press. I'm going to venture a guess that marketing and product/name recognition have a lot to do with it. Let's face facts: You hear a lot in the popular press about RealAudio, Liquid Audio, and Beatnik, but there's little mainstream press in the world of Web audio talking about MPEG. However, this should change.

As I was researching this chapter, I went back to take a second look (or should I say listen) to MPEG audio (and the Web) to see what the story was. Initially, I could never get a good connection and was constantly crashing whenever I did manage to get rolling. I'm going to chalk that up to pilot error on my part, but from what I hear, I wasn't alone.

Still, as I downloaded and listened to how good the MPEG audio sounded, I made one last determined attempt to get this streaming MPEG thing to happen. It did, it does, and you've got to check it out. There's a few free downloadable players that are Netscape Navigator compatible, so I figured I'd start there. The following sections dissect these players in some detail.

Streamworks from Xing Technology

Xing Technology has been around since 1990 and developed the industry's first software-based MPEG audio decoder in 1992. In 1994, Xing released XingMPEG Player, which was the first CD-ROM based MPEG audio/video player in the world. While the history of this company and their achievements is fairly interesting, let's move onto the heart of the matter—the StreamWorks Player.

As you can see in Figure 18-1, the StreamWorks Player is a minimalistic-looking little unit that covers nothing but the basics. It's available as a free download at `http://www.xingtech.com`. I think the download time is something like four minutes on a 28.8 modem. Also, download or make a copy of the set-up instructions if you want to configure the StreamWorks Player to work correctly with your browser. According to Xing Technologies, over 7 million people have downloaded the StreamWorks Player.

I took the StreamWorks Player out on a little test run and I'm very happy to say not only does it work pretty well, but at a connection speed of 28.8, I think it might even actually sound better than any other streaming audio I've heard at this speed. Using the StreamWorks 2.0 Content Guide (found on the Xing Technologies home page), I went and tried out a number of the streaming audio and video sites. Cool content and decent playback.

■ XingMPEG Encoder2

The XingMPEG Encoder2 is a low-cost software solution to expensive encoding hardware. Optimized to take advantage of Intel's MMX technology, the XingMPEG Encoder2 can encode a minute of video in as little 45 seconds. The kicker here is at the time of going to press, there is an introductory price of under $100 plus a 30-day free evaluation for the encode software. You can't ask for much more.

Audioactive

Another of the free downloadable streaming MPEG players comes to you from Audioactive (http://www.audioactive.com). Like pretty much all the other companies promoting streaming audio on the Web, Telos Systems doesn't make anything off of the Audioactive streaming MPEG player but rather by selling the encode and server software that makes it all happen. I won't get into the specifics, but they are very cost-prohibitive for all but those with very deep pockets. This is probably one of the reasons streaming MPEG audio has failed to take off like, say, RealAudio—the initial set-up cost. When the cost comes down, look out!

Streaming MPEG is . . .

In all honesty, MPEG audio sounds incredible. Sticking to this being honest policy, the errors and the connections that never happened using both the StreamWorks and the AudioActive streaming MPEG players say "not ready for primetime." I (and everyone else as well) want to click on a link and hear something. It's like having a great looking, smoother riding, and faster automobile that when it works is the best but most of the time just won't start. Currently, the general public is probably going to go with RealAudio for a lot of reasons, the main one being it works most of the time.

 Java Sound

Speaking of the future (of sound on the Web), the Java Sound API is another definite possibility. At the time of going to press, the Java Sound API has yet to be announced because so many of the final details are not available. Still, I was able to get some basic information and it's going to be cool. For those of you that have actually read this book sequentially, you already know that Sun has licensed the Headspace Audio Engine (see Chapter 14, "Beatnik") and is integrating it as part of Java Sound in the Java VM (Virtual Machine). This opens up some interesting possibilities, not because of the Headspace Audio Engine itself, but because it brings a 32-channel wavetable synthesizer into the Java Sound API.

General MIDI sound set

One of the features included is going to be a high-quality General MIDI sound set that has playback flexibility like nothing else out there. One of the problems I've tried to address in this book is inconsistent playback quality of MIDI files because of such a wide variety of different soundcards. While there's many soft synth browser plug-ins available that do sound pretty good (the Yamaha MIDPLUG being my hands-down favorite), they still need Netscape Navigator (or Internet Explorer) to run. The Java Sound audio engine will change that. It will come with a General MIDI sound set that will be vastly superior to that of the standard set available with the Beatnik plug-in, and have the capability to load in custom sound sets as well.

> **Note**
>
> For more about the Headspace Audio Engine and Beatnik, check out Chapter 14, "Beatnik."

Multiple file playback

Another one of the features that will give Java Sound outstanding flexibility is the ability to play multiple sound files simultaneously. This would include the ability to play two separate MIDI files at the same time. You will also be able to route a streaming audio file through one or two of the channels while playing back a MIDI file. I'm venturing to guess that the speed of the CPU will have a lot to do with just how many different audio channels would actually be able to playback simultaneously.

Open integration

Although I wasn't able to get a confirmation or denial from Sun, it seems as though there will be a number of other sound technologies integrated into Java Sound. The really cool part is they're leaving the system open to integrating different technologies on top of what will already exist. As the streaming audio (which sounds best and is most efficient) debate will probably continue for some time, it's difficult to really say what will be incorporated into the Java VM, but expect all the standard types of audio files to work (AIFF, AU, and WAVE).

I guess the bottom line here is that, with Java Sound, you're going to be able to mix MIDI and audio in ways that were previously not possible. The sound quality will be as good as you wish to make it and the flexibility of the internal mixer will lend itself to creative possibilities that have yet to be exploited in the world of interactive multimedia. If that isn't enough, it's also possible to create 3D sound within a Java applet. It's highly possible that the future of creating and listening to sound on the Web and interactive multimedia may be Java Sound. I'd recommend to any of you that are serious about audio to jump on the Java bandwagon yesterday. It's way better to be standing at the front of the line when the doors open.

 ## Marimba and Castanet

One of the shooting stars to emerge from the jumble of start-ups is, without a doubt, Marimba. With the Castanet tuner, users can zero in on the exact channels of information they want or need. Again, in the world of audio, this can have far-reaching implications. Imagine being able to choose the music you wish to listen to in the order you want to hear it digitally delivered directly to your doorstep via a Castanet tuner. While push technology is already being used today to deliver information and software updates, in the future it will also be one of the methods by which custom music and sound could and will be delivered. Imagine subscribing to an audio channel that updates and changes the music and sound in your computer's desktop on a monthly, weekly, or even a daily basis. All sorts of interesting surprises will be made possible.

DirectX Confusion

Change is constant, and Microsoft has been doing a pretty good job of constantly confusing developers and users in the ActiveMovie, ActiveX, and DirectX arena. The main area of confusion that we'll get straightened out here is what ActiveMovie was and now is.

In layman's terms (before March 31, 1997), the term *ActiveMovie* referred to a subset of ActiveX controls that were essentially a multi-application plug-in environment for processing tools. Two examples of ActiveMovie (plug-ins) that I use in this book are the Waves Native Power Pack (for Windows) and QTools/AX from QSound. These plug-in applications reside in the ActiveMovie environment and were usable for any application that supported ActiveMovie. This included Sound Forge 4.0 and Cakewalk Pro Audio. Because the name change has yet to be implemented into many of the applications used in this book, you see the term ActiveMovie or ActiveMovie plug-in referring to what is now known instead as DirectX. Don't be surprised if it takes as long as a year (or even more) for this little area of confusion to be cleared up.

ActiveMovie now refers to an ActiveX player control that ships with Microsoft Internet Explorer.

PatroNet

Just when you thought it was safe to go back into the water, a very old concept has resurfaced with a new twist. The musician/composer/artist has complained that the insensitive bean counters that run today's record labels not only don't have a clue as to what the fans really want but are keeping way too big of a piece of the pie as well. Look at George Michael and his battle with Sony/Columbia Records or the fact the "The Artist" formerly known as Prince no longer has the right to use his name professionally.

Along comes Todd Rundgren (the artist formerly known as TRi) and his company Waking Dreams with PatroNet. This is a unique opportunity for the artist to create content (musical or otherwise) in any form that he or she feels is relevant. Fans of the artist can then buy a subscription and become a Patron of the Arts! The artist can deliver work as it's finished via the Internet to the subscribers. It's also considerably easier for the artist to get feedback from the end user and find out if what's been created is truly art (in the eyes and ears of the Patrons, anyway) or something altogether different.

Whether you're a musician, artist, author, or just a consumer PatroNet offers possibilities that were not previously available. At the time of going to press, PatroNet was in Beta so instead of me trying to explain it you, go take a look (and listen) for yourself and see what I mean. Go to: `http://www.wakingdreams.com/ni/index.html`.

The Future Is Before Us

The great part about sound on the Web is that we haven't even gotten our feet wet yet. While the general public has yet to figure it out, the Web is to television as television is to radio. Once that nasty little bandwidth problem is straightened out (rewiring the world, in other words), we will have access to anything and everything. I don't even have to tell you what the entertainment and educational possibilities will be.

The motto here is to be prepared. Many of the sound creation and development tutorials in this book may seem a little advanced considering the state of Web audio technology today. Well, they're not. While some are still thinking in basic terms for playback of sound on the Web, you can take the lessons learned in this book and take it a step further. Quality and innovation in not only Web design but sound design and music will make your Web sites stand out in the crowd.

For you to create cutting edge Web content, it's necessary to jump in the water and learn to swim as you go. If you sink, at least you're giving it your best shot. The fear of choking on someone else's heal dust and being sent to the back of the line has been one of my biggest motivations in pursuing the holy grail of high-quality Web audio. It's an incredible experience to be running in this race and I'm looking forward to seeing who will cut to the front of the line next. I hope it's one of you!

Look to the Web

In Table 18-1, you can find the company URLs and a brief description of one or more of the products and technologies mentioned in this chapter.

Table 18-1 Resources On The Web

Company	Description	URL
Gamelan	The Official Java Directory	http://www.gamelan.com
Marimba	The Castanet Tuner	http://www.marimba.com
Sun Microsystems	Java Home Page	http://www.sun.com/java
Xing Technology	The Stream Works MPEG player	http://www.xingtech.com
Telos Systems	Audioactive streaming MPEG player	http://www.audioactive.com
Waking Dreams	PatroNet	http://www.waking dreams.com

Glossary

AFTRA: The American Federation of Television and Radio Artists is a national labor union that represents members in news, broadcasting, entertainment programming, the recording industry, commercials, and not-for-broadcast educational media.

API: The Application Programming Interface is a set of interface subroutines or protocols by which a program can access or modify the operating system.

ASCAP: The American Society of Authors, Composers, and Publishers, a US performing rights licensing organization.

ActiveMovie: Originally a subset of the ActiveX specification. ActiveMovie now refers to a specific ActiveX control that ships with Internet Explorer 4.0.

ActiveX: A software architecture that permits the creation of downloadable software components from a Web server.

AudioSuite: Plug-in environment for Pro Tools 4.0.

BMI: Broadcast Music Inc. is a non-profit performing rights organization.

Bit Depth: Refers to the number of bits used in a sample. Bits are the smallest piece of information processed by a computer.

CODEC: An acronym for a Coder/Decoder, an electronic algorithm used to convert digital signals to analog and vice-versa.

Compressor: An audio device that reduces the dynamic range of a signal. The compressor can be used to smooth out the peaks and the valleys in a sound file.

Compression (File size): This is a technique that is used to reduce the file size for ease of transmission.

Crossfade: A simultaneous fade in between one audio signal while another audio signal fades out.

DAT: Digital Audio Tape is a "rotary head" format for storing music on magnetic tape.

dB (decibel): The most common unit used to measure the level of audio.

DSP: Digital Signal Processing is the manipulation of analog signals converted to digital form.

DC Offset: DC Offset happens when DC current is added (usually by a sound card) to an audio file during the recording process. Many sound recording and editing applications (such as Sound Forge 4.0 or Pro Tools 4.0) can correct this problem.

Digital Delay: An effect that creates a delayed digital repeat of an audio signal.

DirectX: A technology from Microsoft that allows software tools (plug-ins) to operate within a number of different applications. DirectX plug-ins such as those from Waves (Native Power Pack) and QSound (QTools/AX plug-ins) are good examples of DirectX Plug-ins.

EQ or Equalization: Adjusts the volume of selected frequency ranges.

Feedback Loop: This is a situation where the audio output ends up cycling itself back through the audio input. This is sort of like having the sound chase its tail. An example of feedback or a feedback loop would occur if you placed a microphone in front of a speaker. This is a bad thing unless you happen to be a rock guitarist looking for the perfect squeal.

Graphic EQ: A multiband variable equalizer that can boost or cut the volume of selected frequency ranges.

IDR: Increased Digital Resolution. IDR is a noise shaping dithering system used in WaveConvert and WaveConvert Pro. It is also used in a more advanced version as a Waves plug-in.

ISDN: Integrated Services Digital Network is a set of digital communications standards enabling a single fiber to carry voice, digital network services, and video through the telephone network for higher-speed communications.

MPEG: Named after the Motion Pictures Experts Group, MPEG is a data compression scheme for digital audio and video.

Metafile: Metafiles are text files that contain the URL location of a RealAudio file.

Mic: Short for microphone.

NuBus: The expansion bus for versions of Macintosh Computers starting with Mac II and ending with the PowerMac 8100.

Noise Gate: A noise gate removes or *gates out* hiss and background noise in the so-called silent areas of a sound file. The gate can be adjusted in sensitivity to open and close.

Normalize: This amplifies the sound in a file to it's maximum level without causing distortion.

PCI: The Peripheral Connect Interface is a standard for connecting components to a personal computer.

patch: Another name for a synthesizer or sound effects processor program.

pot (or potentiometer): An instrument for measuring electromotive forces. An example would be a volume knob might be called a volume pot.

preamp: Short for preamplifier, which amplifies weak device signals before they are fed to additional amplifier circuits.

RMA: The Real Media Architecture is an open, cross platform, client-server system for streaming media on the Internet.

RTSP: The Real Time Streaming Protocol is a communications protocol for control and delivery of real-time media.

Red Book Audio: Defines the specifications of an audio CD.

Reverb: An effect that simulates multiple reflections of an audio signal in a perceived virtual environment. As an example, a Reverb patch in an audio plug-in might be called "Cathedral." If you were to process a sound file with this patch, it would simulate how the source audio would sound in a Cathedral.

SAG: The Screen Actors Guild is the collective bargaining agent for professional performers. SAG monitors all feature and television film productions as well as those of television series, commercials, and not-for-broadcast education media to ensure the actors' best interests.

SCSI: Pronounced "scuzzy," SCSI stands for Small Computer System Interface, which is a processor-independent standard for system-level interfacing between a computer and peripheral components, such as storage devices, printers, and CD-ROM drives.

SDK: A Software Development Kit is provided by a software vendor to allow their products to be used with those of other software vendors.

SWA: Shockwave Audio is audio created for delivery by the Shockwave plug-in.

Sample Rate: The number of samples used per second to store a sound.

Soft Synth: Refers to a software-based synthesizer. Some good examples include the Yamaha MIDPlug, Apple's QuickTime Musical Instruments, or the Microsoft Synthesizer.

Streaming Audio: Transferring audio in a real time data stream.

Xtra: Macromedia refers to their plug-ins as *xtras*. An example would be the Shockwave Xtra.

CD-ROM

Here's where I tell you what's on the CD-ROM and how it's organized. Basically there are two main categories Mac and Windows. From there, it's broken down into four different folders for each category, as follows:

1. **DEMOSOFT**: This contains demo software, which includes save-disabled versions of some of the applications used for tutorials in the book.

2. **TUTFILES**: All of the tutorial audio files in the book reside in this folder, organized by chapter. When possible, I've duplicated the Mac and Windows files. This was done so you the reader can hear the different results of the tutorial steps even if the tutorial was done on a different platform. Kind of an interactive thing.

3. **PLUG-INS**: While the original intent was to have this folder full of Web audio plug-ins, because of legalities and time it just wasn't possible. What I've done instead is I've created a Web page with links to the Web audio download sites. This gives you the chance to have the latest and best operating version of everything you need to hear sound on the Web.

4. **MISCSOFT**: This is the folder in which I include stuff that didn't fit into the other categories. You just never know what I've run into that needs to get in this book.

The Folders

Here we go boys and girls—Everything you need to know about the CD-ROM but were afraid to ask.

DEMOSOFT

This folder contains save-disabled versions of some of applications featured in the tutorials in this book, as well as a few other surprises.

> **Note**
>
> Each application and demo has different system requirements. Most are listed as read-me files in the individual demo folders. In some cases, you may have to install the demo to find out.

Mac

1. **Arboretum Demo**: This is a demo version of both Hyperprism and the Ionizer (featured in Chapter 10). Hyperprism is a series of effects plug-ins that include reverbs, delays, and whole bunch of other very cool-sounding effects. In at least one case (TDM), there are actually two fully functional plug-ins that you get for free! The supported formats in this case are AudioSuite, Premiere, PPC (standalone Power PC), TDM, and VST (Cubase). Also included is a demo version of the Ionizer. The Ionizer is available as a standalone application or as a plug-in for a variety of different formats. Go click the Arboretum folder and check it out. To install the Arboretum demo, you must drag the folder to your HD.

2. **Director 6 from Macromedia**: For those of you who develop multimedia and Web content, it's more than likely you have at the very least a nodding acquaintance with Director. For the rest of you, here's your chance to check it out. This demo is fully functional except for being save-disabled.

3. **Peak 1.53 from BIAS:** This is a full-featured two-track audio application. Peak is great for both recording and editing sound files and accepts Adobe Premiere plug-ins. This demo is fully functional except for being save-disabled.

4. **SFX Machine from BIAS:** This is probably my favorite application in the whole book. SFX Machine (and demo) are a Premiere plug-in. You've really got to check this one out—It's a blast. Again, this demo is fully functional except for being save-disabled.

5. **SmartSound For Multimedia from Sonic Desktop:** SmartSound For Multimedia is geared for the non-musician who wants professional-sounding results. The best way for you to check out the features is to just go ahead and use it. All the features of this demo work except save, so give it a shot.

6. **Sound Edit 16 (Version 2) from Macromedia**: This demo is a full-featured version of Sound Edit 16 with the exception of being save-disabled. You can complete a number of the tutorial steps in the book using this demo software.

▧ Windows

1. **Cool Edit 96**: The Cool Edit folder contains versions of Cool Edit 96 for Windows 95 and 3.1. Rather than being save-disabled, this application is feature-disabled, but it still enables you to use many of the basic recording and editing functions. For a paltry $50, you can register Cool Edit 96 and it becomes full-featured. This application has the capability to record and edit on two tracks of audio. The recently released Cool Edit Pro has 64 tracks and unfortunately the demo version was not available by this book's deadline. Both of these applications are featured in Chapter 8.

2. **Director 6**: This demo version of Director 6 from Macromedia is full-featured except for being save-disabled.

3. **The Liquifier Pro**: This is a demo (or evaluation) version of Liquid Audio's Liquifier Pro. This demo software is needed to complete the tutorial in Chapter 13.

4. **Sound Forge 4.0**: There are three versions of Sound Forge 4.0 available in this demo folder, Alpha, Windows 3.1, and Windows 95/NT. Sound Forge is a mastering, editing, and recording application with two-track capability. You can do just about everything with this demo application except save or convert a file to different formats.

5. **SmartSound For Multimedia from Sonic Desktop:** SmartSound For Multimedia is geared for the non-musician who wants professional-sounding results. The best way for you to check out the features is to just go ahead and use it. All the features of this demo work except save, so give it a shot.

MISCSOFT

This folder contains that which defies description (in other words, the content didn't fit in the other three folders).

Mac

1. **Shockwave Audio Tools SE16 2.04**: This folder contains all of the components needed to convert and test Shockwave Audio files using SoundEdit 16 Version 2.04.
2. **Shockwave Audio Toolkit**: You are in luck! This is newly released version of the Shockwave Audio Toolkit. This is an updated version of the Shockwave Audio Tools for SoundEdit 16 and corresponds with the release of Director 6.

Note

The updated version of the Shockwave Audio Toolkit was able to be put on this CD-ROM thanks to Buzz Kettles and Brett Stewart at Macromedia. At the time of going to press on this book, the new version of the toolkit was not yet ready for release and we should all give a round of applause for the extra effort made to get it done in time for this book.

Web

There are a number of freeware and shareware Shockwave Audio players available at `http://www.mapenzi.com/shockwave`. This is a great resource for those of you that want to look as cool as you sound.

3. **CyberTunz**: Here's where you get lucky with free music! As I mentioned in Chapter 5, rather than toot my own horn about how good the music on the CyberTunz CD-ROM, is here's a chance to take a listen for yourself. There was some difficulty (my lack of programming savvy with Director) in getting the CyberTunz interface to work on this CD-ROM, so instead I've included both WAVE and AIFF files from all three categories for your use and abuse. Just remember they are protected by US Copyright laws and there are some restrictions. See Chapter 4 if you have any questions.
4. **FREETUNZ**: Just because I'm a nice guy, I filled up what little free space there was on the CD-ROM with some music files from my personal library of original music. In this case, I used a couple of cues from a documentary

I scored a few years back and a couple of cues from a film trailer (preview) that I scored in 1996. Refer to the CyberTunz licensing agreement for restrictions on the music in the FREETUNZ folder.

Windows

1. **CyberTunz**: Here's where you get lucky with free music! As I mentioned in Chapter 5, rather than toot my own horn about how good the music on the CyberTunz CD-ROM, is here's a chance to take a listen for yourself. There was some difficulty (my lack of programming savvy with Director) in getting the CyberTunz interface to work on this CD-ROM, so instead I've included both WAVE and AIFF files from all three categories for your use and abuse. Just remember they are protected by US Copyright laws and there are some restrictions. See Chapter 4 if you have any questions.

2. **FREETUNZ**: Just because I'm a nice guy, I filled up what little free space there was on the CD-ROM with some music files from my personal library of original music. In this case, I used a couple of cues from a documentary I scored a few years back and a couple of cues from a film trailer (preview) that I scored in 1996. Refer to the CyberTunz licensing agreement for restrictions on the music in the FREETUNZ folder.

PLUG-INS

To make it easy to find the plug-ins you really need to hear Web audio, I've created a page in HTML with links to all the relevant sites. Simply go online using Netscape Navigator or Internet Explorer and open this page. By clicking on any of the selected links, you can get to the download page of your choice and get the latest version of the plug-ins you need.

TUTFILES

Mac and Windows

What we have here is all of the tutorial files (audio and otherwise) from the different chapters of the book. When possible, I duplicated the files between Mac and Windows so you can listen to the results of the tutorial steps even if it was done on an application and/or a platform you don't possess. The file folders are named to correspond with each relevant chapter.

Index

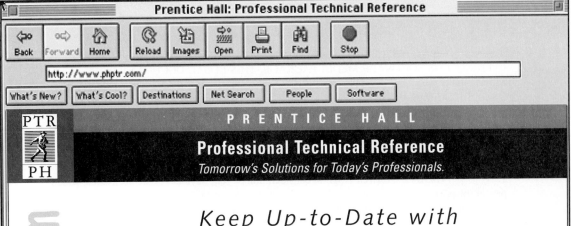

LICENSE AGREEMENT AND LIMITED WARRANTY

READ THE FOLLOWING TERMS AND CONDITIONS CAREFULLY BEFORE OPENING THIS SOFTWARE MEDIA PACKAGE. THIS LEGAL DOCUMENT IS AN AGREEMENT BETWEEN YOU AND PRENTICE-HALL, INC. (THE "COMPANY"). BY OPENING THIS SEALED SOFTWARE MEDIA PACKAGE, YOU ARE AGREEING TO BE BOUND BY THESE TERMS AND CONDITIONS. IF YOU DO NOT AGREE WITH THESE TERMS AND CONDITIONS, DO NOT OPEN THE SOFTWARE MEDIA PACKAGE. PROMPTLY RETURN THE UNOPENED SOFTWARE MEDIA PACKAGE AND ALL ACCOMPANYING ITEMS TO THE PLACE YOU OBTAINED THEM FOR A FULL REFUND OF ANY SUMS YOU HAVE PAID.

1.   **GRANT OF LICENSE:** In consideration of your payment of the license fee, which is part of the price you paid for this product, and your agreement to abide by the terms and conditions of this Agreement, the Company grants to you a nonexclusive right to use and display the copy of the enclosed software program (hereinafter the "SOFTWARE") on a single computer (i.e., with a single CPU) at a single location so long as you comply with the terms of this Agreement. The Company reserves all rights not expressly granted to you under this Agreement.

2.   **OWNERSHIP OF SOFTWARE:** You own only the magnetic or physical media (the enclosed SOFTWARE) on which the SOFTWARE is recorded or fixed, but the Company retains all the rights, title, and ownership to the SOFTWARE recorded on the original SOFTWARE copy(ies) and all subsequent copies of the SOFTWARE, regardless of the form or media on which the original or other copies may exist. This license is not a sale of the original SOFTWARE or any copy to you.

3.   **COPY RESTRICTIONS:** This SOFTWARE and the accompanying printed materials and user manual (the "Documentation") are the subject of copyright. You may not copy the Documentation or the SOFTWARE, except that you may make a single copy of the SOFTWARE for backup or archival purposes only. You may be held legally responsible for any copying or copyright infringement which is caused or encouraged by your failure to abide by the terms of this restriction.

4.   **USE RESTRICTIONS:** You may not network the SOFTWARE or otherwise use it on more than one computer or computer terminal at the same time. You may physically transfer the SOFTWARE from one computer to another provided that the SOFTWARE is used on only one computer at a time. You may not distribute copies of the SOFTWARE or Documentation to others. You may not reverse engineer, disassemble, decompile, modify, adapt, translate, or create derivative works based on the SOFTWARE or the Documentation without the prior written consent of the Company.

5.   **TRANSFER RESTRICTIONS:** The enclosed SOFTWARE is licensed only to you and may not be transferred to any one else without the prior written consent of the Company. Any unauthorized transfer of the SOFTWARE shall result in the immediate termination of this Agreement.

6.   **TERMINATION:** This license is effective until terminated. This license will terminate automatically without notice from the Company and become null and void if you fail to comply with any provisions or limitations of this license. Upon termination, you shall destroy the Documentation and all copies of the SOFTWARE. All provisions of this Agreement as to warranties, limitation of liability, remedies or damages, and our ownership rights shall survive termination.

7.   **MISCELLANEOUS:** This Agreement shall be construed in accordance with the laws of the United States of America and the State of New York and shall benefit the Company, its affiliates, and assignees.

8.   **LIMITED WARRANTY AND DISCLAIMER OF WARRANTY:** The Company warrants that the SOFTWARE, when properly used in accordance with the Documentation, will operate in substantial conformity with the description of the SOFTWARE set forth in the Documentation. The Company does not warrant that the SOFTWARE will meet your requirements or that the operation of the SOFTWARE will be uninterrupted or error-free. The Company warrants that the

media on which the SOFTWARE is delivered shall be free from defects in materials and workmanship under normal use for a period of thirty (30) days from the date of your purchase. Your only remedy and the Company's only obligation under these limited warranties is, at the Company's option, return of the warranted item for a refund of any amounts paid by you or replacement of the item. Any replacement of SOFTWARE or media under the warranties shall not extend the original warranty period. The limited warranty set forth above shall not apply to any SOFTWARE which the Company determines in good faith has been subject to misuse, neglect, improper installation, repair, alteration, or damage by you. EXCEPT FOR THE EXPRESSED WARRANTIES SET FORTH ABOVE, THE COMPANY DISCLAIMS ALL WARRANTIES, EXPRESS OR IMPLIED, INCLUDING WITHOUT LIMITATION, THE IMPLIED WARRANTIES OF MERCHANTABILITY AND FITNESS FOR A PARTICULAR PURPOSE. EXCEPT FOR THE EXPRESS WARRANTY SET FORTH ABOVE, THE COMPANY DOES NOT WARRANT, GUARANTEE, OR MAKE ANY REPRESENTATION REGARDING THE USE OR THE RESULTS OF THE USE OF THE SOFTWARE IN TERMS OF ITS CORRECTNESS, ACCURACY, RELIABILITY, CURRENTNESS, OR OTHERWISE.

IN NO EVENT, SHALL THE COMPANY OR ITS EMPLOYEES, AGENTS, SUPPLIERS, OR CONTRACTORS BE LIABLE FOR ANY INCIDENTAL, INDIRECT, SPECIAL, OR CONSEQUENTIAL DAMAGES ARISING OUT OF OR IN CONNECTION WITH THE LICENSE GRANTED UNDER THIS AGREEMENT, OR FOR LOSS OF USE, LOSS OF DATA, LOSS OF INCOME OR PROFIT, OR OTHER LOSSES, SUSTAINED AS A RESULT OF INJURY TO ANY PERSON, OR LOSS OF OR DAMAGE TO PROPERTY, OR CLAIMS OF THIRD PARTIES, EVEN IF THE COMPANY OR AN AUTHORIZED REPRESENTATIVE OF THE COMPANY HAS BEEN ADVISED OF THE POSSIBILITY OF SUCH DAMAGES. IN NO EVENT SHALL LIABILITY OF THE COMPANY FOR DAMAGES WITH RESPECT TO THE SOFTWARE EXCEED THE AMOUNTS ACTUALLY PAID BY YOU, IF ANY, FOR THE SOFTWARE.

SOME JURISDICTIONS DO NOT ALLOW THE LIMITATION OF IMPLIED WARRANTIES OR LIABILITY FOR INCIDENTAL, INDIRECT, SPECIAL, OR CONSEQUENTIAL DAMAGES, SO THE ABOVE LIMITATIONS MAY NOT ALWAYS APPLY. THE WARRANTIES IN THIS AGREEMENT GIVE YOU SPECIFIC LEGAL RIGHTS AND YOU MAY ALSO HAVE OTHER RIGHTS WHICH VARY IN ACCORDANCE WITH LOCAL LAW.

ACKNOWLEDGMENT

YOU ACKNOWLEDGE THAT YOU HAVE READ THIS AGREEMENT, UNDERSTAND IT, AND AGREE TO BE BOUND BY ITS TERMS AND CONDITIONS. YOU ALSO AGREE THAT THIS AGREEMENT IS THE COMPLETE AND EXCLUSIVE STATEMENT OF THE AGREEMENT BETWEEN YOU AND THE COMPANY AND SUPERSEDES ALL PROPOSALS OR PRIOR AGREEMENTS, ORAL, OR WRITTEN, AND ANY OTHER COMMUNICATIONS BETWEEN YOU AND THE COMPANY OR ANY REPRESENTATIVE OF THE COMPANY RELATING TO THE SUBJECT MATTER OF THIS AGREEMENT.

Should you have any questions concerning this Agreement or if you wish to contact the Company for any reason, please contact in writing at the address below.

Robin Short
Prentice Hall PTR
One Lake Street
Upper Saddle River, New Jersey 07458

About the CD-ROM

The CD-ROM that accompanies this book contains a great many components that will assist you as you work through the tutorials in this book, in both Mac and Windows versions. Please refer to the CD-ROM Appendix for an overview of the contents of the CD-ROM.

System Requirements

Each application and demo has different system requirements. Most are listed as read-me files in the individual demo folders. In some cases, you may have to install the demo to find out. At the very least, this section outlines the minimum system requirements for various platforms for creating and playing back audio content on the Web.

Windows 95/NT

Many of the newer software applications require the use of a Pentium. However, some of the development tools were designed to run on a 486 (these are noted in the book when applicable). To successfully playback audio from the Web, it is necessary to use Netscape Navigator (3.0 or better) or Microsoft Internet Explorer (3.0 or better).

Disk space can also be an issue when dealing with digital audio. If you are recording or editing CD-quality audio files (16-bit, 44.1 kHz, stereo) you will use up 10 MB of disk space per minute.

Because we are dealing with sound in this book, you're going to need a pair of computer speakers. Windows users also need a sound card to playback both MIDI and WAVE files.

MacOS

Many of the newer software applications require the use of a PowerMac. However, some of the development tools were designed to run on a 680X0 Mac (these are noted in the book when applicable). To successfully playback audio from the Web, it is necessary to use Netscape Navigator (3.0 or better) or Microsoft Internet Explorer (3.0 or better).

Disk space can also be an issue when dealing with digital audio. If you are recording or editing CD-quality audio files (16-bit, 44.1 kHz, stereo) you will be using up 10 MB of disk space per minute.

Because we are dealing with sound in this book, you're going to need a pair of computer speakers. With the exception of the really old Macs (pre 68030), all Macs and PowerMacs come with built-in audio capabilities.

Technical Support

Prentice Hall does not offer technical support for this software. However, if there is a problem with the media, you may obtain a replacement copy by emailing us with your problem at:

discexchange@phptr.com